OBJECT ORIENTED
SOFTWARE
TESTING
A HIERARCHICAL
APPROACH

Shel Siegel
with contributions by Robert J. Muller

WILEY COMPUTER PUBLISHING

JOHN WILEY & SONS, INC.
New York • Chichester • Brisbane • Toronto • Singapore

33246139

1/10/97

Publisher: Katherine Schowalter

Editor: Marjorie Spencer

Managing Editor: Robert S. Aronds

Text Design & Composition: Pronto Design & Production Inc.

Designations used by companies to distinguish their products are often claimed as trademarks. In all instances where John Wiley & Sons, Inc. is aware of a claim, the product names appear in initial capital or all capital letters. Readers, however, should contact the appropriate companies for more complete information regarding trademarks and registration.

This text is printed on acid-free paper.

This publication is designed to provide accurate and authoritative information in regard to the subject matter covered. It is sold with the understanding that the publisher is not engaged in rendering legal, accounting, or other professional service. If legal advice or other expert assistance is required, the services of a competent professional person should be sought.

Library of Congress Cataloging-in-Publication Data:

Siegel, Shel, 1951–
    Object-oriented software testing : a hierarchical approach / Shel Siegel.
        p.   cm.
    Includes index.
    ISBN 0-471-13749-9 (alk. paper)
    1. Object-oriented programming (Computer science) 2. Computer
software—Testing. I. Title.
QA76.64.S53   1996
005.1'4—dc20

95-30078
CIP

Printed in the United States of America

10 9 8 7 6 5 4 3 2 1

Acknowledgments

I cannot imagine finding anyone more in tune with my thinking and in possession of the technical muscle than Robert Muller. I brought my seminar material, papers, and ideas to Bob and asked if he would help me turn it into a book. Bob not only succeeded but he also seemed to understand everything I was saying—without me having to say all of it. From a philosophical perspective, Bob and I share a common view of the world of software engineering. Bob is listed on the title page. His contributions were invaluable and I requested that his name be added to the cover of the book to acknowledge the magnitude of his contribution.

Mary-Jean Harrold is the original source and inspiration for "A Hierarchical Approach." To my knowledge Mary-Jean is currently performing the most useful, practical, and ultimately applicable research in the area of testing objects. I am grateful for her research and indebted to her for the concept of hierarchical testing.

Bill Silver has been a friend, colleague, and inspiration to me for many years. He has had a profound effect upon my thought processes. I was privileged to develop the original Total Quality Optimization (TQO) methodology in collaboration with Bill. TQO is the genesis of Quality Optimization Cycles, and of my approach to quality in general. I say we developed Quality Optimization together; we talked through and developed the concepts and the overall system together. Bill did the hard work of transforming the ideas into a detailed method with diagrams. We both modified the original TQO and it evolved into Quality Optimization. Bill has continued to advance Quality Optimization into what he calls Quantum Quality Optimization (QQO). I believe this is the most advanced, comprehensive, and practical system for implementing quality in a software (or any) organization on the planet at this time. Unfortunately, it is slightly ahead of its time. Yet it remains an inspiration and driving force for all of my professional work.

Special thanks to Norman Kashdan of Computer Methods Corporation for his final review of this manuscript, and his input and support over the years. Norm made several significant observations about the original TQO model that led to subsequent improvements. He also made early contributions to my object-oriented testing taxonomy, which later evolved and merged with some of the test integration models described in this book. I am grateful to Norm for his support of Quality Optimization, and his encouragement of my systems thinking over the years.

Thanks to my early reviewers who provided timely feedback into this system:
Brian Lawrence
Doug Hoffman
Norm Kerth
Kelli Kinkella
The HP gang coordinated by Joni Ohta

This book is dedicated to all the teachers in the world who strive to be congruent.
To Michel Abehsera, my first great teacher: I am forever grateful to you.
To: Boris Beizer, Don Gause, and Dani and Gerry Weinberg: You exemplify the struggle and rewards associated with the transformation of personal convictions into professional integrity. Each of you has contributed to my understanding of what it takes to be congruent. Thank you.

To Talis and Cean: You demonstrate every day what is really important—unconditional love!
I love you all.

Shelly Martin Siegel
Souslalex, Valais, Switzerland

Object-Oriented Book Map

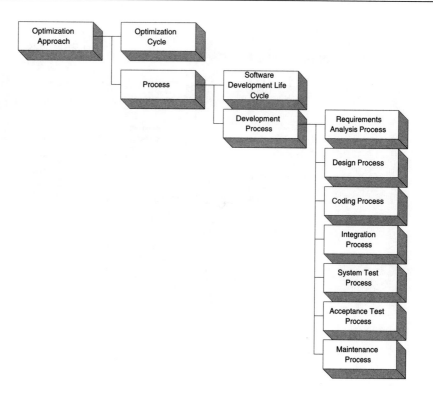

Object-Oriented Book Map

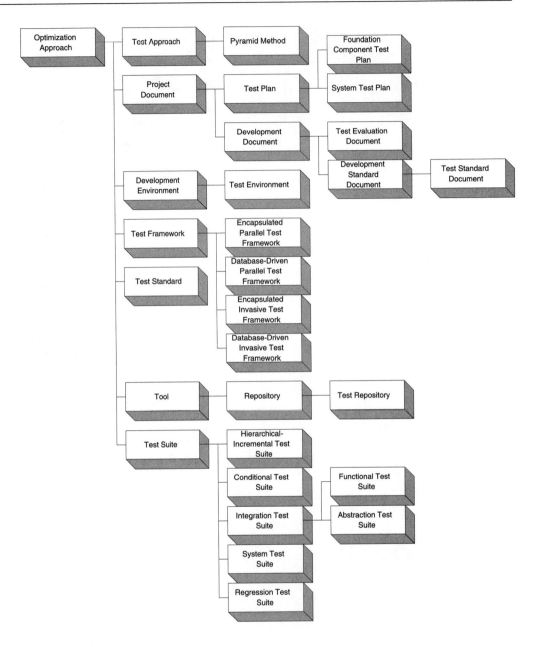

Object-Oriented Book Map

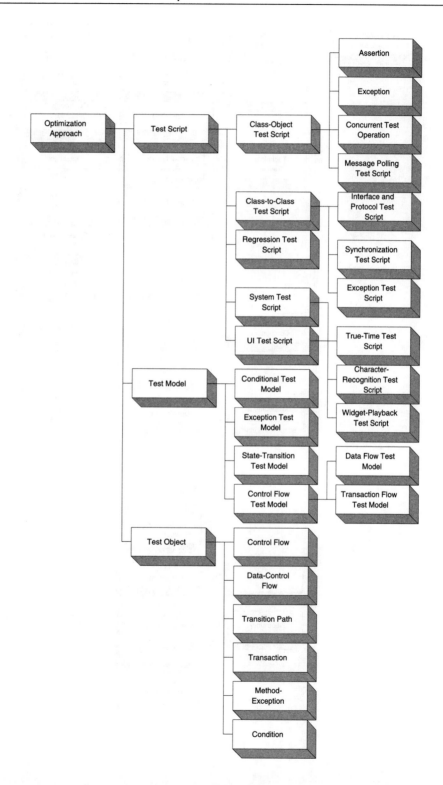

Object-Oriented Book Map

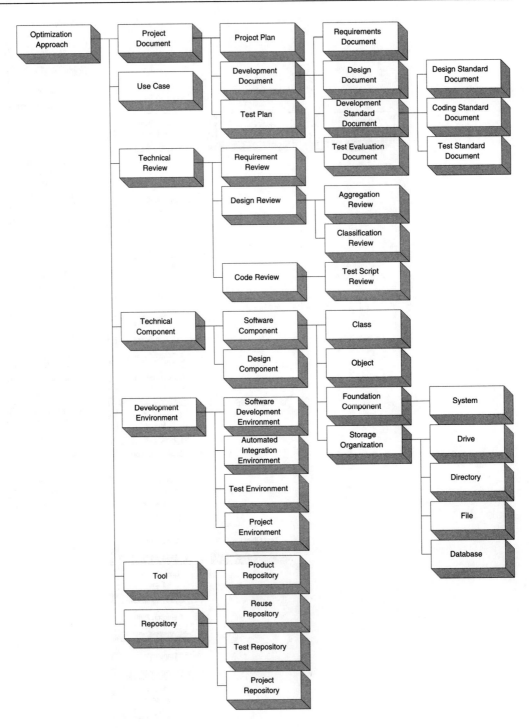

Object-Oriented Book Map

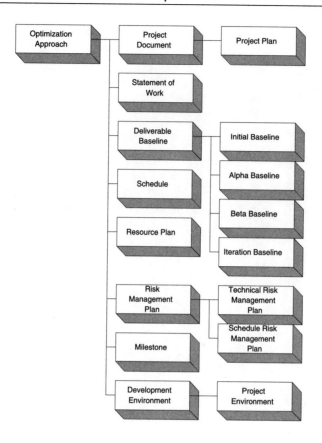

Contents

Foreword

I have known Shel Siegel for almost a decade. That he is an iconoclast is well-known. But he is also an adventurer—an adventurer in the spirit of the freebooting 17th-century explorers, or perhaps more appropriately, in the spirit of the Starship Enterprise because this book goes boldly where no book has gone before.

Most books, even excellent books, on OO design (there have been no previously published books on OO testing) are in a sense profoundly but understandably hypocritical because they are not themselves exemplars of what they espouse: they are not object-oriented. This book concerns testing OO software. As a book, it is to the maximum extent feasible within the linear confines of a paper package, itself an OO system. It defines and discusses the testing of OO software in an OO manner. It describes the testing process (indeed the entire software development process) as an OO system. Furthermore, concepts are illustrated by reference to a single example, an OO defect tracking system. And the test structures created by the methodology of this book are themselves objects and classes.

This is as much a book on OO testing as it is a book on testing OO software. Shel's pervasive application of the OO paradigm to a book on OO testing of OO software is appropriate, but more significant, profoundly honest. It strikes me as the only possible self-consistent approach.

Some readers and reviewers may have problems with this book— especially if they expect linearity and have not really bought into the OO paradigm to the total extent that Shel demands of us. Explorer Shel has gone boldly were few, if any, have gone before and expects us to follow. So this isn't a book to be passively read, but one to be experienced and explored.

Boris Beizer
Huntingdon Valley, PA, April 23, 1996

This Book Is a System

You read this book differently than you read other technical books This book is a system. Understand the system and its parts will be manageable and at your disposal. You are holding an object-oriented testing system in your hands. You might object (no pun intended) and argue that it is just a book— a conceptual system at best. True, but it is more. This book is a specification for an object-oriented test system, an explanation with examples of how to test object-oriented software; and the book itself is an object-oriented system.

The design of this book, its structure and style, is object-oriented. That means that parts are system components, while chapters represent object types. Most concrete objects are specified, while others are just mentioned. Those objects that are fully specified have a consistent form to describe their attributes and methods. Classes are organized into the systems that correspond to the book parts. Think of Parts 1, 2, 3, 4, and 5 as the set of system components that comprise the entire book/system.

Each part (system component) begins with an overview system diagram and specifies one or more object types or objects. Each chapter (object type)

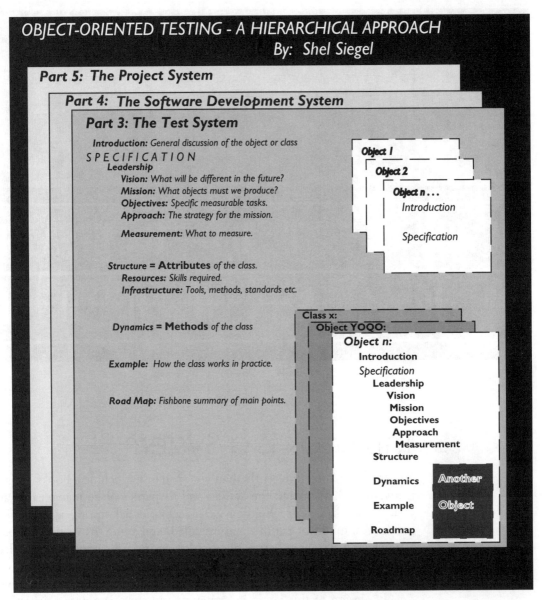

Figure P1.1 Object-Oriented Testing A Hierarchical Approach - Book Structure

consists of objects that are related by inheritance and/or containment. The inheritance and containment diagrams are essential parts of this book/system. Specifications are provided for all the important objects in the class. The specification format is consistent throughout the book and provides the practical information you need to implement the object. The specification format is described in the following Class/Object Specification section. Figure P1.1 illustrates the book's structure.

At the heart of the book is the test system (Part 3). Many of the object types in the process system (Part 2), the software development system (Part 4), and the project system are templates for specific test objects. No attempt has been made to completely represent these other system components. There is no way to do them justice in any one book. Instead we have chosen to provide the larger system context for the test system, and to include the detail about the objects in Parts 2, 4, and 5 that directly impact the test system in a significant way.

Object Type/Object Structure Layout

Each of this book's system components (except for Part 1) has the same structure. To avoid structural absurdity (too many levels of detail), we have not repeated the section structure for literally all of the possible objects, just the major ones. There are dozens of objects just mentioned in passing without having their own class structure. Also, three of the systems in the book (the process, software engineering, and project systems) are overviews of the classes in those systems, rather than a complete exposition of the system. This book is about testing, not process management, software engineering, or project management, but those systems provide a great deal of what a testing system needs to achieve its objectives.

The remainder of this section is a specification for the structure of all class sections in the book.

The introductory paragraph for the section usually introduces the class, states its basic nature, and provides an overall context for the specific discussion in the subsections.

Leadership Section Specification

Vision: A statement of what will be different as a result of having this class of objects.

Mission: Describes the set of objects that will fulfill the vision.

Objective: Enumerates the specific, measurable objectives for achieving the mission.

Approach: States the basic approaches for each objective and shows how each approach addresses the objective.

Measurement: Enumerates the measures for each objective.

The Objective, Approach, and Measurement paragraphs repeat, one for each objective. Each class can have more than one objective, and hence more than one approach and measurement system. This triplet is the leadership section or operational objective. See the chapter on the approach to optimization for full details on these leadership attributes.

The remaining sections detail the different aspects of the class. The existence and extent of these sections depend on the parent class from which the class inherits. If the class has no additional attributes or methods to those of the superclass, for example, there will be no Structure or Dynamics sections in the subclass.

Structure Section Specification

The structure section details the attributes of the class. Each subsection of this section deals with a single attribute, usually an object of another class in the system. See the road map section for pointers to other classes. There are as many subsections as there are attributes. There are also two standard subsections, one describing resources and the other describing infrastructure. Again, remember that each class inherits the attributes of its superclass.

RESOURCES SECTION SPECIFICATION

This subsection describes the skills required for the tasks involved in this class and the required resources, including physical resources, needed to complete the task. It also describes any resource-related estimation techniques.

INFRASTRUCTURE SECTION SPECIFICATION

This subsection describes any tools, methods, standards, guidelines, or environmental objects required by the tasks related to this object.

Dynamics Section Specification

The Dynamics section describes the methods of the class: the actual tasks the class performs to achieve its objectives. Each method subsection describes the nature of the method, any information it needs from outside (*arguments* to the method), and any specific heuristics or algorithms that specify the behavior of the method. There are as many subsections as there are methods.

Again, remember that each class inherits the methods of its superclass.

Example Section Specification

Each class has an example, with source code, illustrations, or description as appropriate, that illustrates how the class works in practice.

Road Map Section Specification

Each class has a fishbone diagram that summarizes the main topics of the class section and guides you to other parts of the book. You can use this road map to get a clear, conceptual overview of the section and its position in the conceptual geography of the book.

The class name appears on the backbone of the fish, with the immediate superclass parent connected with a dashed line. The ribs of the fish are the main topics of the class, with subtopics as minor bones. Figure P1.2 shows a fishbone diagram labeled to show you how to use it.

Reader Road Maps

Depending on the type of personality you have, or the role you are playing on your current project or the tasks or objectives you are working to accomplish, you will have different expectations and needs for the information this book/system contains. Following are a few of the ways you can use the book/system based on some of these classifications. There are many other valid road maps. Experiment, explore, and enjoy.

Hyperlink Road Maps

You can read this book straight through cover to cover if you like, but it will be hard to do. This object-oriented book/system reuses many ideas, but tries not to repeat them. Ideas that are reused or are related to a current object are referred to by **class/object hyperlinks**. Hyperlinks are the little boxes in the margins with the class or object reference embedded in them.

To understand how to successfully implement an object or class, you will have to jump around and read the specifications of other objects. This hyperlink road map is embedded in the *Object-Oriented Testing* system/book for you. You do not need to follow every hyperlink; let the path flow where you need to go.

Object-Oriented Table of Contents

If by nature you enjoy browsing and jumping around a book, you will appreciate the Object-Oriented Table of Contents. It appears immediately after the

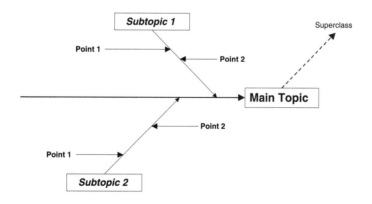

Figure P1.2 Fishbone diagram illustration.

book's dedication. Select any object at any level in this book/system, jump to it, and you will find its specifications as well as hyperlinks to related objects. Have fun; it's a great way to surf the information in this book/system.

Fishbone Road Maps

The fishbone diagrams are yet another way to traverse the objects in this system. They indicate the objects that need to be understood in a linear sequence, and point to related objects. The book uses standard fishbone diagrams to show how a particular class or object relates to others in the overall system. Figure P1.3 illustrates how a fishbone diagram may be used to relate topics or objects in a kind of reader road map.

How to Read the Diagrams

Instead of process diagrams, most concepts in the book have class and object diagrams that show how classes and objects relate to one another. The diagram notation used in this book is based on James Rumbaugh's OMT (Object Modeling Technique). Only a small number of elements are used. Classes are represented as data attributes with methods. A class without methods indicates the methods are defined somewhere else in the system. Connections are always two-way. That means that each box sees the box(es) with which it is connected. Nothing at the end of a line indicates a: to 1 relationship (no options). A black dot at the end of a connection means *0 or more*, that is to say, a *to many* relationship. That is all you need to know to follow the diagrams used in this book.

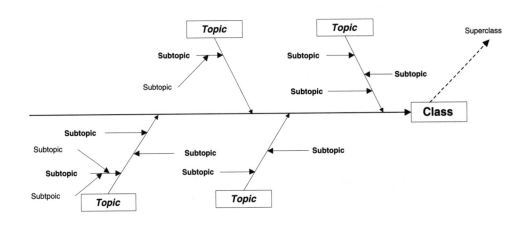

Figure P1.3 Illustration of road map.

CHAPTER 1

EVERY THING IS A SYSTEM

A *system* is a collection of things and their relationships to one another. Interactions characterize relationships; interactions are feedback the system uses as input to modify its behavior. Any system can be viewed as a collection of smaller systems. At any level, from the universe to the subatomic particle, systems comprise things that are themselves systems; and these in turn comprise objects that are themselves systems. We are governed by the immutable order of the universe. Everything is a system!

A system consists of interacting energy. Interactions are the vehicles that provide a system with feedback. Without feedback there is no way for the system to connect to the rest of the universe. Everything in the universe is energy. Without energy there is nothing, no things, no interactions, no feedback to connect systems together. Feedback is glue. This glue is energy. Can you think of anything that is not energy? No thing is not energy.

This book is energy vibrating at frequencies that form the molecular structure of paper and ink. The quantum particles that make up the electrons, protons, and neutrons organize into their own subsystems. At the core of all this is pure energy, at once particle (object) and waveform (relationship). Energy is the basic and most fundamental aspect of a system; the frequency of vibration determines its form. The feedback or interaction with other things (forms of energy) influences the form and directions of those things.

Every thing is energy. No thing is unrelated to some other thing. This universe of which we are a part is a magnificent system, ruled by energy forces that continually amaze us and physicists. As modern physics becomes capable of looking into and dissecting smaller and smaller chunks of energy, we keep discovering smaller and smaller systems made of smaller and smaller parts, and at the extremes of quantum mechanics energy and matter are interchangeable. Energy gets directed and structured into systems. A system is useful if it helps the systems that it interacts with thrive. Systems combine to form larger more complex and more useful systems. Every thing is a system, and every system is part of another system. Our universe is a structured hierarchy of systems made of reusable components.

With the advent of widespread use of object-oriented development, we are entering the era of software component technology. Component technology that has already revolutionized hardware production is now revolutionizing software production. Object orientation may be the first of many component technologies, or it may prove to dominate the software component technology arena for a long time. Today it is on the verge of becoming the dominant software component technology. Unless it suffers the fate of the dinosaurs, it is likely to be around for a long time.

Software is a system, and we regularly use the phrase *"the system"* to refer to our software system: that is to say, the one we are developing or using. The system (software system) comprises subsystems, and each subsystem comprises subsystems of smaller systems. A single line of code is a system. A system that is in relationship with other lines of code, data, its environment, and other elements of the computer.

A project is a system. A project is a thing, and as such, it has all the characteristics of a system. It has relationships to other things (systems) and adjusts itself by feedback mechanisms.

System thinking and object thinking are complementary. Object-oriented software is not alien. It is consistent with the fundamental order of the universe. *Every thing is a system.*

Object-Oriented Software Development Is a System

Object-oriented software development is about things and their relationships. It is an engineering discipline that models some aspect of the world. The form of the model is the object-oriented software system, which comprises objects, things, and their relationships. The objects interact and provide feedback to each other via messages. Object-oriented analysis is used to discover the things that are in the system and their relationships. Object-oriented design organizes the things and relationships into an effective system of code. Object-oriented code is the act of implementing the things and their relationships within the context of a computer system.

The object-oriented software system that we develop has relationships with the system of users, the system of developers, and with their organizations and the people they service. Thus software systems we build have profound relationships with much of humanity.

How can we explain the many books on object-oriented analysis, design, and code and the lack of attention to quality and testing aspects of object-oriented project development? It is as if object-oriented development quality and testing aspects are not considered parts of the development system. Indeed, I've heard those words on numerous occasions. Since 1981 I've traveled the world trying to close software quality gaps. Yet I continue to hear "The testing and quality activities for object-oriented development are the same as for procedural or ad hoc development."

Developers and their managers believe that they can use procedural test strategies on their object-oriented software projects. They believe it until they have had their first real experience trying to test a complex object-oriented system. Often this results in a denial of the value of testing of any sort! While the techniques used to test procedural code are applicable to object-oriented code, object-oriented software requires significantly different strategies, customized testing procedures, and specific tools from other software. Unfortunately, most object-oriented developers have no idea how to engineer the quality of their object-oriented development effort.

The way to do this is by incorporating incremental and iterative testing approaches into development activities. You, as engineer, move to systematic testing at the class and object level and marry the testing to the object-oriented development effort. Object-oriented software development is a system. It is all part of one big integrated quality system.

Quality Is a System

While quality may be a system, what do we mean specifically by quality? Dr. Deming insisted that any useful definition of quality must be operational—that is, measurable. Here is an operational definition of quality:

Quality is a system that is constantly optimizing productivity and value in order to achieve its aim.

Webster's dictionary provides the meaning of *optimize*: (1) to achieve the best possible under restrictions expressed or implied; (2) to realize to the utmost; (3) to obtain the most efficient use of.

Optimization does not mean to maximize or minimize. Definition 1 captures the essence of optimization. The next section provides definitions of software quality.

Definition of Software Quality

From the point of view of the consumer (user and/or customer) of the software: *Software quality is a system that helps its users to optimize their productivity.* If it does so at a fair cost (in time, effort, and dollars), then the software has user *value*.

From the point of view of the producer (developer) of the software: *Software quality is a system with higher development productivity and lower maintenance costs than the competition, so that it generates reasonable profits for its producers.*

If software does so at an acceptable return on investment (ROI)—that is, if the profits justify the effort—then the software has producer value. Measurement is both possible and necessary in each of these definitions. You can measure whether the software system optimizes the user productivity by asking them about the time, effort, and dollar costs relative to some other software system (the previous version perhaps) or relative to a manual procedure. You can record the effort spent to develop a system and track the effort to fix and maintain it. You can relate these measures to the money you pay your development team.

It boils down to the promise of greater value to the organization (in the form of increased productivity) and increased value to the user. The producer organization always expects to reuse code or design or both, to some extent, thus increasing productivity. By purchasing the software, users expect to be more productive in their own endeavors.

Reuse Is a System within the Quality System

Software reuse has been going on for about as long as software has existed. No software professional completely rewrites a sort routine, stack manager, or array processor each time one is needed. Developers use libraries and modify the code available to them. The key issue in reuse is and always has been how to achieve reuse beyond the individual developer. The individual developer encapsulates the reuse system. When two or more developers cooperate on a related project or product, a larger system (the project or product) forms and the individual reuse systems become localized subsystems of each individual. The challenge of reuse is to create a system that developers on the same project can reuse from one release to the next, from project to project, from organization to organization, and ultimately across an entire industry. While object-oriented software technology enables this type of reuse, adjustments in all the other systems that relate to the object-oriented engineering system will be necessary to implement the technology successfully.

Object-Oriented Testing Is a System

Object-oriented testing provides early feedback about how well the object-oriented:
- Analysis has discovered the things and their relationships
- Design organizes the things and their relationships
- Code implements the object-oriented design

Remember: Every thing is a system and every system relates to some other system.

Object-oriented development is a system. Object-oriented testing is a subsystem of that system. The two systems relate via a set of interactions (activities) that provide feedback to each other. They also relate to many other systems. Six subsystems tightly couple to form the object-oriented development system:

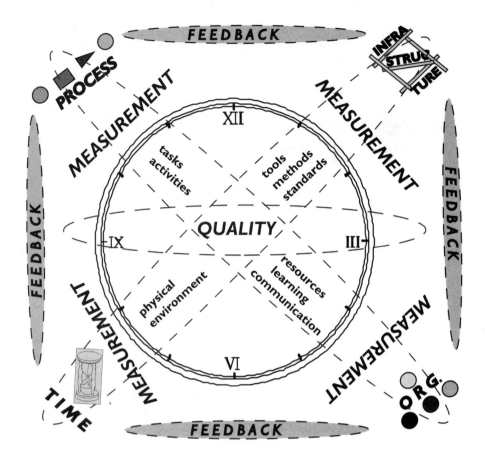

Figure 1.1 The dimensions of quality.

- The resource system
- The process system
- The project system
- The software engineering system
- The testing system
- The quality system

Figure 1.1 shows how the dimensions of quality relate to the overall quality system. The Software Testing subsystem is that part of the overall quality system that measures and therefore provides feedback about how well the other major subsystems meet the overall quality vision, mission, objectives, and approach.

Practice

Ask yourself these questions.

1. What other systems relate to the object-oriented software life cycle subsystem?
2. To the software labor resource subsystem?
3. To the software project subsystem?
4. To the software engineering subsystem?
5. To the software testing subsystem?
6. What other systems relate to the systems you just identified?
7. How do you relate to these systems?

CHAPTER 2

SYSTEMS OF OBJECTS

Having pointed out that everything is a system, let's now look at specific systems. This section itemizes some of the different terms and concepts to which the rest of the book refers. It then compares the system concepts of object and process and shows how an object-oriented system approach differs from a process-oriented system approach. Finally, this section describes the generic layout of the rest of the book: how each section represents, in miniature, the system objects of the quality system.

This book departs somewhat from usual technical volumes on testing in that its organization uses the same concepts that it teaches except for this Part 1, the introduction of these concepts. This format is again based on the principle that each system is essentially related to every other system. In this case, the book organizes its concepts as object types in several interrelated systems. The result is not an object-oriented software system but rather an object-oriented conceptual system. Thus, when you read the following sections explaining object-oriented terminology, bear in mind that that terminology is used throughout the book in structuring its components. Use this book as you would any object-oriented system: reusing parts here and there, following connections from object to object, and taking each object as a separate entity by itself if you want to learn about it.

Object-Oriented Technology

Reuse and Value

Reuse is one of the primary justifications for object-oriented technology. While "reuse" is a simple noun, it is not really a simple system. Like other systems within the quality system, reuse can take on a life of its own when it is applied it in a given environment. Reuse, reusing something—the concept seems very simple. If you think about the last time you tried to reuse some code, however, you will immediately understand why this seemingly simple thing is so complex in practice. Simply put, reuse implies interdependence. When you use what came before, you are relying on the whole system that produced that object. Thus, reuse immediately ties you into the quality system as a whole. If you have no faith in the system as a whole, you will have little reuse in your software environment.

Reuse is important for one reason, however: productivity. Without reuse, object-oriented technology is just another way to try to produce high-quality code, but it doesn't have any innate advantage over the many other ways for producing high-quality code. Object-oriented design and coding, if done right, can dramatically improve your ability to reuse code and thus can dramatically improve your productivity. Part of doing it right is testing to make sure the reusable object is safe to reuse.

Every object is a miniature, open system connected to other systems through input and output. Every class of objects is also a miniature system connected to other classes through inheritance and containment. To assure proper and predictable behavior, and to assure that system interfaces function correctly—both requirements for effective reuse—you must test your classes and objects to an acceptable level of risk. The greater the level of reuse, the greater the chance of something going wrong.

But there are other advantages to an object-oriented approach aside from object reusability. By following such an approach, you increase the flexibility of your system, and thus its value. You can put the system together in new and different ways with little additional effort, thus increasing the number of potential applications for your objects and increasing the value of your system for its customers. If you have a good, reusable design and good documentation, you can learn about and use your objects more easily because of their level of abstraction and the relative decoupling of pieces of the system from one another. That is, you don't need to learn the whole system to use a piece of it. This also improves the quality of the system by reducing the complexity that leads to defects. By testing the objects and classes to an acceptable level of risk, you can assure that this enhanced level of flexibility does in fact contribute value to you and your customers.

Objects and Classes, Attributes and Methods

While we have just justified its existence, what exactly is object-oriented technology? It's a safe bet it has something to do with *objects*. A large part of the paper-and-ink universe has been devoted to explaining, defining, rationalizing, justifying, or whining about exactly what an *object* is. So for the sake of the trees, let's take a simple approach here and simply assume that an object *is*. More specifically, it's a software thing with certain characteristics and relationships to other objects. The term "instance" is synonymous with object. More important is the concept of *class*, an object type (we will use the C++ term class from here on) which is an abstraction of a set (this is where the arguments start) of objects with the same or similar properties. An object is an instance of an object-type/class.

For comparison, here are some definitions of "object" from the literature:
- ". . . an object models some part of reality and is therefore something that exists in time and space" (Booch, 1991, p. 76).
- "We define an *object* as a concept, abstraction, or thing with crisp boundaries and meaning for the problem at hand" (Rumbaugh, 1991, p. 21).
- "An object is an abstraction of a set of real-world things such that:
    all of the real-world things in the set—the instances—have the same characteristics.
    all instances are subject to and conform to the same rules" (Shlaer and Mellor, 1988, pp. 14–15).

You can see the problem. What's an object, and what's a class? This book relies on the relatively standard, English definitions for these terms: An object is a software thing, and a class is a set of those things with similar properties. C++ uses the terms "instance" and "class" for these concepts.

Some other terms that apply to object-oriented technology are "abstraction" and "encapsulation." Abstraction has several definitions; operationally, it's the difference between an object and a class of objects. You abstract the properties of a set of objects into a class, which is therefore an abstract representation of the "ideal" object rather than any specific object. To encapsulate is a long word meaning "to hide within," and the application of this concept to software usually gets the meaning "data hiding." An object conceals its data state from the outside to gain all the design advantages of less coupling of the object to other objects. You can access an object only through its presumably well-defined public properties, and you cannot access its internal properties, thus protecting you from changes to the latter. Encapsulation relates to the functional concept of *modularity*, in which you decompose "modules" functionally into a system to minimize coupling and to maximize cohesion. Modularity and encapsulation are similar concepts in different paradigms.

Figure 2.1 shows the class Person and its properties.

The properties, again in the context of this book, consist of attributes and methods.

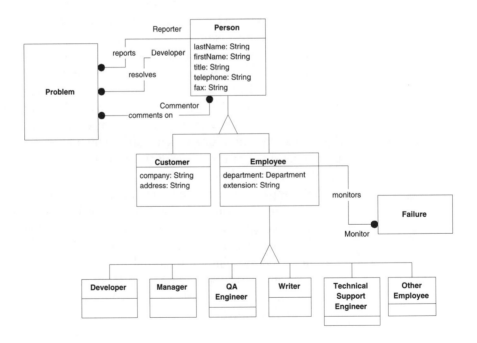

Figure 2.1 Class structure of the DTS Person class.

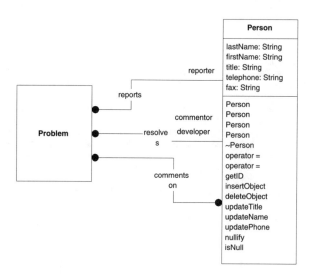

Figure 2.2 DTS class Person with attributes and methods.

An *attribute* "is a data value held by the objects in a class" (Rumbaugh, 1991, p. 23). This is a bit ambiguous, as it could mean a single value shared by all objects in a class (a *class attribute*) or a single value of the same type in each object (an *object attribute*). Abstractly, an attribute is a name, a storage class (class or instance), and a data type.

An operation is an abstraction for some kind of system behavior associated with the objects in a system. Here are two definitions:

- "An operation is some action one object performs upon another in order to elicit a reaction" (Booch, 1991, p. 80).
- "A method is the implementation of an operation for a class." (Rumbaugh, 1991, p. 25).

This book uses the term "method" unless there is some reason to talk about the abstract behavior instead of the concrete implementation of that behavior. C++ calls methods *member functions* and doesn't have the notion of an operation at all. You can also have C++ functions outside any class (*global functions*).

Figure 2.2 shows both attribute and method properties of the class Person. The following C++ code corresponds to this design model.

```
class Person : public DTSSQLObject
{
public:
        Person(Connection & connection, SDWORD id, const String & firstName,
            const String & lastName, const String & title, const String & telephone,
            const String & extension, const String & fax, const String & personType);
        Person(Connection & connection, SDWORD id); // query constructor
```

```
        Person(const Person & person);          // copy constructor
        Person(Connection & connection);
        ~Person() {}
        Person & operator =(const Person & person); // assignment operator
        Person & operator =(SDWORD id);             // query assignment operator
        // Access Methods
        SDWORD getId(void) const {return id;} // unique identifier for the person
        // Insert and Delete Methods
        RETCODE      insertObject(void); // insert the person into the database
        RETCODE      deleteObject(void); // delete the person from the database
        // Update Methods
        RETCODE      updateName(const String & firstName, const String & lastName);
        RETCODE updateTitle(const String & title);
        RETCODE updatePhone(const String & telephone, const String & extension, const String
& fax);
        void nullify(void) {id = 0;}
        BOOL isNull(void) const {return (id ? FALSE : TRUE);}

protected:
        SDWORD      id;                      // unique identifier
        String      firstName;               // first name of person
        String      lastName;                // last name of person
        String      title;                       // work title of person
        String      telephone;               // voice phone for person
        String      extension;               // extension for person
        String      fax;                         // facsimile phone for person
        String      personType;              // type of person (Employee, Customer)
};
```

Class Relationships: Inheritance and Polymorphism

Now that you know what class and object are, how do you unite them into a system of interacting things? There are two ways to look at a system of classes: as a system of class relationships (inheritance) or as a system of object relationships (composition or containment).

INHERITANCE

"Inheritance" is an active term for a passive relationship. The fundamental idea of inheritance is that two classes share some properties.

- "Inheritance means that we can develop a new class merely by stating how it differs from another, already existing class" (Jacobson, 1992, p. 94).

The classes in a system relate to one another in a directed, acyclic network based on their properties, and this network therefore represents the network of "is-a" relationships between the classes. Classes higher in the network represent generalizations of classes lower in it. A class higher in the network is a superclass of those below it, while a class lower in the network is a subclass of those above it. Reasonably loosely speaking, you can think of this network of classes

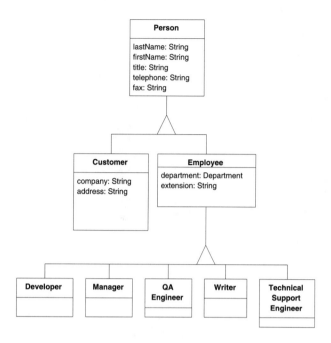

Figure 2.3 DTS Person class hierarchy.

as a semantic network, a set of "meaning" relationships. Figure 2.3 shows the class relationships of the DTS Person system. Person is the superclass of Customer and Employee; a Customer is a Person, and an Employee is a Person.

Note: Another relationship exists between classes, that of *aggregation* in the sense of being mutually exclusive. For example, you can constrain objects so that a Customer is not an Employee, and thus the class of Persons is really an aggregation of two subsets: Customers and Employees. In some situations class or integration testing needs to test such a relationship.

MULTIPLE INHERITANCE

Multiple inheritance happens when a class has two or more superclasses. A simple example combines the properties of the classes Time and Date into a new subclass TimeStamp. The TimeStamp class has both a Date and a Time and all the methods and attributes apply; it also adds fraction, which is the number of milliseconds. You overload certain methods (see the next section) to apply them to the combined data structure. Figure 2.4 shows the TimeStamp hierarchy.

POLYMORPHISM, OVERRIDING, AND OVERLOADING

Polymorphism is the ability to use the same name and protocol interchangeably with objects of different classes. A lot of complexities are associated with poly-

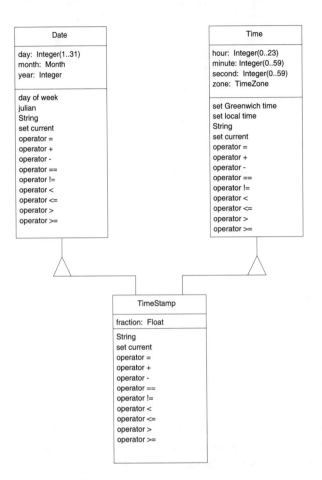

Figure 2.4 Class structure of DTS TimeStamp class.

morphism, and this book will stick with the relatively simple varieties found in the C++ language.

Overriding lets you redefine an operation in a subclass.

C++ in fact only lets you override methods, not attributes, and you have to take into account the full method signature, not just the method name when considering whether a subclass method overrides a superclass method. C++ lets you have several methods with the same name as long as the arguments are different in some way, and you can override each one in a subclass. Overriding a method in C++ means that when you call the method on an object of the subclass, you get the subclass behavior, not the overridden superclass behavior.

For example, in the TimeStamp example in Figure 2.4, the method **setCurrent()** in the TimeStamp class overrides the methods with the same signature in the base classes Time and Date. When you call **setCurrent()**

against a Date object, for example, it sets the object to the current date. When you call **setCurrent()** against a TimeStamp object, it sets both the current date and time and the fraction as well. On the other hand, the class doesn't override the operator methods because the arguments they take are different. For example, operator +() on Time takes another Time object; operator +() on TimeStamp takes another TimeStamp. You could override the base class operators by adding additional operator +() methods to add times and dates to time stamps.

Using the same name for a method but specifying a different protocol or signature by changing the types or number of the parameters is not, strictly speaking, overriding. To override a method, the method must have exactly the same signature. Methods that use the same name but change the signature are newly defined methods for the subclass.

Overloading takes this one step further and lets the language decide what kind of object is involved. C++ calls this feature a *virtual function*. When you overload a function, you can call a method without knowing what kind of object is involved and the runtime system will call the right method for the actual object. Here's an explanation: ". . . the ability to attach more than one meaning to the same name, ambiguities being resolved by looking at the context of each occurrence of the name, either at compile . . . or run time" (Meyer, 1988, p. 399).

Again in Figure 2.4, if you made the **setCurrent()** method a virtual function in C++, it would become an overloaded method. If you had a pointer to a Date object, but the object was really a TimeStamp, C++ would call the TimeStamp **setCurrent()** method. If the method weren't virtual, C++ would call the **Date** method. In this case, the class overrides the method but does not overload it, and if you are pointing at a Date, you get Date behavior regardless of the actual nature of the underlying object.

Object Relationships

You can relate objects in several different ways. The primary one is containment: the ability to contain objects inside other objects. You can send a message from one object to another one; you can have objects operating concurrently or asynchronously, performing actions at the same time. Finally, and related to inheritance, you can have compatible and incompatible objects: Some objects are appropriate in a given context while others are not.

It's also important to realize the basic distinction between classes (object types) and objects. Classes are conceptual in nature and can exist independently of any particular execution of your software system. The running software system instantiates objects from classes, and thus objects cannot exist independently of a particular running of the system. Object relationships are therefore an artifact of a dynamic software environment, although you can describe them statically. Runtime testing of one sort or another is required to test such relationships.

Containment

When you define a class, you can add as part of its definition the presence of attributes that contain objects instantiated from other classes. This results in a *containment hierarchy*, a network of interrelated objects of different types. The inheritance hierarchy is the conceptual structure of the system; the containment hierarchy is the physical structure of the system. You can use the inheritance hierarchy to share properties and the containment hierarchy to share objects.

Figure 2.5 shows the containment hierarchy based on the Fault class. You'll notice that there are many different kinds of relationships between objects (one to many, many to many, zero or one to one, etc.). These correspond to the kinds of relationships you find in data models, and often object-oriented design strongly resembles data modeling.

Figure 2.6 shows an alternative to using multiple inheritance for the TimeStamp object in Figure 2.4. Instead of inheriting the properties of Time and Date, this version of TimeStamp includes a Time object and a Date object directly, then adds the fraction object. This differs from the multiple-inheritance solution because the TimeStamp class does not get any of the properties of Time and Date. It can refer to the ones in the encapsulated objects, and the C++ storage structure is (probably) the same. This

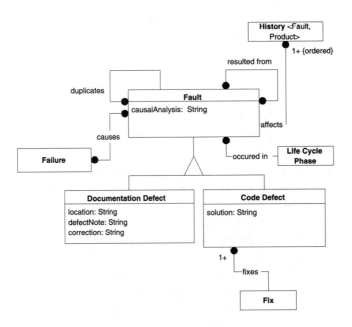

Figure 2.5 DTS Fault class containment hierarchy.

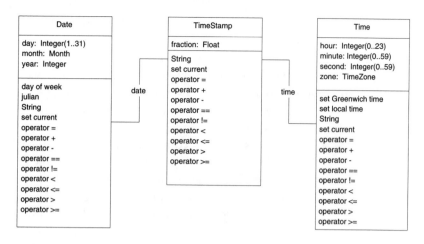

Date	TimeStamp	Time
day: Integer(1..31) month: Month year: Integer	fraction: Float	hour: Integer(0..23) minute: Integer(0..59) second: Integer(0..59) zone: TimeZone
day of week julian String set current operator = operator + operator - operator == operator != operator < operator <= operator > operator >=	String set current operator = operator + operator - operator == operator != operator < operator <= operator > operator >=	set Greenwich time set local time String set current operator = operator + operator - operator == operator != operator < operator <= operator > operator >=

Figure 2.6 Alternative class stucture of DTS TimeStamp class.

procedure might be appropriate if those properties did not apply reasonably to the TimeStamp class. So, for example, TimeStamp in Figure 2.6 does not have a **setGreenwichTime()** method, as it is not really appropriate for a time stamp.

MESSAGES AND VISIBILITY

The second major way that objects relate to one another is through messages. A *message* is a call from one object to a method of another object with optional arguments and a return value. *Visibility* is the ability of an object to send a message to another object. In some languages, you can control visibility directly at the class level; in C++, if you can get a pointer to the object, you can send a message to it (call its member functions). You control visibility of specific objects by encapsulating them within classes so that objects outside the encapsulating object cannot see the hidden object.

The message and visibility structure is the dynamic structure of your system; the sequence of messages is the behavior of the system outside the performance of a specific method.

Messages are useful to make objects visible to other objects. If a particular object is visible to a second one, that second one can call a third one, passing a reference from the first object to the third one. The third one can then call the first one's methods. Of course, the more of this you do, the less encapsulation you have, and therefore the more tightly coupled your system becomes. Loosely coupled systems are generally more conducive to reuse.

CONCURRENCY AND TIMING

Although not particularly a C++ issue, since that language doesn't support concurrency directly, many software systems make use of operating system or language facilities to have objects that execute in different *threads*, or sequences of dynamic behavior. Concurrency means that two objects are in separate threads and hence they can execute their methods independently of one another. Concurrency relations come into play when these objects send messages to one another. Note that one method must:

- Execute within a certain time of the end of a method of another object (timing)
- Send a message to a concurrent object and return without waiting for that object to finish processing (concurrent execution)
- Send a message to a concurrent object and wait for that object to finish processing (blocked execution)
- Send a message to another object, which must then asynchronously send a further message on to another object (buffered execution)

And so on. Concurrency introduces enormous complexity into the relationships between objects (and into the testing of these relationships). A conceptual example of concurrency is the sequencing of tasks in a project life cycle: Some tasks move in parallel, some depend on others to finish, and some are completely independent of one another.

COMPATIBILITY

Compatibility is the ability of one object to send a message to another object based on the nature of the message. That is, the calling object has a certain message that it wants to send, while the receiving object understands exactly that sort of message. It is an error to send a message to an object that doesn't understand the message.

A *protocol* is the structure of a message; an *interface* is the structure of a method (or the set of methods of a class, taken in the large). The protocol of a message must match the interface of the called method.

C++ is a *type-safe* language, which means that the language itself enforces the compatibility requirement. C++ compilers generate compile-time errors if you make an incompatible call, which saves you time and effort later in the programming process. Other languages, such as Smalltalk, enforce the compatibility requirement at runtime; they let you send the message, but the system keeps moving up the inheritance tree until it decides no interface matches the message protocol. You hope there's some code to handle the situation when that happens. These latter languages can be more flexible and easier to use, but type safety generally does reduce your overall risk of technical failure.

A more general issue with compatibility, particularly of interest with respect to reusability, is whether an interface provides what the caller needs. For example, two versions of a software package may want to use the same class, but the second version needs additional information from the call and is therefore incompatible with the class. Another example is when a standard interface meets up with a calling object that doesn't use the standard protocol, such as a database program that uses a different dialect of SQL. This kind of compatibility relationship is the basis for judging whether a system meets compatibility requirements.

System Relationships

Each system has internal and external relationships. External relationships *couple* the system to other systems. Moving beyond the class and object as systems (externally related to other objects and classes), systems of objects may send messages to objects in other systems of objects. The boundary of a system of objects is always slightly arbitrary, but you will find your architecture breaks up into such systems based on whether the objects tend to communicate with each other more than with other objects. Figure 2.7 shows the system structure of our Defect Tracking System (DTS). The Person system never calls anything outside itself, while the Problem and Product systems call each other and the Person system. Each of these systems has strong relationships between the classes and objects within itself but much more tenuous relationships with objects outside the system. Often systems reside in separate, and possibly dynamically loaded, libraries (DLLS). Generally, the lower the degree of *coupling*, the easier it is to reuse a system. For example, you could move the Person system to a completely different product without changing a line of code.

Each system may be more or less complex in terms of its internal relationships. The degree of *system complexity* depends on how control transfers around the system. Note that this is similar to the complexity of the individual method or class. The more complex the system, the more difficult it is to test and to maintain.

Finally, and more abstractly, the system relates to its specifications or requirements through consistency and correctness. *Correctness* is the ability of

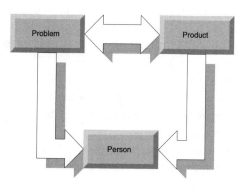

Figure 2.7 DTS subsystem visibility relationships.

the system to do what its specification says it does without errors. *Consistency* is the ability of the system to be correct reliably across multiple executions.

Object versus Process

Before looking at the structure of the book, you need to understand the fundamental organizing principle behind it: the object. The last section introduced the various concepts comprising the object-oriented approach; now we compare it briefly to the process approach and note some major differences.

The quality system, of which testing is a key part, is all about quality. But what is quality? It's an object—value. Quality is value. In the object-oriented approach, quality is the object of concern. In the process approach to quality, the focus is on the quality process, not on quality (value) itself. This is a perfectly valid way of looking at the world, but it results in a process-oriented structure rather than a value-oriented one. By using an object-oriented approach in this book, we hope to refocus testing on its object: value. Value means productivity for the development organization while value may be expressed as "satisfaction" from the end user perspective.

To take full advantage of this book, you need to reorient your thinking from processes to objects. For example, when you think about the process life cycle, think about it as an object (with a vision, mission, and objectives as well as attributes and methods). It contains other objects (processes, milestones, infrastructure). Thus "process" is itself an object (with vision and so on) with all that implies. Instead of thinking about process steps, you should think about the results of the process—or, rather, how the dynamic behavior of the objects ("results" such as a requirements document) interacts with other objects to become a system.

For example, in studying the automation of system integration, this book focuses on the system as a software object that is part of the testing system. It does not focus on the process, or sequence of steps, by which you integrate the software. You see the different components of the object (tools, software system, test suites, resources, and so on) and a series of methods that show you how the object dynamically interacts with other objects (building the automation system, running it, etc.).

This way of looking at the quality system tends to make the system much more concrete. As you use different parts of the book, you will become more and more familiar with those concrete structures and dynamics you need to know to make everything work.

Instead of process diagrams, most concepts in the book have class and object diagrams that show how classes and objects relate to one another. The book uses standard fishbone diagrams (see Part 1: How to Read this Book) to show how a particular class or object relates to others in the overall system.

Part 1

How to Read
This Book

CHAPTER 3

OBJECT ROAD MAP

The object road map in this chapter shows you how the overall quality system functions as a collection of objects. Chapter 4 pulls the system inside out and shows you the inheritance hierarchy of the quality system. Looking at the containment hierarchy shows you a *system structure*, which groups objects into clusters by the way other objects use them. It shows the containment relationships between the classes.

The class diagrams in this chapter use a high-level diagramming technique to represent just the class and the containment relationships between classes. Figure 3.1 shows classes as beveled boxes and the containment relationships as the lines between those boxes. That is, when you see two boxes connected by a line, it means that one class refers to the other. The lines are not directed (that is, they aren't arrows pointing one way) because visibility is both ways along the line.

The diagrams in the part introductions are similar but focus on the classes for a particular system, such as the process or test system. These diagrams, and the text accompanying them, go to the next level of detail. They tell you

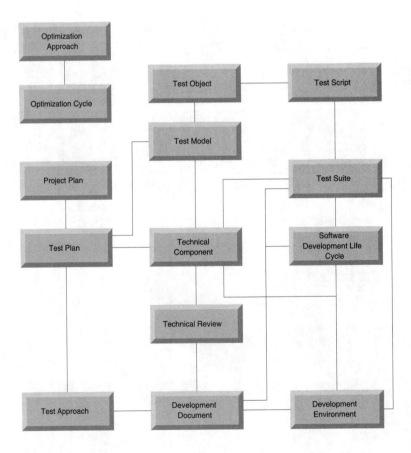

Figure 3.1 Summary of the quality system containment relationships.

specifically how the classes in the system interact with one another and with classes outside the system. Two shades of gray represent classes within the system and classes outside the system in other systems. See Figure P2.1 for an example. This chapter presents the highest level overview, while the part introductions provide an intermediate level.

The more detailed diagrams in each chapter show you the details of the class, such as attributes and methods, as well as the inheritance and containment relationships. This chapter provides an overview that can help you see just the structural relationships between the different types of things in the system. Some people get more out of the inheritance diagrams in Chapter 4; others want to take a more structural approach to understanding the quality system.

Most of the text in this chapter duplicates material you will find in the introduction to each part, tying all the descriptions together and showing the pieces from different systems organized around central classes that use them.

Figure 3.1 shows the containment relationships between the classes at a very high level and summarizes the fundamental objects in the quality system.

The *optimization approach*, though of central importance in the quality system, contains only the *optimization cycle* class. As all classes in the system inherit the optimization approach, however, it the most used class in the system. See Part II for a complete discussion of optimization.

The *project plan* is the most important object in the project system. It contains virtually every object in that system and many in the test, process, and software development systems. If everything is a system, and if optimization is the central ethic of the quality system, the project plan represents the everyday cycle of getting things done. In Figure 3.1, the project plan contains the test plan, which is the driver for the entire test system. See Part V for a complete discussion of the project plan and its components.

Although omitted from the figure for clarity reasons, the project plan also contains the software development life cycle, which comprises a set of development processes. Each development process has inputs and outputs that, although they can be any object in the system, focus on technical components, development documents, test suites, and the development environment. The project drives the life cycle processes, which in turn drive everything else. See Part II for a complete discussion of the life cycle and its processes.

Because this is a book on testing, the quality system focuses on the details of the test plan more than on any other object. The test plan contains the test approach, the technical components under test, and the test models. See Part III for everything you ever wanted to know about testing objects.

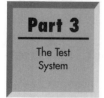

The *test approach*, and in particular the subclass *hierarchical method*, is what this book is about. As an object, it is one of many, but the test approach is a system that contains the rest of the testing system. It contains development documents of interest to testing and details the infrastructure of tools and resources the test system uses (the test environment).

The *test model* is the key technical object in the test system because it contains the whole complex of the actual tests: test objects, test suites, technical components under test, and test scripts. Understanding the test model is central to understanding the hierarchical approach. If you carry away nothing else from this book, understanding test models and their position in the test system will provide the best rewards for your investment of time.

In summary, the test model is an abstract model of the technical component you want to test. It provides a different way of looking at the software or other technical material that is better suited to developing tests. Programmers don't need test models to code classes; but the code they write is not of much use to testers. The things testers need to know are different from the things programmers need to know. Hence, the test model. The *test objects* are the components of the test model that correspond to individual tests. The kind of test object varies with the kind of test model. From the test object, you can develop *test scripts* that implement one or more test objects. *Test suites* collect test scripts to fit them into development phases or other categories of your choice.

Technical components are the meat of the system, the software and design components that make up the actual system you produce. All the other classes are for support services in one way or another. While you can't do technical components without them, the components are the result while the other things are the means for getting that result. See Chapter 10 for a complete discussion of technical components.

Development documents are the various kinds of technical documents that make up the project's library of documents. Documents live in the development environment. They document characteristics of technical components, test suites and their scripts, and the life cycle processes. The test approach refers to development documents and their components, such as requirements use cases or designs. See Chapter 18 for a complete discussion of development documents.

Technical reviews are a key part of the software development system. They relate technical components (the thing you are producing) to development documents (the description in various forms of the thing you are producing). Reviews are essential to quality; you often can catch more problems with reviews that compare documents to reality than you can by testing the reality. See Chapter 19 for a complete discussion of technical reviews.

At the bottom of Figure 3.1, and rightfully so, lives the *development environment*. This class provides the infrastructure for the entire game: tools, resources, repositories, and so on. Without a development environment that serves all the systems (process, development, testing, and project management), you wouldn't get very far with your project. See Chapter 21 for a complete discussion of the development environment.

Ch. 10

Test Repository

Ch. 18

Development Document

Ch. 19

Technical Reviews

Ch. 21

Development Environment

CHAPTER 4

CLASS
TAXONOMY

Chapter 3 looked at the quality system from the perspective of the containment hierarchy. That way of looking at the system shows you how the overall system functions as a collection of objects. This chapter pulls the system inside out and shows you the inheritance hierarchy of the quality system. Looking at this hierarchy shows you a *taxonomy* of the system, which classifies the objects into meaningful classes. It shows the generalization and specialization relationships between the classes and tells you how to categorize the different types of things in the system.

The class diagrams in this chapter use a high-level diagramming technique to represent just the class and the inheritance relationships between classes. Figure 4.1 shows a root class on the left and the subclasses extending to the right connected by branch lines. A connection from a class box on the left to a class box on the right means that the class on the right inherits from the class on the left. If more than one line flows into a box on the right, it means the class inherits from two or more classes. There is only one instance of multiple inheritance in the quality system: the user-interface test scripts in the test system.

The more detailed diagrams in each chapter show you the details of the

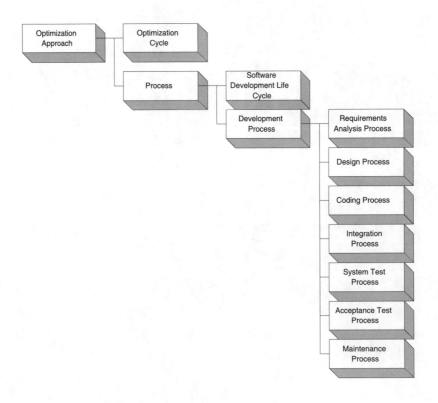

Figure 4.1 Optimization and process inheritance hierarchy.

class, such as attributes and methods, as well as the inheritance and containment relationships. The overview in this chapter can help you see just the semantic relationships between the different types of things in the system. Some people get more out of the containment diagrams in Chapter 3; others want to take a more taxonomic approach to understanding the quality system.

Most of the text in this chapter duplicates material you will find in the introduction to each part, tying all the descriptions together and showing the pieces from different systems organized under their parent classes rather than in separate systems.

Ch. 3

Object
Road Map

The *optimization approach* is the basic class in the quality system and is the root class for all the other classes in this book. The optimization cycle is a kind of optimization approach; each optimization approach in this book also contains an optimization cycle. (See Chapter 3.) Figure 4.1 is the optimization and process-related class hierarchy.

The software development life cycle comprises a set of development processes. Each development process has inputs and outputs that, although they can be any object in the system, focus on technical components, development documents, test suites, and test scripts. Specific relationships exist between subclasses of development process and specific technical objects, but the details are beyond the scope of this book.

Figure 4.2 shows the document and technical object class hierarchy. The *project document* hierarchy contains all the documents that are part of a project. There are three kinds of project document: the project plan, the development document, and the test plan.

The statement of work, schedule, resource plan, risk management plan, and milestone are all parts of the *project plan*.

There are four kinds of *development document*: requirements, design, standards, and test evaluation documents. The *requirements document* contains the requirements and use cases for the system. The *design document* contains architectural and low-level designs for the system. *Standards documents* come in three types: the design standard, the code standard, and the test standard. *Design standards* are rules for what a design must do. *Code standards* are the rules you must follow when writing code. *Test standards* are criteria for test success, test script documentation standards, and test report formatting standards. The *test evaluation document* summarizes the results of a test using the test standards for each kind of test.

The *test plan*, a part of the overall project plan, lays out the test approach and contains the guts of the test abstractions (test models and objects). The test plan contains the test approach and the individual test models for the particular technical component under test. A test plan can be either a foundation component test plan or a system test plan. A system test plan applies to testing a system and may have some structural differences from a functional component test plan, which applies to any foundation component.

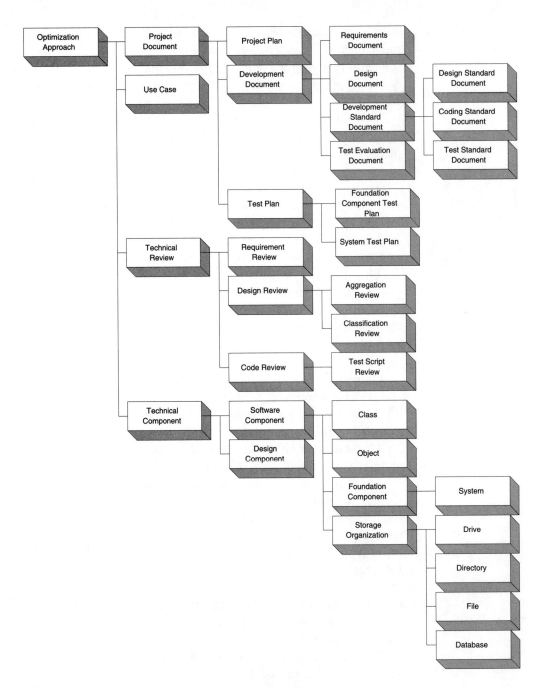

Figure 4.2 Document and technical object inheritance hierarchy.

The *use case* is the primary component of requirements documents; it is a
sequence of transactions from the point of view of system users playing dif-

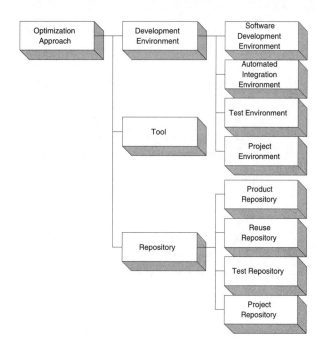

Figure 4.3 Environment (infrastructure) inheritance hierarchy.

ferent roles in using the system.

Technical reviews include reviews of *requirements*, *designs* (including both composition and inheritance hierarchies, the *aggregation* and *classification* reviews, respectively), and *code*. *Test script reviews* are a kind of code review.

Technical components include both *software* and *design components*. The technical component is an abstraction that represents a technical "thing" to which various parts of the system refer. Sometimes, parts of the system refer directly to software or design components. Software components include *classes* and *objects*, unsurprisingly; most object-oriented programming systems have these components. A great deal of software development concerns collections of classes and objects as well; the *foundation component* (a meaningful collection of classes) and its subclass *system* (a meaningful collection of foundation components) represent such collections. Finally, the *storage organization* (*drives*, *directories*, *files*, and *databases*) represents the static data component of software.

Figure 4.3 shows the class hierarchy for the environment and infrastructure classes. Software development happens in the context of a *development environment*, of which there are four types: the *software development* and *automated integration environments* of interest to developers, the *test environment* of interest to testers, and the *project environment* of interest to project managers.

The *tool* and *repository* are both components of the development environment and thus part of the infrastructure of software development (as well as of testing and project management). There are four kinds of repository:

- **Product Repository:** Contains the software and data for the product itself.
- **Reuse Repository:** Contains reusable software and data.
- **Test Repository:** Contains test scripts, plans, data, and results.
- **Project Repository:** Contains project documents and data.

Figure 4.4 shows the test support class inheritance hierarchy. While these classes are not tests themselves, they provide important services to the testing system.

The *test approach*, and in particular the subclass *hierarchical method*, is what this book is about. As an object, it is one of many, but the test approach is a system that contains the rest of the testing system.

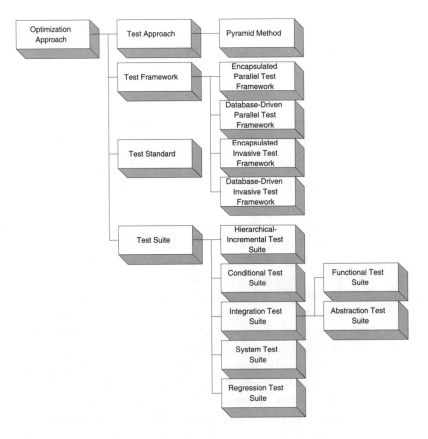

Figure 4.4 Test support inheritance hierarchy.

The *test framework* provides the software drivers for many of the test scripts. There are four approaches to test frameworks; we recommend the *database-driven, invasive test framework* approach.

The *test standard* is a criterion by which you judge the success or failure of a test script. The test standard document contains the test standards.

The *test suite* is a collection of test scripts and serves to group the scripts into meaningful components. A different kind of test suite exists for the major types of testing that we recommend as part of the hierarchical method.

Figure 4.5 shows the specific test classes and their inheritance hierarchy.

The *test model* models a technical component from the tester's perspective, as opposed to the coder's or architect's perspective. While there are more kinds of test model than the figure shows, these are the important ones to the hierarchical method.

The *test object* represents a single test that is part of the larger test model. Again, only the ones important to the hierarchical method are shown.

The *test script* is the executable form of the test object that actually implements the test. There are class-based scripts (*class-object test script*), integration scripts (*class-to-class test script*), *system test scripts*, user-interface (*UI*) *test scripts*, and the *regression test script*. The UI test script and system test script are both parents to the three user-interface scripts. They can be both integration and system tests depending on how you go about testing the UI. The regression test script represents any kind of test script that becomes part of a regression test suite that runs against a technical component to retest it after changes.

Figure 4.6 shows the inheritance structure of the project-related classes.

The statement of work, schedule, resource plan, risk management plan, and milestone are all pieces of the project plan. A *statement of work* lays out the scope, or extent, of the project, including the project requirements, the test plan, the documentation plan, and the work breakdown structure. The *schedule* takes the work breakdown structure tasks, and *milestone* specifies the dependencies between tasks and assigns resources to tasks, then specifies the timing of tasks based on estimates of effort, dependency relationships, and resource availability. The *resource plan* lays out the organizational and authority structure of the resource system. The *risk management plan* analyzes risk in the schedule or technical components and provides a plan for managing that risk.

A *deliverable baseline* is a configuration of technical components, usually under the control of a configuration management system, that gives you a foundation on which to build additional baselines. The ultimate baseline is the system baseline, when you finish coding and testing your system. There are several types of baseline. The *initial baseline* is your "first draft" of a component. The *alpha baseline* is your "final draft." The *beta baseline* is the production release to external users. The *iteration baselines* are the iterations on

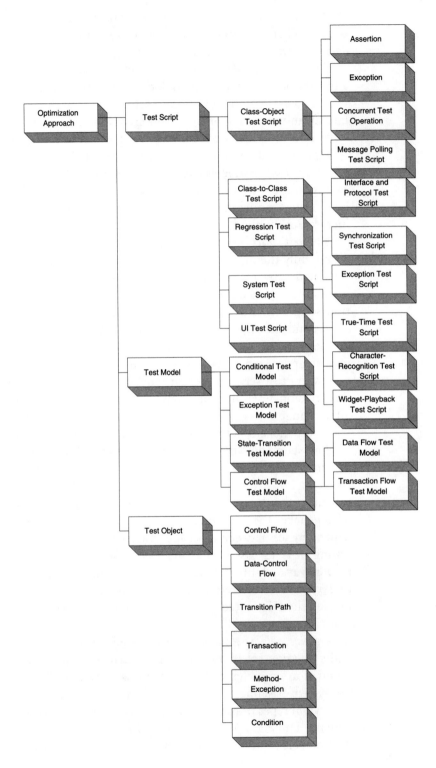

Figure 4.5 Test inheritance hierarchy.

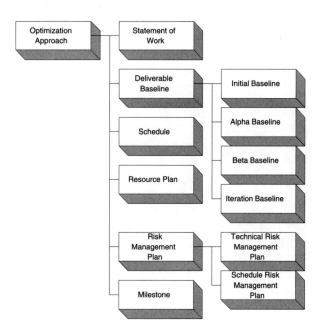

Figure 4.6 Project inheritance hierarchy.

this final release to fix problems or add features as your life cycle continues. It is vital to understand that these baselines include not only the standard waterfall phase deliverables but also delivery of the smallest foundation component. *Every* component of the system goes through baselining in the hierarchical method to guarantee that it can serve as a reusable foundation for further work.

REQUIREMENTS DOCUMENT FOR THE DEFECT TRACKING SYSTEM EXAMPLE

This chapter provides you with the original Requirements Document for the Defect Tracking System, the software development project used to illustrate all the nooks and crannies of object-oriented testing in this book. All examples in the following chapters come from the same example. Reading this chapter along with the previous two chapters will give you the understanding you need to follow the example sections in the rest of the book.

Introduction: Defect Tracking System Requirements

The Defect Tracking System (DTS) is a software system for improving the quality of software products through the management of information about defects in the software, including reporting, auditing, and measurement functions. The DTS is a state-of-the-art information management application that supports the entire life cycle of defect discovery, tracking, and removal. The DTS also provides a working example of software design and coding that seminars on software development can use to illustrate concepts.

Modern defect tracking distinguishes between software faults and software failures. A software *failure* is "the departure of the external results of program operation from requirements." A software *fault* is "the defect in the program that, when executed under particular conditions, causes a failure."[1] A software *enhancement* is an improvement in the program that, when executed under particular conditions, removes a problem that is not a failure (an *opportunity*); you can see an opportunity as a failure if you treat some requirements as latent rather than explicit. It's worth stating that very few sets of requirements can be exhaustive given the limitations of human cognition, so failure is relative to recognition of the true requirements, which is necessarily incomplete over time.

The DTS tracks defects in multiple software *products* supported by a single organization, the *software producer*. The DTS supports several audiences:

- **Customers**—those who license the software form the software producer
- **Technical Support**—those who support the software; employed by the software producer
- **Quality Assurance**—those who test the software; employed by the software producer
- **Documentation**—those who create documents that assist customers in using the software product or products
- **Development**—those who build the software; employed by the software producer

---

[1] J. D. Musa, A. Iannino, and K. Okumoto, *Software Reliability: Measurement, Prediction, Application.* New York, McGraw-Hill, 1987. Cited in G. M. Weinberg, *Quality Software Management, Volume 1: Systems Thinking.* Dorset House Publishing, 1991. Chapter 12 in Weinberg contains an excellent and approachable discussion of the purpose of tracking defects, and supplies most of the requirements in this document.

- **Management**—those responsible for managing Technical Support, Quality Assurance, Documentation, and Development, including general and project management; employed by the software producer
- **Other Producer**—those employees of the producer other than those in the groups above; these employees can act as customers with respect to failures, but the DTS must distinguish them from customers, because they don't pay for the product

There is one section following that describes the specific requirements for each of these audiences. In addition to these requirements, there is a second class of requirements for the DTS software based on its didactic orientation. There is a section following the audience sections, detailing specific requirements for the DTS software design relating to its use in seminars on testing object-oriented software systems.

Defect Life Cycle

the DTS assumes the following life cycle transitions. The process may start at the different events marked as *entry*.

1. Product Fails (entry)
2. Failure Reported
3. Failure Assigned for Verification
4. Failure Verified or Unfounded
5. Failure Assigned for Investigation by Management
6. Fault Discovered (entry) or Enhancement Recommended (entry)
7. Fault or Enhancement Associated with Failure
8. Fault or Enhancement on Hold or Assigned for Development
9. Fault or Enhancement Resolved
10. Failure Resolved

The DTS makes no assumptions about the exact status of persons who can assign responsibility roles.

Customer Requirements

A *customer* is a company or person that licenses the software product or products that the DTS tracks. Customers experience failures and report them to the software producer, usually through Technical Support. These requirements permit the customer to report problems directly into the DTS, although the software producer must permit that by making the system available to customers through access paths in its network, or by other means such as paper-based forms for entering reports. None of this access is formally a part of the DTS itself or these requirements.

Customers may or may not be exposed to the actual DTS software at the discretion of the company. To let customers access the DTS, the DTS must handle the following requirements and limitations:

1. Customers must be able to enter failure reports, including test cases that will allow Technical Support to reproduce the error (Reporter responsibility role).

2. Customers must be able to query status on failures they have entered without requiring them to enter numeric keys. They should be able to select and sort the reports by date and reporter (the individual who entered the report).

3. Customers may be able to query those failures published to the customer community, but must not be able to query failures not explicitly published. Publishing is community-wide, not on a per-customer basis.

4. Customer access must be through a client application running on Microsoft Windows 3.1 or above. It must access a server database running at the company through a SQL-based, client/server interface accessible by a modem running at 9600 bps or above.

5. Also, the failure report must contain the following information:
   - A unique identifier for the failure
   - The software product that failed, including the name of the product and the specific version of the product that failed
   - Customer reporting the failure, with information sufficient for the software producer to contact the individual who reported the failure with updated information
   - Date of report
   - Description of the failure
   - Description of the hardware and software configuration under which the software failed
   - Any supporting materials (test cases) required to reproduce the failure

6. Customers must be able to prioritize the failure, using a set of ordinal severity categories.

Technical Support Requirements

Technical Support is a part of the software producer that handles the interface between the customer and the software producer.

1. Technical Support must be able to enter failure reports (Reporter responsibility role) containing the following information:
   - A unique identifier for the failure
   - The software product that failed, including the name of the product and the specific version of the product that failed

- Customer reporting the failure, with information sufficient for Technical Support to contact the individual who reported the failure with updated information
- Date of report
- Person reporting the failure
- Description of the failure
- Description of the hardware and software configuration under which the software failed
- Any supporting materials (test cases) required to reproduce the failure

2. Technical Support must be able to query all the above information for all failures in the database, selecting and sorting on date, customer, and reporter.

3. Technical Support must be able to prioritize failures, using a set of ordinal severity categories; they should be able to enter both the customer's priority and Technical Support's priority.

Quality Assurance Requirements

Quality Assurance (QA) is a part of the software producer that tests the software product or products as its main responsibility. QA may experience failures directly as a result of testing the software product.

1. AW must be able to enter failure reports, playing the Reporter role. A failure report contains the following information:

- A unique identifier for the failure
- The software product that failed, including the name of the product and the specific version of the product that failed
- Test case or cases that resulted in the failure
- Date of report
- Person reporting the failure
- Description of the failure
- Description of the hardware and software configuration under which the software failed
- Any supporting materials required to reproduce the failure

2. A person must take responsibility for monitoring changes to the status of a failure (Monitor responsibility role). All failures must have a person playing the Monitor role. The Monitor must be able to resolve the failure, which removes any Action role from the failure and notifies the Reporter if possible. The type of failure solution is one of several possibilities:

- Fault Removal
- Acceptable Failure (too low priority to fix)

- Unreproducible
- User Error (not a failure of the software but of the user's use of the software)
- Feature (not a failure but intentionally the way the software works)

3. QA must be able to report on the life cycle status of all failures to enable QA to track the failures for measurement and management purposes.

4. QA must be able to report the failure rate of the product relative to some meaningful time interval, such as a week, month, or quarter (including a fiscal quarter).

5. QA must be able to prioritize failures, using a set of ordinal severity categories; this priority must be separate from any other priority entered for the failure.

Documentation Requirements

Documentation is a part of the software producer that documents the software product or products as its main responsibility. Documentation employees use the software while documenting it; these requirements are similar to those of other producers (see the following). Documentation also documents faults and failures so that customers and others know what to expect or how to work around problems in a product that Development has not yet fixed. The DTS assumes this documentation is in the form of *release notes*, published text that describes the problem and any temporary solutions to it.

1. Documentation must be able to enter a release note different from the problem description, which may not conform to documentation style guidelines or requirements.

2. Documentation must be able to specify the exact product (name and version) for a release note, since a problem may exist in more than one version of the software product.

3. There is no requirement for style information to be associated with the release note; documentation is responsible for application of style in the published form of the note.

Development Requirements

Development is a part of the software producer that builds, or produces, the software product. A developer may report failures as an *other producer* (see the following). Also, developers are responsible for investigating and fixing faults that lead to failures, as well as for developing software enhancements to address failures.

1. Developers must be able to query failures, enhancements, and faults currently assigned to them in the Developer responsibility role, and to order

them by management priority and date. Developers should be able to select enhancements and faults by unique identifier to permit easy communication of work status.

2. Developers must be able to enter faults and to link faults to failures; faults can exist without failures, failures can link to more than one fault, and faults can link to more than one failure. Fault information must include this information to permit marking them as resolved:

- A unique identifier for the fault
- The person entering the fault
- A description of the fault
- A brief analysis of the root cause of the fault
- The software product or products in which the fault exists
- Life cycle phase in which the fault occurred (Requirements, High-Level Design, Low-Level Design, Coding, Testing, Maintenance)
- Whether the fault is the result of fixing another fault (identified by a unique identifier)

3. Managers must be able to get a list of the faults that Developers resolve.

4. Developers must be able to mark faults assigned to them (and no others) as duplicates of other faults if one derives from the other according to the root-cause analysis; marking a fault as duplicate links the faults. Managers must be able to get a list of the faults a Developer has marked as duplicating other faults.

5. Developers must be able to enter the following information about fixes to the software product, and to link the fix to one or more faults:

- Developer's identity
- Date of the fix
- Software product to which the fix applies (possibly several)
- Description of the fix
- List of software configuration units (SCUs) the fix affects

Management Requirements

Management is the group of employees of the software producer, who are responsible for managing the efforts of the other employees in the groups previously mentioned, and specifically for assigning work to employees. Managers include group managers, project managers, senior managers, and corporate executives.

1. A manager must be able to assign the Monitor and Developer roles for failures, enhancements, and faults.

2. The manager must be able to query any changes to the status of the enhancement over time.

3. A manager must be able to give a failure, enhancement, or fault a *holding* status that acknowledges receipt of responsibility but puts the work involved on hold until further notice; usually this implies a lack of adequate resources to handle the work or some dependency, and there should be an explanation of the reason for the status associated with the status.

4. The DTS must notify a manager when a person finishes a task assigned by the manager.

5. Managers must be able to query failures, enhancements, and faults of any description for possible assignment to employees.

6. Managers must be able to query failures, enhancements, and faults assigned to particular employees, selecting and ordering by status, date, and priority.

7. Managers must be able to resolve faults.

8. Managers should be able to generate reports on failure and fault occurrence rates for all work done by the software producer (implying that the DTS must support storing all such work in a single database rather than in separate databases, though without the requirement to do so).

Other Producer Requirements

An *other producer* is an employee of the software producer other than a member of the Technical Support, QA, Documentation, Development, or Management groups. Often, members of the marketing, MIS, or other organizations will encounter failures while experimenting or using the software. While these software product users have similar characteristics to customers, the DTS must distinguish them from customers, since they don't actually pay for using the software product.

1. Other producers must be able to enter failure reports, including test cases that will allow Technical Support to reproduce the error (Reporter responsibility role).

2. Other producers must be able to query status on failure reports they have entered without requiring them to enter numeric keys. They should be able to select and sort the reports by date and reporter (the individual who entered the report).

3. Other producers may be able to query those failures published to the company outside of development and QA, but must not be able to query failures not explicitly published. Publishing is company-wide, not on a per-employee basis.

4. Producer access must be through a client application running on Microsoft Windows 3.1 or above. It must access a server database running at the

company through a SQL-based, client/server interface accessible by a modem running at 9600 bps or above.

5. Also, the failure report must contain the following information:
   - A unique identifier for the failure
   - The software product that failed, including the name of the product and the specific version of the product that failed
   - Customer reporting the failure, with information sufficient for the software producer to contact the individual who reported the failure with updated information
   - Date of report
   - Description of the failure
   - Description of the hardware and software configuration under which the software failed
   - Any supporting materials required to reproduce the failure

6. A customer must be able to prioritize the failure, using a set of ordinal severity categories.

Priorities and Status

Priority in the DTS is an ordinal scale, where 1 is the highest priority:

1. Kills People
2. Data Loss
3. System Crash
4. Unrecoverable Error
5. Error with Workaround
6. Cosmetic

Status is a nominal scale with no implied order:
- Reported
- Verified
- Unfounded (not an error)
- Holding (not being dealt with)
- Underway (being dealt with)
- Resolved

Part 1 References

1. Grady Booch. *Object-Oriented Design with Applications.* Benjamin/Cummings, Redwood City, CA: 1991.

This book was one of the first on the subject to teach a relatively large audience. Rumbaugh and Jacobsen have recently joined forces with Booch at Rational and are working on a unified methodology.

2. Ivar Jacobsen et al. *Object-Oriented Software Engineering: A Use Case Driven Approach.* Addison-Wesley, Menlo Park, CA: 1992.

This book introduced the world to the applicability of use cases. It is a seminal work in that a test object (use case) is deployed as a major artifact of the software modeling activity.

3. Bertrand Meyer. *Object-Oriented Software Construction.* Prentice Hall, New York, NY: 1988.

An excellent source for additional conceptual material, Meyer focuses more on Eiffel as an implementation language than most Americans would appreciate.

4. James Rumbaugh et al. *Object-Oriented Modeling and Design.* Prentice Hall, Englewood Cliffs, NJ: 1991.

We chose Rumbaugh's notation for our diagrams. His methodology is a popular and generally good, all-around approach. However, Fusion and some of the more recent developments warrant serious consideration. Perhaps this is behind the attempt at Rational to forge a comprehensive composite methodology from the approaches of Rumbaugh, Booch, and Jacobsen.

5. Sally Shlaer and Stephen J. Mellor. *Object-Oriented Systems Analysis.* Yourdon Press, Englewood Cliffs, NJ: 1989.

Excellent introduction to the subject. Well written with simple, easily understood examples to illustrate the concepts.

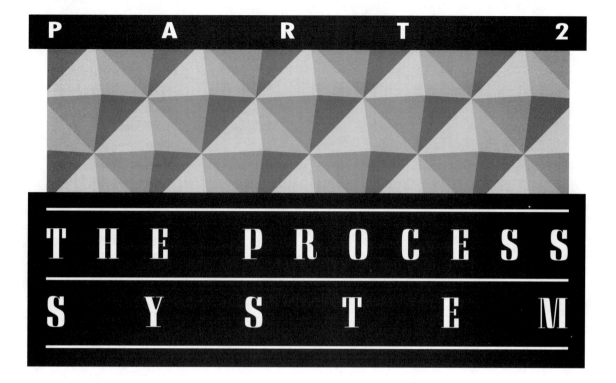

The *process system* is the part of the quality system that relates to the dynamic structure of the system: the way the system operates. The process system contains the optimization approach and the software development processes that are part of the software development life cycle.

Figure P2.1 shows the inheritance hierarchy of the process system. The optimization approach is the basic class in the quality system and is the root class for all of the other classes in this book. The optimization cycle, process, software development life cycle, and all the development processes are part of the process system.

Figure P2.2 shows the containment relationships between the classes at a high level.

The optimization approach, though of central importance in the quality system, contains only the optimization cycle class; all classes in the system inherit the optimization approach, however.

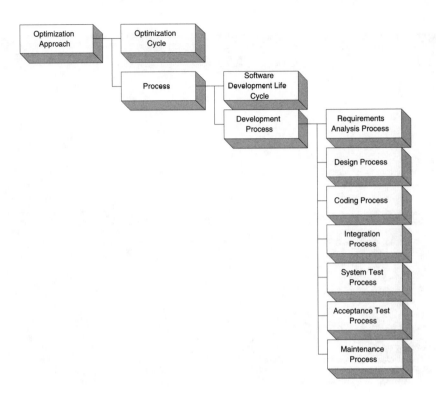

Figure P2.1 Process system inheritance hierarchy.

The software development life cycle comprises a set of development processes. Each development process has inputs and outputs that, although they can be any object in the system, focus on technical components, development documents, test suites, and test scripts. Specific relationships exist between subclasses of development process and specific technical objects, but the details are beyond the scope of this book.

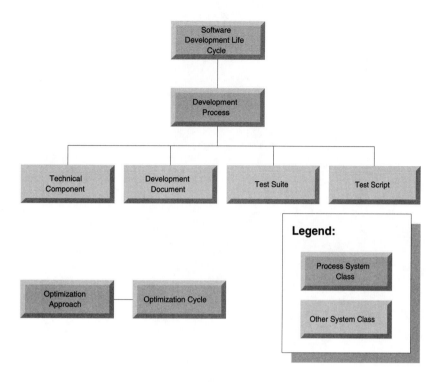

Figure P2.2 Process system containment hierarchy.

CHAPTER 6

THE APPROACH TO OPTIMIZATION

The Approach to Optimization

Optimization is the process of improving something to an optimal state. The *approach to optimization* in this book is an abstract class of objects that represents a specific approach to optimizing some object. Each object class in this book contains a leadership section listing the optimization approach attributes. The approach is the root class for all the classes in the system, so all classes inherit the attributes and override them. Each class must override the abstract vision, mission, and *operational objectives* (objective-approach-measurement triplets). You can think of these attributes as a special set of *class-level attributes* that apply to all objects of a class.

The driving object for optimizing the system is the optimization cycle, the class developed in the next section of this chapter. The section provides details of the optimization process and discusses the attributes of the approach, as opposed to the attributes of the process itself. The approach is static, while the cycle is dynamic in nature.

Ch. 1

Every Thing
Is a System

This approach to optimization derives primarily from the primitive concepts of *value* and *productivity*. Everything we do as part of the quality system assumes that we want to optimize value and productivity. These assumptions—that "value" is valuable and that "productivity" is something we want to increase—are fundamental assumptions behind this book. Chapter 1 lays out these assumptions and shows how they work as universal principles.

Figure 6.1 shows the class structure of the approach to optimization class.

Leadership

Vision: A visionary, mission-driven quality system of optimization of value and productivity.

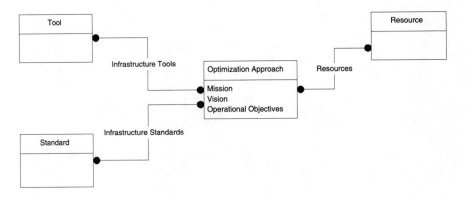

Figure 6.1 Structure of optimization approach class.

Mission: To define the purpose of an object in operational, measurable terms.

Objective 6.1: To optimize value or quality in the system during an accounting period with respect to the business objectives of the system during that period.

Measurement 6.1: Return on investment from application of the optimization approach in an optimization cycle during the accounting period.

Objective 6.2: To optimize productivity in the system with respect to value during an accounting period.

Measurement 6.2: Effort-hours per function point in the accounting period.

Structure

THE VISION STATEMENT

The *vision statement* is a brief, textual statement that tells the reader what will be different because of the existence of the class. The vision statement should be terse, clear, and well thought out. It should make the reader discern the nature of the object's quest for value. It should, in short, be *visionary*.

THE MISSION STATEMENT

The mission statement operationalizes the vision into a specific purpose for the object. It is also a brief, textual statement that tells the reader something: in this case, the reason for the existence of the object, its basic goal or target. Usually this is quite simple: The mission is the concrete version of the vision. For example, in the "Leadership" section, the mission "To define the purpose of an object in operational, measurable terms" introduces the operational meaning of the vision, "A visionary, mission-driven quality system of optimization of value and productivity." It takes "optimization" and defines it in terms of "operational, measurable terms" to ground the vision in the object's system.

THE OPERATIONAL OBJECTIVES

The *operational objectives* break down the mission into a set of specific, measurable goals that you can use to drive optimization. There may be more than one operational objective; for example, if you want to optimize both quality and value with an object, you need separate objectives for each optimization. Separate objectives need not necessarily avoid conflict or contradiction, as long as you understand the nature of the trade-offs.

The first component of the operational objective is the statement of the *objective*. This statement should again be a brief, textual statement of a measurable goal. It usually will express a *value*: to increase something, to optimize something, and so on. You also can have *enabling objectives*, objectives that create the possibility for something else to exist or happen. In composing the objective, you should answer this question: What is the specific, measurable purpose for this object? What is the specific problem we're trying to solve?

The second component of the operational objective is the statement of the *approach*. This component describes the proposed solution to the problem or the way in which you will go about achieving the objective. This is a reasonably short paragraph that describes the series of actions you will take. This approach statement should touch on the attributes and methods of the object and thus tie them into the achievement of the objective.

The third component of the operational objective is the *measurement*. This is a specific data item or statistic that you will collect or compute to measure the achievement of the objective. This data provides the feedback information in the optimization system. The measurement should relate directly to the objective, and the approach should facilitate the measurement process.

There are three levels of measurement:

- **Measure:** A dimension, attribute, or amount of any thing; *data*.
- **Metric:** A primitive or computed set of measures you use to compare to other values or to predict values; a *statistic*.
- **Meter:** A metric or measure that you have calibrated to help managers and other resources to make operational decisions; a *benchmark*.

For example, a measure might be the fact that a test tested a test object; a metric might be the coverage of the test model containing the test objects, and a meter might compare the coverage with a benchmark for an acceptable level of risk.

A special kind of measurement is survey data, which you gather by questioning other people. The construction of surveys is a specialty; it can be tricky, depending on your objectives and the nature of the process or thing you're trying to measure. Our advice is to get professional help with surveys unless you're an expert at them.

Measures, metrics, and meters are all part of the operational objectives of an object, and they're all subject to optimization during an optimization cycle. As part of the cycle, you should not only collect and look at the measurements; you should validate them and decide whether to change or improve the measurement process. A hint: Automate measurement as much as possible.

RESOURCES

The "Resources" subsection appears in the "Structure" section of each class. Every object in the quality system has zero or more resources associated with it. The particular aggregation of resources depends on the needs of the class. The specific section in the class overloads this attribute to contain the specific resource roles that the class requires.

INFRASTRUCTURE

The Infrastructure subsection in the Structure section of each class details the zero or more tools, methods, standards, guidelines, or environmental objects that objects of the class require (or might require) to achieve their objectives. There are separate objects for Tools and Standards connected as relationships in the root optimization approach class. Other objects appear in subclasses in the overloaded infrastructure attribute.

Road Map

Figure 6.2 is the road map to the optimization approach class.

Optimization Cycle

The optimization cycle comprises a set of ordered activities with a goal. A single optimization cycle focuses on one objective of one specific class of objects. All object classes are subject to optimization, as all have objectives. The ultimate goal of any optimization cycle is to adjust some thing or activity to improve an aspect of productivity and/or value. The improvement is relative to some set of objectives based on a higher-level mission with its corresponding vision and objectives. Optimization cycles have ten discrete steps to follow, each of which has input and output from the attributes of the cycle.

Webster's Dictionary defines *to optimize*, a transitive verb, as: (1) to achieve the best possible under restrictions expressed or implied; (2) to realize to the utmost; (3) to obtain the most efficient use of.

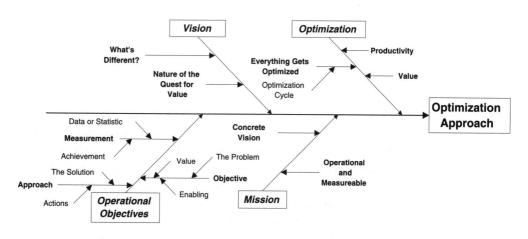

Figure 6.2 Road map for the optimization approach class.

These definitions are very different from the concepts of maximization or minimization. To optimize, you need a clear idea of what the "best possible," or "the utmost," or "the most efficient use of" actually means. Without a definition of your aim and a way to measure progress toward that aim, you cannot optimize.

Optimization is probably not the extremes of a set nor ordinal values in a range. The spirit of optimization is the notion of *balance*. Balance and extreme positions are mutually exclusive. What is possible given constraints imposed by reality—this phrase captures the sense of optimization. To achieve it, you must know what you are trying to accomplish and realistically work within this set of real-world constraints. Optimization is a *continuous* activity because the real world is constantly changing around us and we are constantly reacting to those changes. Optimization is a *key* activity for any system that wants to stay alive.

Optimization cycles are an extension and expansion of the classic Plan, Do, Check, Act cycle (PDCA) that originated with Walter Shewhart around 1929. The PDCA looks very much like an adaptation of the scientific method indelibly etched into our memories in grade school. Can you recall "Form a hypothesis, design an experiment, carry out the experiment and observe the results, then form a conclusion or a new hypothesis"? The scientific method is the engine that drives much of the advances in scientific knowledge for Western civilization.

Champions of the quality movement further refined the original PDCA cycle into the notion of *continuous improvement*. Continuous improvement is a flawed and outdated approach that does not account for the interrelation and interdependence of open systems. It treats each improvement as a closed system unaffected by surrounding systems. The optimization cycle represents a quantum leap beyond the idea of continuous improvement because it is based on the realization that everything is a system.

Every system adjusts itself. For example, the success or failure of biological systems depends on the ability of their feedback mechanisms to monitor the environment (real world) and to make adjustments based on those observations. Small tremors and massive earthquakes represent the geological expression of optimization.

Put a frog in a pot of boiling water, and it jumps out. Put the same frog in a pot of water and gradually increase the temperature, and the frog cooks. Biological optimization in action! The feedback mechanism of the frog, its skin, is capable of detecting large changes in the water temperature but not steadily increasing small ones. It dies because it cannot optimize for this type of change. Of course, in its natural environment it does not need to. Humans seem to adapt more readily to minor changes. At any rate, you would be hard-pressed to find a more dynamic, changing, and rapidly evolving environment than the software industry.

The optimization cycle thus represents an evolutionary leap forward from the notion of continuous improvement (*kaizen* in Japanese). Any system that seeks continually to improve itself—that is, to maximize what is good and minimize what is bad—runs a very real risk of obsolescence because it exists in a rapidly changing environment. Optimization cycles are a formal approach for deploying quality in the competitive and rapidly evolving technological environment of software production.

Optimization cycles are *fractal* structures. A fractal is an object that has a similar structure and composition to something that looks like it but is itself unique. You can think of fractals as self-similar objects that are scaleable. Optimization cycles are fractal. Optimization cycles are scaleable because individuals, project teams, entire organizations, and even companies can apply them. Every optimization cycle has the same structure and the same ten steps, even though the optimized objects may vary widely. The amount of time, energy, and attention to detail may vary from step to step and from cycle to cycle, just as a structural fractal in nature looks the same as another but has differences in the specifics and details of its design. (Think of a snowflake.)

You can selectively apply optimization cycles to improve one or more specific aspects of an object-oriented software project. You can, more comprehensively, apply them to improve an entire process area, such as class or integration testing. On a larger scale, it is very reasonable to optimize the entire product testing process. On the most comprehensive scale, it is possible to optimize the entire software development organization and the company in the large. When we abstract the attributes of an optimization cycle, we clearly demonstrate the fractal nature of any and all other such cycles.

The optimization cycle is the engine that powers both incremental improvements and massive breakthroughs in either productivity or value or both. Have you ever wondered why it is possible to achieve great gains in some aspect of product development, your own personal productivity, for example; or to buy some new tool that automates a significant portion of your project and still have the project finish late? Lack of optimization is a likely explanation. To improve overall project productivity and to achieve significant breakthroughs in functionality or performance, it is necessary to optimize across an entire project. If individual goals and project goals do not align properly, advances in some areas translate into setbacks in other areas. Everything is a system that is in a dynamic relationship with the other systems around it. The productivity or value of a system can be improved only to the extent that we apply optimization at the system level. Optimization cycles represent a formal answer to managing both incremental and quantum breakthroughs in productivity or value or both at whatever level you apply the optimization.

Figure 6.3 Structure of optimization cycle class.

Optimization cycles are at the heart of what it means to be a *learning* organization. To improve we must learn from our mistakes and stop making the same mistakes over again. Peter Senge, in his book *The Fifth Discipline* (1994), explains why it is important to become a learning organization but does not tell us how to achieve it. Optimization cycles are the best method to transform systematically an organization of any size and complexity into a learning organization. Optimization cycles need to become endemic and systemic, applied at every level of your organization, and part of everything that you do as a professional. When this happens, quality will be systemic, a part of everything that you do, as opposed to an activity that is separate and apart from how you do your job.

As with everything else in the quality system, the optimization cycle is a kind of optimization approach with vision, mission, and goals subject to an optimization cycle: a self-improving, recursive system of optimization and quality!

Figure 6.3 shows the class structure of the optimization cycle.

Leadership

Vision: A learning system capable of sustaining optimized productivity and value. The individual, project teams, organization, and ultimately the company will become one learning system capable of sustaining optimized productivity and value. Rapid adaptation and evolution of all aspects of product development will become a reality when optimization cycles are endemic and systemic to projects and the organization. As individuals or teams learn and apply the knowledge from optimization cycles, they cease making the same mistakes over and over again. The optimizing entity becomes a learning machine that is capable of adjusting constantly to a changing environment.

Mission: To adjust some thing or activity to improve an aspect of productivity and/or value with respect to some set of objectives based on a higher-level mission with its corresponding vision and objectives.

Objective: To increase the ability of the object to achieve its objectives by changing some aspect of the object.

Approach: Every object has an owner or person responsible and accountable for it. The people who are in the best position to suggest changes to the object are those people who actually work with it. The approach is the same for each objective: A subject-area expert uses his or her experience and expertise to produce the deliverables for each step in the optimization cycle. The first step in the cycle, align, assures the integrity of the proposed change. The benchmark and evaluate steps, which define and apply the criteria for success, act as a check-and-balance mechanism. The suppliers to and customers of the optimized object must review and accept the proposed change and the success criteria.

Measurement: The significance of the improvement in the measurements associated with the objectives of the object, as measured by appropriate statistics of difference between the benchmark and the new values.

Structure

GOAL
The *goal* is a textual statement of the mission and vision of the specific optimization cycle object that is in alignment with the rest of the system and its overall aim.

BENCHMARK
The *benchmark* is a text description of your current practice that you can use for comparison to the measurements you take during the optimization cycle.

ASSESSMENT
An *assessment* compares current practices to some standard or otherwise desirable situation. This lets you determine the scope or importance of the problem you're trying to resolve.

PROPOSED SOLUTIONS

The *proposed solutions* list is a list of possible changes to the current practice that have the potential to optimize the overall system.

SUCCESS CRITERIA

The *success criteria* are statements of how you will know if or when each change is successful.

CHECKLIST

The optimization *checklist* is a checklist of all of the infrastructure items, processes, organizational issues, and time dependencies that you will need to address if the change(s) are to succeed.

REPORT

The optimization cycle report is a document that analyzes and evaluates the entire optimization cycle, with recommendations regarding what to do next.

Dynamics

The following methods are a ten-step series of activities you perform in order during an optimization cycle. Each step in the cycle process is a method.

ALIGN

The optimizing group must first align its vision, mission, and objectives for the optimization cycle with the vision, mission, and objectives of other system components. If objectives for this object do not align well with objectives for higher-level objects, the group should realign its objectives or get the higher-level objectives realigned before proceeding. The output of this method is the goal. (See the "Structure" section on page 65.)

UNDERSTAND

Members of the optimization team research and document the vision, mission, and operational objectives of the object they are going to optimize. Each team member should fully comprehend the objectives, approaches, and measurements that are part of the current object. The team should then collect and analyze an appropriate set of measurements from the current object to use as a *benchmark* of the current system. (See the "Structure" section above.)

BENCHMARK

The team *benchmarks* the system formally when it compares the benchmark statistics from the Understand method to some standard set of values or other desirable target. The result of this comparison is a formal *assessment* of the current object. (See the "Structure" section on page 65.)

IDENTIFY CHANGES

Considering your goal and informed by your benchmark and assessment, identify, prioritize, and justify the changes you want to make to the object. This becomes the *proposed solutions* list.

DEFINE SUCCESS

Given the benchmark, assessment, and measurements for the optimization cycle, define the criteria for the metrics that will indicate the success of the cycle. This becomes the *success criteria* for the cycle.

PLAN

Develop a schedule and resource plan for the cycle based on the list of proposed solutions. The output is a checklist of issues and items you need during the cycle.

DO

Make the proposed changes in the object and collect measurements as you use the object.

CHECK

Evaluate the results of the change. The output of this method is the optimization cycle *report*. This report should compare the measurements and metrics to the benchmark of the object before you changed it and to the success criteria.

LEVERAGE

Take what you have learned and communicate it to other parts of the project or organization, feeding the information back into the system as a whole. Remember, the optimization cycle is an *open system* with outputs and inputs to and from the rest of the quality system.

ITERATE

Start a new optimization cycle to make further improvements in the object. You will, of course, have to prioritize the new cycle with the other cycles you can create based on their value and chances for significant improvement.

Example

As part of the ongoing effort to improve the quality of the product, the research and development (R&D) team responsible for the Person system of the DTS has decided they want to start an optimization cycle for the Hierarchical Incremental Test Script. The first implementation of this object used state-transition tests and control flow tests but had no specification tests.

The team members first looked at the overall system context to align itself with the system. They saw teams responsible for other parts of the product using specification tests; they saw general support from management and quality assurance for using such tests (and for acquiring the test case generation tools that would make it easy to do). The team leader wrote up a description of the current HIT test system, including the vision, mission, and operational objectives. He then had a brainstorming session with the team to determine what the optimization goal should be. They decided that, since the key objective was finding message and exception errors, measuring these kinds of failures would be an appropriate benchmark.

The team leader then went to the other groups and gathered their numbers on this metric. He also came across a published article describing an industry survey that published some statistics on this kind of error. The team used this information to assess the current HIT object and discovered their discovery rate in new code was only 25 percent of the industry average. But the Person HIT discovery rate was 75 percent of the average of the other DTS teams, indicating that the other teams weren't as effective as they might have been. The team leader briefly reflected that it might be that there were fewer errors . . . well, maybe not.

The team then had another brainstorming session to come up with proposals. Everyone read the articles and course notes they had on HIT and brought ideas. The team came up with over 50 different kinds of HIT tests based on specification techniques to add to the class/object test suite for the Person system. Of those, the team decided to implement the top five, because those seemed easy to implement and very productive of failures. The team then wrote a memo on these five tests and implemented them in the automated testing system. It also chose a target of 80 percent of the industry average as a success criterion, and just to be fair, decided that a validated target of 25 percent based on not finding errors later in the process would also indicate success. (Discovery that they were luckier programmers than they thought!)

Over the next several builds, the team collected the measurements of number of specification-type failures discovered in the system. The rate more than tripled, bringing it much closer to the industry average. After the agreed-upon three-month cycle period, the rate was still up.

The team then evaluated the cycle to evaluate its success. Tracing the failures back to the tests, they found that 80 percent came from the new tests. This indicated that the tests were, in fact, successful in improving the system. But the discovery rate fell short of the target of 80 percent by 5 percent.

The team then presented their results at the weekly R&D meeting, and other teams quickly decided to include the two or three tests they had not been doing. Management then handed out small bonuses to the successful team.

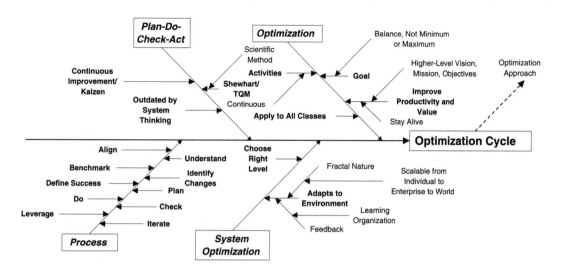

Figure 6.4 Road map for the optimization cycle class.

The team then decided to start a new optimization cycle to implement two more of the original set of 50 tests to see if they could get that extra 5 percent out of the system.

Road Map

Figure 6.4 shows a road map of the optimization cycle class.

CHAPTER 7

THE SOFTWARE DEVELOPMENT LIFE CYCLE

The Process

The generic optimization approach and the optimization cycle are powerful abstractions that give you solid tools for improving any system. But they are still abstractions, not real tools. They aren't real until you apply them to a specific process.

Ch. 1

Every Thing
Is a System

While you can optimize anything, there is one class of things that is central to productive work: the process. A process is a system of processes for producing something. This recursive definition may seem odd; if so, go back and read Chapter 1. Everything is a system, including systems, and the essence of anything usually includes itself. The ultimate process is a single, dynamic action; but how far can you take that, down to the cellular level? What about atoms? What about particles? There are ultimate building blocks for processes—and for everything else in the universe. We stay at a higher level in that we end the block party with a process that does not contain any other processes, a leaf in the process tree.

A process consists of a system that takes inputs (material, labor, ideas—anything, really) and turns these inputs into outputs (also anything). Because optimization is key to the quality system, we see these inputs and outputs as optimization approaches—the essence of things in the quality system.

No process is instantaneous: All have some duration in time during which the system of processes operates on the inputs to produce the output. Specific kinds of processes have the typical project management attributes, such as planned start date, actual start date, planned cost, actual cost, and so on. The generic process has none of this, just duration and effort (the amount of time the process takes and the amount of effort spent during the process). It also has a status that varies with the type of process but includes the basic states "started" and "finished." There is no reason to limit the system of processes to a sequence; the system can be parallel and concurrent. That means that the process state includes any number of operating processes at a single instant in time. Because there is no such thing as a process that operates indefinitely, the duration is always less than infinity.

Some specific processes are of interest in the software quality system:

- **The Software Development Life Cycle:** The overall system of software development processes.
- **Development Process:** A process belonging to the software development life cycle process.

Figure 7.1 shows the structure of the process class.

Leadership

Vision: An optimizing system for producing value.

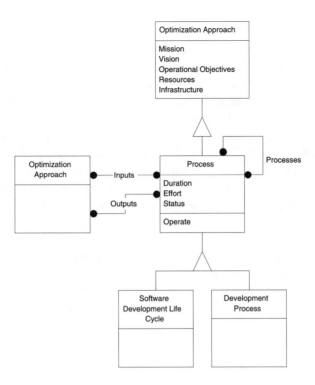

Figure 7.1 Structure of the process class.

Mission: To define and optimize the system processes that produce something of value.

Objective 7.1: To optimize value or quality in the process during an accounting period with respect to the business objectives of the system during that period.

Measurement 7.1: Return on investment from the process during the accounting period.

Objective 7.2: To optimize productivity in the system with respect to value during an accounting period.

Measurement 7.2: Effort-hours per output unit in the accounting period.

Structure

INPUTS

You can't start a process unless you have some kind of input, whether it's a bar of metal or an idea. The set of *inputs* to the process comprises a set of optimization approach objects. These objects can be the outputs of some other process, or they can be primary inputs into your system from other systems.

Processes

Each process comprises a system of *processes* that operate on the inputs to produce the outputs. The system operates by starting and finishing these processes, with the particular configuration forming during operation.

We do not make any attempt to model the process here; process modeling is an optimization technique that lets you see how the system works. Using this knowledge, you can figure out ways to improve its operation. Process modeling usually includes flows of objects between the processes and imposes ordering and dependencies on the system. In practice, the model does not always reflect the way the system actually operates. We prefer to leave modeling to you rather than canonizing structure that is really amorphous.

Outputs

You can't stop a process unless you have some kind of output, whether it's a bar of metal or an idea. The set of *outputs* to the process comprises a set of optimization approach objects. The value of the system, whatever system it might be, is its outputs. These objects can be the inputs to another process, or they can be the final result and value in your overall system.

Duration

Every process has a duration in time—the amount of real time the process takes to operate from start to finish.

Effort

Every process that produces value has effort associated with it, however minimal; an effortless process would require no optimization for productivity and no way to affect value and is hence irrelevant. At this level of the system, the effort applies to units of production for the measures associated with the process.

Dynamics

Operate

Only one method is associated with the process: operate. Operating moves the system forward dynamically from start to finish; the system is either operating or not operating at any point in time. The same is true, of course, for the processes belonging to the process. The duration of the process is the time it takes to move from start to finish in a particular instance of the process.

Road Map

Figure 7.2 is the road map for the process class.

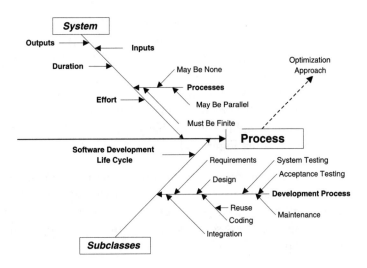

Figure 7.2 Road map for the process class.

The Software Development Life Cycle

Again, an abstract process with a system of abstract processes isn't of much practical use; you have to make the process concrete. The next step in doing this is the *software development life cycle*: the system of processes that takes an idea for a software system and realizes it in working software.

The term "software" should include any results of the development processes, including paper or online documentation or services, such as training, if that makes sense from a system point of view.

Because this process is more concrete, there are more constraints on how the system works. Some restrictions come from the innate physical qualities of the inputs and outputs: You can't test software until you compile it, for example; you can't test a system against requirements if there are no requirements and no software. Other restrictions apply optimization techniques to the process system to improve its quality or productivity.

Certain specific optimization ideas apply to many different visions of the development life cycle. Without judging whether these are valuable in any specific case, here are some of interest:

- **Life Cycle Phase:** Divide the process into major subprocesses, such as requirements analysis, design, coding, and testing.
- **Phase Commitment:** Make one output of a life cycle phase the signature of one or more persons with authority; make this sign-off the

required input to another phase. This creates an ordered sequence of phases with intermediate approvals by authorities. A more sophisticated version of this commitment adds a risk analysis to the sign-offs for each phase (the spiral model in Figure 7.3).

- **Waterfall Model:** Make the transition between phases relatively rigid with only limited feedback so that you do the work in major, complete, and thoroughly controllable steps rather than as a process of repeating phases. (See Figure 7.4.)

The waterfall model reminds us of the concrete steps wildlife managers build beside dams to let salmon spawn by going upriver: the steps are necessary from the salmon's point of view only because somebody fouled up somewhere up the line, so to speak. Definitely suboptimal—again, from the salmon's point of view.

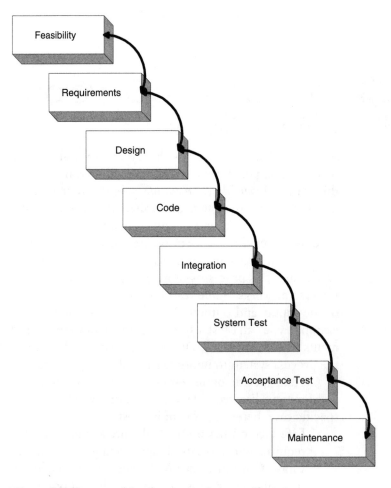

Figure 7.3 The waterfall software development life cycle.

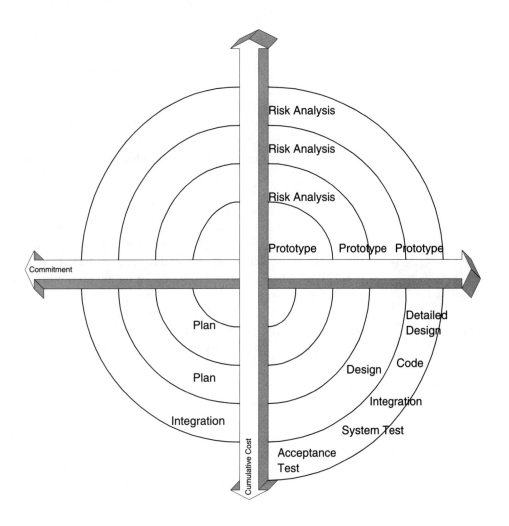

Figure 7.4 The spiral software development life cycle.

- **Rolling Wave:** Commit resources and materials for a limited set of processes or a phase rather than for the entire life cycle, enabling replanning and reworking of inputs as the process operates.
- **Standard Objects:** Create a standard set of objects, such as development documents, reviews, or test suites, that each project has to complete as the output of some task; optionally, make some or all of these objects required, or designate some as relevant or irrelevant in different situations.

Again, the point of these constraints is to guide you toward a particular objective of interest in a given situation. You should decide on these restrictions based on a full optimization cycle.

We do have some specific recommendations to make. Some life cycle arrangements are definitely better than others when you are constructing object-oriented software systems. Object orientation is not in itself particularly suited to any form of life cycle, but the style of design and programming it encourages definitely works better with iterative life cycles.

A two-week delivery cycle is the most appropriate constraint on the level of deliverable processes (that is, processes with outputs consisting of deliverable objects of some kind, such as development documents, software, or test results). As you plan your project, break processes down to at least a two-week delivery schedule. For example, instead of scheduling a month for requirements analysis, break this into a series of two or three requirements analysis processes that iterate with interim deliverables. The purpose of this shortened delivery cycle is to improve the feedback rate in the system, delivering at least part of the technical object as a draft or prototype that others can review. See the "Schedule" section in Chapter 23 for details on planning for process delivery cycles.

Ch. 23

Schedule

A small piece of advice: If you confront a situation where you think having others look at the product of a process before it's "done" is useless, *rethink*. The purpose of such reviews is feedback, keeping people in the loop, communicating, and building trust, confidence, and credibility. Train people to expect drafts or interim deliverables, and remind them that these are *not* the final deliverable. Clarify your reasons for these interim reviews: You are looking for constructive feedback in order to optimize your development process.

In some circumstances, even two weeks may be too long without feedback. When working with a small team or for a relatively small, short project, one week or less may be more appropriate. You should not, however, reduce the duration below about a day, or people will start to thrash. This doesn't apply to processes such as reviews or other brief, scheduled events of a couple of hours, just to longer development processes.

Many books develop particular life cycle approaches in detail; good ones are those by Boehm (1985), DeGrace and Stahl (1990), and King (1992).

Figure 7.5 shows the structure of the software development life cycle class.

Leadership

Vision: An optimizing system for producing software.

Mission: To define and optimize the system processes that produce software.

Objective 7.3: To optimize value or quality of software you produce during an accounting period with respect to the business objectives of the system during that period.

Approach 7.3: Define and implement a software development life cycle aligned with the business objectives of the quality system.

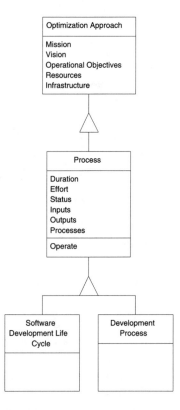

Figure 7.5 Structure of the software development life cycle class.

Measurement 7.3: Return on investment from the software during the accounting period.

Objective 7.4: To optimize productivity in the system with respect to value during an accounting period.

Approach 7.4: Define and implement a software development life cycle that optimizes productivity through process optimization and optimal process inputs and outputs.

Measurement 7.4: Effort-hours per software function point in the accounting period.

Example

The DTS project adapted the corporate software development life cycle, itself a modified spiral model, to its own purposes and needs. The most important need for the DTS project was to provide value to its clients by giving them what they wanted. Doing so required a strong prototyping and user

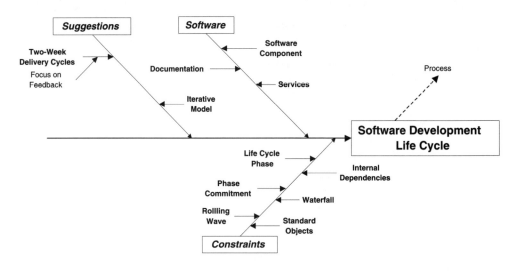

Figure 7.6 Road map for the system development life cycle class.

review approach to development. Instead of two or three iterations on a prototype and continued development along a basic waterfall model, the DTS project team decided to iterate on the prototype until a user survey of 16 separate satisfaction measures had proved the requirements and design to be adequate. This took six iterations. The final prototype then served as the input to the final detailed design, coding, and other processes.

Due to the nature of this development life cycle, the team also decided that a rolling wave commitment process was in order. The project manager took the project proposal to senior management on this basis and convinced them that the modified life cycle was the right thing to do. The senior management monitored the satisfaction survey results, which were impressive enough to make the senior management revise the corporate standard to use the same techniques.

Road Map

Figure 7.6 is the road map for the software development life cycle class.

The Development Process

A *development process* is a kind of process that produces outputs relevant to some aspect of software development. Any system object can be an input; relevant outputs include such things as development documents, technical components, test suites, and test scripts, although a development process could produce any object, theoretically, as a side product.

The development process has several subclasses for specific kinds of processes:

- **Requirements Analysis:** The development process that states the problem to solve and produces the requirements document.
- **Software Design:** The development process that states the software solution to the problem and produces the design document.
- **Software Coding:** The development process that produces new software components.
- **Software Integration:** The development process of assembling the software components into larger software components such as systems.
- **Software System Testing:** The process of testing the software system as a whole from the perspective of the producer.
- **Software Acceptance Testing:** The process of testing the software system as a whole from the perspective of the client.
- **Software Maintenance:** The process of maintaining the value of the software system over time from delivery until product death.

These subclasses don't cover all the possible processes for producing specific objects, but they are the most important for this book. Each of the following sections provides an overview of the process.

We believe here that development processes in object-oriented systems are better off with one of two work models: a buddy system or a collaborative system. See the "Operate" section that follows for details.

Figure 7.7 shows the structure of the development process class.

Leadership

Vision: An optimizing system for producing a technical component.

Mission: To define and optimize the system processes that produce a technical component.

Objective 7.5: To optimize value or quality of technical components you produce during an accounting period with respect to the business objectives of the software development system during that period.

Approach 7.5: Define and implement an optimal development process that adds significant value to the technical components it produces.

Measurement 7.5: Return on investment from the technical component during the accounting period.

Objective 7.6: To optimize productivity in the system with respect to value during an accounting period.

Approach 7.6: Define and implement an optimal development process that contributes value to the technical components with a minimum of effort.

Measurement 7.6: Effort-hours per component function point in the accounting period.

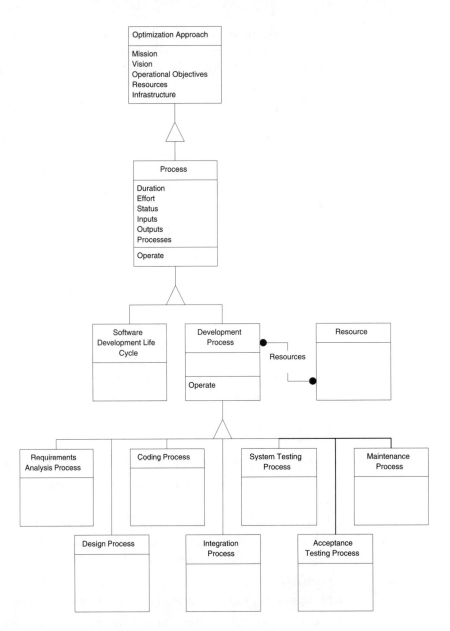

Figure 7.7 Structure of the development process class.

Structure

RESOURCES

Development processes require resources—people— trained in the particular technical discipline that produces the technical output. Using either of our recommended operating organizations, you will have both developers and testers working in the process; these people need training to a level appropriate for their jobs.

Dynamics

OPERATE

The nature of the software development life cycle for object-oriented software leads to an iterative model for development processes. We also suggest that you integrate development and testing into development processes to optimize the creative production of the technical outputs. As mentioned, we recommend either of two models for process operation, the buddy system or the collaborative system.

As in diving and elsewhere, the buddy system teams up two or more individuals to work on a process on the theory that if one makes a mistake, his or her buddy will correct it immediately and keep the process on track. For a development process, this means teaming up two developers with joint responsibility for producing the technical components, including reviews and tests. Each works on the task with around 75 percent of the effort required for the task, leaving the other 25 percent for testing and review of each other's effort. To function in this manner, both developers need training in both development and testing of the output object.

The collaborative system is a looser coupling that makes one developer responsible for all the development effort and associates him or her with a tester who reviews format and tests what is developed in collaboration with the developer. This is looser than the buddy system in that here development and testing are divided between two individuals; it is tighter than a normal development process because the two people collaborate in a single, integrated, parallel task rather than in sequential tasks. The collaborative system requires the test person to have more technical knowledge than would be required in the buddy system, but a full-scale second developer person is not needed.

Both development models provide a better way to approach development of any technical object by integrating the production and quality efforts into a single effort that gets synergy from the team interaction.

Requirements Analysis

The requirements analysis process transforms ideas, current technologies, and client needs into a statement of the problem that you intend to solve with a software system. The output is a requirements document. You can reuse requirements, especially use cases, from other systems as appropriate.

Software Design

The software design process transforms the requirements in the requirements document into a software system architecture and a low-level design of the classes, files, databases, and other technical components of the system. You can reuse design components from other systems as appropriate. The result of the design process is a design document.

Software Coding

The software coding process transforms the design and existing, reusable technical components into new, working software components. Hierarchical-incremental and conditional testing are part of this process.

Software Integration

The software integration process assembles software components, both new and reused, into larger software components as systems. The ultimate integration is the system as a whole.

Software System Testing

The software system testing process takes the software system as a whole (including documentation and other such objects) and runs a series of system test suites against it. This tests the system from the perspective of the *producer*, verifying that the system as a whole functions according to requirements. The objective of the process is to make the system fail.

Software Acceptance Testing

The software acceptance testing process takes the software system as a whole (including documentation and other such objects) and runs a series of system test suites against it. This tests the system from the perspective of the *client*, verifying that the system as a whole functions according to requirements. This is not strictly a part of the quality system but rather a part of the environment with which it must deal as an open system.

Software Maintenance

The software maintenance process takes the tested system and maintains it through its life cycle as a product, from delivery to the client through its death. Maintenance generally involves fixing problems with the system and enhancing it to provide additional value. The maintenance process is an iterative sequence of life cycles, with each release of the product defining a distinct life cycle. "Distinct" is perhaps too strong a word; the maintenance process seems to be fraught with many configuration-management and product-marketing issues beyond the scope of a straightforward, simple book on quality. In other words, we don't have any answers to these problems yet. Another book, perhaps.

Example

Two DTS team members teamed up using the buddy system to code the Problem class. Each developed some of the methods, and the other developed the hierarchical-incremental and conditional test suite scripts for them. Toward the end of the process, the two teamed up to brainstorm class invariants and to look at the class as a whole; then one developer coded the **verify()** method to reflect the results of the brainstorming session. The pair then scheduled a code review for the class with an SQA representative.

During system test of the DTS, a developer and a tester teamed up using the collaborative model to test the performance of the system. The tester developed the test scripts and test data, and the developer observed the results and tuned the system to improve performance where appropriate. The developer also investigated a couple of performance failures and determined the faults that led to them without fixing them; fixing them required some redesign and recoding.

Road Map

Figure 7.8 is the road map for the development process class.

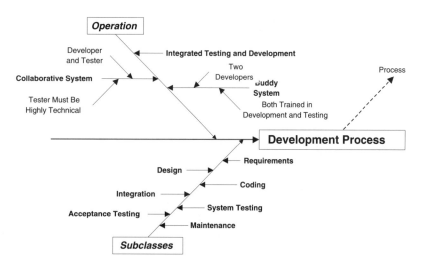

Figure 7.8 Road map for the development process class.

Part 2 References

1. Barry W. Boehm. *Software Engineering Economics.* Prentice-Hall, Englewood Cliffs, NJ: 1981.

This book is the reference on the waterfall life cycle. It also has a complete analysis of software estimation and costing.

2. Barry W. Boehm. "A Spiral Model of Software Development and Enhancement." In *Proceedings of an International Workshop on the Software Process and Software Environments*, March 27–29, 1985, edited by Jack C. Wileden and Mark Downson. Published as ACM SIGSOFT Proceedings.

This paper lays out the spiral development life cycle that emphasizes prototyping, iteration, and risk analysis.

3. Peter DeGrace and Leslie Hulet Stahl. *Wicked Problems, Righteous Solutions: A Catalogue of Modern Software Engineering Paradigms.* Yourdon Press, Englewood Cliffs, NJ: 1990.

This is a delightfully well-written account of the major system development life cycles.

4. David King, *Project Management Made Simple: A Guide to Successful Management of Computer Systems Projects.* Yourdon Press, Englewood Cliffs, NJ: 1992.

This short book has a good, prescriptive model of the software development life cycle and its place in the management of software development projects.

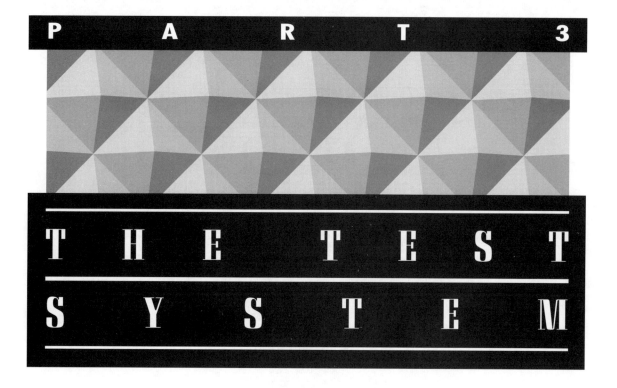

THE TEST SYSTEM

The *test system* is the part of the quality system that relates to *testing*: the specification, design, and building of the software testing system. The test system contains the tests and the things you use to build it, including extensive models of the software under test.

Ch. 6

Process System

Figures P3.1 and P3.2 show the inheritance hierarchy of the test system. As with all the different parts of the quality system, all the classes have the *optimization approach* as the root; see Part 2 for details on that class. Each class can and should go through optimization cycles to optimize value and productivity.

The *test approach*, and in particular the subclass *hierarchical approach*, is what this book is about. As an object, it is one of many, but the test approach is a system that contains the rest of the testing system.

The three kinds of *project document* of specific interest to the test system include the test plan, the test evaluation document, and the test

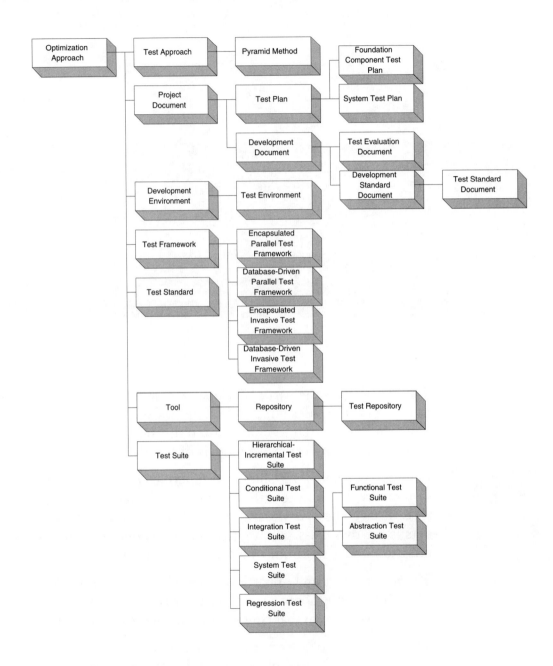

Figure P3.1 Test system inheritance hierarchy.

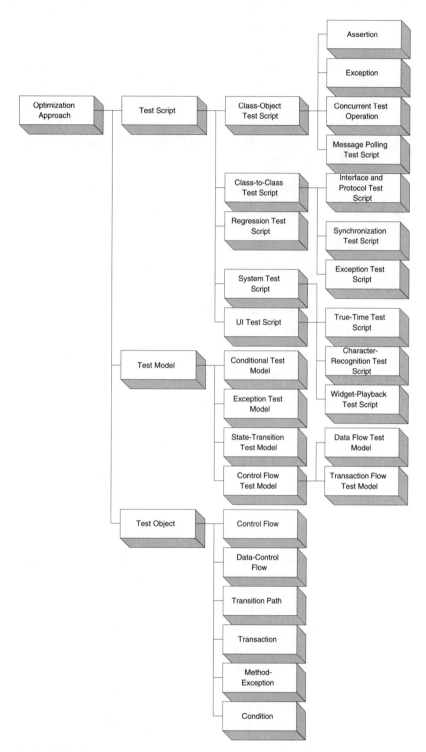

Figure P3.2 Test system inheritance hierarchy (continued).

standard document. The *test plan*, a part of the overall project plan, lays out the test approach and contains the guts of the test abstractions (test models and objects). There is a test plan for *foundation components* and one for *systems*. These foundation components and systems have slightly different testing requirements. The *test evaluation document* summarizes the results of a test using the test standards for each kind of test. The *test standard document* contains those test standards.

The *test environment*, a kind of *development environment*, provides the infrastructure for the test system. It contains the *test repository*, which in turn contains the test suites, test documents, and other test-related data.

The *test framework* provides the software drivers for many of the test scripts. You can take any of four approaches to building test frameworks; this book recommends the database-driven, invasive approach.

The *test standard* is a criterion by which you judge the success or failure of a test script.

The *test suite* is a collection of test scripts; it serves to group test scripts into meaningful components. There is a different kind of test suite for the major types of testing that we recommend as part of the hierarchical approach.

Continuing with Figure P3.2, the test script, test model, and test object are the central components of the test system. The *test model* models a technical component from the tester's perspective, as opposed to the coder's or architect's perspective. There are more kinds of test model than depicted in the figure; it shows the important ones to the hierarchical approach.

The *test object* represents a single test that is part of the larger test model. Again, there are more kinds of test object than the figure shows, but these are the important ones to the hierarchical approach.

The *test script* is the executable form of the test object that actually implements the test. There are class-based scripts (*class-object test script*), integration scripts (*class-to-class test script*), *system test scripts*, user-interface (*UI*) *test scripts*, and the *regression test script*. The UI test script and system test script are both parents to the three user-interface scripts. They can be both integration and system tests depending on how you go about testing the UI. The regression test script represents any kind of test script that becomes part of a regression test suite that runs against a technical component to retest it after changes.

Figure P3.3 shows the containment relationships between the classes at a high level.

The test plan and test approach are central objects to the test system. The test plan contains the test approach, the test models, and the technical components relevant to testing. It is a part of the statement of work, which in turn constitutes the major part of the project plan.

The test approach contains development documents of interest to testing and details the infrastructure of tools and resources the test system uses (the test environment). The test framework is the part of the test environment that automates the test scripts, the major contributor to productivity in the environment.

The test model is the key technical object in the system because it contains the whole complex of the actual tests: test objects, test suites, technical components under test, and test scripts. Understanding the test model is central to understanding the hierarchical approach. If you carry away nothing else from this book, understanding test models and their position in the test system will provide the best rewards for your investment of time.

Although it is not part of the system, the technical component does drive the test system. Because the product consists of technical components, they of necessity drive the testing. Without technical components, there would be nothing to test.

Development documents also play a strong role in the testing system. The documents that are a part of the system (test evaluations and test standards) and those from other systems (requirements and design documents) provide much of the structure for testing models. Testers don't start with code, they start with requirements, continue to design, then make sure the code satisfies the requirements and at least resembles the design. The test plan, as a project document, also

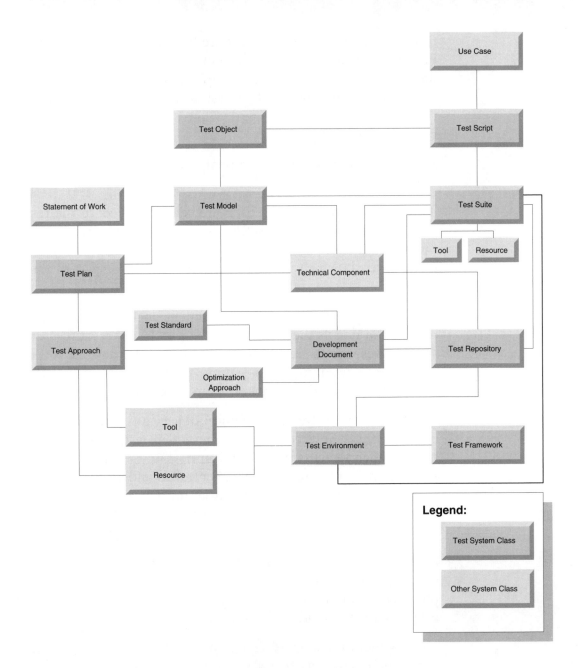

Figure P3.3 Test system containment hierarchy.

plays a major role in the test system. To find out what something means, look at the test plan and its components.

CHAPTER 8

THE HIERARCHICAL APPROACH

Test Approach

A *test approach* is the way you go about testing a system. This abstract class has many possible subclasses; this book is all about one of those subclasses, the hierarchical approach. This chapter presents this approach in detail.

Ch. 8

Test
Plan

Your organization should have a standard test approach as part of its standards documents. You can refer to this standards document in your test plan, modifying the standard test approach with new optimizations appropriate to the specific project. The result becomes the test approach in your test plan. (See the "Test Plan") The job of the test approach is twofold.

First, the test approach must describe in detail how to build test models, test objects, and test scripts. It must describe how to combine test scripts into coherent test suites that you run against the designated technical components.

Second, the test approach must explicitly specify the optimization approach characteristics of all these objects: the vision, mission, and operational objectives. The objectives (objective, approach, and measurement) serve as criteria for the success of the test: model coverage, risk reduction, failure rate, and so on. Because all of these objects are a kind of optimization approach, all have such operational objectives; the job of the test approach is to make these objectives *explicit*, in writing, in a standards document.

Simply put, what are the goals for this phase of testing? Managing risk is the driving force that dictates the testing goals. Testing focuses on technical risk that you manage by using appropriate test techniques. The hard thing to do is to establish measurable coverage criteria within an acceptable project time frame. From the testers' point of view, there is hardly ever enough time to test to an acceptable level of risk. This is why optimization plays a critical role. Optimization introduces a healthy dose of reality to an otherwise utopian view of what we should do. Please reread Chapter 6 if you are even the least bit uncertain about what this means in practical terms.

Customers must drive the objectives of the test plan. It is imperative that you identify and consult with the customers and users: those who will use the product you produce and test at this development level. It is your responsibility to make your customers aware of the technical risks and to advise and make recommendations regarding what you believe you should test. It is their responsibility to make the decision regarding how much resources to allocate to the testing effort. If customers do not understand the technological risks, then you must do your best to make them aware. If customers decide to cut

Ch. 23

Risk
Management

testing resources, then they must be willing to take responsibility for the quality of the product they receive, assuming you have done your job and apprised them of the technical risks.

This is captured in the risk management plans. (See the section on risk management plans in Chapter 23.) Producing the technical risk management plan is clearly the responsibility of the software developers. Our experience is that most of the time customers will make the right decision about testing resources if they are made aware of the risks. After all, if you invest the time and effort to analyze the technical risks and to produce a risk management plan, no one is more expert than you regarding the scope of testing. In a very real sense, that is what customers pay us for. On the other hand, the old saying remains true: "You can lead a horse to water but you can't make him drink." Sometimes customers will do the wrong thing from your perspective and cut back testing. That is their decision and their right. You must accept that they have a different and wider set of risks to assess than simple technical ones.

Specific and measurable quality objectives make it easy for the project team to allocate the correct resources to optimize productivity and value. As part of the optimization approach for your test plan and its components, you should accomplish the following tasks in the document:

- Enumerate a set of acceptable and measurable testing goals that sufficiently address (minimize) the quality risks.
- Produce a check list of measurable testing goals the entire team, including the customers and users, agree upon and recognize as the goals of this testing effort.
- Prepare a vision and/or mission statement. Propose a set of objectives, then review, negotiate, and revise with customers until you achieve sign-off. This iterative process ultimately results in a formal acceptance of the set of objectives.

When a customer and production team sign off on the test objectives, you have an acceptable list of testing goals. Sign-off is an explicit act of empowerment that effectively creates a shared responsibility regarding the testing objectives.

As with any standard, you should review the test approach thoroughly for both technical content and practical applicability to the target projects. Reviewers should include representatives of functional management, project management, development, and quality assurance to make sure that all points of view find their way into the standard.

Figure 8.1 shows the structure of the test approach class.

Class Bang Approach: An Example of Ad Hoc Testing (What Not to Do)

Before getting into the details of the general test approach, it might be useful to provide an example of what not to do: the class bang approach.

This approach has the modest goal of performing a compile-link-and-execute cycle at the individual class level. All developers integrate their class methods within their class hierarchy and test (or don't test) to their own unspecified level of acceptability. This approach is a kind of minimal class

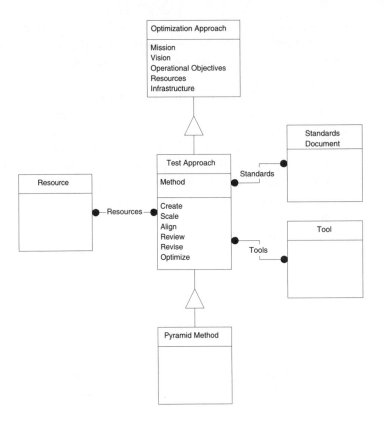

Figure 8.1 Structure of the test approach class.

integration test. To integration-test the objects within the class hierarchy, the class must be compiled. However, no standard or systematic approach exists to test the integration of the individual methods or objects within the class. The class bang approach represents the very minimum level of acceptable testing for object-oriented development—namely, that a class compiles. This is a necessary but by no means sufficient test criterion.

If each class developer integrates his or her class methods to this level and then passes the class into the next phase of testing, undesirable consequences are likely to ensue. If you assume that someone has tested the individual methods within the class hierarchy (not at all a safe assumption in many organizations) but that no one has tested interactions systematically within the class, then we have the big bang theory of integration applied on a small scale. The developer will wait for someone to test his or her code in the heat of integration with other class methods outside their realm of development responsibility. When tests find anomalies, all of the classic integration and regression problems become manifest. In case you have forgotten, here are a few of the indications:

- Tester says developer must fix; developer says it is tester or user error.
- Developer error but two or more developers argue over who must change the source code to fix the problem.
- Developer accepts responsibility and fixes but fix breaks (regresses) something else in the system. Now repeat the previous scenarios.

You might succeed in producing reusable methods and objects; there is nothing inherent in the development of a class hierarchy that suggests the objects will be reusable or useful or even good code. But you certainly will have failed to significantly increase time to market or developer productivity.

The class bang approach is functionally equivalent to ad hoc testing. At its best, the project might get lucky. If all the developers do a super job of designing and testing their class methods and code, a solid software system can be produced. At worst, you have the nightmare of a late release delayed again and again. In between the extremes (the likely scenario), you have all the problems you always had with testing. This leads to a long function or system test phase of project development, long product cycle times, and developer and tester productivity that is not significantly different from before. Your organization tries to improve precisely these things when it invests in component or object technology.

Leadership

Vision: A method of testing that you can reuse in many projects to achieve an acceptable level of risk with a high degree of productivity.

Mission: To provide an optimized testing approach that you can reuse in many projects to get an acceptable level of risk and a high level of productivity in testing a software system.

Objective 8.1: To provide a test method that you can reuse to achieve an acceptable level of risk in your software projects.

Approach 8.1: Develop a written, standard test method that shows how to build test models, test objects, test scripts, and test suites and that gives the specific objectives, approaches, and measurements for those objects that will achieve your acceptable level of risk.

Measurement 8.1.1: Number of projects that reuse the test approach.

Measurement 8.1.2: Level of risk for project using test approach.

Objective 8.2: To provide a test method that you can reuse to achieve a high level of productivity in testing your software projects.

Approach 8.2: Develop a test method as in 8.1 with the additional objective of efficient testing: taking optimal amounts of effort to create and run the tests against the technical components.

Measurement 8.2: Schedule performance index for testing tasks in the project (earned value divided by baseline cost of work scheduled).

Ch. 23
Project
Plan

See Chapter 23 for an explanation of this measure. Essentially it measures how well the resources performed the testing tasks against what your project plan specified.

Structure

METHOD

The *method* is the abstract textual description of the test method. It includes a description of each test model to use along with the criteria for deciding when to apply it. It includes a description of how to go about choosing test models for technical components and how to use them to develop test suites. It also includes any standards for test documentation and reporting. The method may be algorithmic, heuristic, or informal as long as it meets the objectives of reusability, risk management, and productivity.

RESOURCES

Developing a test approach requires a lot of experience in testing methods and theory. The resources—people—who develop the test approach should have formal training in quality assurance for software development with emphasis on testing models at all levels (object, integration, and system). These people must be capable of seeing the big picture and writing it down so that others can see it too.

INFRASTRUCTURE

The test approach must be a part of the standards documents for the project, as it contains standard test methods. If specific tools support the test approach, the approach should list the tools and refer to any standards for their use.

You can modify any standard test approach to suit a particular component, but you must explain this variance in the test plan. To justify a different approach, the test approach section should clearly explain the variance using the risk analysis in light of the test objectives. Approval of the test plan constitutes approval of the variant approach.

Dynamics

CREATE

The Create task creates the test approach within a test plan based on the standard test approach. This task, begun by the process of creating the test plan, scales the test approach to the project's statement of work and aligns the approach with the project schedule (the Scale and Align tasks, to be discussed next).

SCALE

The Scale task takes the general, standard test approach and scales it to fit a particular test plan. Your overall statement of work in the project plan identifies the classes, foundation components, and systems as the technical components subject to test. Your technical and schedule risk management plans identify the risks to manage through testing. The combination of the components and the risk management tasks gives you the basis for scaling the test approach to your project's requirements. You may not need to apply the entire method, or you may need additional methods to test unusual components or requirements. In any case, you must carefully analyze the test approach and scale it to fit.

ALIGN

Include the appropriate testing objects and their associated tasks in the project schedule through the WBS. This is an important dynamic because it "officially" includes (and therefore recognizes) the testing objects as part of the development system. If the testing objects do not appear as part of the project schedule, you will find it is very difficult to use them to achieve their vision, mission, and objectives.

REVIEW

As with every significant object in the development system, review the approach with technical peers and customers of the objects.

REVISE

Add to, reduce, and change the method as necessary to reach agreement from the customers of the testing objects.

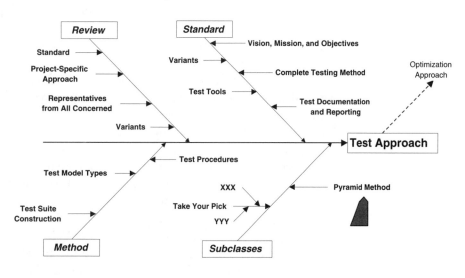

Figure 8.2 Road map for the test approach class.

Optimize

This may be your first time using some or all of the testing objects from the approach. As your project progresses, apply the optimization cycle that is part of the approach. Learn from your successes and failures and feed back the learning in real time to achieve optimum results.

Road Map

Figure 8.2 is the road map for the test approach class.

The Hierarchical Approach

The *hierarchical approach* is at the heart of the object-oriented testing system. This test approach uses and builds upon several well-understood testing techniques, tying them together into a comprehensive testing system. The hierarchical approach leverages the fact that "everything is a system." It defines and applies testing standards for several levels of software component: objects, classes, foundation components, and systems. The hierarchical approach designates as *SAFE* those components that meet the testing standards for that kind of component. Once you designate a component as SAFE, you can integrate it with other SAFE components to produce the next-level component. In turn, you test this component to the level of safety associated with the component level it represents. SAFE is always a relative state. It depends entirely on the standards you choose to enforce, your application, your attitude toward risk, and the specific risks and risk management practices you adopt in your project. The hierarchical approach provides guidelines for minimum safety; you decide what is right for you.

The hierarchical approach focuses on foundation components. A *foundation component* may be one complete class hierarchy or some other cluster of classes that performs a core function or that represents a logical or physical architectural component.

After you test a foundation component to a safe level, you can integrate it with other foundation components. Integration testing of safe foundation components then needs to address only the interconnections between the foundation components and any new composite functionality. The hierarchical approach eliminates the need to test all of the combinations of states during integration testing, thus improving productivity.

This approach views integration testing as a daily activity for the development team. The integrated and SAFE foundation components combine with each other, eventually combining into systems. Foundation components and systems appear as baseline components in the WBS and as milestones on the project schedule. The project milestones are the actual expected deliveries of architectural baselines of the final software product. The hierarchical approach is completely consistent with and supports the iterative incremental and recursive development process. You can adopt, adapt, and apply any piece of the hierarchical approach to work with any other software development process.

Earned value and its associated measures and metrics are a consistent way to track project progress as well as product quality. As you designate foundation components SAFE, they earn value points. You award points based on the relative value of the foundation component to other system components within the context of the overall project. Foundation components eventually integrate into systems. Each system earns its own value upon SAFE designation. These systems correspond to the functional, logical, or architectural layers that are major project milestones and baselines. The development effort progresses up the pyramid in a parallel, iterative, and recursive manner. The goal of the hierarchical approach is to optimize development team productivity and the final value the product delivers to the customers.

Figure 8.3 is a graphical representation of the hierarchical approach. Time moves forward by ascending the pyramid. At the base of the pyramid, you

HIERARCHICAL TESTING APPROACH

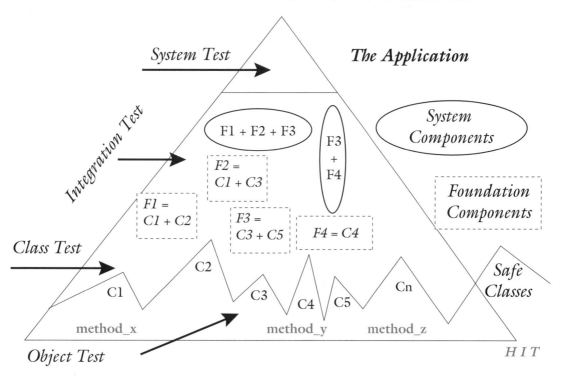

Figure 8.3 The hierarchical approach.

Ch. 11

Hierarchical-
Incremental Test
Suite

Ch. 12

Conditional
Test Suite

Ch. 13

Integration
Test Suite

Ch. 14

System
Component
Test Suite

thoroughly test individual methods to a SAFE designation. (See the operational objective criteria for success in the sections on the different test models.) The methods integrate into classes and you test whole class hierarchies to a SAFE level. (See Chapters 11 and 12.) The collections of SAFE classes (foundation components) form the foundation of your final product. The large integration area of the pyramid is where you integrate the foundation components into the different architectural, functional, and logical structures. (See Chapter 13.) They form the systems. At the apex of the pyramid is a short and concentrated system test. (See Chapter 14.)

The shortened system test phase represents the harvest of the testing labors sown lower in the pyramid. System test concentrates on the "Illities" (ill at ease) system tests (usability, reliability, flexibility, performability, securability, and so on). You spend minimal time regression-testing a system you successfully develop with the hierarchical approach. Most if not all of the regression and system tests suites are already complete from test cases, scripts, and use cases developed and executed lower in the pyramid, so you reuse them in various combinations.

The pyramid has been designed with a rhomboidal foundation. The foundation is the result of applying the approach explained later in this section through following the test plan. This pyramid, common as a tomb for rulers in ancient Egypt, is one of the most stable forms of construction (Mendelssohn, 1974, pp. 114–132). When the basic building blocks of your system are sound and your mortar (integration material) is applied correctly, your system can survive, even thrive for a long time (perhaps not millennia, though) with minimum maintenance and maximum functionality. Implementing the optimization approach, the basis for the pyramid test method, results in system longevity.

Figure 8.4 shows the structure of the hierarchical approach class.

LEADERSHIP

Vision: A comprehensive method of testing object-oriented software components that you can reuse in many projects to achieve an acceptable level of risk with a high degree of productivity.

Mission: To provide a testing approach optimized for object-oriented software components that you can reuse in many projects to get an acceptable level of risk and a high level of productivity.

Objective 8.1: To provide a pyramidal test method that you can reuse to achieve an acceptable level of risk in your object-oriented software projects.

Approach 8.1: Develop a written, standard test method using hierarchical incremental, conditional, integration, and system test models that gives the specific objectives, approaches, and measurements for those objects that will achieve your acceptable level of risk.

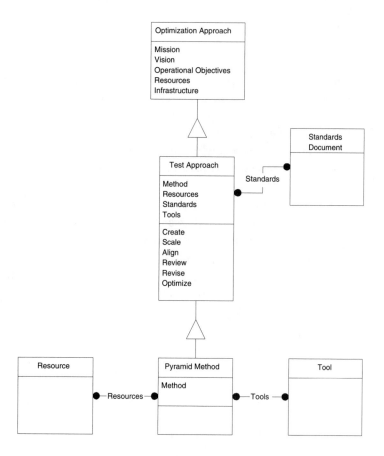

Figure 8.4 Structure of the pyramid method class.

Chapters 15 to 19 constitute the details of this hierarchical test method.

Measurement 8.1.1: Number of projects that reuse the test approach.

Measurement 8.1.2: Level of risk for project using test approach.

Objective 8.2: To provide a pyramidal test method that you can reuse to achieve a high level of productivity in testing your object-oriented software projects.

Approach 8.2: Develop a test method as in 8.1 with the additional objective of efficient testing: taking optimal amounts of effort to create and run the tests against the components.

Measurement 8.2: Schedule performance index for testing tasks in the project (earned value divided by baseline cost of work scheduled).

Structure

The hierarchical approach provides a structured set of test suites and test models. When you scale and apply these suites and models, your project will reduce your risk to acceptable levels and will increase your testing and development productivity.

The rest of Part 3 contains the details of the hierarchical approach for testing object-oriented software. The following test suites make up the structure of the pyramid:

- **Conditional Test Suite:** Tests classes using the conditional test model and its accompanying assertions, exceptions, concurrent test operations, and message polling test scripts.
- **Hierarchical Incremental Test Suite:** Tests foundation components using various test models and scripts (see the following paragraphs for details), possibly with stubbed references to other components.
- **Integration Test Suite:** Tests combinations of foundation components using the hierarchical incremental models with scripts that use all the components, not just stubs.
- **System Test Suite:** Tests systems of foundation components using system test models.
- **Regression Test Suite:** Tests foundation components and systems.

The hierarchical incremental test suite is the most complex of the test suites. You can build the suite using any or all of the following test models:

- **State-Transition Test Model:** Models the dynamic behavior of classes as states and transitions, with the test object being the life cycle flows through the model.
- **Transaction-Flow Test Model:** Models the dynamic behavior of classes as black-box transactions, with the test object being transaction flows.
- **Exception Test Model:** Models the exception behavior of classes.
- **Control-Flow Test Model:** Models the dynamic behavior of methods as a flow of control through a method; the test object is a single flow through the model.
- **Data-Flow Test Model:** Models the dynamic behavior of methods as a flow of both control and data through a method; the test object again is a single flow through the model.

See the individual chapters for a comprehensive, detailed method for choosing which models and objects to use, building the test scripts into test suites, and automating the execution and result-gathering procedures. Each object has its own optimization approach details; the operational objectives for each object constitute the test standards for that object.

RESOURCES

The proverbial good news and bad news applies here. The bad news first. The hierarchical approach represents a complete evolution beyond the best current software engineering practices. The SEI CMM would refer to successful development with the hierarchical approach as level 5, if it addressed testing or quality adequately, which it does not. In quality terms, the hierarchical approach implements quality optimization principles for software development. To implement the hierarchical approach completely, you need an organization that has mastered everything presented in this book. Mastery of these skills requires in-depth technical training and detailed technical capabilities beyond the scope of this book.

There is also plenty of good news. The hierarchical approach is not an all-or-nothing approach. You can use it in an incremental and piecemeal manner. You can benefit from any and all of the approaches and build upon them as you move toward a vision of software engineering that encompasses many if not all of them. You can implement the full hierarchical approach in phases, in parallel, and incrementally. If you apply the principles from the quality system and practice and implement optimization cycles, you will be able to evolve quickly into the hierarchical approach. A list of what we believe to be the minimum level of training and technical capabilities for a project team to start working with some of the objects in the hierarchical test system follows.

- Object-oriented analysis and design (minimum of 3 to 5 days of seminars or the equivalent in experience)
- Mastery of object-oriented programming language
- Object-oriented testing
- Basic test techniques

INFRASTRUCTURE

Adoption of any method benefits from tools that support and automate aspects of it. At press time, several tool vendors have expressed interest in developing a tool set to implement the hierarchical approach. Some of the pieces have already been implemented, and others are being developed piecemeal. I invite any of my readers to contact me personally for an update on work in this area; my Internet address is listed in the frontmatter of this book. There is a forum on hierarchical approach test automation on the Internet.

Example

The DTS project was the first project in the company to use the new hierarchical approach. The project manager hired a consultant who provided courseware and degapping services using the method and, with the quality assurance manager, developed the test approach standard to use in the DTS project and in future object-oriented software projects.

Because the DTS team had had extensive exposure to object-oriented programming and design in previous projects, and because there was already a basic measurement and quality optimization program in place, the project manager felt that the test approach could use most if not all the hierarchical testing method.

The final draft standard included most of the material that appears in the following chapters of this book. The project manager and quality assurance manager brought together the senior executives and functional managers who would need to work with the method for a review meeting. Also present were several representatives from the design, programming, and quality assurance groups. The review eliminated some items and added some standards, but the overall reaction was positive, and the company adopted the test approach as its standard.

During the creation of the DTS project plan statement of work, the quality assurance (QA) manager created the test plans and created the specific project test approaches as a part of the plans. The QA manager trimmed some of the hierarchical incremental test models, focusing on transaction flow and data flow models, and decided to add some specific performance modeling and testing during the system test to address some risks in that area. Because the team had acquired a strong UI test tool, the QA manager decided to focus on widget-playback testing of the user interface. The QA manager and the project manager systematically revised the metrics to specify using earned value measured in function points rather than in terms of cost.

The QA manager incorporated the finished test approach into the test plan, won approval for the plan, and started the process of test model development.

As the project progressed, the project manager conducted several optimization cycles on both the standard test approach and the project-specific one. The benefits from the performance test model were so great that it moved into the standard. The testing team also decided to use a state-transition model for a particular foundation component, to which it seemed very well suited.

Road Map

Figure 8.5 is the road map for the hierarchical approach class.

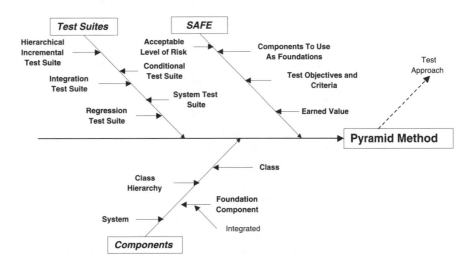

Figure 8.5 Road map for the pyramid method class.

Test Plan

Ch. 23

Project
Plan

Test plans are a type of project document. (See Chapter 23.) A project plan statement of work contains one or more test plans, each corresponding to some software component in the WBS. All test plans share a common structure; the structure presented here is an object-oriented version based on the IEEE standard for test plans. You should be able to reuse the organization and structure of test plans. Most projects store test plans as complete documents in the project or test repository. If you create a standard repository or directory structure with naming conventions you can include your documents. We suggest treating sections of your documents as reusable objects. Select the individual objects (sections) for each project appropriate to the type of plan you are writing. You can modify each individual section as necessary in accordance with the specifics of your current project needs. You may or may not be able to reuse specific test models and objects.

Object-oriented test plans differ based on the type of object to test and the amount of detail that you include in your plan. The test approach that you create as part of the test plan, the scope and size of your project (statement of work), and the objectives and resources (schedule) determine how many test plans you produce. How you organize your test plans—the order of the sections—is a matter of style. Use our approach as a template. Create your own specific instances of plans based on your company culture and experience. You may choose to combine or cross two or more plans (an example of multiple inheritance and reuse in action).

You must provide enough background information about your project for the reader to make sense out of the scope and scale of the testing you are planning. Describe relevant events or customer needs that led to this project or the features or functionality you will test. Describe what the plan does and does not cover. Your introduction is successful if your customer (target audience) can read it and come away with a description of the product to test, its scope, and its scale. Have several potential users of the plan review this section and provide feedback. The content in the rest of the plan should answer their questions. If they have general questions about the product to test or the scale or scope of what this test plan covers, then you must add information. It is acceptable to provide references to other documents with more detail about the product, such as the statement of work, without repeating the detail in the test plan. It's all part of the statement of work.

The test approach should identify the test objectives for the test suites. Identify and interview the customers of the testing effort. Usually this includes the project manager (representing the organization), developers of the system, and actual end users, as well as anyone else with a contribution to make. Ask each of the customers what they expect in the way of quality and productivity. Make a list of the expectations and transform the expectations into reasonable test objectives. Use the test models to map the user or customer expectations to the test objectives. Reasonable objectives are realistic and measurable. Hint: The objectives must map to the test models for the component. If one or more objectives are not reasonable, then you must negotiate with the customers to set reasonable objectives.

Every product has time and quality trade-offs. Your task in the test plan is to quantify the minimum level of acceptability within a specific time frame. Always state the test objectives in a numerically verifiable way. For example, it is possible to set as an objective a percentage of code or path coverage and then actually to count the coverage achieved. Since numerous tools are available to automate this for you, it is both a reasonable and realistic test objective. It is also possible to state the test objective relative to the project requirements, specification, or functionality. If all of these do not yet exist—a highly likely and common occurrence on the projects we work on—then set your objectives as a percentage of the final number as of some future date. Another valid approach is to remove a quantifiable amount of risk from the product. As long as it is possible to discretely measure against the criteria at any given time and to state unambiguously where the development effort is in relation to the test objectives, you have reasonable test objectives.

You should develop test objectives by and with the customer and/or end user community. If the customer and end user do not participate in setting the quality objectives, they should at least approve them. The end user may not be in a position either technically or otherwise to participate at this level. If that is the case, then a test or quality assurance function must act on their behalf. Often the immediate customers and end users are not one and the same party. The fact that the immediate customer is an internal function or even another developer or tester may complicate the situation. It is imperative that customers participate in the negotiations that lead to the setting of the test criteria.

Once you develop the test plan, enter the planned test models and suites into the WBS as deliverables, and enter the tasks associated with those deliverables into the project schedule. This integrates the testing plans into the project and ensures adequate feedback on progress to all concerned.

Track the resolution of issues and concerns just as you would project progress. In a very real sense they are accurate indicators of project progress. Unresolved items have a time open (today's date minus the date first opened) as well as an importance factor or severity. A useful metric is to multiply the importance factor by the time open and then add together all the items from the three lists. If the number is getting larger, week to week, your project is likely in big trouble. If the number remains relatively stable, the project team may have an unrealistic attitude that if they ignore them long enough, they will probably just go away. This almost never happens. The only acceptable situation is for the absolute value of the number to decrease consistently. The rate that this occurs is a good heuristic for predicting how likely it is that the project will meet its objectives.

There are two subclasses of test plan, each corresponding to a particular type of software component or test suite:

- **Foundation Component Test Plan:** A plan to test a foundation component, including hierarchical incremental tests, conditional tests, and integration tests.
- **System Test Plan:** A plan to test a system, including system and regression tests.

You also can create one test suite per test plan and hence one test plan for each software component, but you can combine several test plans into a single test suite if that makes sense.

Once you have gotten approval of the basic test plan, you need to develop the test model and from it the test objects, scripts, and suites required to do the testing. You should consider the test model part of the test plan. As you develop and revise the test model, you should revise the test plan in accordance with standard change management procedures. As are all project documents, the project repository (or the test repository) stores the test plan.

Figure 8.6 shows the structure of the test plan class.

Leadership

Vision: A comprehensive set of models of software components that provide a contract that permits the productive development of comprehensive test suites.

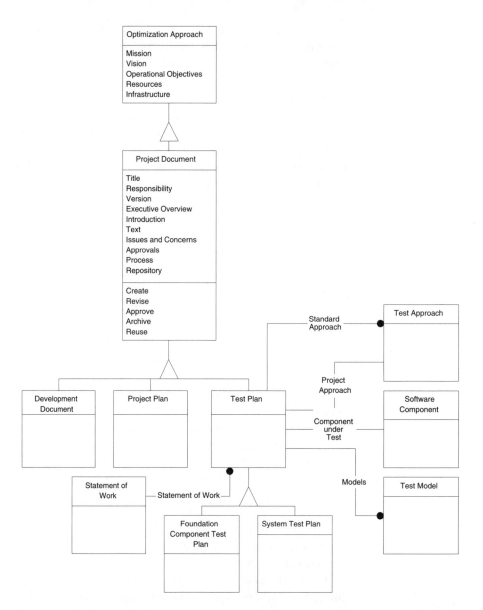

Figure 8.6 Structure of the test plan class.

Mission: To serve as a document of understanding or contract between the project team members regarding their quality objectives and the basic tasks and responsibilities for each member of the development team.

In a very real sense the test plan serves as a living, evolving contract between the various cross-functional elements that contribute to any product team. In many cases, it is the only repository for information regarding the testing and quality objectives for the project or product. Test plans link individual project team members with specific testing tasks, and these link directly to the test objectives. You must perform these tasks or reach an agreement to change the objectives before you can baseline the product.

When the pressure to ship a product becomes overwhelming, the test plan must serve as an artifact of calmer times and saner minds. It is always possible to meet a ship date. The difficult task is to ship with an acceptable amount and severity of defects. This translates into failures that do not occur too often and are not too severe from the customer's perspective. The purpose of the plan is to state the acceptable level and propose an approach to achieve it before the pressure to meet a ship date becomes overwhelming. Thus, if the plan exists and everyone has agreed to it before the schedule pressures obliterate common sense, the team should be able to make the optimum decisions based on the situation at hand.

Objective 8.3: To understand and communicate what the project needs to accomplish to achieve high quality.

Approach 8.3: Construct and maintain a test plan consisting of a test approach, a software component, and a test model that comprehensively lays out the testing requirements for the software component to ensure that the project resources understand what they need to do to achieve adequate component quality.

Measurement 8.3: Schedule performance index for the resulting WBS testing tasks (earned value at completion divided by the median plan baseline cost of work scheduled; see the following earned value section for details).

Objective 8.4: To increase productivity through understanding and communicating how to achieve the project goals.

Approach 8.4: Construct a test plan as in 8.3 that optimizes the effort of test resources by comprehensively presenting the test approach and criteria for success and the test model on which to base test suites.

Measurement 8.4: Ratio of median test productivity (effort per tested [SAFE] function point) to benchmark productivity.

Structure

COMPONENT UNDER TEST
The *component under test* is the software component that you are planning to test. The test models apply to this software component.

STANDARD APPROACH
The standard approach is the test approach that is standard in your project environment. The project approach is the adaptation of this standard approach to this particular project.

Project Approach

The project approach is the test approach that you adapt from the standard approach. It can be a simple list of variations on the standard approach, or it can be a full-blown test approach all its own. In the latter case, you will need to justify the departure from the standard approach to get approval of the plan.

Models

The set of test models that model the component under test provide the basis for all of the testing work done under this test plan. You create the basic test models when you have access to the initial design for the software component. As you get more detailed design documents, you refine the test models to reflect that design. Test models can be any test model approved by the project test approach.

Statement of Work

The statement of work is part of the project plan. It contains entries for all the deliverable objects (test objects, scripts, and suites) that you develop as part of the test plan. It also contains the tasks the project manager derives from those deliverable objects. These tasks relate directly to the project schedule, which sets the timing, resources, and dependencies for the tasks.

Resources

Writing a test plan requires the following skills:
- Knowledge of the test approach and its methods.
- Ability to read and understand technical documentation such as object-oriented designs and code.
- Ability to identify and communicate with the customer and end user.
- Ability to analyze and negotiate trade-offs.

Infrastructure

Reuse existing test plan sections' templates. If they do not exist, create them based on the templates in this book. You will need a standard word processor, spreadsheets to manipulate lists, and access to printing and reproduction machines.

Example

The next software component for test planning was the problem hierarchy foundation component. Its several classes comprise the small hierarchy of problem-related classes. The QA manager assigned the test plan for this class to a test engineer, who produced the following draft based on the architectural design for the class hierarchy in Figure 8.7.

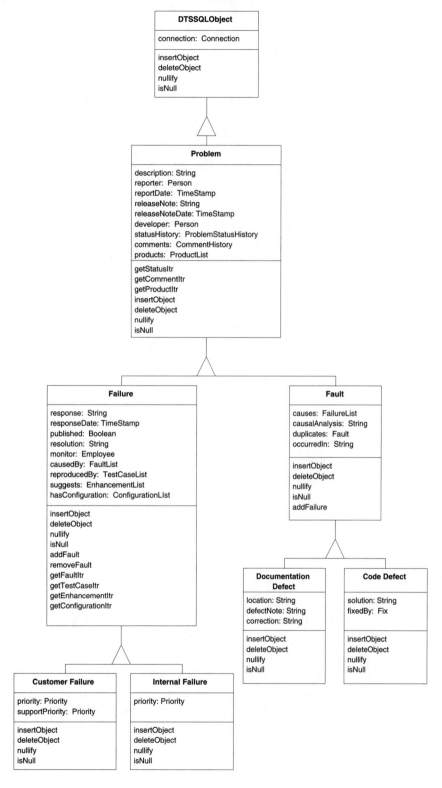

Figure 8.7 DTS Problem inheritance hierarchy.

Title: Problem Foundation Component Test Plan

Responsibility: DTS Test Engineer

Version: 1.0

Introduction: The requirements document in the project statement of work contains the use cases, the source of the architectural design decisions that this design represents. The essential idea is to distinguish faults from failures and to record the basic information for each. The hierarchy inherits from the DTSSQLObject class in the utilities system because the classes all represent database objects. The DTSSQLObject class is part of another foundation component and is not under test.

The test plan uses the standard hierarchical approach for its test approach with no variations. The operational objectives for the different classes of test model are the test objectives for the test models that are described next.

Text: Include project/component specific text here.

Test Model: Problem Transaction-Flow Model

This test model will model the abstract life cycle of a problem from creation to destruction. The test objects will become test scripts in the Problem Transaction-Flow Test Suite.

Test Model: Problem::insertObject Data-Flow Test Model

This test model tests the **insertObject** method, which overrides the parent method. Although the class is abstract, the method is not, because it inserts data into the database. The test objects will become test scripts in the Problem::insertObject Data Flow Test Model Test Suite.

Test Model: Problem::deleteObject Data Flow Test Model

This test model tests the deleteObject method, which overrides the parent method. Although the class is abstract, the method is not, because it inserts data into the database. The test objects will become test scripts in the Problem::insertObject Data Flow Test Model Test Suite.

Test Model: CodeDefect Synchronization Test Model

The CodeDefect class is a concrete class that must interact with other objects in database transactions. The test objects from this model test the CodeDefect objects synchronously committing to the database with other code defects and problems of various kinds.

Issues and Concerns: Apparently marketing has raised an issue that we may need to include a separate kind of failure relating to internal failures not caused by developers (that is, marketing or technical support failures). The argument is ongoing, but this will result in another 16 test models for this test plan.

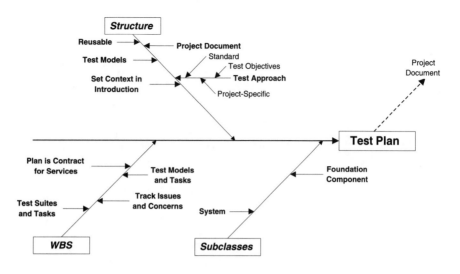

Figure 8.8 Road map for the test plan class.

Approvals: Initial approval from the QA manager and the project manager for inclusion in the project plan.

After completing the first draft of the test plan, the engineer checked the document into the project repository as part of the project plan's statement of work. The project manager created a deliverable in the WBS for each test model and created a tentative test suite for each test model as well. The project manager then scheduled the tasks in the project schedule, working with the QA manager to assign resources.

Road Map

Figure 8.8 is the road map for the test plan class.

CHAPTER 9

TEST ENVIRONMENT

Test Environment

The test environment contains the infrastructure for testing and is a kind of development environment. (See Chapter 21.) The automated integration environment contains automated testing elements as well; see the "Automated Integration Environment" section in Chapter 21.

Ch. 21

The Development Environment

- **Test repository:** The storage system to organize and keep track of the test objects.
- **Test framework:** The system that manages the execution of the testing.
- **Test standards:** The rules for construction, processing, and evaluation of test objects.

All objects in the test environment are under the control of the configuration management system, which the test environment includes as a development environment. The test environment has an owner, the integration autarch, who is responsible for its maintenance and integrity.

According to the dictionary, design (verb) means the following: (1) to arrange or organize objects, (2) to plan.

Both of these meanings must be applied to the objects in the test environment and the objects it contains. When you design the test environment itself, you are modeling real relationships between the objects in the environment and the users of the environment. The way you plan your system and arrange the objects in the system must reflect how you will use the system. The design of the objects within the test environment follows the same principle. If your test environment contains no standards, then you and your peers will use the system in nonstandard and ad hoc ways. If the standards are bureaucratic and overbearing, the usefulness of the system disintegrates, and you will not use it.

Good or effective design is an optimization process, and the test environment is a kind of optimization approach. Effective design seeks to impose real-world constraints upon the requirements in such a way as to fulfill the requirements while optimizing development productivity and value to the customer. One objective of this book is to present the design of an object-oriented testing system. The book at once represents (is an instance of) and applies the principles of object-oriented design. The relationships of the various objects, the order of presentation, the amount of detail, and where the detail appears are the result of careful design decisions. One of our goals was for this book to be an example of the application of object-oriented analysis and design principles to real-world problems. Another goal was for the design to demonstrate clearly the relationship of the testing objects in the test system to one another and to the other major systems in the development environment. The measure of a good design is reflected in the practicality and ease of use of the end product. The test environment is the major infrastructure object for the hierarchical method. Without it, the test system is an ad hoc affair.

Figure 9.1 shows the structure of the test environment class.

Leadership

Vision: A practical test environment that is easy to learn and use and that facilitates the reuse of test objects.

Reuse of test objects will contribute to increased testing productivity and products with greater value. Increased testing productivity from release to release, project to project, and organization to organization will lead to a competitive advantage in the marketplace.

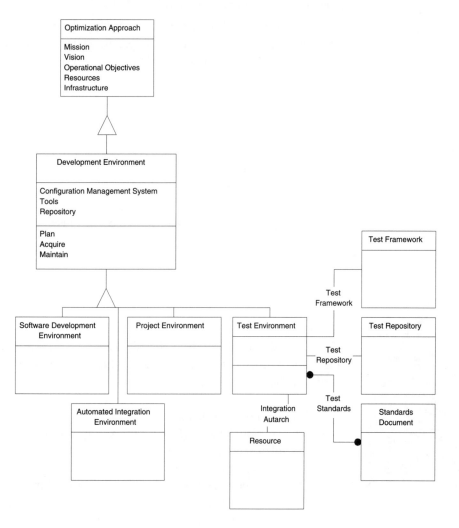

Figure 9.1 Structure of the test environment class.

Mission: To design and deploy a test environment that facilitates productivity through reuse of test objects and ease of use.

Objective 9.1: To create a reusable test environment.

Approach 9.1: Build the different aspects of the test environment in the same way you would build any object-oriented software system.

Measurement 9.1: Ratio of earned value from reused test environment components to total project earned value.

Objective 9.2: To create an easy-to-use test environment.

Approach 9.2: Build the different aspects of the test environment from requirements expressed as use cases in the same way you would build any object-oriented software system.

Measurement 9.2: Productivity of testing tasks using environment components compared to a benchmark productivity (productivity measured in effort-hours per unit of earned value).

Structure

TEST FRAMEWORK

An object-oriented *test framework* contains the following objects:

- User interface
- Set of common testing methods
- Database
- Runtime procedures to automate certain tasks

See the "Test Framework" section that follows for details of this class.

TEST REPOSITORY

See the section on the test repository in Chapter 10 for details of this class.

TEST STANDARDS

Test standards are meters (see the discussion of measurement in Chapter 6) applied to a broad category of objects. The hierarchical method suggests standards for the following objects:

- Directory structure
- Naming conventions
- Objects associated with different test approaches
- Test plan sections
- Test approach guidelines
- Entry and coverage objectives for conditional models
- Entry and coverage objectives for hierarchical incremental models
- Entry and coverage objectives for integration models
- Entry and coverage objectives for system models

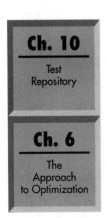

Ch. 10
Test Repository

Ch. 6
The Approach to Optimization

Ch. 17
Test
Standards

Ch. 11
Hierarchical-
Incremental
Test Suite

- Baseline exit criteria

Standards accompany the classes to which they apply either as operational objectives in the leadership sections or as specific standards in infrastructure sections. See Chapter 17 for a complete analysis of test standards and standards documents.

RESOURCES

It is essential to have an integration autarch who owns or is responsible for the test environment. See the section on the automated integration environment in Chapter 11.

Example

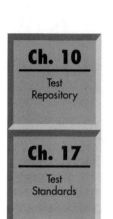

Ch. 10
Test
Repository

Ch. 17
Test
Standards

The DTS project was the fourth in a series of projects using the basic tools of the test environment. The test framework consists of templates from a proprietary testing framework system; see the example in the section below on the test framework. The test repository is a custom collection of relational database tables and files; see the example in the test repository section of Chapter 10. The test standards include the process standards for the different kinds of test objects and the documentation and report standards for test scripts and test output. See Chapter 17 for examples of these objects in the DTS project.

The DTS project team planned the environment by identifying the reusable frameworks, repository, and standards from other projects and designing new repository elements and standards for test objects that had changed. Because the project was the first to use the pyramid method's hierarchical-incremental testing for foundation components, for example, the team had to design test standards for these test objects and repository tables to store and track the objects and their results.

The team then acquired the environment in the usual way, buying parts and building others. The team paid an additional licensing fee for using the test framework in a new project. The team proposed and reviewed the new test standards. Finally, the team developed the revised repository and some additional testing tools as small software development projects. After finishing development of the environment early in the project, the project team turned over environment maintenance to the quality assurance team for the project.

Road Map

Figure 9.2 is the road map for the test environment class.

Test Framework

A *test framework* manages the interface among a developer, the test code, and the product code. It provides a consistent interface to the tester. It also serves as the test driver and test manager.

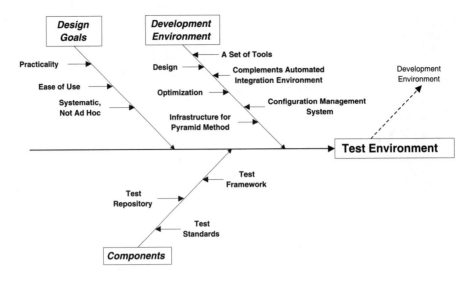

Figure 9.2 Road map for the test environment class.

Object-oriented test drivers are not a new idea. A common architecture for testing classes is the parallel test class, which serves as a test driver for the class under test (CUT). Developers using C++ readily seize the opportunity to use the C++ *friend* relationship to implement this parallel, mirror test system. We first implemented such a parallel test system in 1989. The parallel architecture worked! However, the overhead of developing, testing, and maintaining the parallel test system was almost 75 percent of the effort to develop the software system we were testing. There had to be a better way, and there is.

A test framework provides a set of generic classes and a generic repository for managing the object-oriented test environment. Since you design and implement the framework using the same tools and techniques as your object-oriented code, you have the same kind of classes and methods. You can reuse, refine, overload, and override the framework class methods just as in your product code. The framework provides a standard core set of working test methods that empower the developer or tester to be creative and flexible in approaching testing class methods.

You can design test frameworks as very simple test drivers or as highly automated tools. Figure 9.3 shows four framework architectures. You can either encapsulate the test data in the parallel test class or store it as an independent and reusable object in a relational or object database. You can make the test methods external to the product source code you are testing (*parallel*) or inherit them as part of the product source code classes (*invasive*). In either case you still need an external test driver and manager. In the parallel system, there is one test driver per foundation component. In the invasive system, there is one common test driver/manager for all the development classes.

The encapsulated, parallel framework is the easiest to implement and to understand but requires the most overhead. Creating, documenting, debugging, and maintaining a parallel test system can be hazardous to your schedule. Also, you cannot reuse your test objects beyond reusing an entire class hierarchy. Whenever you reuse and modify a class, you can reuse and modify the parallel test class, but the tests themselves, encapsulated within the test objects, are not available to other classes or projects. You can replace only entire test methods, not the individual tests within them.

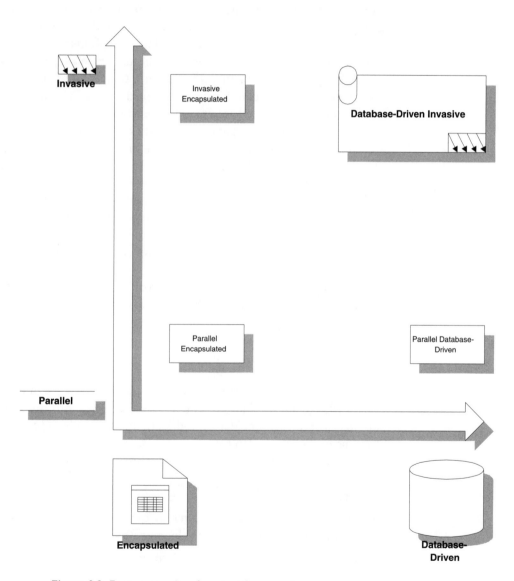

Figure 9.3 Four approaches for a test framework.

The encapsulated, invasive framework has two advantages: reuse of the test methods and a common test harness. Developers do not need to code their own test drivers for each class, and they have a common and consistent test interface. The invasive test methods also permit developers to modify the test methods in the context of their classes. What are the negatives? One is possible performance and memory overhead. If you are developing an embedded application, or one that is sensitive to performance, you will have to analyze whether you can afford to include the test methods. You can always bracket the invasive methods out using precompiler conditions after testing your class to SAFE. Having many precompiler conditions tends to make your code less readable, but if you design the test methods into an abstract class, the problem disappears from your product code. This is also an advantage of the parallel approach, which removes the test code into a separate, parallel class. The biggest problem with the encapsulated, invasive approach is the unavailability of test data for reuse out of the context of the class, the same problem as with the encapsulated, parallel framework.

The database-driven, parallel approach combines the advantages and disadvantages of the parallel approach, but the test data is available for reuse. The overhead incurred for the reuse of the test data is the design, documentation, and maintenance of the test repository. We think it is well worth the effort but understand that many developers are currently (always?) in the middle of a project and need to do some testing quickly (now) for this project. Many developers do not have the time to implement the separate database architecture. *C'est la guerre!* Or as we Americans say, "You can pay now or pay later!"

The database-driven, invasive approach has all the advantages of the encapsulated, invasive approach plus the advantages of separate data. The overhead for the design, documentation, education, and maintenance remains, but we believe if you do it right, it is worth it. Reuse, productivity, and time to market were some of the reasons that compelled your organization to move to object-oriented technology. We also expect to see a proliferation of tools that support automation of the maintenance of the test system, as knowledge about object-oriented testing diffuses into the software development workplace. The database-driven, invasive architecture represents the first major step toward automating the hierarchical testing method.

Figure 9.4 shows the structure of the test framework class.

LEADERSHIP

Vision: An automated testing system with standard, reusable test objects that results in high productivity and value in software product development.

Mission: To create an automated testing system that provides standard, reusable test objects.

Figure 9.4 Structure of the test framework class.

Objective 9.3: To create high productivity in testing

Approach 9.3: Build or buy a test framework using the database-driven, invasive approach to test automation.

Measurement 9.3: Earned value in function points per effort-hour spent in testing tasks compared to a benchmark productivity value.

Objective 9.4: To create high value in tested components.

Approach 9.4: Build or buy a test framework using the database-driven, invasive approach to test automation and use it to build test objects that achieve the test standards.

Measurement 9.4: SAFE schedule performance index, counting earned value only from components that meet test standards (earned value for standard-meeting components divided by baseline value for all components).

STRUCTURE

TEST ENVIRONMENT

The test environment is the development environment of which this test framework is a component. See the test environment section.

GENERIC TEST CLASSES

The test framework provides a set of *generic test classes* that serve as the basis for your extensions into database-driven, invasive test suites. These classes use all the features of the target programming language such as C++ to provide generic and virtual testing methods that you can call or overload in your subclasses.

As with any programming framework, the completed test framework should include

- Class design diagrams (Rumbaugh-OMT and Booch)
- Test model documentation with test object specifications
- Commented and tested test script code
- Descriptions of how to use each method and class in the framework

GRAPHICAL USER INTERFACE

The test framework may or may not provide a simple *graphical user interface* for entering and saving ad hoc tests and for querying objects. (See the "Dynamics" section below.)

GENERIC REPOSITORY

The test framework should provide a generic repository for storing test data and scripts, including

- Design documentation
- Low-level database specification
- Database creation scripts such as SQL scripts

RESOURCES

As with any software component, the test framework requires that the resources assigned to it be skilled in the object-oriented programming language in which the framework is built. Since the framework architecture and the product code architecture in combination determine the architecture for the framework, no design skills are necessary.

INFRASTRUCTURE

You need the following tools:

- A software development environment
- A database manager
- A script or macro language that allows you to access the file system of the operating system, such as REXX, Visual Basic, shell scripts, or a programming language with operating system function calls.

All these tools are part of the test environment of which the test framework is a component.

DYNAMICS

CREATE

Create the test scripts and test data from your test models and objects and store them in the database. The script and data objects must have these stored attributes:

- Developer's identity
- Date of creation
- Association between objects and test script
- Description of any external test setup and cleanup requirements
- Expected results

EXECUTE AD HOC TEST

You must be able to execute ad hoc tests. The test framework should support ad hoc, on-the-fly, manual creation of messages and data. Many developers prefer this manner of debugging and testing; but because you need to capture and document this sort of ad hoc testing, it is best done through the test framework. Many developers simply do not have the time to save and document their ad hoc tests.

QUERY

Ch. 12
Conditional
Test Suite

The Query method lets you interact with a program object while the program runs. If you implement the message-polling test script (see Chapter 12), each object can validate itself and report various states, such as the current values for various conditions, the current state, the set of objects that are currently active, and the set of objects that the program has destroyed. You should be able to get this information through a simple graphical user interface.

INITIALIZE

Besides the standard maintenance activities (the development environment **Maintain** method), you also must do certain things to start tests. The **Initialize** method takes care of test initialization, setting up any data or other environmental components the test needs to run. It also provides an audit trail of the environment initialization.

EXECUTE

The **Execute** method runs the test framework. Some possibilities for differing executions include running:

- All tests
- A specific test script
- A set of specific test scripts

- A specific test suite
- Several specific test suites
- A manual, ad hoc test (and record it for reuse into an existing suite)

Executing the test framework runs the indicated tests and produces test results in the test repository.

COMMENT

The **Comment** method lets you enter a comment in the audit trail for a particular test execution. This comment becomes part of the test results and hence part of the test reports.

CLEAN UP

The **Clean Up** method cleans up the test framework and environment after executing the framework. The cleanup process might include destroying any active objects and creating an audit trail of this destruction.

REPORT

The Report task generates reports from the test results and sends them to the appropriate people for evaluation.

EXAMPLE

The DTS adopted the INFACT!™ test framework and developed all the hierarchical-incremental test scripts and integration test suites using its classes.

INFACT! stands for Invasive Framework Architecture for Class Testing. The original version of INFACT! runs under Microsoft Windows. INFACT! is an object-oriented software framework that provides a set of generic methods for managing your class and object testing. It is most useful for the hierarchical-incremental and integration test approaches. (See Chapters 15 and 17, respectively). There is no reason that you could not extend INFACT! to support most if not all the hierarchical method.

The INFACT! system met the following set of functional requirements:
- Execute a specified combination of test scripts and suites.
- Execute a manual test.
- Add a manual test to an existing test suite in the test repository.
- Automatically log errors in the test repository.
- Log comments on tests in the test repository.
- Store test results in the test repository.
- List all objects that the test creates or destroys in the test repository.
- List invariant conditions for the class under test in the test repository.
- List the current state of the class under test in the test repository.

The DTS project team also considered modifying INFACT! to adapt it to a parallel approach but concluded after a prototype study that the results would be less productive than the invasive approach.

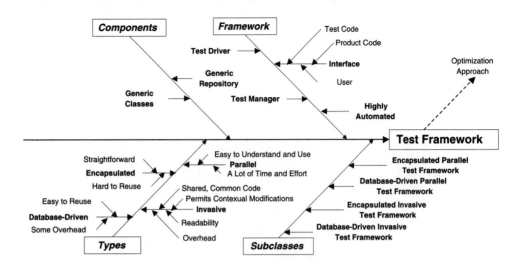

Figure 9.5 Road map for the test framework class.

ROAD MAP

Figure 9.5 is the road map for the test framework class.

CHAPTER 10

TEST REPOSITORY

Test Repository

The *test repository* is a kind of repository that contains the test suites, test data, and results data for a system. The test repository may overlap physically and conceptually with the product and project repositories. Tests may be an integral part of the product, and the results of tests may be part of the project data.

The test repository is like any repository, a collection of one or more storage structures. Your repository doesn't need to be integrated (that is, accessible through a single, consistent technology). You could have some test scripts on paper in a file drawer, some in files in two or more file systems, and some in two or more databases. At some point, though, you need to balance technology with complexity. If your primary approach is to enhance productivity by technological means, having many different storage structures amenable to the testing technologies for the scripts, you will find your setup time increasing as you have more difficulty finding the tests to run. If your primary approach to enhance productivity is to simplify things by constraining all tests to conform to a single storage standard, you may find your testing time lengthening as you translate scripts to a form more amenable to your tools. Your best bet, as always, is an optimizing compromise that gets closer to the technology of your testing tools while maintaining relative simplicity in your storage arrangements. See Chapter 6 for a way to improve your decisions here.

Ch. 6

The
Approach to
Optimization

The organization of the test suites depends largely on your software system structure and your approach to testing. The extremes are to organize all your test scripts as a single sequence regardless of type or to organize them into small clusters according to some extensive organizing principle. Your testing team should use optimization cycle techniques to make and improve this decision as you move forward.

This book divides the test suites by type, as it presents the different types of test script in separate chapters. Your repository could in practice be organized along system lines, with one test suite per system. Another possibility might be to break up the tests that are reusable with the ones specific to a given class or system. In any case, your approach to organizing test suites should align carefully with your objectives for the repository and the objectives for the rest of the testing and development system.

Figure 10.1 shows the class structure of the test repository class.

Leadership

Vision: An effective test storage organization.

Mission: To provide test storage services in a way that promotes productivity.

Objective 10.1: To increase testing productivity through organizing automatic and manual test script storage for easy storage and retrieval.

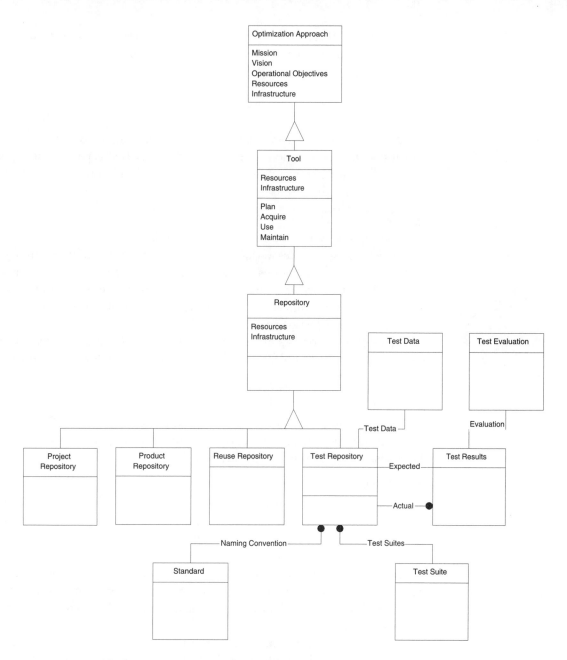

Figure 10.1 Structure of the test repository class.

Approach 10.1: Buy or build a database or file structure that provides storage and retrieval services for test scripts of all kinds.

Measurement 10.1: Developer and tester productivity in effort-hours per function point of product while repository is available.

Structure

NAMING CONVENTION

For the test repository, you will need a specific naming convention aimed at your test script organization. Use the basic strategy that is part of the repository object naming convention, but consider specifically those users who will actually be using the scripts.

TEST SUITES

Ch. 14

System
Component
Test Suite

The test repository is a file structure and/or relational database that uses the naming convention. At least, that's the most common way of doing things. It contains a series of test suites that apply to systems or the entire system as a whole. This latter organization aligns with our approach: structuring a software system as a carefully divided set of systems with minimized connections. (See the "System" section in Chapter14.)

Each test suite consists of a series of test scripts. See the sections that follow on the test suite object and the test script object for details on these classes of object.

TEST DATA

The test data of the system consists of all the database rows or files the test scripts need to perform the series of tests you have designed. This element of the repository often is called the *test bed*.

TEST RESULTS

Test results comprise data that represents the output of a test run. This can be anything from the specific data output into the database, to text you "print" out (into the test repository) to describe what is happening. There are two kinds of results data: expected results and actual results.

Expected results are data that represent what you expect to come out of the system for a test run. You can create these results by saving the test data from a successful test run, or you can create the data manually based on some kind of specification.

Actual results are data from a given test run. You compare the actual results to the expected results and flag any differences as potential errors. A test evaluation evaluates the results and feeds the conclusions back into the system as fixes and test system updates.

Example

The DTS test repository consists of a combination of storage structures: a relational database and a file system.

The relational database contains a set of tables that describes test scripts, test data, and test results used by the built-in testing mechanisms in the various test suites. The DTS team developed this database specifically for this project as part of the automated integration environment toolset. The tables include identifiers for the different systems so that system builds can access the appropriate test scripts and data in the database.

The file structure for each system of the DTS contains a set of files relating to several tools (such as the GUI testing tool) that require flat files to store scripts, data, and results. The DTS project acquired all of these tools from third-party vendors, and the file structure and naming conventions correspond to the defaults of the tools.

The test data in the DTS represent a thorough domain analysis of the database design. This permits the careful selection of data to test boundaries, input and output categories, and so on. A component of random data is also inserted for system testing. Since the DTS is primarily a relational database application, all the test data is in the relational database except for some initialization file test data, part of the system test.

Road Map

Figure 10.2 is the road map for the test repository class.

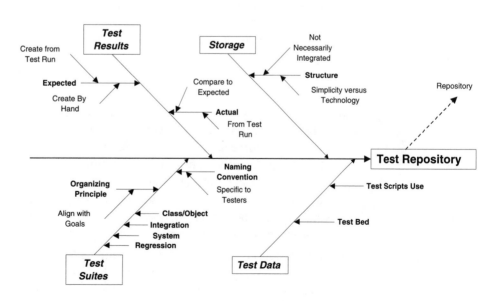

Figure 10.2 Road map for the test repository class.

Test Model

A *test* makes a technical component fail, if it can. The *test script* models a test (that is, represents the series of actions in a practical form, whether automatic or manual). To *fail*, in this context, means to not meet expectations, which in turn depends on a model of what to expect. Software development models the system so that you know what to expect of it.

The requirements document is the model of the problem. The design document is the model of the solution to the problem. The source code is a high-level programming language model of the system that implements the design. The object code and executable program are models of the working system that you get when you run the program. All of these are the *base models* for the system.

A simple view of testing says that if you exercise each statement in your program at least once, you have completely tested it. *Coverage analyzers* are automatic tools for measuring this kind of testing. In their most simple form, *coverage analyzers* put counters in your source code and increment the counters whenever the associated code is executed. Thus for a given set of input data, the analyzers tell you how many and what lines of code were executed. Unfortunately, this kind of testing is totally inadequate for most systems because tests based on the source code model of the system do not make the system fail enough to reduce risk to appropriate levels.

To approach the level of risk reduction that most software systems require, you need to model the system structure and behavior in ways that better map to failures. There are three major issues with using source code as a model for testing:

1. Paths through source code can be infinite; that is, with loops and recursion and arbitrary entrances and exits from code, you can have an infinite number of possible sequences of statements. Of course, the better your code structure is, the more likely you are to find failures with source code test approaches; but the sort of coding required to achieve this is quite limiting for creative developers.

2. The source code model touches on the things that make programs fail only indirectly. For example, you can figure out what a control flow is by looking at source code, but the code does not represent it directly. Nor does the code automatically represent things such as preconditions and postconditions, or class-invariant conditions. You don't need these conditions in the code to run, as generations of programmers have demonstrated. The code certainly doesn't represent the relationships between class properties, design components, and requirements use cases.

3. Not all source code is directly executable when compiled into object code. For example, you cannot directly test abstract classes, since you can't instantiate them into objects. You have to test them through subclass objects. Also, frameworks and other reusable systems often have no

objects that are directly testable; you have to build another system to use them, then test the integration rather than test the library directly.

So, if source code is a weak reed, what do you test? Books on testing provide dozens of interesting constructs, such as control flows, transaction flows, use cases, pre- and postconditions, and so on. You don't read about these things in programming texts (more's the pity), so they aren't really programming constructs. So why do you need these things?

You need to abstract your technical component, whether it is requirements, design, or source code, into something that is testable and that reflects the things that make programs fail. This means that you need to analyze the base model to discover the underlying concepts. The intermediary between your tests and your base model is the *test model*.

A test model lets you abstract the characteristics of the component under test using structures and relationships that make the component fail. Certain kinds of base models, such as use cases or state-transition diagrams, lend themselves to direct testing, as long as you realize what you're testing. (See below.) Other kinds, such as abstract classes and method source code, require further abstraction into quite different test models before they become useful.

Each of these models has a set of model constructs that serve as the basis of test scripts and reviews that make the component fail. These test model components are the *test objects*. A review or a test script tests one or more test objects in the test model. In requirements reviews, you inspect the use cases in the requirements model. In state-transition tests, you test the paths through the state-transition graph from construction to destruction of the object. In control-flow tests, you test the control flows through the flow graph from start to finish. In classification reviews, you inspect the inheritance relationships between classes. Different test models are appropriate for different technical components.

Each path, flow, or inheritance graph is a model component that defines a specific review or test script in a test suite. In this book, we use these test objects to organize the different classes of test script and test suite: A test script type corresponds to the test object that it tests, and a test suite collects all the test scripts that apply to the underlying base model.

Figure 10.3 shows the relationships between all of these model abstractions. The base models appear along the right, cascading down the life cycle to a working software system. You can transform each base model into a test model, and you can develop the test suite from the test model. The magnifying glass shows the specific relationships among test suites, test scripts, test models, and test objects. The test script (and reviews as well) test the test object, which the test model contains.

The section on the test suite discusses *test coverage*: how to evaluate the completeness of your test over the test model.

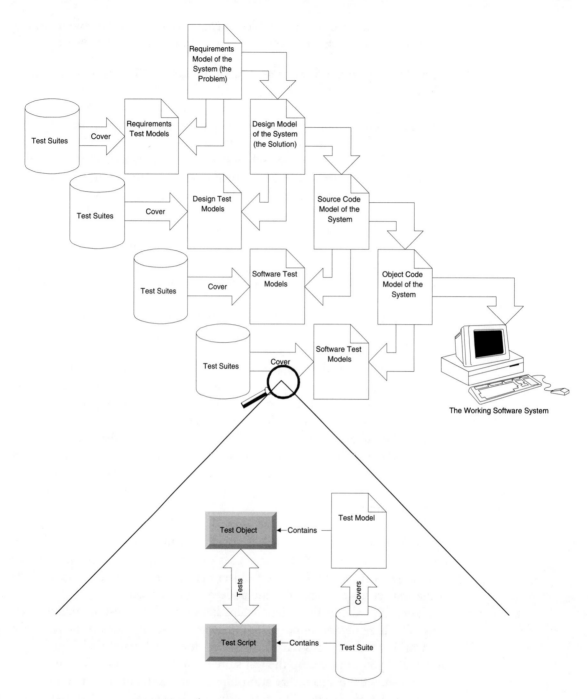

Figure 10.3 Model transformations in the testing system.

Table 10.1 shows the different classes of test model, test object, and the corresponding test scripts or reviews.

Table 10.1

Test Model	Test Object	Description	Review or Test Script
Requirements model	Requirements use case	A series of actions that comprise a single requirement at the system level, a scenario that shows a particular feature that the user drives	Requirements review
Design object model	Inheritance hierarchy	An inheritance hierarchy of classes from the object model of the design; may be some cohesive portion of the overall inheritance hierarchy	Classification review
Design object model	Composition hierarchy	A composition hierarchy of classes from the object model of the design; may be some cohesive portion of the overall composition hierarchy	Aggregation review
Design dynamic model	State-transition life cycle	A sequence of states and transitions from the dynamic model of a class that represents one behavioral life cycle for an object of the class from initial state to terminal state (construction to destruction)	State-transition test script
Domain model	Domain partition	A partitioning of the inputs and outputs of a class method by some domain criterion	Domain test script
Exception model	Exception condition	A collection of conditions that will raise an exception when you send a particular message to an object of the class	Exception test script
Control-flow model	Control flow	A sequence of linked control nodes that models the flow of control through a method	Control-flow test script
Transaction-flow model	Transaction flow	A sequence of linked control nodes that models an object through its life cycle	Transaction-flow test script
Data-flow model	Data flow	A sequence of linked control nodes annotated with data that models the flow of data through a method	Data-flow test script

Table 10.1 (cont.)

Test Model	Test Object	Description	Review or Test Script
Condition model	Error condition	A logical predicate that, if false, asserts that the object is not valid	Assertion
Condition model	Exception condition	A logical predicate that, if false, raises an exception from a method	Exception
Condition model	Concurrent error condition	A continuously monitored logical predicate within an object that, if false, asserts that the object is not valid	Concurrent test operation
Condition model	On-demand error condition	A logical predicate that, if false when requested by message, asserts that the object is not valid	Message polling test
Design interface model	Protocol	Definition of message structure for a class method	Interface and protocol test script
Design concurrency model	Concurrent operations	Sequences of object behavior operating concurrently in separate objects that require synchronization	Synchronization test script
Exception model	Exception handler	Sequences of object behavior following the raising of an exception	Exception test script
Design user interface model	User interface bitmap	A bitmap sequence that, together with event timing, represents the expected outcome of a series of input GUI events	True-time test script
Design user interface model	Style-independent bitmap	A bitmap sequence that brackets certain specific elements such as object location and font style as irrelevant	Character-recognition test script
Design user interface model	User interface widget	A sequence of output events associated with a GUI object that represents the expected outcome of a set of input events	Widget playback test script
Requirements model	Requirements use case	The relationships between the finished system and the requirements use cases	System validation test script
Requirements model	System resource	A specific thing that the system "consumes" while processing, such as memory, network packets, or disk space	System stress test script

Table 10.1 (cont.)

Test Model	Test Object	Description	Review or Test Script
Requirements model	System performance requirement	A use case that specifies the performance charac- teristics of part or all of the system	System performance test script
Requirements model	System configuration	A configuration of logical and physical devices on which the system depends	System configuration test script
Requirements model	System malfunction	A specific failure in the software and hardware on which the system runs	System recovery test script
System security model	System vulnerability	A specific weakness in the system, the exploitation of which could result in sabotage, deliberate sys- tem damage, loss of sys- tem control, or other security breaches	System security test script

See Boris Beizer's books (1984, 1990, 1995) on testing techniques for the best, in-depth review of test models, test objects, and the tests you can develop from them.

Each specific kind of test object addresses some aspect of the system that contributes to the overall risk of failure. These divisions are by no means mutually exclusive; the test objects often overlap when you map them to the base model. That's why, for example, control-flow tests often exercise source code statements multiple times.

Sometimes, however, even the test model has limitations, particularly in terms of being intractable. For example, in control-flow analysis, you still have loops that can make the number of paths through the flow graph infi- nite, or at least very large. As another example, in domain testing of methods, you can have several inputs and outputs that can take on any real number. You may be type safe (at least you know it's a number), but you don't have any way to generate a test script for each possible number. As a final example, state- transition models are notorious for quickly becoming intractable for large, complex objects. There can be a very large number of states and transitions during the life cycle of the object. While there are ways to reduce the model complexity (Harel statecharts, for example, use nested states to reduce com- plexity), the models still translate into very complicated test scripts. The fun- damental question to ask about a model (base or test) is whether the model is *testable*; that is, can you develop a set of test scripts that achieves your accept- able level of risk?

A way around this intractability is the *equivalence class*, based on the *equiv- alence relation*. This is a mathematical relationship between two or more objects that says the objects are "the same" in some sense. Mathematically, "the same" means the relationship is reflexive (O1 = O1), symmetric (O1 = O2 implies O2 = O1), and transitive (O1 = O2 and O2 = O3 implies O1 = O3). Ordinarily, equivalence means object identity: references to exactly the same thing. But an equivalence relation can attach other meanings to the "same" relationship. In particular, two objects that belong to the same class of objects can be equivalent.

In testing, an *equivalence class* is a collection of objects such that testing any object yields the same risk of failure as testing any other object in the class: The objects are equivalent with respect to testing. But what are these objects? They are aggregations of the test objects in the underlying test models. For example, in domain testing, you partition inputs and outputs of methods into classes of inputs and outputs that are the same with respect to testing. The domain model is thus based on an equivalence model of the interface model. If you start by modeling your class method with control flows through the control graph, you can abstract it into a higher-level and less complex model by forming equivalence classes of flows that are the same with respect to testing.

In looking at any test, you can improve your productivity by analyzing the equivalence relations between the objects you are testing. If you can find some reason why a set of these objects will yield the same failures, then you don't have to test all of them, just one. Taking this logic further, if you can determine that a higher-level, simpler model gets you to your acceptable level of risk, you can improve productivity by simplifying the test model using equivalence classes, up to the point where risk outweighs productivity.

In testing things that depend on data values, a specific set of classes are usually interesting:

- The minimum legal data value
- The minimum legal data value − 1
- The minimum legal data value + 1
- The maximum legal data value
- The maximum legal data value − 1
- The maximum legal data value + 1
- Zero
- Null
- Special characters

If data represents a partitioning in itself (a *nominal data type* in the lingo of the data theory world), values may consist of one of a series of distinct values, such as True and False or Monday, Tuesday, Wednesday, and so on. C++ represents this kind of data as an enumerated data type. Nominal data has no inherent order; the next step up is ordinal data, which has order. To construct appropriate equivalence classes, you need to understand clearly which is which. For example, True and False or a list of modules as sources for bugs are value sets that have no inherent order and thus can group arbitrarily into equivalence classes. The days of the week or months of the year have an inherent order, so you have to group them taking that order into account.

Object-oriented systems tend to do away with many of these nominal types, replacing them using the class structure. Smalltalk even makes True and False classes with single instances; everything's an object in Smalltalk. C++ still has enumerated types, and designers often use them to simplify object-oriented designs by moving some of the messy class structure into simpler, procedural code. Almost invariably, however, use of nominal data leads to a lot more control-oriented code in methods, so you need to be particularly aware of data like this for class-object testing.

See Boris Beizer's *Software Testing Techniques* (1990) or Glenford Myers's *The Art of Software Testing* (1979) for a more complete discussion of equivalence classes and relations in the context of software testing.

In the quality system, modeling using test models has one additional advantage. Often you find requirement, design, or code failures while you are analyzing the system to build the model. That is, you can find failures through analysis instead of through review or testing. This is even more productive than reviews for finding failures, as you don't need to involve other people at all. Test modeling is really the first step in finding failures in your system.

This book does not attempt a serious classification of test models and test objects, which would be a good subject for an academic paper but is beyond the scope of a practical book on testing. Figure 10.4 shows the basic structure of the test model classes without attempting a more formal classification based on theoretical attributes and relationships. Some overlap probably exists between the test model subclasses and certain development documents, such as the requirements document. This is all beyond the scope of this book.

Leadership

Vision: A productive, risk-averting set of abstractions of technical components of use in reviews and test construction.

Mission: To abstract the technical component model into objects that make the technical component under test fail to an acceptable level of risk with optimal productivity.

Objective 10.2: To model the technical component to produce tests with an optimal level of failure in the component relative to the acceptable level of risk for the component.

Approach 10.2: Model the technical component using test-related objects that form the basis for effective reviews and test scripts.

Measurement 10.2: Ratio of technical risk using test model and objects to technical risk using base model.

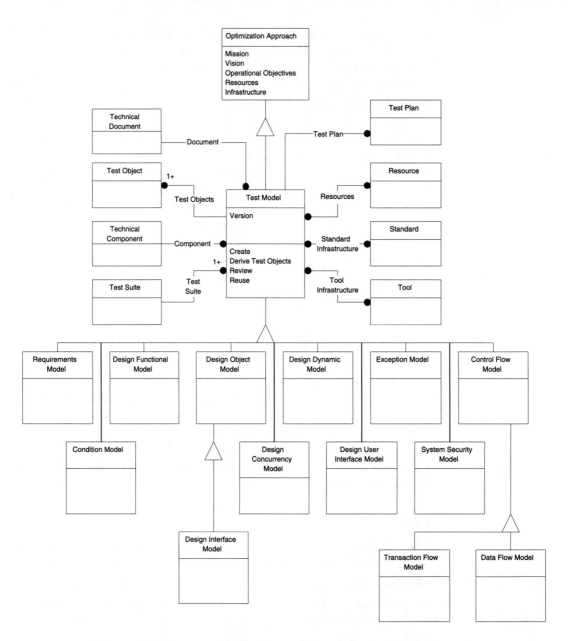

Figure 10.4 Structure of the test model class.

Objective 10.3: To model the technical component to produce tests with an optimal level of productivity.

Approach 10.3: Model the technical component using test-related objects in a tractable model that provides a minimal set of test scripts that achieves the acceptable level of risk for the technical component.

Measurement 10.3: Ratio of effort to test technical component based on test model and objects to effort to test based on base model.

As part of the optimization cycle for this approach, both of these measurements require benchmarking based on the base models.

Structure

COMPONENT

The *component* is the technical component under test. Usually it will be a class or some kind of other software object, though it could be a use case or design component if you develop varieties of test scripts for those component types.

TEST OBJECTS

The *test objects* are the components of the test model. Each specific kind of test model uses specific kinds of test objects. For example, the requirements model comprises a set of use cases as test objects. The object model comprises a set of class boxes (with attributes and methods) and a set of relationships between those classes (inheritance and composition). The control-flow model comprises a set of nodes (control points) and edges (flows between control points). See the "Test Object" section that follows for the structure of that class. Part of the art and science of test development is the derivation of test objects from the test model; see the "Derive Test Objects" method below for a general discussion.

TEST SUITE

Each test model corresponds to a single *test suite*. That suite contains the test scripts that test the test objects contained in the the test model. A suite can cover more than one test model.

DOCUMENT

The test model *document* is the physical representation of the test model in whatever medium is appropriate: paper, tool files, repository database records, or online documents. This representation of the model as a technical document serves to communicate the model for the purposes of review and reuse.

VERSION

The test model is dynamic: It changes over time as you change the tested component and the test objects. Because of this, you must track the model using a version number. Whenever you modify the test model and/or its component test objects, you give the result a new version number. This version of the test model associates with a specific version of the component under test and the test objects in the test repository.

RESOURCES

Test modeling is a distinct skill that requires training beyond the standard programming training most developers receive. Resources for this task can be developers trained in modeling techniques or specialized technical resources training specifically in requirements, design, and software test modeling, usually associated with a software quality assurance function. In large organizations, even more specialized resources, such as requirements test analysts and state-transition test designers, could devote their entire effort to very specific modeling.

INFRASTRUCTURE

As with any modeling activity, the resources use tools for building the models. There exist many test modeling tools for modeling control flows and other test models. Related to this effort are the test frameworks for running test scripts; these tools frame not only the operational testing effort but the practicality of using one or another test model to produce those test scripts. The organization also may standardize certain aspects of test modeling for communication and productivity.

Dynamics

CREATE

Creating a test model is an analytical process of abstracting an abstraction into a test model document. Sounds bad, but the results are invariably good. In the process of thinking about a technical component (an abstraction of one kind or another), you clarify in your mind both the purpose and the structure of that component. As with any kind of creative process, committing the thought to another medium invariably makes you discover holes and flaws in the original abstraction. The creation of the test model is thus the first stage in risk reduction. It also enables the later creation of the tests that are the fundamental basis for limiting risk in your system.

The creation process itself uses whatever tools are available to build the model, in paper or online form (the document). The document then becomes part of the test suite in the test repository.

DERIVE TEST OBJECTS

This abstract or pure method lets you develop a set of test objects for the test model. It is specific to the type of test model, so each test model class must implement it. Test object derivation requires the test model to be complete.

Generally, test object derivation from the test model analyzes the elements of the model into higher-level components. See the "Test Model" and "Object" sections for further information. For example, from a control-flow model of a method, you develop a series of control-flow equivalence classes out of the nodes and edges of the control-flow graph. From a state-transition or dynamic model of the class, you use the state-transition test object algorithm to build a series of birth-to-death transition paths for the objects.

The adequacy of your test object derivation depends on the relationship between the test model and the risk model you adopt. Most techniques produce more or less comprehensive sets of test objects; how thorough you want to be is based on your acceptable level of risk. The better models have well-understood ways to generate complete sets of test objects; this lets you automate the process and lower your risk levels without impacting your productivity.

REVIEW

As with any abstraction process, you always will benefit from getting another person look at your thinking in concrete form. The review process takes the test model document and reviews it as part of the test suite review. This review looks at the adequacy of the model in reducing technical risk for the component under test and determines whether the model is testable.

REUSE

As with any abstraction, it is the more productive for your organization if you can reuse the abstraction along with its concrete implementation. You can reuse requirements, design, and software models; you also can reuse test models along with their underlying base models. Having the analysis done makes it much simpler to develop (or reuse) test scripts for the new technical component.

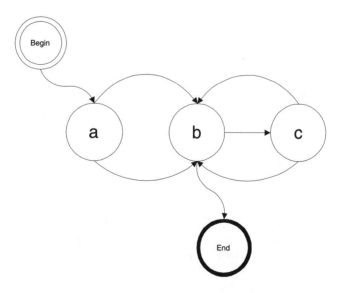

Figure 10.5 DTS Connection:errorHandler method control flow model.

Example

The following function is a method of the DTS Connection class that handles errors in the ODBC connection. Because it involves several control points, it makes a good example of a relatively complex, but not intractable, control-flow model. The lower-case letters in comments relate the statements to the control nodes in the control-flow diagram in Figure 10.5.

The following source code below represents the source code model of the technical component, in this case the method Connection::handleError. The diagram in Figure 10.5 represents the test model for this technical component.

```
// Function: Connection::handleError
//
// Description: Handles an error in the ODBC connection with the appropriate
//       action based on the nature of the error. Handles situations in
//       which there are more than one error in the ODBC error handling
//       stack (i.e., when the return code is not SQL_NO_DATA_FOUND).
void   Connection::handleError(HSTMT handle, RETCODE returnCode)
{
     UCHAR        SQLState[6];                    // SQL State code
     SDWORD       nativeErrorCode;          // Server DBMS error code
     UCHAR        errorText[200];            // Server DBMS error text
     if (returnCode == SQL_ERROR)           // a
        (void) rollback();                   // b
     while (returnCode != SQL_NO_DATA_FOUND)     // c
     {
        returnCode = SQLError(SQL_NULL_HENV, pDatabaseObject->m_hdbc,
                                 handle, SQLState, &nativeErrorCode, errorText,
                                 sizeof(errorText), NULL);
        if (returnCode != SQL_NO_DATA_FOUND)     // d
        {         // e
                TRACE("\nODBC Error:\n\tSQL State: %s", SQLState);
                TRACE("\n\tServer Code: %ld", nativeErrorCode);
                TRACE("\n\t%s\n", errorText);
        }
     }
}
```

Road Map

Figure 10.6 is the road map for the test model class.

Test Object

The *test object* is a component of a test model. See the "Test Model" section on page 136 for a complete contextual discussion of test objects and test models. Figure 10.7 shows the structure of the test object class. Again, the subclasses represent the kinds of test objects we use in this book without attempting to build a more formal classification of the objects.

LEADERSHIP

Vision: A test model component that you can use to produce a test script that contributes effectively to reducing risk for a technical component.

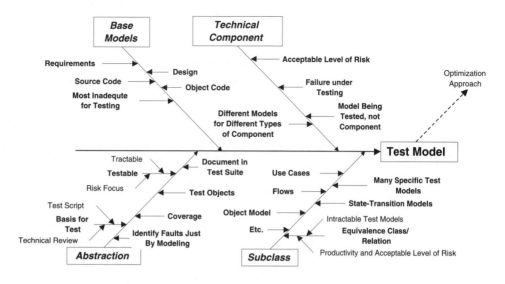

Figure 10.6 Road map for the test model class.

Mission: To contribute significantly to the effectiveness of a test model.

Objective 10.4: To model a specific aspect of a technical component to produce a test with an optimal level of failure in the component relative to the acceptable level of risk for the component.

Approach 10.4: Model the aspect of the technical component using a technique that forms the basis for effective reviews and test scripts.

Measurement 10.4: Ratio of technical risk using test object to technical risk using base model object (control flow versus statement, for example).

Again, this measurement requires a benchmark.

STRUCTURE

OBJECTS

The objects of the test object are the test model constructs the test object uses. The test object itself is not usually a low-level component of the test model but rather an aggregation of several such components. For example, a control-flow test object is a path of nodes and links through the overall control-flow graph. A state-transition test object is a path through the state-transition graph.

TEST MODEL

The *test model* is the model with which this particular test object associates. The test object belongs to exactly one test model.

TEST SCRIPT

The *test script* is the script that tests this test object. A test script can cover more than one test object if it makes sense for initialization or other reasons.

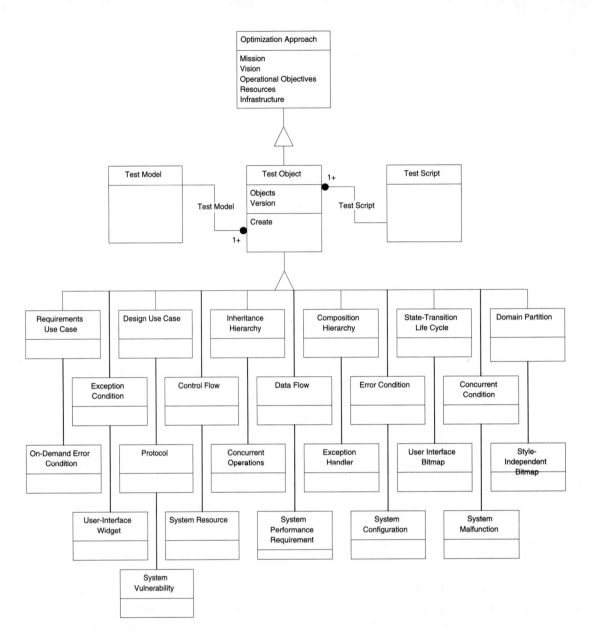

Figure 10.7 Structure of the test object class.

VERSION

The test object is dynamic: It changes over time as you change the tested component and the test model. This means that you must track the object using a version number. Whenever you modify the test object, you give the result a new version number. This version of the test object associates with a specific version of the component under test and the test model in the test repository.

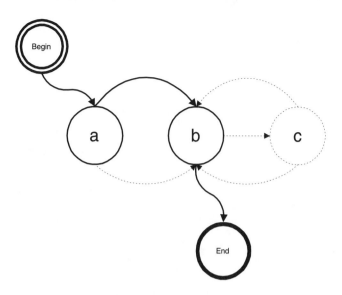

Figure 10.8 DTS Connection:errorHandler method control-flow object.

DYNAMICS

CREATE

Usually the test objects in a test model don't just pop out at you automatically. As the theory of testing and test models gets more sophisticated, modeling techniques creators are building in algorithms or heuristics for determining test objects as well as just building test models automatically from base models. The state of the art is not very advanced, however. Expect to spend a good portion of your time in determining just what the test objects in test models are.

EXAMPLE

Taking the control-flow model from the test model example just given, Figure 10.8 represents a single control-flow path through the model. This control-flow path corresponds to a single test that tests the situation where ODBC reports the status message SQL_DATA_NOT_FOUND, which requires no rollback or error reporting.

ROAD MAP

Figure 10.9 is the road map for the test object class.

Test Suite

A *test suite* is a collection of test scripts. The basis for membership in the collection can be arbitrary: You can call any random collection of test scripts a

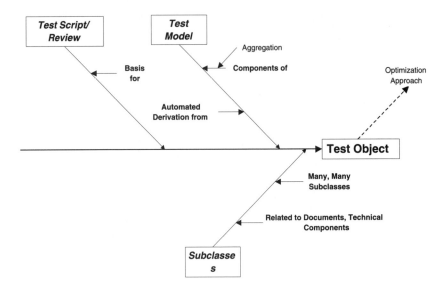

Figure 10.9 Road map for the test object class.

test suite. One way to organize test suites is to define them as a set of test scripts executed as a set, all at once. Yet another way is to organize all the tests that apply to a particular stage in a life cycle into a test suite that applies to that cycle. You also can use a test suite to have an ordered sequence of test scripts. One script can leave the test data and results in a specific state, ready for input into the next test script. Also, you can overlap test suites by having a test script in more than one suite. By definition, a regression test suite has scripts that have run in other test suites.

We find that organizing test suites systemically yields a better overall picture of testing and ties the suite to the objectives of the overall quality system. Building test suites centered on the different kinds of test models, or aggregations of them, produces a systematic classification of test suites aligned with the structure of the system. Adding test suites that represent a specific system focus, such as cluster, system, and regression test suites, permits a strong systemic focus for testing.

- **Hierarchical-incremental Test Suite:** The suite of test scripts corresponding to test models based on the design object, dynamic, and functional test models: state-transition test scripts, transaction-flow test scripts, exception test scripts, control-flow test scripts, and data-flow test scripts. These scripts operate in the context of the inheritence hierarchy for a single class, which provides a way to reuse tests at different levels of the hierarchy—hence the term "hierarchical." This term is also appropriate because this test suite is the primary set of tests that fulfills the promise of the pyramid describing the overall quality system.

- **Conditional Test Suite:** The suite of test scripts that cover the conditional model of a single class: the set of conditions (conditional errors, exceptions, concurrent or on-demand errors) that define the logical validity of the class.
- **Integration Test Suite:** A suite of test scripts of any model that test a cluster of classes; standard clusters include functional tests that test a set of vertical functions in a system and abstraction tests that test a horizontal API in a system; includes tests of objects relative to other objects (protocols and interfaces, concurrency and synchronization, exception handling, and user interfaces); another term for this suite is the cluster test suite.
- **System Test Suite:** The suite of test scripts of any model that operate over the system as a whole instead of to a specific class or system; based on the system quality of the whole being different from the sum of the parts; requires not only a complete system but a working, external environment similar to that in which the system will deploy.
- **Regression Test Suite:** The suite of test scripts already run against some class, system, or system; based on the system objectives of ensuring that a change in the system doesn't break something that works and that fixes do fix what they're supposed to fix.

Test coverage is the extent to which your test suite is complete with respect to the test model of the system. If you have a control-flow model, for example, coverage means the extent to which your test scripts test all the control-flow test objects in the control-flow model. If you are testing class-invariant conditions in the condition model of a class, coverage means the extent to which your class test scripts test all the condition objects in the condition model of the class.

The point here is that you are covering the test model, not the design or code itself. You can cover the code (*statement coverage* is an example of this), but doing so usually is not a particularly good way to lower risk of failure, as it doesn't model failure very well. That is, a test criterion of exercising every statement at least once, using the source code as a model of itself, misses a lot of the things that can cause code to fail. Modeling control and data flows and testing those will exercise statements more than once with different parameters and paths that may fail. The more interesting test models (state-transition models, control- and data-flow models, and so on) are much more productive in causing your system to fail.

The obvious target for coverage is 100 percent. The target may be obvious, but achieving it is usually impossible, sometimes probably so: Many approaches involve test objects with infinite possible combinations. We still suggest 100 percent, but with two major qualifiers: the acceptable level of risk and the equivalence class.

Testing to an *acceptable level of risk* means accepting a certain risk of failure at later stages of the life cycle. Risk consists of two components: the probability of failure and the consequence of failure. An acceptable level of risk is the degree to which you are willing to accept the combination of probability and consequence. For example, in the case of a private-circulation game program, you may be quite comfortable with a 50 percent risk of class/object failure, given the consequence is minimal and the users don't have your phone number. For a key system in a solar energy system on which 10,000 people will depend for their lives in a harsh environment, and where they *all* have your phone number, you may be comfortable with .01 percent risk of failure or less, given the catastrophic consequences. Most systems are going to be somewhere in between. But you cannot expect zero risk of failure if you cannot test every possible combination of test object (flow, partition, exception, or whatever).

Reuse introduces both a way to limit risk and the need for careful evaluation of risk. By reusing technical components, you can add the benefits of the component system to your system with much less effort than developing the component from scratch would take. On the other hand, reusing components in this way requires components to be of higher quality than might otherwise be the case. By committing your organization to reuse, you are committing your organization to a relatively low level of acceptable risk. You are unlikely to want to reuse high-risk components in other projects or other parts of your project simply because adding the component raises your overall level of risk in the system.

Having defined the risks you are willing to take on behalf of the system users (hint: Ask them too) and on behalf of future reusers of the components, you now can define the equivalence classes of test object in the different kinds of test scripts. What this does is to model the test model, using equivalence relations to reduce the number of test objects to a tractable number. You can define many equivalence classes using simple arithmetic. For example, it may not matter whether the input is 3 or 300, the exact same code executes with the exact same result. In flow testing, as another example, you can test the flow by testing all the paths through the flow graph. But what about loops? How many times around the loop is enough: 0? 1? 2? 200? Again, you need to determine the equivalence classes. A minimum requirement might be at least to touch all the flows once.

So, let's come back to the term "complete" for a minute. Here's a good approximation to the facts of life:

- **Complete** *coverage of all test model components is not possible.*

That said, your coverage should be as complete as your acceptable level of risk and equivalence classes allow and no less. As we state this in the metrics that follows, "complete coverage with respect to risk and equivalence." This is not a contradiction, merely a qualified definition.

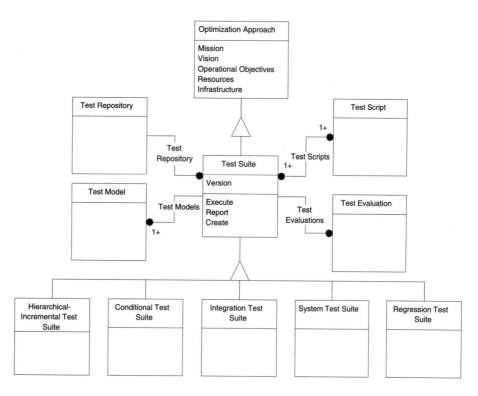

Figure 10.10 Structure of the test suite class.

Beizer's *Software Testing Techniques* (1990) has an extensive discussion of testing criteria and coverage. Although it is in the context of flow testing, Beizer's points are relevant to any kind of coverage.

The test suite class is thus an abstract class that represents all these different kinds of test suites. It has some basic elements, but the key element is the ownership of a set of test scripts. The test suite plays a role as an intermediary, higher-level object that gives you access to a particular group of test scripts. Its mission is to provide a big-picture perspective on the composition of test scripts that the individual test script cannot provide.

Figure 10.10 shows the class structure of the test suite class.

Leadership

Vision: A unified collection of test scripts that test the system to an acceptable level of risk.

Mission: To aggregate test scripts into a whole that provides a clear perspective on the contribution of each test script to an overall acceptable level of risk.

Objective 10.5: To test the object(s) under test to an acceptable level of risk.

Approach 10.5: Build a set of test scripts that test the equivalence classes of behaviors of the object(s) under test using techniques that make the objects fail with respect to your acceptable level of risk.

Measurement 10.5: Ratio of actual test coverage to complete test coverage with respect to risk and equivalence of test objects.

Structure

TEST REPOSITORY

Each test suite belongs to a *test repository*. That repository also holds the test data used by test scripts within the test suite.

TEST MODELS

The test suite corresponds to one or more *test models*. These models contain the test objects that correspond to the test scripts in the test suite.

VERSION

The test suite has a *version* number, just as do the test scripts in the test suite and the components under test. When you add a test, modify a test, or delete a test, you increment the test suite version number. Test reports should refer to the test suite version number to ensure that the correct test suite has run.

TEST SCRIPTS

In this abstract class, the group of *test scripts* can contain any kind of test script. In subclasses, the subclass restricts the class to contain the specific kind of test scripts for which you design the class. The test scripts are in a fixed order in the group so that you can predict the results of running the series of scripts.

TEST EVALUATIONS

Each test suite has a set of test evaluation objects. Every time you execute the test suite, you get a test report. You then evaluate that report and feed the results back into the test suite. See the test evaluation object for details.

Dynamics

CREATE

This operation has a corresponding method overloading it in each of the specific test suite classes. Creating a test suite is the primary task that test engineers perform. Creating the suite, as opposed to the test scripts that are part of it, requires analyzing the entire domain under test: the class, the system, or the entire system as a whole. Through this method you will find the specific approaches and techniques for developing complete sets of tests that cover the entire domain under test.

Also, this is not a one-time process. Each time you run the test suite and evaluate the results, you should feed the results back into additional test development.

EXECUTE

Run the test scripts, executing each in turn in the order they appear in the test scripts group.

REPORT

Once you've executed the test suite, you must report the results. You analyze these results in the light of the test objectives and feed the results back into further test development through the test evaluation.

Example

The DTS organizes its testing by system, then by project management deliverable within the system. Each test suite thus corresponds to a set of test scripts that apply to one or more classes within a system that the team delivers as an assembly as part of the project plan.

For example, the project plan for developing the Product system calls for deriving the product history list class, then later creating the Product class that embeds it. The product history integration test suite runs several integration test scripts on the product history and product history iterator classes. The product hierarchical-incremental test suite runs object tests on the Product class. The product regression test suite runs all the test scripts that apply to the whole system once they have successfully run against their target components.

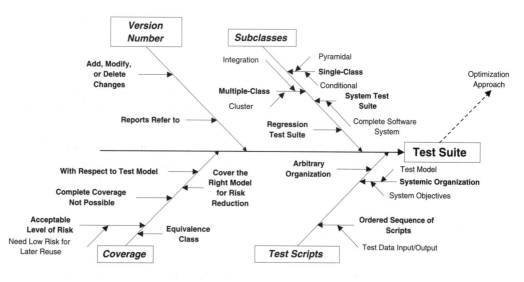

Figure 10.11 Road map for the test suite class.

Road Map

Figure 10.11 is the road map for the test suite class.

Test Script

A test script is a sequential set of instructions for performing a specific test on a specific software component based on a particular test object in a test model. You can write a script in a special language that the automated integration system can execute. You also can write a script in some form of structured natural language that gives instructions for manually executing a test.

There are several different kinds of test script, differentiated by the kind of test they represent:

- **Class/Object Test:** A test that applies to a single class of objects (corresponding to state-transition, transaction flow, exception, control flow, data flow, and condition test objects).
- **Integration Test:** A test that applies to the integration of two or more classes of objects (interface-protocol, synchronization, exception, and GUI test scripts).
- **System Test:** A test that applies to the software system as a whole (validation, stress, performance, configuration, recovery, and security test scripts).

Besides using the basic script, test scripts also make use of test data and use cases.

Figure 10.12 shows the class structure of the test script class.

Leadership

Vision: A clear, concise, and effective procedure to test a test object modeling a software component to an acceptable level of risk.

Mission: To test, using appropriate technology and data, a particular test object.

Objective 10.6: To test a test object to an acceptable level of risk.

Approach 10.6: Use the test technique appropriate to the test object to test any and all possibilities for failure in the component under test, whether a class or system.

Measurement 10.6: The ratio of the number of failures during a test run using this test script to the expected number of failures.

Structure

TEST OBJECT

Every test script tests an abstraction of the component under test that represents the expectations for the behavior of the component. This is the *test*

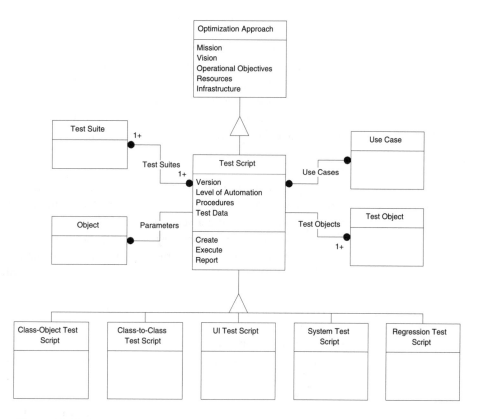

Figure 10.12 Structure of test script class.

object. A test script can test one or more test objects that model some aspect of a technical component.

VERSION

The test script is dynamic: It changes over time as you change the tested component and/or the test model. This means that you must track the script using a version number. Whenever you modify the test script, you give the result a new version number. This version of the test script associates with a specific version of the component under test in the test repository. You always know which version of which script tests which version of which component and test object. The test suites combine test script versions based on the versions of the components they test.

LEVEL OF AUTOMATION

You can test automatically using an automated test environment that executes the script, or you can test manually, entering commands from a manual script. The more you automate, the more productive you can be with respect to regression testing objectives. The *level of automation* can be manual, automated, or mixed.

PARAMETERS

The automated test framework can allow you to pass data into a test script, giving you a lot of flexibility in programming the tests. You even can program test scripts that call other test scripts with different parameters to test a sequence of test cases, much as you would reuse a method in a program. You also can use parameters to pass in concrete instantiations for test scripts that test abstract classes. (See the class-object test script.)

PROCEDURES

The sequence of *procedures* can vary in format. You can develop a test script as a textual statement of a series of instructions for manual testing, or you can develop the script using a scripting language that lets you automate the test. You can use various proprietary scripting languages, such as WinRunner's Test Script Language (TSL), operating system scripting languages such as the DOS batch file language or UNIX csh, or even programming languages such as C, C++, or Smalltalk.

Even a simple assertion or exception statement contained within the source code in the product repository can constitute a test script. This is a concept, not a particular format.

Running the test script creates a set of test results in the repository.

TEST DATA

Certain tests use *test data* acquired from the test repository or embedded into the test script. The structure of this data usually should reflect the appropriate level of analysis for the test. If you build a test based on some kind of domain analysis or other way of partitioning the system, the test data should reflect that same partitioning. You also can use randomly generated test data, although usually this will be less effective than well-structured data that tests boundaries and classes of inputs and outputs, for example.

USE CASES

Certain tests (many of them, actually) correspond to one or more *use cases*. See the "Requirements Document" section in Chapter 18 for details on use cases. These requirements statements describe what the component under test should do under a particular set of circumstances, and the set of use cases should fully elaborate the different circumstances that exercise the component under test. You also should note that a use case may correspond to one or more test scripts (a many-to-many relationship).

Ch. 18

Requirements
Document

RESOURCES

The test developer must have technical skills appropriate to the test script he or she is constructing, including skills for: test development of the indicated type; technology required to create, modify, and execute the script; and interpreting the results.

INFRASTRUCTURE

The test script relies upon the test repository for storage. The automatic script also relies on the tool that lets you execute the script. If there are reports to generate, the script relies on a report generator of some kind. The script may or may not be the subject of coding and design standards.

Dynamics

CREATE

When you create the test script, you implement the test design in the scripting language appropriate to the kind of test and to the tools you have chosen to use. You create the test script in the context of creating a test suite as one of a series of test scripts that cover the set of test objects to an acceptable level of risk.

You implement this abstract method differently in each of the different kinds of test script.

EXECUTE

When you execute the test script, you execute the series of instructions in it, either automatically or manually. Those instructions may or may not read and write test data to and from the test repository.

REPORT

After executing the test, the Report method lets you generate the appropriate reports for the type of test involved. See the Automated Integration Environment for details of the various kinds of report.

Example

A simple example of an object test script is the following built-in assertion sequence in some DTS code:

```
BOOL Person::verify(void) const          // test the Person class-invariant conditions
{
    ASSERT(id>0);
    ASSERT(personType=="Customer" || personType == "Employee");
    return TRUE;
}
```

This example script tests two conditions on object data that must evaluate to true at any given time.

Here is an example of a manual test to test the architecture of the Problem hierarchy for classification failures:

1. Per Use Case 7.45.3, verify that each Fault can relate to zero or more Failure objects.
2. Per Use Case 7.45.5, verify that each Fault can have one or more problem status history entries with the first one being the creation of the fault.
3. Per use Case 7.45.6, verify that the Fault can be either a Documentation Defect or a Code defect.

Road Map

Figure 10.13 is the road map for the test script class.

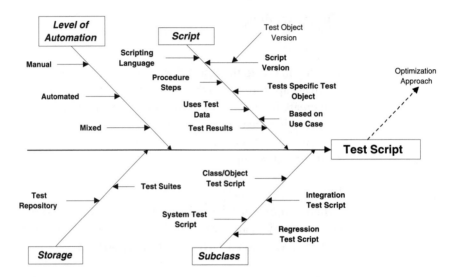

Figure 10.13 Road map for the test script class.

CHAPTER 11

HIERARCHICAL-INCREMENTAL TEST SUITE

Hierarchical-Incremental Test Suite

The *hierarchical-incremental test suite* is a set of test scripts that test objects as instances of classes and as part of a system of interrelated systems. The term "hierarchical-incremental" expresses the test objective of testing the object in the context of its inheritance hierarchy and system pyramid. That is, any object consists not only of the properties you give it but also of those it inherits from its more general and abstract parents. You need to test the object taking all of this into account.

At one extreme, you can have a single hierarchical-incremental test suite for your entire system or, at the other, a single suite for each class. Something in between is usually more appropriate. Focusing on the system is a good way to start; the system usually contains all the classes that are appropriate subjects of a single group of tests. As a developer, you likely will be working with a single system, testing the individual class hierarchies as you build them. Later on, automated integration and regression testing will reuse the tests to verify the operations in a system. It may make sense in some cases to deal with subsets of classes in a system if there is some synergy to gain by doing so; this is similar to the concept of cluster testing during integration.

It's important to note the difference between abstract and concrete classes. You can test concrete classes directly, but you cannot test abstract classes directly because you cannot instantiate them. Structurally, you build the test scripts for the abstract classes separately but run them as part of the testing of concrete subclasses. Keeping the test scripts separate lets you reuse the tests for different subclasses, taking full advantage of inheritance to reuse tests. When you instantiate an object and run tests on it, those tests test both the class of which the object is an instance and its superclasses, going up the pyramid.

The essence of the hierarchical-incremental test suite is the inheritance relationship between classes. In the object-oriented world, when you test a class, you also are testing its parent classes and constructing tests you can later reuse in testing its subclasses. Each class is the result of combining the structure and behavior of the parent class or classes with new attributes and methods. Harrold and McGregor (1992) distinguish three kinds of methods:

- **New methods:** Methods you define in the subclass, including ones with the same name as methods in a superclass but with different parameters.
- **Recursive methods:** Methods you define in a superclass that you don't override or overload in the subclass.
- **Redefined methods:** Methods you define in a superclass that you override or overload in the subclass.

Abstract methods are methods of any type associated with an abstract class. Abstract methods may or may not have an implementation. If they don't, the subclasses must redefine the method by overloading it.

Why are these different types important? Each has a different requirement for testing in the context of the class.

- **New methods:** Complete testing
- **Recursive methods:** Limited retesting if the method interacts with new or redefined member functions; you need only retest test objects relating to the interaction, not all of them.
- **Redefined methods:** Retesting with reuse of test models and objects you developed from specifications rather than from internal control logic.

This means that you don't need to test each kind of object if it were completely new; you only have to test the parts that really are new. This can boost testing productivity (as well as programming and design productivity) enormously. Structural reuse of this kind is a key part of the object-oriented paradigm. Your test plan should work out the detailed list of classes and methods to test; see the example below.

Multiple inheritance makes this categorization more difficult, but it doesn't affect the categories themselves. Certain models of multiple inheritance, such as that of C++, let you have the same superclass exist in two or more instances in the object, creating more than a single recursive method. That is, you can call a "different" method that is actually the same method by qualifying the method with the path to the superclass. As long as the method is recursive, you don't need to test this. If you redefine the method, you don't need to test the superclass ones, just the redefinition. The only situation where you might need to test multiple paths to the same method is when the method interacts with virtual methods that you redefine in a subclass.

Ch. 13

Integration
Test Suite

Note that dynamic binding plays a role in determining testing needs too, but only in the context of integration tests. See Chapter 13. Dynamic binding creates the possibility of a set of messages (sender and receiver combinations), which means you need several tests instead of one to test a specific message. When you are just testing methods, as opposed to messages, you have no concern with this except for the variety of possible data values that messages could pass into the method.

Depending on what kind of test model you use and how your test suite develops, you may need to add some test objects to test conditions that arise in recursive methods. For example, if a recursive method uses some data attribute, and the subclass adds a new range of values to that attribute, you should add test objects and scripts to test the new range as part of a control- or data-flow model. This situation is relatively unusual, but you always should reexamine the test models for superclasses to make sure the coverage is adequate.

Hierarchical-incremental testing covers a range of test models. Two structural models apply to methods:

- **Control-Flow Model:** This models the class as a series of control-flow graphs deriving from the method implementations.

- **Data-Flow Model:** This models the class as a series of control-flow graphs with data annotations showing the flow of data values through the method implementations.

Three functional models apply to classes:
- **State-Transition Model:** In OMT, the *dynamic* model; this models the states and transitions for a particular class in the context of its position in an inheritance hierarchy and comprises a set of state-transition path test objects.
- **Transaction-Flow Model:** This models the object life cycle as a *transaction* from construction of the object to its destruction; you can derive this from either the OMT functional model, which models class behavior as processes, or the requirements model use cases.
- **Exception Model:** OMT does not model exceptions, and the control- and data-flow models don't either, so you need to have a model that specifies what methods raise what exceptions under what conditions; this leads to both exception-raising test objects and test objects that do not result in exceptions.

See the methods below for details on modeling and transforming the model into test objects and scripts.

As you build your test suite into your development test framework, you also are building up a suite of regression tests. You should document and automate your hierarchical-incremental tests for later reuse, either in subclasses or as regression tests.

Figure 11.1 shows the structure of the hierarchical-incremental test script.

Leadership

Vision: A system of objects with an acceptable risk of failure.

Mission: To test the system of objects to an acceptable level of risk, taking into account time and resources.

Objective 11.1: To test the system of objects to an acceptable level of risk based on structural features.

Approach 11.1: Model the objects using structural test models (control and data flow models) that use available information to specify test scripts with a maximum probability of causing failures.

Measurement 11.1: Branch coverage (the degree to which each decision, or branch, in the objects' behavior has each alternative outcome at least once).

Branch coverage (see Myers, 1979, pp. 38–44; Beizer, 1984, pp. 75–77) is still a relatively weak form of coverage, and it forms a minimum requirement for safe testing of a class. Strictly speaking, if you achieve 100 percent branch coverage, you also must also have achieved 100 percent statement coverage

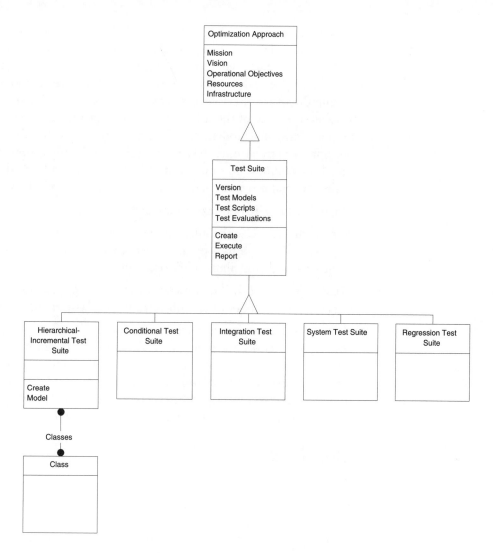

Figure 11.1 Structure of the hierarchical-incremental test suite class.

(executing all executable statements at least once). But branch coverage does not uncover requirements failures.

Objective 11.2: To test the system of objects to an acceptable level of risk, taking into account functional requirements.

Approach 11.2: Model the system of objects using functional test models (state-transition, transaction-flow, and exception test models) that specify test scripts with a maximum probability of causing failures using dynamic models and use cases.

Measurement 11.2: Model coverage (the degree to which you exercise each test object in the test model at least once).

This measure is relative to the process by which you derive the test objects in the test models. You can make the measure stronger or weaker by strengthening or weakening your equivalence classes or your criteria for generating test objects. To evaluate risk over time, you should relate model coverage data to fault discovery effectiveness data. This kind of benchmark produces direct, absolute evidence of the level of risk your coverage criteria produce. Also, as the individual test models and objects detail, this is a minimal testing criterion, not an optimal one. Test object selection heuristics provide many additional possibilities. You must optimize the test suite by trading off coverage against time and resources using your acceptable level of risk.

Objective 11.3: To optimize productivity in testing to an acceptable level of risk.

Approach 11.3: Use the inheritance structure of the system to structure testing incrementally into a pyramid that ensures that you test only those elements that will contribute additional failures.

Measurement 11.3: The ratio of the number of test objects in the suite to the estimated number of test objects for the classes treated separately.

For this measure, you need to estimate how many test objects you would have if you collapsed the inheritance hierarchy and duplicated all the code in the different concrete subclasses. This estimate tells you how much effort you save by reusing tests at higher levels in the hierarchy. Note that you must duplicate some tests due to interdependencies between methods higher in the hierarchy with virtual methods. See the individual test model objects for details.

Structure

CLASSES

Each hierarchical-incremental test suite tests a specific set of classes in the system. Usually this set of classes is a complete inheritance hierarchy of some kind, since the hierarchical-incremental suite emphasizes inheritance as an organizing factor for the test models.

Dynamics

CREATE

To create the test suite, you need to build a series of test models for the classes that are the subjects of your testing. Here's a process for creating a hierarchical-incremental test suite:

1. List the classes, both abstract and concrete, that comprise the set of classes under test for the suite.

2. For each class, build an appropriate series of test models, or adapt design models to the purpose. See the "Model" section that follows.

3. For each test model, derive the set of test objects. This may be as simple as taking the components of the model, it may involve collecting model components into aggregates such as flows or paths, or it may involve equivalence class development. See the method Derive Test Objects on the test model class.

4. For each test object, develop a test script in the appropriate format. You can optimize this by collecting several test objects into a single script with a shared setup and cleanup of the test environment such as shared test data, shared object instances, shared initialization, and shared destruction. For example, if you can test three control flows using a single object instance with a sequence of messages, you could use three test scripts, but a single one would be better.

5. Build the test scripts into an automated test suite using the test framework appropriate for the test scripts. See the section on test frameworks for a discussion of how scripts interact in frameworks. This building includes developing test drivers and stubs in the test framework.

6. Build any test data the scripts require into the test repository. You can do this through a combination of random data generation and specific data development based on the test scripts. For example, the test data usually will contain values that test models specify as likely to cause failures (zero, values less than or greater than some boundary condition, and so on).

MODEL

After deciding which classes you are going to test with this test suite, you must then model the classes using the different test modeling techniques. Part of the job here is to decide which techniques are appropriate, and the rest is building the model or models.

Looking at the available test models, you have several choices. This section gives you some guidelines. Your choice depends on what you know about the class, your acceptable level of risk, and the available time and resources.

First, what do you know about the classes?

If you have a complete dynamic model of the classes under test (that is, state-transition diagrams that specify the behavior of the objects without reference to the internal processing of the class), you should just use that model as your test model. If you can build such a model from other information, and if the result is tractable and testable, this model is one of the best ways to generate test objects and scripts.

If you don't have a complete dynamic design for the class, but you have requirements use cases from which you can specify the behavioral life cycle of an object, you can build a transaction-flow model that shows the different possibilities for objects moving through their life cycles from construction to destruction. This kind of model is higher level and less formal than the state-transition model.

If you have enough information to understand the internals of the methods—source code, for example—you can build a control-flow or data-flow model. You can build a control-flow model from the source code for each method, and you usually can annotate it with data value information from the source code as well.

The advantage in using a state-transition or transaction-flow model (a *black-box* or *functional* model) over a control or data-flow model (a *white-box* or *structural* model) is a much better and more productive level of coverage. The state-transition or transaction-flow model covers the entire object rather than just individual methods and so is much more appropriate for testing objects; control flows test individual methods rather than the objects of which they are methods. The structural models miss the shared elements such as the common class attributes, for example, and the methods don't work well in the context of exceptions and concurrency.

The disadvantages to the state-transition and transaction-flow models come from several areas:

- Because these models derive from requirements, not code, it can easily be wrong. You have to test the model extensively as well as the code.
- Because the model includes all of the class behavior and that of its superclasses, the model can become very complex very quickly. Using hierarchical state-transition models helps reduce complexity, but you still may run into trouble with intractability for objects with any degree of complex behavior. Breaking the problem down into individual methods gets rid of the overall complexity; but this strategy usually will just transfer the problem to integration testing as you use the object with other ones.
- Because these models model behavior rather than internal logic, even good coverage of the model may miss control and data faults. Your assumptions about the behavior based on requirements may not reflect the equivalence assumptions that the programmer makes. Hence you may think two transaction paths are the same, when in fact they do different things to control or data.

If you decide to construct a control- or data-flow model, your next question is whether to model data flows. Look at your risk: If you have a lot of data declarations in your methods or a lot of attributes in your classes, or if you use data for any kind of control decision, you should model the data as well as the control to look for such things as uninitialized variables, variables the code uses after destruction of the value, values defined that the code never uses, or values the code defines and then redefines without any use in between. In our opinion, most modern code will benefit from data-flow testing.

The next question is whether the classes can generate exceptions from messages. If so, you should build or adapt a model of exceptions that shows the conditions for the raising of each exception. If the classes do not raise exceptions under any circumstances, you can ignore this test model.

Now, having gone through all the choices having to do with the level of information you have, it's important to step back and look at your modeling choices in light of your acceptable level of risk in combination with your available time and resources. Again, the point of testing is to reduce risk to an acceptable level. You need to be aware of the extent to which your test model choice affects your risk level. Unfortunately, there's really no way to measure this without a lot of accumulated data about what test models produce what expected failure rates and so on. In the initial stages of adopting a quality optimization approach, you will need to evaluate your choice subjectively to decide how many different test models to adopt to get to your acceptable level of risk. For example, just testing transaction flows based on use cases may not be enough if you know there are many control and data elements and a lot of internal complexity within the classes. For a simple management information system (MIS) application that just reads and writes data in simple transactions, you can make do with a simple transaction-flow test suite. In more complex systems, or in systems with greater consequences of failure, your risk level will require more thorough assurance about system behavior, and hence you will want to adopt more models and have more tests. You should validate your decision and intuition with peers, clients, and/or domain experts by reviewing the test approach with them.

In the best of all possible worlds, you have a detailed state-transition model, well-defined use cases and a complete functional model, access to source code, and a complete specification of exception conditions. You usually will want to develop an approach combining all the different test models. One way to do this systematically is to structure your test suite around state-transition test objects and transaction flows, then to develop tests for the individual methods using control and data flows based on the structures from the functional tests. You can then feed back the flow analysis into the functional tests to cover any cases you may have missed. This approach gives you complete coverage from the perspective of both the requirements for the classes and the actual structure of the classes.

Example

The DTS system broke up into clearly defined systems based on the several inheritance hierarchies, and the hierarchical-incremental test suites for the DTS followed. For example, there was a single hierarchical-incremental test suite for each of the three data model systems: Person, Product, and Problem.

The Problem hierarchical-incremental test suite tested the classes in the problem inheritance hierarchy in Figure 11.2. There were four concrete

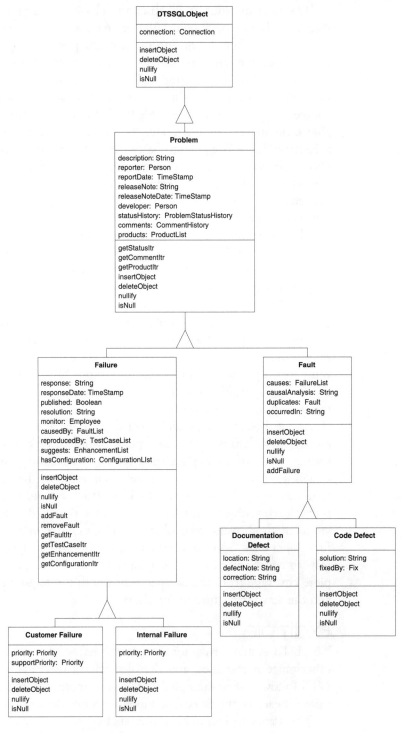

Figure 11.2 DTS Problem inheritance hierarchy.

classes (Code Defect, Documentation Defect, Customer Failure, and Internal Failure) and four abstract classes (DTSSQLObject, Problem, Failure, and Fault). Note that DTSSQLObject was not in the Problem system proper (that is, it wasn't in a separate DLL because it's shared between several systems); since it was part of the overall hierarchy, the DTS testing team had to test it in that context.

The test plan contained Table 11.1 showing the inheritance implications for testing (for brevity's sake, this table covers only part of the hierarchy table):

Table 11.1

Class	Method	Type	Abstract
DTSSQLObject	DTSSQLObject	New	
	insertObject	New	Yes
	deleteObject	New	Yes
	nullify	New	Yes
	isNull	New	Yes
Problem	Problem	New	
	Problem	New	
	Problem	New	
	getDescription	New	
	getReporter	New	
	getReleaseNote	New	
	getDeveloper	New	
	getStatusItr	New	
	getCommentItr	New	
	getProductItr	New	
	updateDescription	New	
	updateReporter	New	
	updateReleaseNote	New	
	updateDeveloper	New	
	updateProductHistory	New	
	updateStatusHistory	New	
	insertObject	Redefined	
	deleteObject	Redefined	
	nullify	Redefined	
	isNull	Redefined	
Failure	Failure	New	
	Failure	New	

Table 11.1 (cont.)

Class	Method	Type	Abstract
Failure *(cont.)*	Failure	New	
	getResponse	New	
	getPublished	New	
	getResolution	New	
	getMonitor	New	
	getFaultItr	New	
	getTestCaseItr	New	
	getEnhancementItr	New	
	getConfigurationItr	New	
	updateResponse	New	
	updatePublished	New	
	updateResolution	New	
	updateMonitor	New	
	addFault	New	
	removeFault	New	
	addTestCase	New	
	removeTestCase	New	
	updateConfiguration	New	
	insertObject	Redefined	
	deleteObject	Redefined	
	nullify	Redefined	
	isNull	Redefined	

There are no recursive methods that interact with virtual methods, so the table does not list any recursive methods that need testing for this hierarchy.

Scanning the source code for the methods of these classes, the DTS team found very few conditional branches in the individual methods. The architect had stressed the data modeling aspects of the design and so had very little in the way of control embedded into the system. That is, this system serves other systems, such as the user interface and document systems, by manipulating data and leaving control to the service requester.

As a consequence, the hierarchical-incremental test suite for the Problem hierarchy focused on a combination of state-transition testing and a transaction model for each of the four concrete classes based on the use cases for the system. For the few methods that have conditional branching, the test suite added a data-flow model (Failure::addFault(), Failure::removeFault(), and Fault::addFailure()). The team discussed adding data-flow models to validate the various data flows, since data was important, but decided to use a thorough code review instead.

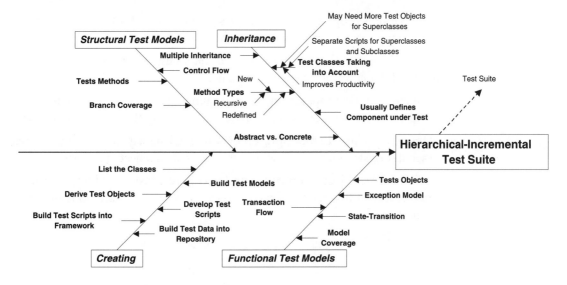

Figure 11.3 Road map for the hierarchical-incremental test suite class.

Road Map

Figure 11.3 is the road map for the hierarchical-incremental test suite class.

Class-Object Test Script

Object-oriented testing begins with testing objects. Well, perhaps not begins: Everything is a system, and you have to test (and optimize) everything in the system, including the requirements and design you have before you even get objects. You even have to test the tests before you can test the objects. Still, the first actual code you test is going to be an object. Well, perhaps not an object: There are lots of objects, but there's no real reason to test them all.

So, how do you group the objects in the system for testing purposes? The first step is using the natural group: the class. The *class-object test script* tests some aspect of a class of objects. But which aspects? That question is the genesis of most of the theory of software testing. The rest of this chapter discusses the various test suites and models that define the test scripts for object-oriented software. However, the set of test models here is by no means exhaustive; with ingenuity, you can come up with many new and different ways to test objects of a class. Ultimately, however, you need to put the test in executable form in a class-object test script.

All class-object tests operate within the test framework. The test drivers for a class create the objects required to run all the hierarchical-incremental tests as well as exercising all the built-in conditional tests.

There are four specific subclasses of the class-object test, all of which operate through the conditional test suite:

Assertion: A programming language statement that aborts the program during debugging if a condition evalutes to false.

Exception: A programming language statement that raises an exception in a method if a condition evaluates to true.

Concurrent Test Operation: A programming language statement that tests for valid conditions and takes appropriate action during the execution of a method.

Message Polling Test Script: A programming language statement that is part of a set of such statements that validate the status of an object of the class at any time.

The class-object test script is itself a concrete class; the hierarchical-incremental test suite consists of class-object test scripts that are none of the above four classes.

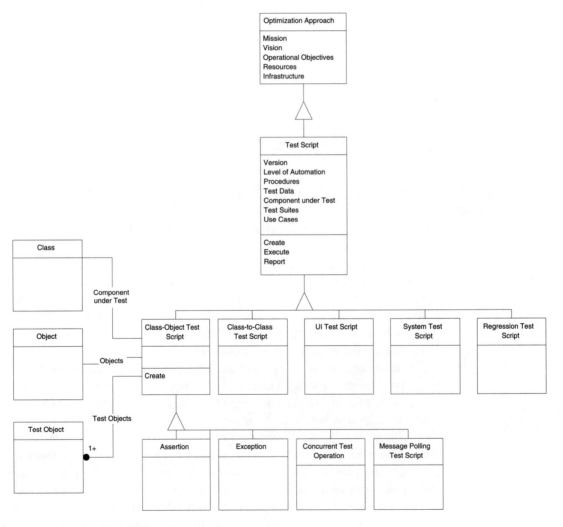

Figure 11.4 Structure of class-object test script class.

Although it's not a part of the test script hierarchy, the *code review* is one of the best class-object testing tools you have. Going through a code review on a class, with no objects in sight, will find many failures much more efficiently than spending years writing tests. Although you have to test to get an acceptable level of risk, it's a good idea just to look at what you're testing before you test. Along the same line of logic, requirements and design reviews are also a good way to find errors before you start writing test scripts for the class. See Chapter 19 for an in-depth exhortation to review before you run.

Ch. 19

Technical
Review

Figure 11.4 shows the structure of the class-object test script class.

Leadership

Vision: A set of objects (a class) capable of performing all required behaviors to an acceptable level of risk.

Mission: To discover failures in a specific class or its superclasses.

Objective 11.2: To test the class to an acceptable level of risk.

Approach 11.2: Build a test script that tests an equivalence classes of test objects of the class using techniques that make the class fail with respect to your acceptable level of risk.

Measurement 11.2: Number of failures versus the expected number of failures

This measure depends on your ability to estimate the expected number of failures, but it gives a clear metric of the performance of the test against expectations. If the test discovers fewer failures than expected, you may need more tests of the class to ensure that you've reached an acceptable level of risk. This may seem counterintuitive: Isn't the purpose of a test to prove that a class is okay? NO! The purpose is to make the class fail in order to reduce the risk of later failure. You can never prove something always works, but you can easily prove it fails.

Structure

Component under Test
The *component under test* in this case is the class, the source code that maps to the test objects for the test script. The class supplies the structure for the test in the script. You don't directly test the class, since it's not executable; you test the objects of the class. You cover the test objects in the class by these tests, however.

Objects
You create one or more *objects* of the class under test as part of the test script. The script then sends messages to the objects to perform the test on the test objects (such as the control flows or conditions).

TEST OBJECTS

The *test objects* are the specific test model components that this test script tests. If you test more than a single test object in a test script, the script should identify all the objects.

Dynamics

CREATE

Creating the class-object test script requires an understanding of the specific test object you want to test, which in turn requires creating a test model for the class. You do this in creating either the hierarchical-incremental or conditional test suite, since the test model spans several test scripts and classes. Once you have derived the test objects, you can create the test script. The actual process of doing this depends largely on the language in which you express the script procedures. This can vary from a programming language, such as for conditional tests coded in C++, to structured English for manual test scripts. It all depends on the nature of the test framework. In any case, the job is to transform the test object into a series of procedures that generate test results for evaluation.

The test script can test just one test object or several. You may find that it's possible to group several related tests for a class together into a single test script. Typically, you will create an object, then send it messages. You also can base groups of tests on shared test data.

You also can run other test scripts from the current one. This is how you can run test scripts associated with abstract classes. These do not, create objects for testing; they cannot. When you test a concrete subclass, you call the test scripts associated with the superclass using the objects you create in the subclass. That implies at least one parameter to the test script, letting you pass in the object to test. You also can parameterize a single test script so that you can reuse it for several test objects. You create a driver test script, then call the parameterized one several times with different parameters. Again, the exact format depends on the nature of the test framework.

Example

The DTS test framework is a database-driven, proprietary tool that lets you construct test scripts from descriptions of test objects in a database. A precompiler reads the source code and your test object description and embeds C++ test drivers and stubs in the code.

As an example of a test script in the hierarchical-incremental suite for the Problem hierarchy, the test script that tests the following transaction:

1. Create a customer failure with a specific set of initialization parameters (an equivalence class), including a Connection object.

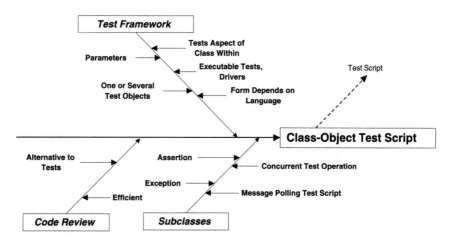

Figure 11.5 Road map for the class-object test script class.

2. Run a specified test case that verifies the behavior of the Failure class attributes response, published, and monitor.

3. Set the priority.

4. Set the support priority.

5. Insert the object into the database.

6. Commit the database transaction.

7. Destroy the customer failure.

The precompiler creates the following C++ code in the customer failure implementation file:

```
#ifdef DTS_PROBLEM_PYR_TEST
void
DTS_PROBLEM_PYR_TEST_1(CustomerFailure * pTest1, Connection & connection, SDWORD id,
                const String & description, const Person & reporter,
                    TimeStamp & reportDate, SWORD published, const Employee & monitor,
                TestReport & report)
{
    // 1. Create a customer failure with a specific set of initialization parameters (an
    // equivalence class), including a Connection object.
      if (!pTest1) // only create if not already created by subclass
      pTest1 = new CustomerFailure(connection, id, description, reporter,
                                          reportDate, published, monitor);
    // 2. Run a specified test case that verifies the behavior of the Failure class
    //    attributes response, published, and monitor.
      String response = "Test response.";
      DTS_FAILURE_PYR_TEST_6(pTest1, response, TRUE, monitor, report);
    // 3. Set the priority.
      report << pTest1->updatePriority(eVeryHighPriority);
    // 4. Set the support priority.
      report << pTest1->updateSupportPriority(eModeratePriority);
```

```
        // 5. Insert the object into the database.
           report << pTest1->insertObject();
        // 6. Commit the database transaction.
           report << connection.commit();
        // 7. Destroy the customer failure.
           delete pTest1;
}
#endif DTS_PROBLEM_PYR_TEST
```

Road Map

Figure 11.5 is the road map for the class-object test script class.

Control-Flow Test Model

The *control-flow test model* models a class method as a sequence of nodes and edges (a graph). This *control-flow graph* represents the control structure of the method and hence is a structural model of the class. Figure 11.6 shows a sample flow graph.

The circles in the graph represent one of two things:

- *Decisions:* Points in the method where control can pass to any of two or more different alternative statements.
- *Junctions:* Points in the method where control passes from any of two or more different alternative statements.

Decisions are nodes with multiple arrows emerging from the circle; nodes a, b, and c are decisions. Junctions are nodes with multiple arrows entering

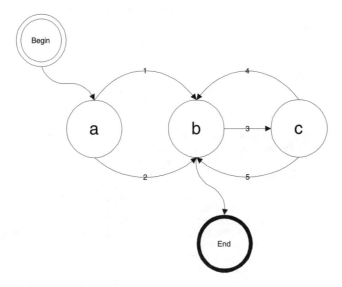

Figure 11.6 Example of a control-flow graph.

the circle; node b is a junction. Node b is thus both a junction and a decision. The double circles represent the beginning and end of the method, to make clear where the process starts and ends.

Note that you cannot have a node that has only one entrance and exit, as this would represent a statement with no relevance to the control structure. Another way to look at this restriction is that you need to combine a series of statements with no control decisions into a single node. Thus, there is no one-to-one relationship between source code statements and control nodes.

The edges, or links, between the nodes represent the flows between control decisions and junctions. These correspond to the sequence of program statements that don't involve decisions.

There are two subclasses of the control-flow test model, both of which use a similar graph structure of nodes and edges representing control behavior.

- **Data-Flow Test Model:** This test model adds data flows to the control flows.
- **Transaction-Flow Test Model:** Models an entire class with control flows based on use cases.

The transaction-flow test model appears above with the functional test models, even though it uses the same structural components as the structural models. It provides a strictly functional view of the class.

Figure 11.7 shows the structure of the control-flow test model and the control-flow test object.

Leadership

Vision: A method with an acceptable risk of failure.

Mission: To test the method to an acceptable level of risk, taking into account time and resources.

Objective 11.3: To test the method to an acceptable level of risk based on structural features.

Approach 11.3: Model the objects using a control-flow model and derive control-flow paths from that model as test objects with a maximum probability of causing failures.

Measurement 11.3: Branch coverage (exercising each flow in the flow graph at least once).

Structure

Test Objects

The *test objects* for the control-flow model are specifically *control flows*, the paths through the control-flow graph that satisfy your objectives.

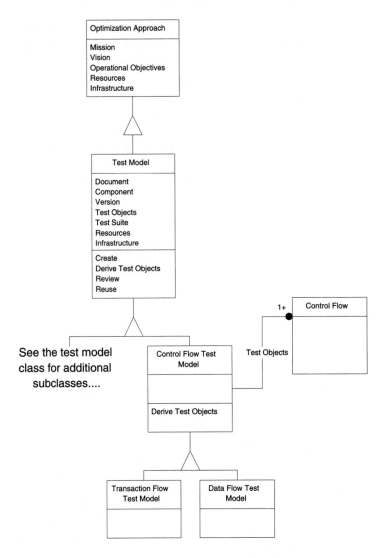

Figure 11.7 Structure of the control-flow test model.

Dynamics

DERIVE TEST OBJECTS

Deriving control-flow test objects is more of an art than a science. A control-flow test object is a path through the control-flow diagram that goes from the method initialization to the method termination.

Because the control-flow model allows loops, there is no guarantee of a finite number of paths through the graph. Figure 11.6, for example, has an infinite number of paths because of the loop between nodes b and c. Thus, you cannot often achieve 100 percent path testing. That's why the hierarchi-cal-incremental test suite relies on branch coverage for test object generation. In a control-flow model, branch coverage means having a sufficient number of control-flow paths to exercise all the links at least once.

Again, this is a minimal test coverage criterion; it ignores missing require-ments and bugs involving multiple passes through the flow paths. It also ignores data problems. (See the "Data-Flow Test Model" section below.)

If control-flow modeling is part of your test suite, you should follow these guidelines:

- Ensure that your test suite also includes requirements-based, function-al test models such as state-transition and transaction-flow models.
- Choose paths through the system that represent the sensible paths the method is likely to take, even if this duplicates coverage of some links.
- Develop equivalence classes of variations on the initial paths based on your intuitive feel for what could cause problems.
- If you've picked all the sensible paths and you find you haven't achieved branch coverage, ask yourself why—there are probably control-flow problems, absurd situations, or dead code issues with the method.

Note that not all paths are achievable. Data values can control predicate evaluation to make a given decision impossible. There are different faults associated with control predicates, so you should look at the predicates care-fully to derive your test objects. For example, predicates with side effects are always a joy for testing control. (Remember, you're supposed to be making the thing fail, that's what makes you happy.) Predicates with multiple, com-plex terms are also a good bet. And there's always the old, reliable "> versus >=" problem (let's see now . . .). Predicates and the data values they use should guide a lot of your thinking about test object derivation from control models. You may find data-flow models somewhat more useful if you have a lot of complex, data-dependent predicates.

See Boris Beizer's books (1984, 1990, 1995) for a more detailed set of guidelines for analyzing specific situations, especially predicates, loops, and multiple-entry or multiple-exit situations.

Example

Figure 11.6 shows a sample control-flow graph. The following code is the source from which the DTS testing team generated the flow graph. The let-ters in comments correspond to the control nodes in the flow graph.

```
// Function: Connection::handleError
// Description: Handles an error in the ODBC connection with the appropriate
//              action based on the nature of the error. Handles situations in
//              which there is more than one error in the ODBC error handling
//              stack (i.e., when the return code is not SQL_NO_DATA_FOUND).
void   Connection::handleError(HSTMT handle, RETCODE returnCode)
```

```
{
    UCHAR        SQLState[6];                // SQL State code
    SDWORD       nativeErrorCode;            // Server DBMS error code
    UCHAR        errorText[200];             // Server DBMS error text
    if (returnCode == SQL_ERROR)             // a
        (void) rollback();                   // flow 2
    while (returnCode != SQL_NO_DATA_FOUND)     // b
    {               // flow 3
        returnCode = SQLError(SQL_NULL_HENV, pDatabaseObject->m_hdbc,
                    handle, SQLState, &nativeErrorCode, errorText,
                    sizeof(errorText), NULL);
        if (returnCode != SQL_NO_DATA_FOUND)      // c
        {               // flow 5
            TRACE("\nODBC Error:\n\tSQL State: %s", SQLState);
            TRACE("\n\tServer Code: %ld", nativeErrorCode);
            TRACE("\n\t%s\n", errorText);
        }
    }
}
```

Figure 11.8 shows a single test object, a path through the control-flow graph. This test object is the case where the ODBC return code is **SQL_NO_DATA_FOUND**, indicating the case where you fetched a data row and there was no result. At node a, the condition fails, skipping the rollback. At node b, the condition again fails, skipping the error processing block. The method then terminates.

The DTS tester took the following approach to generating possible test objects. First, the tester thought about the sensible paths through this method. The first thing to come to mind was whether the code was

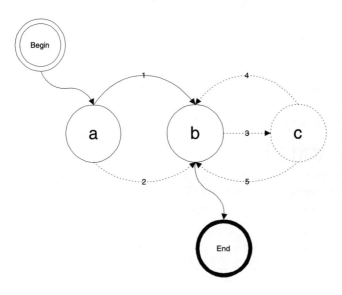

Figure 11.8 Example of a control-flow object.

SQL_ERROR, leading to the test object in Figure 11.8. The next was to sketch some possibilities if the error was **SQL_ERROR**. The tester read the design document for the method, which noted that ODBC sends back multiple errors. When you retrieve the last error, you get the return code **SQL_NO_DATA_FOUND** from the call to SQLError(). This was the reason for node c, the if statement that tests the return code from SQLError(). Therefore, the following obvious cases existed:

- A single error in the error stack
- Two errors in the error stack

Figure 11.9 shows the test objects for these two cases, with the actual path below the diagram. Notice that the path for the first test object achieves full, 100 percent branch coverage of the method. Minimal testing, thus, did not require testing the second test object. The DTS tester, however, knew that that second error printing loop constituted a relatively high risk for failure, both because ODBC drivers sometimes didn't implement this error handling correctly and because of the possibility of a logic error in the code or the conditions. So the tester included both test scripts in the test suite.

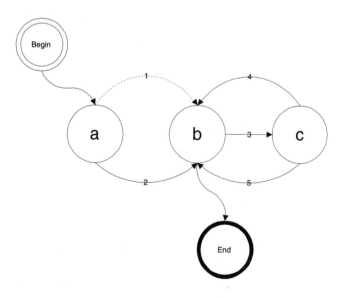

Single Error: Begin-a-2-b-3-c-5-b-3-c-4-b-End

Double Error: Begin-a-2-b-3-c-5-b-3-c-5-b-3-c-4-b-End

Figure 11.9 Single- and double-error DTS control-flow test objects.

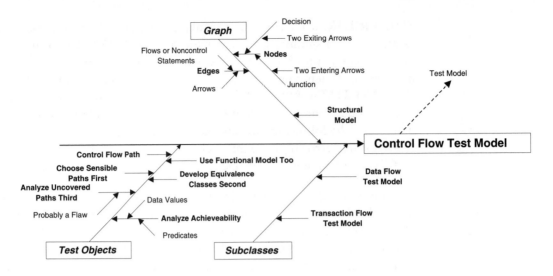

Figure 11.10 Road map for the control-flow test model class.

Thus, in testing the **Connection::handleError** method, the DTS tester constructed three test scripts:

- Construct a connection, then generate a **SQL_NO_DATA_FOUND** warning and pass the handle to the method, then destroy the connection.
- Construct a connection, then generate a single SQL error and pass the handle to the method, then destroy the connection.
- Construct a connection, then generate two SQL errors and pass the handle to the method, then destroy the connection.

In terms of equivalence classes, this test suite considers two equivalence classes based on return code (**SQL_NO_DATA_FOUND** and anything else) and two equivalence classes based on the handle (one error and two errors).

Road Map
Figure 11.10 is the road map for the control-flow test model class.

Data-Flow Test Model

The data-flow test model is a kind of control-flow test model annotated with data elements that shows what happens to those data as you move through a method execution.

The data-flow model is thus a graph with nodes and edges that represent the same control information for the method as does the control-flow model. It also includes annotations on the edges that represent the data objects of interest to the method. For most object-oriented languages, this includes several kinds of data elements:

- **Global variables:** Variables outside the scope of any class.
- **Class variables:** Data members of the class with a value shared between all objects of the class to which the method belongs.
- **Object variables:** Data members of the class with separate values for each object of the class.
- **Parameters:** Values the caller passes to the method by value or by reference, thus making the outside value visible inside the method regardless of its defining scope.
- **Local variables:** Variables the method defines that exist only when the method runs.

Figure 11.11 shows the control-flow example of Figure 11.6 with annotations that explain how the data elements of the method flow through the method execution. The following symbols designate specific events that happen to the data items:

d Define or construct or change the data value.

k Kill or destroy the data value.

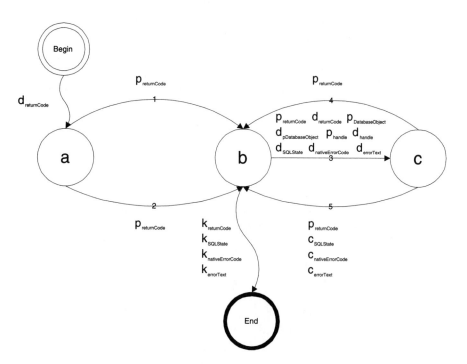

Figure 11.11 Data-flow model of DTS Connection::handleError method.

c Use the data value in a calculation.

p Use the data value in a predicate.

At the beginning of the graph, the method defines the input parameter returnCode (passed by value). Notice that there is no definition for the first parameter, handle, which the caller passes by reference, and that the method does not initialize the three local variables.

The decision in node a uses the returnCode variable in a predicate, as does the decision in node b. Depending on the decision in node b, the method either kills all the variables defined earlier or changes the values of all six variables in the method. Node c uses the returnCode in a predicate and either does or does not use three of the variables based on the result.

Sometimes figuring out what should be a use and what should be a definition, particularly in the context of subroutine calls, can be a bit tricky. All parameters to subroutine calls are uses (the c symbol); if the call changes the value, such as for an in-out variable, you should specify an additional definition (the d symbol). Thus you need to know from the function definition what the subroutine does to variables passed by reference. By implication, it also means you need to know that the method is passing the variable by reference. For example, looking at the call to SQLError in the **handleError** method in the last section, the handle variable seems to be a by-value parameter. In fact, it is a by-reference parameter, because the HSTMT defined constant hides the fact that it's a pointer. As we said, it can be a bit tricky.

The testing objects are the different paths through the graph: control-data flows. Look for several specific data anomalies in these flows:

- A sequence of two definitions for the same variable (possibly harmless; required if the redefinition is an alternative to some path that uses the variables).
- A destruction immediately following a definition (harmless but worthless).
- A destruction following a destruction (possibly harmful, depending on the language and the context).
- A use following a destruction (either an immediate eruption or a quiet trickle of smoke).
- A destruction by itself. (Did you really define it elsewhere?)
- A use by itself. (Ditto.)
- A definition by itself. (Destroyed somewhere else? Used somewhere else?)

The last of these anomalies is the most important, but the others can cause both faults and confusion in future maintenance. Many compilers detect the other ones, though by no means all, and some situations are undetectable.

Look for several specific problematic data situations in this model:

- An array use that uses an uninitialized or out-of-bounds element. (See the example below.)

- A variable use as a consequence of a variable use (multiple dereferencing of pointers, variables carrying function pointers).
- Use of data of an unknown type (void pointers and unions, typedefs of typedefs of types, defined constants replacing variables).
- Assumptions about data that may not be true.

The encapsulation techniques of object-oriented programming by design avoid many of the problems that data-flow testing catches. Hybrid languages such as C++ do let you violate encapsulated design principles, so data-flow testing still has its place. For best results, your method design should follow some specific rules (summarized from Beizer, 1990, pp. 171–172):

- Avoid modifying variables you pass into the method; pass by value, not by reference.

This rule is a guideline, not a law. The common practice of passing data into methods, modifying the data, and returning (the in-out variable or pass-by-reference variable), while it is quite flexible, renders data-flow testing very hard. Essentially, you are moving the testing to the integration stage, with all the associated increase in risk and cost.

- Keep data construction and destruction at the same level in your program.

This rule is closer to a law, just to maintain your testing team's sanity. It probably should be a rule in your coding standards. A really good way to introduce data problems into your program is to construct a value belonging to a class by dynamically allocating it in a constructor, then to destroy it randomly before destroying the object. Use the default construction/destruction mechanisms, such as automatic construction and destruction of member attributes, to the fullest. If you construct a member explicitly, destroy it in the appropriate place. A good rule of thumb is to designate some object as the owner of the data, then have that object both create and destroy the data object it owns. It also helps to decide on some consistent rule and to follow it religiously.

A corollary of these rules is to avoid overloading variables with multiple uses. (Bit strings and unions come immediately to mind.) Using the variable can affect more than one value, making testing harder. Another corollary is to avoid using the variables in predicates at different program levels, since you can find problems only during integration testing.

- Avoid avoiding strong typing.

Situations commonly arise in which you usually find it expedient to dispense with the strong type checking of most object-oriented languages. Doing so is a bad idea simply because it makes testing impossible. For example, "casting away const" or "downcasting" in C++, while it increases your flexibility and reduces the amount of code you must write, almost guarantees problems for the unit testing of the class and its later maintenance. If you cast

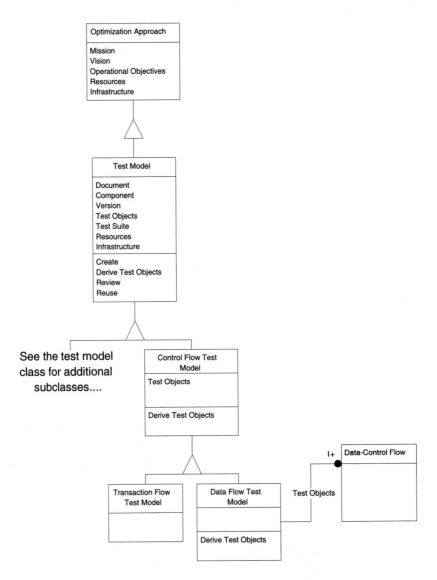

Figure 11.12 Structure of the data-flow model class.

away a const specifier for a variable passed by reference for efficiency, then change it (or call a method that changes it, even worse), the tester looking at the method that passed the variable has just assumed that the value will not change and so made the wrong testing choices. This law also should be in your coding standards.

- Always initialize data members and other data elements.

Another law; uninitialized data causes many of the severe failures associated with program crashes, such as dereferencing bad pointers or trying to call a method on an object that doesn't exist. Making all initialization explicit also makes the data-flow testing job easier, as the tester can see immediately where the initialization occurs.

See Beizer's *Software Testing Techniques* (1990, pp. 145–172), for an extended discussion of data-flow testing. Beizer notes that you can generalize data-flow graphs into a data-flow architecture that does not assume a single control stream but rather allows for parallelism. Should you have to test such a program, the data-flow model is not optional, it's required. However, most object-oriented languages of interest to you are going to be Von Neumann architecture languages that assume no parallelism.

Figure 11.12 shows the class structure of the data-flow test model class.

Leadership

Vision: A method with an acceptable risk of failure.

Mission: To test the method to an acceptable level of risk, taking into account time and resources.

Objective 11.4: Test the method to an acceptable level of risk based on structural features.

Approach 11.4: Model the objects using a data-flow model and derive data-control flow paths from that model as test objects with a maximum probability of causing failures.

Measurement 11.4: Model coverage (using each data value in the flow graph at least once; see below).

Structure

Test Objects
The *test objects* for the data-flow model are specifically *data-control flows*, the paths through the data-flow graph that satisfy your objectives.

Dynamics

Derive Test Objects
Deriving the test objects for a data-flow model assumes the basic work done in the control-flow model with some additional work needed to satisfy the additional coverage required.

The coverage measure we chose to apply for this model is to test all uses of the data at least once, similar to branch coverage of a control-flow model. Specifically, we want to test all the paths through the graph from a definition of a variable to a use of that variable with no intervening definition. To do this, start with the definition of the variable and trace through the paths until you find a use of it. After doing this for all the variables and all uses of them, reduce the number of test objects through evaluating which paths cover multiple variables.

Example

The DTS tester added some test scripts for the hierarchical-incremental test suite that included the Connection class, as in Figure 11.6, by building a data-flow model of the **handleError** method (Figure 11.11). The code for the method is in the example for the control-flow model.

There was one array variable, errorText, with a fixed bound of 200. Some thinking about this indicated a couple of problems. First, although the use of the variable correctly told ODBC's SQLError routine to use 200 as the size, there is no indication in the design that this is the right length. Second, the coding standards call for use of a defined constant or const variable in this context rather than an explicit number. They also call for using a number plus one to indicate the terminating null value at the end of the array. ODBC assumes the last element is the null value, but it still should be explicit in the code.

Next, some quick analysis showed that the method uses, and possibly changes, the handle variables defined elsewhere (the handle variable and the database object handle). The handle is a kind of control structure that ODBC uses to maintain a state, and ODBC in some sense owns this variable, so this was probably okay.

The method did not kill any variable that it did not previously define.

The various uses of the returnCode variable were all in the context of control predicates; hence, the control-flow paths cover this variable.

The method uses the SQLState, nativeErrorCode, and errorText variables only after defining them after node b (flow 3). Thus initialization at the beginning of the routine is unnecessary. The path that covers flows 2, 3, and 5 (the single-error test object from the control-flow test model) also covers the three definitions and uses.

Finally, it is possible to redefine the various ODBC variables after using them, so there are an infinite number of use paths looping through nodes b and c. Using intuition, the DTS tester selected (again) the double-error test case as the second equivalence class (one error message versus two or more error messages).

So in this particular case, the control-flow test objects proved to be much the same as the data-flow test objects—at least, after some thinking and analysis. Furthermore, the DTS tester identified one code standard violation that missed the code review.

Road Map

Figure 11.13 is the road map for the data-flow test model class.

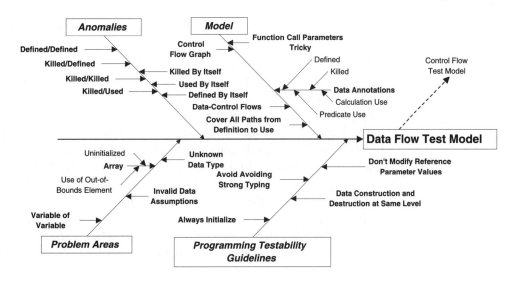

Figure 11.13 Road map for the data-flow test model class.

State-Transition Test Model

Transitioning from testing individual methods to classes introduces the concept of class behavior. Each individual method of a class expresses some element of the overall behavior of the class. Most methods in good object-oriented designs are quite amenable to testing as separate entities, but at some point you start missing things if you look only at individual behaviors in isolation. This effect is yet another example of scaling up from system to system.

In particular, when you express requirements in a design, you need to express behavior at a level that is beyond the individual task or activity. The use cases that specify requirements translate into a sequence of such activities. Scaling up requires moving to a higher-level system; that system can either be the class or the integration of several classes (a system or a cluster). Chapter 13 deals with the latter; the former is the subject of this and the following sections.

Many different object-oriented design methods use the state-transition model to represent the behavior of a class. The OMT method, for example, uses the state-transition model as its dynamic model (Rumbaugh et al., 1991, pp. 84–122). There are many variations on state-transition model notation, including diagram and tabular representations. We adopt the notation from the OMT model, a state-transition diagram adapted from the work of David Harel (1987, 1988).

The *state* of an object is the combination of all the attribute values and objects the object contains; unsurprisingly, a state is *static*, at a point in time, rather than dynamic. To model dynamics of the object, you add transitions, movement from a state to a state. When the object is in a given state, an *event* occurs that moves it to another state (or back to the same state). During the transition from state to state, an *action* occurs.

Figure 11.14 shows the state-transition model for the DTS ProblemStatus-History class, which is a double-linked list that can be in one of three states: empty, a single node in the list, or multiple nodes in the list (the three state nodes in the diagram). The notation shows the entry (constructor) and exit (destructor) points as smaller nodes. If different constructors can put the object into different states, you will have multiple entries; this of course makes the testing harder.

The edges in the graph are the transitions; the labels on these consist of the events and the actions that occur in the transition from state to state. The actions correspond to class method names, while the events are simply named user interface or other events in the system, such as conditions or messages. The condition in brackets coming out of the Multiple Nodes and One Node states is an automatic transition that occurs when the condition, or guard, is true. In this case, for example, the removing of the second to last node causes the Multiple Node state to transition to One Node. Where the event is a message sent to an object of the class, the event and the action are the same, as in Figure 11.14; otherwise, a slash separates the action and event.

For example, if some transition occurs because the user presses the OK button in a dialog box to set a series of Fault response attributes, you might see the event/action pair labeled "OK Button Down/updateResponse" on a transition for the Fault class. This convention implies that you have the object model with methods and so on complete before you develop the dynamic model, but this is not necessarily true; you generally develop them iteratively, adding methods as the transitions require or changing names on the transitions as appropriate to a new design. You can develop a state-transition diagram with

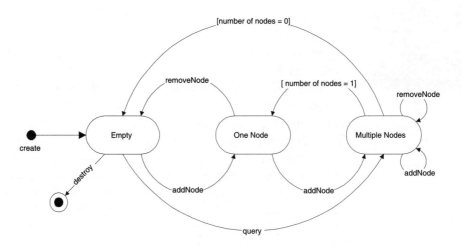

Figure 11.14 State-transition model for DTS ProblemStatusHistory class.

little besides the requirements and a preliminary architectural design. This is a functional model, not a structural model; it represents a description of how the system should behave, not how you actually design or implement it.

We use the Mealy-model version of this notation, where the events and actions label the transition edges, not the state nodes. Boris Beizer also discusses the different forms of state-transition modeling (calling events inputs and actions outputs) in his books on *Software Testing Techniques* (1984) and *Black-Box Testing* (1995).

This is a functional model you derive from requirements. Because it does not necessarily correspond directly to the processing logic of the program, you need to pay attention to the modeling rules, or you can have an invalid model. Such a model is useful for generating test scripts only to the extent it is correct. Beizer details many rules for checking state-transition models; in summary:

1. Verify that the states represent the true set of states: make sure that, for example, there is one state for each possible (or equivalent) value of the underlying state variables, usually the data attributes of the class. It's a good idea to list impossible states and review them to make sure they really are impossible. It's a good idea to make equivalence of states explicit and review that too.

2. Check that the model accounts for all possible events that you require the class to acknowledge. Thus there should be a transition from each state for every method of a class. For example, there is no transition from the Empty state in Figure 11.14 for the message remove Node. You should query this and check that the design specifies an error in this case. That is, if the list has no nodes and you attempt to remove one, what happens? Similarly, what happens if you destroy the object when in One Node or Multiple Node states? In this case, a destroy message (the destructor in C++) triggers a sequence of removeNode actions to get the state back to empty.

3. You also should check that there is exactly one transition for each event-state combination; otherwise, you have an ambiguity or contradiction. Doing this kind of check is easier if you have a matrix representation showing all possible combinations of states and events:

State	Empty	One Node	Multiple Nodes
Event			
create	Empty	Empty	Empty
destroy	Exit	?	?
query	Multiple Nodes	Multiple Nodes?	Multiple Nodes?
addNode	One Node	Multiple Nodes	Multiple Nodes
removeNode	?	Empty	Multiple Nodes
[number of nodes = 1]	NA	NA	One Node
[number of nodes = 0]	NA	NA	Empty

A question mark indicates a potential problem with the model; an NA indicates a logically or procedurally impossible situation. Note that create assumes an arbitrary, uninitialized state and transitions to Empty without showing this detail in the state-transition diagram. The destructor event transitions only from the empty state; what does this mean for one and multiple node states? The design might call for an automatic transition to remove the nodes to bring the state back to empty before destruction. Removing an empty node should raise an error of some kind; otherwise a loop could remove nodes endlessly. The query always puts the list into multiple node state; the guarded automatic transitions take care of transitioning the object to the appropriate state based on the actual number of nodes the query creates. Thus, building the state-transition matrix immediately identifies three problems that you should test.

4. Check for unreachable and dead states. An unreachable state is one you cannot get to by any path through the model. A dead state is one you cannot leave (no transitions from the state). You can have valid unreachable states that represent some kind of impossible state that you want to test. Generally, dead states are not valid in object-oriented systems, as the objects should always have a clear destruction path.

5. Check for invalid actions, including methods that don't exist or methods that do not satisfy the requirements for the transition. That is, make sure the actions are the right ones for the given transition.

The test objects for the state-transition model are transition paths, the paths through the graph that represent a full object life cycle from creation to destruction. That is, each test object represents one possible sequence of states between the birth and the death of an object of the class. See the "Derive Test Objects" section below for an algorithm for deriving the covering set of life cycle transition paths.

Minimal test coverage for state-transition models is model coverage, testing so that each transition occurs at least once.

Figure 11.15 shows the structure of the state-transition test model and the state-transition path object.

Leadership

Vision: A class with an acceptable risk of failure.

Mission: To test the class to an acceptable level of risk, taking into account time and resources.

Objective 11.5: Test the class to an acceptable level of risk based on functional features.

Approach 11.5: Model the objects using a state-transition model and derive

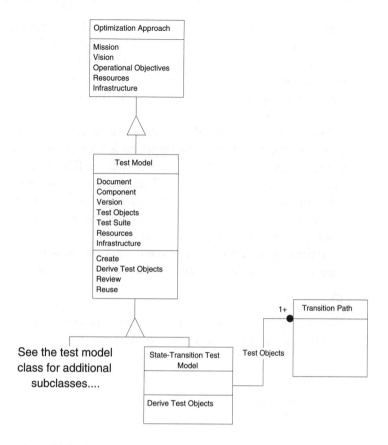

Figure 11.15 Structure of the state-transition test model class.

transition paths from that model as test objects with a maximum probability of causing failures.

Measurement 11.5: Model coverage (exercising each transition in the model at least once).

Structure

TEST OBJECTS

The *test objects* for the state-transition model are specifically the *transition paths* through the model. See the "Derive Test Objects" method below for details on transition paths.

Dynamics

DERIVE TEST OBJECTS

This method develops the test objects from a state-transition model. You want to pick a set of paths through the state-transition model that exercises each transition at least once. Transition paths for object-oriented models start with the construction of the object and end with the destruction of the object.

When you have multiple constructors that transition to different states, you should treat your test object derivation as a sequence of derivations, one for each possible combination of constructor and destructor. A matrix of these will help.

You can trace through the network using a depth-first approach and choosing the next transition based on a sensible sequence of events, as for control-flow diagrams. Some of your paths will be very short (construct, then destroy, for example); others will be very long, packing in many transitions into one path. One approach proposed by McGregor and Dyer (1994) iterates through the set of transitions systematically, deriving the test object by finding a path back to the constructor.

If the set of reasonable transitions doesn't get you to a complete coverage of the transitions, go back and reexamine your model for problems or special situations.

Example

Figure 11.14 shows the state-transition model for the DTS ProblemStatus-History class, which is a double-linked list:

```
// Class:            ProblemStatusHistory


#include "prstnode.h"   // ProblemStatusNode class
#include "connect.h"  // Connection class and ODBC defines

class ProblemStatusHistory
{
public:
                        ProblemStatusHistory() : pYoungest(NULL), pOldest(NULL) {}
    BOOL                addNode(ProblemStatusNode & node);
    BOOL                removeNode(ProblemStatusNode & node);
    RETCODE             query(Connection & connection, SDWORD id);
protected:
    ProblemStatusNode * pYoungest;
    ProblemStatusNode * pOldest;
};
```

When you create the list using a constructor, it is empty. While empty, you can either add a node or query the nodes from the database or destroy the list. When you add or query nodes, the list is no longer empty. With a not-empty list, you can either add additional nodes (but not query them) or remove nodes; removing the last node makes the list empty.

Figure 11.16 illustrates the test objects the DTS testing team developed as state-transition diagrams:
- create, empty, destroy
- create, empty, addNode, one node, removeNode, empty, destroy

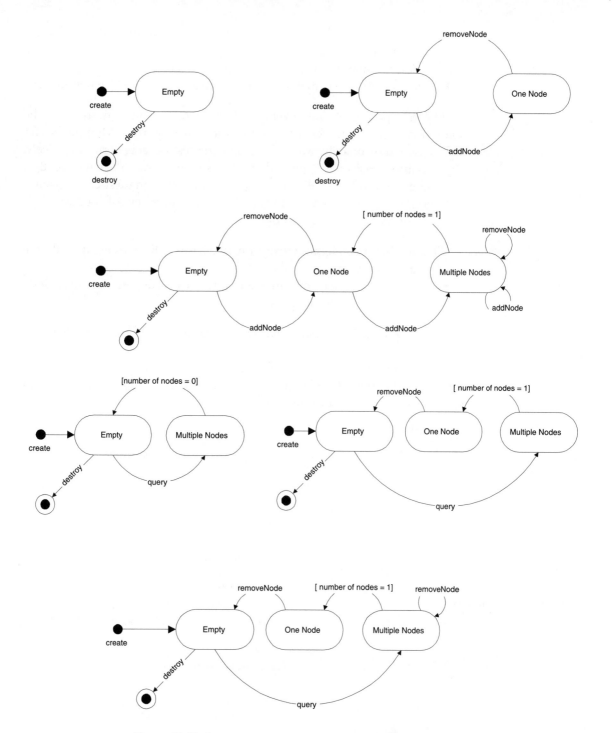

Figure 11.16 State-transition path test objects for ProblemStatusHistory.

- create, empty, addNode, one node, addNode, multiple nodes, addNode, multiple nodes, removeNode, multiple nodes, removeNode, multiple nodes, [number of nodes = 1], removeNode, empty, destroy
- create, empty, query, multiple nodes, [number of nodes = 0], empty, destroy

This last path provided coverage of the two remaining transitions, the query transition and the guarded, automatic transition from Multiple Nodes to Empty. Unfortunately, while this meets the test coverage criterion nicely, it is a relatively rare case: a query that returns no data from the database, thus creating no nodes. It seemed wise to include the following test case as well:

- create, empty, query, multiple nodes, [number of nodes = 1], removeNode, empty, destroy

This queries a single node from the database. A little thought made the tester add one more case as well:

- create, empty, query, multiple nodes, removeNode, [number of nodes = 1], removeNode, empty, destroy

This case tested the retrieval of two nodes, a typical boundary condition test case.

These transition paths convert directly into test scripts that create, process, and destroy ProblemStatusHistory objects. Running this set of test scripts covers all the transitions in the class.

Road Map

Figure 11.17 is the road map for the state-transition test model class.

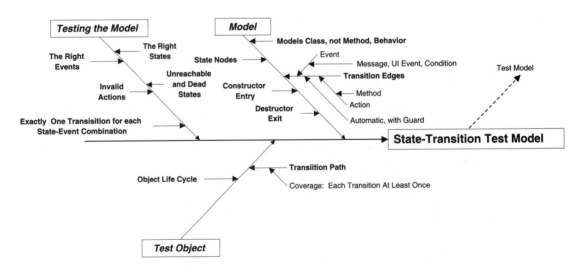

Figure 11.17 Road map for the state-transition test model class.

Transaction-Flow Test Model

A *transaction-flow test model* is a kind of control-flow test model that applies to the class as a whole rather than to just a method of the class. Using the same structures and approaches as the control-flow model, the transaction-flow model scales the control logic up to deal with object life cycles rather than with method life cycles. The model is functional rather than structural because it deals only with the testable behavior of the object, not the internal logic and structure.

A *transaction* is a unit of work. A transaction-flow model shows the processes, decisions, and junctions that make up that unit of work. You can also think of this as a *work-flow* model for the object. In the context of a class, we define the unit of work as the creation, processing, and destruction of the object. Thus, each transaction model consists of the different ways to create an object, the different tasks or processes the object undertakes during its life cycle, and the different ways that you can destroy the object. An individual transaction—a test object—is a path through the transaction-flow graph from birth to death of the object.

The flow graph that models the transaction begins with the construction of the object, possibly with multiple constructions. The flows then model how the object responds to its environment by calling its methods, much as with the state-transition model. Each node in the diagram represents a control point in the sequence of behaviors, as for the control-flow model, or a process or task of interest. Finally, the model terminates the flows when you destroy the object, calling the destructor for the class. The nodes reflect the public attributes and methods of the class, encapsulating all references to other objects and to internal methods and data. The purpose is to create functional tests of this class, not to build a full system test suite. The processing that goes on inside each node may well be very complex, but it belongs to the transaction model of another class, not the one under test. As with all forms of class/object test, the class methods may depend on stubs that return the results you want for testing purposes rather than a full-scale integration; that comes later.

When you've fully constructed your model, review it with a test review. List any class methods that don't appear in the model, and ask the designers whether these methods correspond to missing requirements or whether they should be internal methods instead of public ones. It's also a good idea to have a set of derived transactions listed for review, particularly the grotesque ones. It clears the air wonderfully when designers confront the limits of what their design does.

It is possible that a single object could exhibit concurrent behavior. That would mean that a transaction could be running along multiple paths at once. If this is the case with your system, certainly modify your test scripts to test this possibility. The flow model in this section will help you to identify the transactions, but it does not help much in identifying the concurrent ones, as it has no way to distinguish such paths.

You build the transaction-flow model from the requirements use cases, focusing on the sequence of control decisions that affect the object. The model is thus a functional model, with no direct relationship to the underlying implementation code.

The best place to start building the transaction-flow model is with the traceability matrix associated with the class under test. Usually that will be part of the design documentation for the class. Should your design documentation not link design elements back to requirements (bad) or should you not have any design documentation at all (worse), you can start with the use cases themselves and build the transaction-flow models for all the classes involved. This way of doing it tends to be a lot more work because it doesn't focus on the class but on the use case. Traceability to requirements is an important part of your overall productivity in class testing.

Once you have the use cases, build the model in a series of iterations:

- Eliminate any external references, such as to databases, files, or methods in other classes.
- Simplify the model where possible by combining methods into a single process.
- Review any remaining use case references that don't appear in the class design with the designers; this lack of reference may indicate unfulfilled requirements.
- Review any public methods that don't appear in the model with the designers; this lack of reference may indicate missing requirements or methods that the designers could encapsulate as private to the class.

The techniques in this section derive from the transaction system test model that Boris Beizer details in *Software System Testing and Quality Assurance* (1984) and *Software Testing Techniques* (1990). He applies the techniques at the system testing level, while we also apply them at the object testing level as a functional test of the class.

Figure 11.18 shows the structure of the transaction-flow test model class.

Leadership

Vision: A class with an acceptable risk of failure.

Mission: To test the class to an acceptable level of risk, taking into account time and resources.

Objective 11.6: To test the class to an acceptable level of risk based on functional features.

Approach 11.6: Model the objects using a transaction-flow model and derive transaction paths from that model as test objects with a maximum probability of causing failures.

Measurement 11.6: Model coverage (exercising each flow in the model at least once).

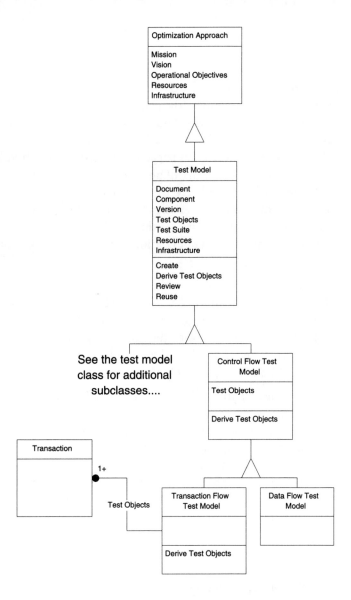

Figure 11.18 Structure of the transaction-flow test model.

Structure

Test Objects

The *test objects* for the transaction-flow model are specifically the *transactions* through the model. See the "Derive Test Objects" section for details on transaction test object derivation.

Dynamics

DERIVE TEST OBJECTS

Once you have defined the transaction model for the class, you must derive the individual transaction-flow paths that exercise each individual flow at least once. Generally this is the same process that you use for control-flow and data-flow test object derivation, but with here you need to think about the object life cycle as a whole instead of just a single method life cycle.

According to Beizer, the minimal covering tests for a transaction-flow test model generally are unlikely to yield many failures. This lower productivity comes from the tendency of designers to understand the "easy" transaction flows better. Your best bet is to find particularly long and involved tests that reflect situations the designers did not consider, or that reflect missing requirements.

Example

The assignment of the DTS testing team was to create a transaction-flow model for the Failure class. The design document for the requirements class referred the modeler back to the requirements for the problem system. The requirements document that addresses the requirements of Technical Support for the DTS provides a simple problem statement for the Problem system:

> Technical Support is a part of the software producer that handles the interface between the customer and the software producer. Technical Support shall be able to enter failure reports (Reporter responsibility role) containing the following information:
> - A unique identifier for the failure
> - The software product that failed, including the name of the product and the specific version of the product that failed
> - Customer reporting the failure, with information sufficient for Technical Support to contact the individual who reported the failure with updated information
> - Date of report
> - Person reporting the failure
> - Description of the failure
> - Description of the hardware and software configuration under which the software failed
> - Any supporting materials (test cases) required to reproduce the failure

The requirements use case for entering a failure report is one use case to which the design for the class refers:

```
1. Create a Failure object.
2. Assign a unique identifier to the failure.
3. Assign a Product object to the failure.
4. Assign a Customer object to the failure.
```

5. Assign today's date to the failure.
6. Assign a Technical Support Engineer object to the failure.
7. Create a String object containing text that describes the failure and assign it to the failure.
8. Create a String object containing text that describes the hardware and software configuration under which the software failed and assign it to the failure.
9. Create OLE objects for any supporting materials required to reproduce the failure and assign links to those objects to the failure.
10. Insert the failure in the database.
11. Repeatedly handle events from the user interface that affect the object (see additional use cases).
12. Update the database as required and repeat handling events.
13. When the document closes, or on deletion of the failure in the database, or on closing the application, destroy the failure object.

Figure 11.19 shows the data-flow diagram representation for this use case. Starting with this data-flow diagram, the modeler developed the transaction-flow model for the Failure class in Figure 11.20. First, the modeler eliminated the data stores, which are external to the object. The purpose is to test the class, not the database into which it stores data. Next, the modeler converted the processes to reflect the methods in the preliminary design for the class:

```
// Class:          Failure
// Description:    A Failure is a defect found in a program.
#include "problem.h"      // Problem base class and system header
#include <emp.h>          // Employee class
#include "faultlst.h"     // FaultList and FaultItr classes
class Fault;
class Failure : public Problem
{
public:
        Failure(Connection & connection, SDWORD id, const String & description,
                const Person & reporter, const TimeStamp & reportDate,
                SWORD published, const Employee & monitor);
        Failure(Connection & connection, SDWORD id);    // query constructor
        Failure(const Failure & Failure);               // copy constructor
        ~Failure() {}
    Failure & operator =(const Failure &);      // assignment operator
    Failure & operator =(SDWORD id);            // query assignment operator
    // Access Methods
    const String & getResponse(TimeStamp &responseDate) const;
    const String & getResolution(void) const {return resolution;}
    const Employee & getMonitor(void) const {return monitor;}
    FaultItr & getFaultItr(void);
    TestCaseItr & getTestCaseItr(void);
    EnhancementItr & getEnhancementItr(void);
    ConfigurationItr & getConfigurationItr(void);
    // Insert and Delete Methods
    RETCODE       insertObject(void); // insert the Failure into the database
    RETCODE       deleteObject(void); // delete the Failure from the database
    // Update Methods
    RETCODE       updateResponse(const String & response, const TimeStamp & responseDate);
    RETCODE       updateResolution(const String &resolution);
    RETCODE       updateMonitor(const Employee & monitor);
    RETCODE       addFault(const Fault & fault);
    RETCODE       removeFault(const Fault & fault);
    };
```

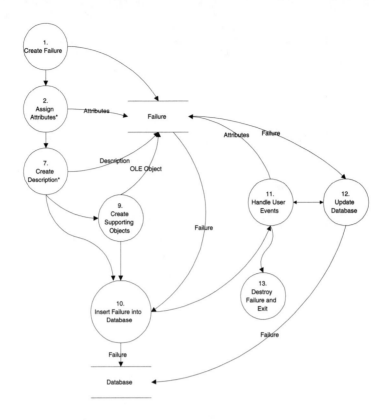

Figure 11.19 DTS Failure class use case diagram.

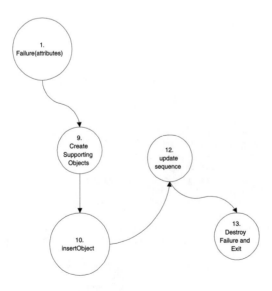

Figure 11.20 Preliminary DTS Failure class transaction-flow model.

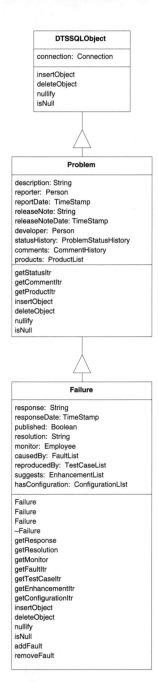

DTSSQLObject

connection: Connection

insertObject
deleteObject
nullify
isNull

Problem

description: String
reporter: Person
reportDate: TimeStamp
releaseNote: String
releaseNoteDate: TimeStamp
developer: Person
statusHistory: ProblemStatusHistory
comments: CommentHistory
products: ProductList

getStatusItr
getCommentItr
getProductItr
insertObject
deleteObject
nullify
isNull

Failure

response: String
responseDate: TimeStamp
published: Boolean
resolution: String
monitor: Employee
causedBy: FaultList
reproducedBy: TestCaseList
suggests: EnhancementList
hasConfiguration: ConfigurationLIst

Failure
Failure
Failure
~Failure
getResponse
getResolution
getMonitor
getFaultItr
getTestCaseItr
getEnhancementItr
getConfigurationItr
insertObject
deleteObject
nullify
isNull
addFault
removeFault

Figure 11.21 DTS Failure class design.

Figure 11.21 shows the OMT object model diagram for this class.

Looking at the processes remaining, the modeler consolidated steps 2 and 7 into the attribute constructor and steps 11 and 12 into a sequence (any sequence) of update method calls. Process 11 is external to the object, and process 12 could

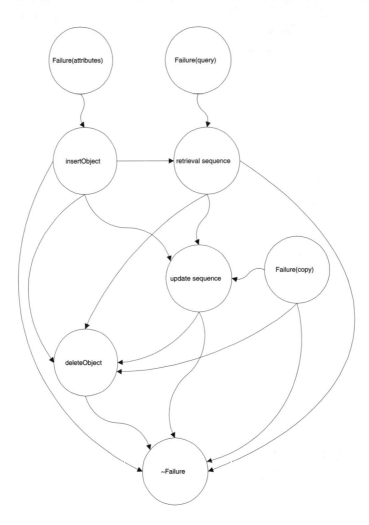

Figure 11.22 Final DTS Failure class transaction-flow model.

be any specific update method. That left process 9, Create Supporting Objects. Looking at the preliminary design, the modeler saw no methods that create test cases, enhancements, or configuration descriptions. At the resulting test review, the designer confirmed that this was a fault, an oversight. There should be a series of update methods for adding to these embedded object lists. Thus, the eventual test model removed the process entirely, absorbing it into the update sequence process.

Further examination of the requirements elicited another constructor for creating the object using a database query and the consequent retrieval of data into the UI. Other requirements use cases specified the processes of adding and removing links to faults (part of the updating process) and of deleting failures from the system.

Figure 11.22 shows the final transaction-flow model for the class. From this model, the DTS testing team derived the following test objects to cover the model:

- Failure(attributes), insertObject, ~Failure
- Failure(attributes), insertObject, deleteObject, ~Failure
- Failure(attributes), insertObject, retrieval sequence, update sequence, ~Failure
- Failure(attributes), insertObject, update sequence, deleteObject, ~Failure
- Failure(query), retrieval sequence, ~Failure
- Failure(query), retrieval sequence, deleteObject, ~Failure
- Failure(copy), ~Failure
- Failure(copy), update sequence, ~Failure
- Failure(copy), deleteObject, ~Failure

After reviewing these test objects, the DTS team decided to add another object for a possibility that would occur fairly often:

- Failure(query), retrieval sequence, update sequence, ~Failure

Because the object life cycle in this case was fairly straightforward, the basic insertion and retrieval test objects were the most tortuous this class has to offer; not much could have gone very wrong in terms of transaction complexity.

One tricky element is the assumption that the two "sequence" items are any valid sequence of methods. However, the essence of the transaction model approach is to encapsulate the class: The actual internal processing of the methods is irrelevant to this model. All of these methods just access attributes or write to the database. These issues get more complicated during integration and system test, where what happens inside the methods starts to matter.

Road Map

Figure 11.23 is the road map for the transaction-flow test model class.

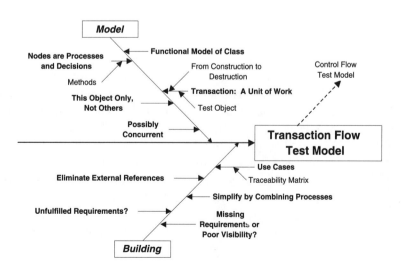

Figure 11.23 Road map for the transaction-flow test model class.

Exception Test Model

The exception test model is a kind of test model that makes explicit certain kinds of behavior that might not be evident in other functional models of the class. An exception, in the abstract sense, is an anomaly in a running program. For example, you can divide by zero, overflow arrays, run out of memory, or use somebody else's class framework (that's a joke), all of which constitute anomalies in your running program. How your program handles these situations is between you and your programming language. Most object-oriented languages now provide some kind of direct support for raising named exceptions and handling them with some designated piece of code. You can use these language features (exceptions in Ada, try and catch blocks in C++, and so on), or you can test for the situation where needed and deal with it right then and there.

Next to providing exceptions and exception handling, the nicest thing an object-oriented design or programming language can do is to let you specify which specific exceptions a method can raise. Many design notations do not let you specify this, OMT included. Many programming languages don't either (Smalltalk doesn't; C++ does with the throw list).

So the justification for yet another test model, the exception test model, comes to two questions:

- Does your base model support the specification of exceptions?
- Does your program raise exceptions in some special way, such as crashing or handling them?

If you answered the first question no and the second question yes, which is the most likely combination of answers, you have a problem. You need to test exceptions (question 2), but you don't know what to test (question 1). You need another test model.

The exception test model consists of the object model (the classes and methods with their relationships) as well as a designation for each method listing the exceptions it can raise—system as well as user-defined exceptions—and the conditions under which the exceptions can be raised. This includes system exceptions as well as user-defined exceptions. The model does not include any information about exception handling; that's an integration issue. See the "Exception Test Model" section in Chapter 11. In the exception test model, we focus on raising the exception, not handling it. We don't look at the internal logic of creating the conditions that lead to the anomaly: This is a functional, not structural, model.

In building the set of exceptions, you should consider all the system exceptions for each class method. Most methods will not contain the elements that could lead to the program anomaly. Some methods turn off the exception in one way or another.

Ch. 11

Exception
Test Model

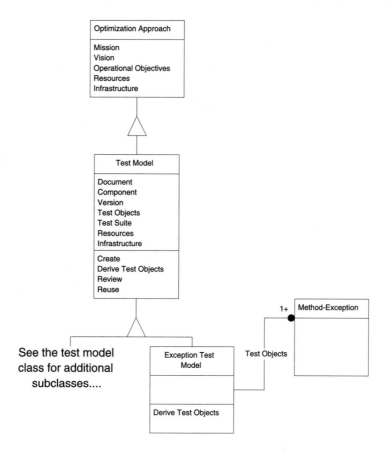

Figure 11.24 Structure of the exception test model class.

Inheritance plays a role in determining exceptions through the inheritance of methods from superclasses. If overloaded methods or situations that arise only in the context of the subclass (such as dividing by a member that can't be zero in the superclass but can in the subclass) affect the exceptional conditions, you need to test the exception again; otherwise, the exception model for the superclass covers inherited exceptions.

To test exceptions, you need to create the situation that causes the method to raise the exception. Thus, the test object for the exception test model is the individual exception for a method. You also may want to add some tests that try to raise exceptions that the program is not supposed to be able to raise. For example, if the method specifies no divide-by-zero exceptions, pass in zero-valued parameters and see what happens.

Figure 11.24 shows the structure of the exception test model class.

Leadership

Vision: A class with an acceptable risk of failure.

Mission: To test the class to an acceptable level of risk, taking into account time and resources.

Objective 11.7: To test the class to an acceptable level of risk based on functional features.

Approach 11.7: Model the objects using a state-transition model and derive transition paths from that model as test objects with a maximum probability of causing failures.

Measurement 11.7: Model coverage (exercising each transition in the model at least once).

Structure

TEST OBJECTS

The test objects in the exception test model are the exception-method combinations, which include the conditions under which the method raises the exception.

Dynamics

DERIVE TEST OBJECTS

Deriving test objects from the exception model is straightforward: Test all combinations of exception and methods for the class.

Example

The DTS Connection class is an interface class that wraps the Microsoft Foundation Class (MFC) Library ODBC cDatabase class for portability. The designers of the class have taken care to isolate exceptions to the single Connection::Connection constructor method, which can only raise a memory exception. MFC raises a standard database exception for problems connecting to the ODBC server, but the Connection class handles all of these.

The DTS tester assigned to this class built a simple test model showing the single method/exception combination, which also became a test object: Create a connection in a situation where there is no free memory. He added another test object: Connect to an invalid ODBC server to make sure the constructor correctly defused the resulting exception. The tester also looked at the standard system exceptions in Visual C++ to make sure that he covered all the bases: archive, file, OLE, user, not supported, and resource exceptions for MFC. None of these were likely to occur; if they did, they would do so during object or integration testing as a fault.

Road Map

Figure 11.25 is the road map for the exception test model class.

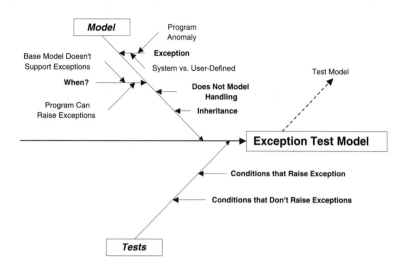

Figure 11.25 Road map for the exception test model class.

Practice

Given the test objects in the state-transition test model example, can you think of tests that would be likely to yield failures beyond those indicated by the test object derivation algorithm? Why do you think the algorithm and the coverage criterion did not consider those test cases?

CHAPTER 12

CONDITIONAL TEST SUITE

Conditional Test Suite

The *conditional test suite* is the suite of test scripts based on conditional models of the class. A *conditional model* describes the logical contract of the class to its clients. Conditional models range from a simple assertion that a single variable must have a certain value at a certain point in a method, through a complex condition that raises an exception, to a complete model of the behavior of a class through a decision table or other logical model.

We limit discussion here to the simpler forms of conditional modeling, as we've found that the more complex forms are beyond the resources and training of most developers and testers. Perhaps if formal specification and design methods become more popular and more automated, formal testing based on complete logical specifications and modeling of classes will be easier. In any case, this kind of test model leads to test objects and scripts as a functional or structural model suitable for inclusion in the hierarchical-incremental test suite. These models are similar in many ways to control-flow, data-flow, transaction-flow, and state-transition models. See Beizer's *Software Testing Techniques* (1990, pp. 320–362) for an introduction to more complex logical modeling techniques.

The conditional test suite brings several benefits to the testing process for classes and objects. It makes assumptions about the class and methods explicit and documents those assumptions in the class code, which makes for both easier debugging and easier maintenance. The process of working through the assumptions using logic often catches obvious mistakes in the code.

This process can serve as a basis for improving other class-object models, thus improving the coverage of the hierarchical-incremental test suite. For example, modeling the class-invariant conditions often makes assumptions about the different states of the object much clearer for the state-transition model. Conditions can serve as discriminants for equivalence classes, partitioning the allowed data values into appropriate domains that you can use in testing control and data flows. You should add test cases to test methods for these equivalence classes. There should be one test case for each disjoint (OR) term in a condition, and you should have at least one test case that violates each condition in your hierarchical-incremental test suite. You can, of course, combine tests into single test scripts as appropriate.

Making the logical assumptions about the class and its behavior explicit also makes the contract between the class and its clients much clearer. The test scripts monitor the degree to which the class fulfills its contract when servicing a request.

Because of its limited modeling, the conditional test suite focuses more on the individual class or method, with less need to take the inheritance or containment hierarchies into account. You are testing the logic of the class to an acceptable level of risk. The actual test scripts tend to be code embedded in your class implementation rather than externally driven scripts. The suite, as such, really consists of a series of checks built into your code as well as some code that other classes and test drivers can access to validate an object at runtime.

You can use four types of test script in the conditional test suite:

- **Assertions:** Program language statements that abort the program if the condition fails.

- **Exceptions:** Program language statements that raise an exception if the condition succeeds.

- **Concurrent test operations:** Program language statements that monitor the condition continuously and handle the situation when the condition succeeds.

- **Message polling test scripts:** Program language statements that evaluate the condition on demand from a client of the class.

The suite thus maps naturally to the class, and there tends to be one such suite of tests for each class in your system. Because the tests follow the coding structure of the system, that structure also guides the planning for the suites. You can plan for a single verification method on each class, for example, and for blocks of code in each method to enforce method-related conditions. Also, since you build your tests into the running code, you naturally reflect the abstract/concrete class and method distinctions. Abstract classes and methods without implementations have no conditional test scripts, since such scripts are fundamentally a part of the implementation.

You do have some restrictions on the conditions that inheritance imposes. The nature of inheritance and dynamic binding means that you can refer to an object of a subclass as if it were an object of a superclass. For this reason, no condition you impose on specific data elements in a subclass can restrict values more than conditions on the same elements in a superclass of that class. That means that you have to specify things that always apply to an object at the highest level in the class hierarchy at which the condition applies. It also means you can't refine conditions in subclasses to be more restrictive. For example, if you have a condition that says a data attribute can be one of three values in a particular class, you have to apply the same condition to all levels of the hierarchy to which that data attribute is visible, which means you put the condition in the class that defines the attribute. If you let one subclass have four values, referring to that subclass as the superclass would violate its contract. Methods must have input conditions that are the same or more general and output conditions that are the same or more restrictive for the same reason.

Coding these test scripts as part of the class has some drawbacks. First, because some test scripts are publicly available or require friendly access to the class internals, the code may violate strict encapsulation. The fact that the code is part of the class may tempt clients to use the test scripts to get at class internals to ìimprove performanceî or other such dubious goals. Doing so can lead to a lot of maintenance problems. Second, adding a lot of conditional testing to every method may have a measurable impact on class performance.

Often you can code these test scripts as code available only during testing or debugging. For example, in C++, you can enclose these scripts in conditionally compiled blocks that vanish when you change a single defined constant on the compiler command line or in a header file. You can have a constant, **CONDITIONAL_TEST**, that if true lets the compiler compile the scripts and if false removes them. When you build your production system, this code vanishes. That means that production code can't use it, preserving encapsulation and improving performance. If you treat conditional tests in this way, you should be sure that you don't need the checks at runtime. For example, if you test for array bounds to make sure nothing uses an array index greater than the number of elements in the array, you should compile it conditionally only if you can ensure that the conditions it tests for won't happen to an acceptable level of risk. To ensure this, you must test the method or methods with the hierarchical-incremental test suite. Also, you should use exceptions for code that needs evaluation in production code and assertions for conditions that need evaluation only during testing and integration. Exceptions make explicit the integration implications for clients through exception handlers, while assertions and other method-based code approaches do not.

If there are any interactions with similarly conditionally compiled code in other classes such as superclasses, make sure you compile all the necessary code conditionally; otherwise you will get compilation or linking errors.

As with hierarchical-incremental tests, conditional tests become part of the regression testing process. You should document your suite, usually in code comments, and you always should make sure to execute these tests during a regression test. For example, if you add code to a class and run a regression test, be sure to turn on the conditional compilation of your conditional tests.

Figure 12.1 shows the structure of the conditional test suite class.

Leadership

Vision: A class that fulfills its contract for services without failure.

Mission: To test the class for adherence to its logical contract to an acceptable level of risk, taking into account time and resources.

Objective 12.1: To test the logical correctness of the class to an acceptable level of risk.

Approach 12.1: Model the class contract using a conditional test model, then derive test objects and build test scripts that implement them.

Measurement 12.1: Model coverage (the degree to which you test each condition at least once).

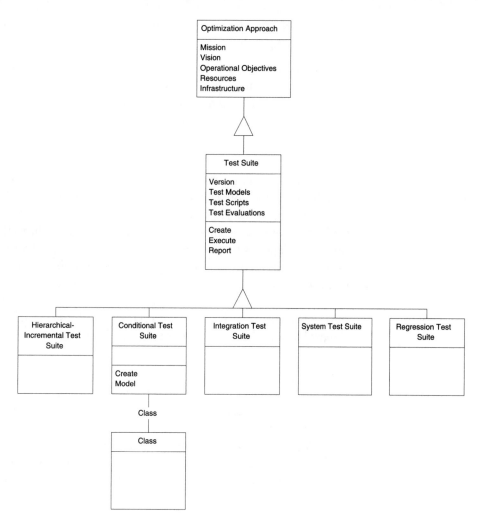

Figure 12.1 Structure of the conditional test suite class.

Structure

CLASS

Each conditional test suite tests a specific class in the system.

Dynamics

CREATE

The process of creating a conditional test suite for a class is relatively straight-forward:

1. Create a conditional test model for the class and its methods. (See the

"Model" section and the "Conditional Test Model" section which follow.)

2. Derive the individual test objects from the model.

3. Translate the test objects into the appropriate format for a test script and put the script in the appropriate place. If possible, combine individual test scripts into aggregate ones to reduce overall size and complexity.

4. Document the test object.

MODEL

The modeling task for a conditional test suite is a matter of thinking systematically about the contract for the class in logical terms, making explicit what is implicit. Since there really is only one model involved, which uses a relatively straightforward modeling technique, this is technically simple. Its real simplicity depends on the fiendishness with which the class designer has done his or her job in contracting. Logic may be pure, but it's not necessarily easy. Contracts may be explicit, but unenforceable—in law and in software.

At some point in your analysis, you will have to decide whether it makes sense to continue modeling or to rely on other test models and suites to find the problems. This is a matter of time and resources.

Example

The DTS testing team had a test standard and test plan that called for conditional testing of specific sorts. For example, a tester developed a model for the fault class that consisted of a series of conditions relating to the pre- and postconditions of the methods and the conditions that applied to all faults at all times. The tester then developed each of the propositions into a C++ relational expression and encoded it in the class implementation.

Road Map

Figure 12.2 is the road map for the conditional test suite class.

Conditional Test Model

The conditional test model describes the contract of the class for services to its clients in logical conditions or sentences (Helm, Holland and Gangopadhyay, 1990). A *logical sentence* is a series of constants related by some combination of *sentential* operators:

> AND: Logical conjunction; the sentence is true if both terms are true.

> OR: Logical disjunction; the sentence is true if either term is true or both terms are true.

> NOT: Logical negation; the sentence is true if the term is not true.

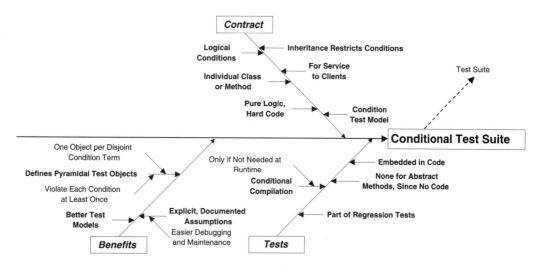

Figure 12.2 Road map for the conditional test suite.

IF-THEN: Logical conditional; the consequent (THEN part) is true if the antecedent (IF part) is true.

IF-AND-ONLY-IF: Logical biconditional; the sentence is true if both terms are true or if both terms are false.

Starting with data attributes in the class and including any other data visible to the class, you can build up a sentence from the individual attributes and the logical operators. We use the term "conditional" for the sentences in this test model because many, if not most, of those you use to model a class are conditional sentences: IF-THEN combinations such as IF the id value is greater than zero, THEN the class is valid.

For more help with how symbolic logic works, see any text on symbolic logic or discrete mathematics, such as Klenk's *Understanding Symbolic Logic* (1989).

As noted earlier in the section on the conditional test suite, we don't intend to model every aspect of the class through sentential logic, just the part of it that ensures that the class will fulfill its contract for services to its client. To do this, you need to model the following types of conditions:

- **Class invariant:** A condition that must be true if the class is valid.
- **Precondition:** A condition that must be true when you execute a method.
- **Postcondition:** A condition that must be true when a method finishes executing.
- **Loop invariant:** A condition that must be true at all times during execution of a loop.

If a class-invariant condition is false, then the class is invalid. Class-invariant conditions hold for all methods of the class and all its super- and subclasses

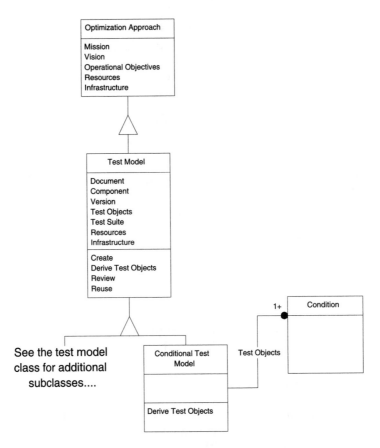

Figure 12.3 Structure of the conditional test model class.

at all times. Since the condition applies everywhere, you must define it where you define its terms. If you define the class attributes over one or more classes, you define the class-invariant condition in the class that defines the last attribute to which it refers. Superclasses that don't define one or more attributes don't need the condition; it doesn't apply to them. Subclasses need to enforce the condition, but you want to enforce it at all the levels, so you need to put it at the first point at which it applies. You generally code class-invariant conditions in verification methods; see "Message Polling Test Scripts."

The pre- and postconditions apply to individual methods. Preconditions apply to the input to the method, while postconditions apply to its output. The combination of the two kinds of condition covers the entire contract for a method: what it needs to do its work and what it promises to supply when it finishes that work. Preconditions usually mean failure to deliver on the part of the client, while postconditions mean failure to deliver on the part of the server. Often the preconditions reflect equivalence classes of inputs that you should test in the hierarchical-incremental test suite. You usually code these conditions as assertions or exceptions (Meyer, 1992).

The loop-invariant condition applies to a specific loop in a method. Because the loop can change data values other than the ones that drive it (the loop condition in a while or until loop, the counters in for loops, and so on), you need to know when certain conditions apply throughout the loop. These conditions are relevant in some way to loop processing, such as the availability of a reference through a pointer. You want to make sure the reference is always valid, that the loop has not wrongly disrupted the reference. Again, you usually code these with assertions or exceptions.

Figure 12.3 shows the structure of the conditional test model.

Leadership

Vision: A class that fulfills its contract for services to its clients with an acceptable level of risk.

Mission: To test the contract to an acceptable level of risk, taking into account time and resources.

Objective 12.2: To test the logical contract of the class to an acceptable level of risk.

Approach 12.2: Model the class using a series of logical propositions that describe class invariants for the class as a whole and pre- and postconditions, loop invariants, exception conditions, and other validity issues.

Measurement 12.2: Model coverage (exercising each condition in the logical model once).

Structure

Test Objects
The *test objects* are sentences, well-formed formulas, that you can express in the sentential calculus using the AND, OR, NOT, IF-THEN, and IF-AND-ONLY-IF operators. Typically these are conditional (IF-THEN) sentences.

Dynamics

Create Test Objects
Look at the data attributes and the class requirements for the class to which the model applies. Work out any logical conditions that apply to the class at all times (class invariants) using the sentential calculus. Make sure the expression applies only to this class and its subclasses, or move it up the hierarchy until that is true. If you focus on the attributes you define in this particular

class, this shouldn't be an issue, since the attributes don't exist for superclasses. But you do have to look at the superclasses to make sure your condition doesn't contradict or even change a condition that applies at a higher level. If it does, it would mean that the current condition allows values that the higher condition does not for attributes the superclass defines.

For each method in the class, work out the pre- and postconditions. Be sure you examine all data the method has available and uses, including global variables, parameters, class (and superclass) data attributes, and local variables. Determine which data come from outside, which are purely internal, and which the method exports back to the client. Create preconditions for the outside variables and postconditions for the exported ones. You should ensure that the method properly initializes or sets the purely internal ones with data-flow test scripts. This is a good time to do domain analysis if you haven't already done it for hierarchical-incremental tests. Think about the domains of individual and joint variables and break the possible sets of values into equivalence classes. Each such class then constitutes a test object. Be clear when the language data typing takes care of the condition and when it requires a test script; express the condition anyway.

For each loop in each method in the class, work out the invariant conditions. Look at the data objects the loop uses. Think about what happens if the value changes during the course of an iteration of the loop. A common issue here is the continuing validity of a pointer to some object that you dereference; another is the possibility of a changing return code from a function or method you call during the course of an iteration. You can express the condition as part of the condition associated with the loop (looping while the return code is okay, for example). Sometimes the looping condition differs from the driving condition; you can add it to the loop test, since it's invariant. But you may want to eliminate the test from production code, or you may want to handle it as an exception.

Example

The Person class was a pretty simple class to analyze for invariants:

```
// Class: Person
// Description: A person is a customer or employee that is part of the system
//              of tracking defects.
#include <sqlobj.h>// DTSSQLObject base class
#include <dtsstr.h>// String class

// static constants for lengths
static const size_tcTitleLength = 100+1;    // Title length + NULL
static const size_tcPhoneLength = 20+1;     // Telephone number length + NULL
static const size_tcExtLength   = 10+1;     // Telephone extension length + NULL
static const size_tcTypeLength  = 8+1;      // Type length + NULL
class Person : public DTSSQLObject
{
public:
                Person(Connection & connection, SDWORD id, const String & firstName,
```

```
                      const String & lastName, const String & title,
                      const String & telephone, const String & extension,
                      const String & fax, const String & personType);
              Person(Connection & connection, SDWORD id);  // query constructor
              Person(const Person & person);      // copy constructor
              Person(Connection &    connection);
              ~Person() {}
Person &      operator =(const Person & person);    // assignment operator
Person &      operator =(SDWORD id);                // query assignment operator
// Access Methods
SDWORD        getId(void) const {return id;}        // return the unique identifier
// Insert and Delete Methods
RETCODE       insertObject(void); // insert the person into the database
RETCODE       deleteObject(void); // delete the person from the database
// Update Methods
RETCODE       updateName(const String & firstName, const String & lastName);
RETCODE       updateTitle(const String & title);
RETCODE       updatePhone(const String & telephone, const String & extension,
              const String & fax);
void          nullify(void) {id = 0;}
BOOL          isNull(void) const {return (id ? FALSE : TRUE);}

protected:
// Primary data members
     SDWORD        id;                      // unique identifier
     String        firstName;               // first name of person
     String        lastName;                // last name of person
     String        title;                   // work title of person
     String        telephone;               // voice phone for person
     String        extension;               // extension for person
     String        fax;                     // facscimile phone for person
     String        personType;              // type of person (Employee, Customer)
};
```

Examining the data members of the Person class, the DTS tester derived the following test objects:

- If id <= 0, then the class is invalid.
- If the title length is greater than 100, then the class is invalid.
- If the telephone is not a valid telephone number, then the class is invalid.
- If the extension is not a valid extension number, then the class is invalid.
- If the fax number is not a valid telephone number, then the class is invalid.
- If the person type is not one of Employee or Customer, then the class is invalid.

The test condition for the length of names was part of the DTSSQLObject class, which ruled over all the different kinds of names in the database. That condition applied here as well by inheritance.

The class-invariant conditions were all relatively simple expressions in C++, so the tester implemented the test script as a **verify()** method on the class to enable message polling and self verification by the class.

The next step was to examine the methods of the Person class. Most of the methods, such as the following **updatePhone** method, were straightforward:

```
RETCODE    Person::updatePhone(const String & telephone, const String & extension,
                    const String & fax)
{
    RETCODE returnCode = SQL_SUCCESS;
    HSTMT       updateHandle;
    SDWORD      nullData = SQL_NULL_DATA; // tells DB to update with a NULL value

    // copy the inputs to the SQL buffers
    telephone.copyToBuffer(telephoneBuffer);
    extension.copyToBuffer(extensionBuffer);
    fax.copyToBuffer(faxBuffer);

    // Allocate the ODBC UPDATE handle
    returnCode = SQLAllocStmt(connection.handle(), &updateHandle);
    RETURN_CODE_IF_ERROR(updateHandle, connection, returnCode);
    // bind the phone numbers to the SET clause
    returnCode = SQLSetParam(updateHandle, 1, SQL_C_CHAR, SQL_VARCHAR,
                cPhoneLength, 0, telephoneBuffer, telephone.size() ? NULL : &nullData);
    RETURN_CODE_IF_ERROR(updateHandle, connection, returnCode);
    returnCode = SQLSetParam(updateHandle, 2, SQL_C_CHAR, SQL_VARCHAR,
                cExtLength, 0, extensionBuffer, extension.size() ? NULL : &nullData);
    RETURN_CODE_IF_ERROR(updateHandle, connection, returnCode);
    returnCode = SQLSetParam(updateHandle, 3, SQL_C_CHAR, SQL_VARCHAR,
                cPhoneLength, 0, faxBuffer, fax.size() ? NULL : &nullData);
    RETURN_CODE_IF_ERROR(updateHandle, connection, returnCode);
    // bind person_ID to the WHERE clause
    returnCode = SQLSetParam(updateHandle, 4, SQL_C_LONG, SQL_INTEGER, 0, 0, &id, NULL);
    RETURN_CODE_IF_ERROR(updateHandle, connection, returnCode);
    // Execute the UPDATE
    returnCode = SQLExecDirect(updateHandle, phoneUpdate, SQL_NTS);
    RETURN_CODE_IF_ERROR(updateHandle, connection, returnCode);
    // Free the handle
    returnCode = SQLFreeStmt(updateHandle, SQL_DROP);
    RETURN_CODE_IF_ERROR(updateHandle, connection, returnCode);

    // Everything succeeded, so copy the inputs to the data members
    Person::telephone = telephone;
    Person::extension = extension;
    Person::fax = fax;
    return(returnCode);
}
```

This method takes input telephone, extension, and fax phone numbers,
updates the attributes in the database, then updates the data attributes of the
Person object. The following test conditions were preconditions for the
method:

- If the telephone is not a valid telephone number, then the class is
  invalid.
- If the extension is not a valid extension number, then the class is invalid.
- If the fax number is not a valid telephone number, then the class is
  invalid.

Looking over the variables the method uses, the tester decided all but the
return code were internal only. The other outputs were the database attribute
value changes and the changes to the data attribute values of the object, but

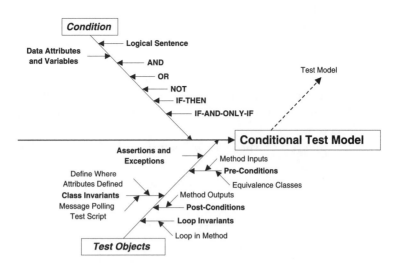

Figure 12.4 Road map for the conditional test model.

neither of these is a relevant conditional test object. The following test condition is the only postcondition for the method:

- If the return code from the method is anything other than SQL_ SUCCESS, then the method is invalid.

There were no loops at all in the Person class, so there was no need for a loop-invariant condition.

Road Map

Figure 12.4 is the road map for the conditional test model class.

Assertion

An *assertion* is a program statement that evaluates a programming language expression to true or false and takes some well-defined action if the expression evaluates to false. Typically, an assertion terminates the program, but only in the debugging mode. When you run the program in production mode, the program ignores assertions. In the quality system, you use assertions as a kind of class-object test script to test condition test objects that you don't want to impose on the production system.

By definition, assertions use the programming language to express the condition. You thus can typically use variable names, constants, expressions, and the various relational, logical, and arithmetic operators. The format of an assertion assumes a conditional test: IF the expression is false, THEN abort the program. The translation of your sentential logic into the programming language may be more or less easy depending on the complexity of your logic.

Assertions are a simple, efficient way to embed conditional tests into your program to facilitate class testing. If you want to test the condition and enforce it at runtime, use exceptions. (See the following "Exception" section.)

Figure 12.5 shows the structure of the assertion test script class.

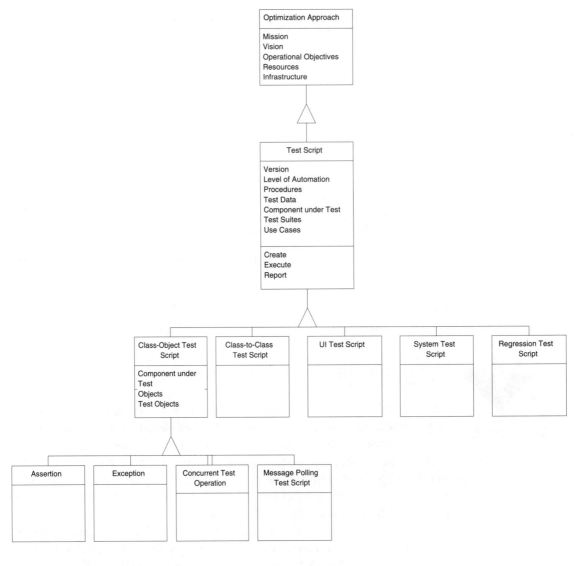

Figure 12.5 Structure of the conditonal testing subclasses.

Leadership

Vision: A clear, concise, and effective procedure to test a test object modeling a condition for a class to an acceptable level of risk.

Mission: To test a condition for a class to an acceptable level of risk.

Objective 12.3: To test a conditional test object to an acceptable level of risk.

Approach 12.3: Embed an assertion into the class implementation that asserts the truth of the condition and fails if it is false.

Measurement 12.3: The ratio of the number of assertion failures during a test run of this class to the expected number of such failures.

EXAMPLE

To assert method preconditions for the Fault class constructor, the DTS tester inserted two assertions about the reporter and reportDate:

```
Fault::Fault(Connection & connection, SDWORD id, const String & description,
             const Person & reporter, const TimeStamp &reportDate)
        : Problem(connection, id, description, reporter, reportDate),
              °pDuplicates((Fault *)0)
{
        ASSERT(!reporter.isNull());
        ASSERT(!reportDate.isNull());
        initializeSQL();
        causalAnalysis.nullify();
        occurredIn.nullify();
}
```

Road Map

Figure 12.6 is the road map for the assertion class.

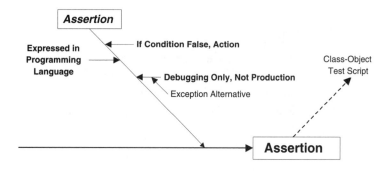

Figure 12.6 Road map for the assertion class.

Exception

An exception is a programming language statement that evaluates a condition and raises an exception if the condition is true. Unlike the assertion, the program raises the exception both in debugging and production environments. You should think of the exception as validating the class or method, as opposed to testing it. The exact sequence of events and transfer of control that occurs when you raise an exception depends on the specific programming language and the exception model you use. For example, in C++ you can use C++ exceptions, compiler exception macros, framework exception macros and functions, and library functions such as signal (a bad idea in C++ because of its inability to handle C++ object destruction properly). While the multiplicity of models makes your job as a coder harder, validating of the class becomes easier.

One major use for exceptions in C++ is to handle validation in constructors, which cannot return data to the client. Exceptions are thus the only mechanism available for handling errors in a constructor, and condition validation is one set of such errors.

Figure 12.7 shows the structure of the exception class.

Leadership

Vision: A clear, concise, and effective procedure to test a test object modeling a condition for a class to an acceptable level of risk.

Mission: To validate a condition in the class.

Objective 12.4: To validate a condition in the class.

Approach 12.4: Embed an exception in the class implementation that raises when the test object condition occurs, either during testing or during a production run.

Measurement 12.4: The ratio of the number of exceptions during a test run of this class to the expected number of exceptions.

Example

The constructor for the Connection class creates a Microsoft Foundation Class object for an ODBC connection. The code following handles the several MFC exceptions, but it also raises a memory exception (AfxThrowMemoryException()) if it can't allocate a CDatabase object on the heap.

```
#include "connect.h"
Connection::Connection(void)
{
    pDatabaseObject = new CDatabase();
    if (pDatabaseObject)
    {
        TRY
        {
```

```
            pDatabaseObject->Open(NULL);
    }
    CATCH(CDBException, pDBException)
    {
            TRACE("Database exception %s on opening connection \n",
                pDBException->m_strError);
    }
    AND_CATCH(CMemoryException, pMemException)
    {
            TRACE("Memory exception on opening connection\n");
    }
    END_CATCH
}
else
{
    AfxThrowMemoryException();
}
}
```

Road Map

Figure 12.7 is the road map for the exception class.

Concurrent Test Operation

The *concurrent test operation* is a programming language statement that continuously validates a condition. The objective for this validation test script is to allow recovery or at least to permit graceful failure. Because of the critical nature of the validation, the operation runs in both production and testing in the same way as an exception, but instead of transferring control up the stack, the concurrent test operation handles the problem on the spot.

The most common form of concurrent test operation in C++ is the test for a null pointer. Null pointers are less common in C++ than in C because of references and the tendency to embed objects in classes rather than dynamically allocating them, but they still exist for many idioms. This test script also often monitors critical hardware failure situations and other vital conditions.

As exception handling improves in object-oriented languages, exceptions tend to replace concurrent test operations. As a nonlocal transfer of control, however,

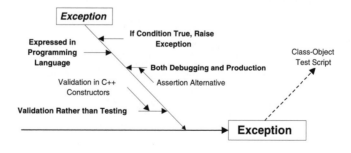

Figure 12.7 Road map for the exception class.

an exception always implies some risk of program failure; a concurrent test operation guarantees that you retain as much control as possible given the failure.

The negative aspect of the concurrent test operation is the overhead. The condition evaluates continuously, consuming possibly precious resources. If performance is critical, more so than recovering from the error gracefully, then assertions or exceptions may provide a better mechanism.

Figure 12.8 shows the structure of the concurrent test object class.

Leadership

Vision: A clear, concise, and effective procedure to test a condition modeling a class to an acceptable level of risk.

Mission: To test a condition for a class to detect critical failures to an acceptable level of risk.

Objective 12.5: To test a condition to an acceptable level of risk.

Approach 12.5: Embed code in the class implementation that concurrently monitors the condition to detect failures.

Measurement 12.5: The ratio of the number of failures during a test run of the class to the expected number of failures.

Example

The DTS isolated most critical failures in the ODBC layer and dealt with them by handling exceptions. The DTS code itself relied on the error-handling mechanisms of ODBC rather than incurring the overhead of a lot of concurrent testing of the database connections and handles.

In several places, however, a method needs to test for a particular result rather than just ignore it. The **deleteObject()** method in the Failure class, for example, checks the ODBC return code after deleting the Problem object from the database to make sure everything happened correctly. If not, the method does not update the class data attributes. It notifies the sender of the error by passing back the return code. This is your normal, everyday concurrent test operation.

```
RETCODE        Failure::deleteObject(void) // delete the Failure from the database
{
    RETCODE returnCode = SQL_SUCCESS;
    returnCode = Problem::deleteObject();   // Delete the Problem first
    if (returnCode == SQL_SUCCESS)
    {
        // copy the id into its buffer, then execute the prepared statement

        idBuffer = id;
        returnCode = SQLExecute(dStmtHandle); // See implementation headers for
dStmtHandle
        RETURN_CODE_IF_ERROR(dStmtHandle, connection, returnCode);
    }
    return(returnCode);
}
```

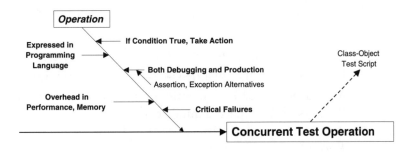

Figure 12.8 Road map for the concurrent test operation class.

Road Map

Figure 12.8 is the road map for the concurrent test operation class.

Message Polling Test Script

A message polling test script is a programming language statement that is part of a set of such statements that validate the status of an object of the class at any time. You package these scripts in a class method called **verify()**, **assertValid()**, or something similar, and clients call the method to validate the status of the class on demand.

Message polling evaluates class-invariant conditions, conditions that are true at all times for all the objects of a class. It's possible that you could find other uses for the validation method, such as specific conditions valid only in a single object, but this is rare.

Message polling as an approach to validating the class has two disadvantages. First, the object relies on the client to ask about problems; it doesn't validate itself automatically (See "Concurrent Test Operation" above.) Second, because the client has access to the method, if you return information from the encapsulated data in the class, you've broken encapsulation. If a production client uses this information through this trapdoor, you have negated most of the benefits of object-oriented programming for maintenance. You should fully encapsulate the validation as much as possible. You also should make the validation method a debug-only method that the compiler ignores in the production compilation.

Figure 12.9 shows the structure of the message polling test script.

Leadership

Vision: A clear, concise, and effective procedure to test a condition modeling a class to an acceptable level of risk.

Mission: To test a class-invariant condition to an acceptable level of risk.

Objective 12.6: To test a class-invariant condition of a class to an acceptable level of risk.

Approach 12.6: Embed the class-invariant condition for a class as an assertion or an exception in a special verification method on the class.

Measurement 12.6: The ratio of the number of failures during a test run of the class to the expected number of failures.

Example

The DTS testers created the following method in the Person class. Various clients would call this function to validate a Person object, including various test scripts in the hierarchical-incremental test suite.

```
// Method:          verify
// Description:        Request verification of object state

#ifdef DEBUG
BOOL Person::verify(void) const
{
    // verify the base class
    BOOL isValid = DTSSQLObject::verify();
    if (isValid)
    {
        ASSERT(id > 0);
        ASSERT(personType == "Customer" || personType == "Employee");
    }
    return(TRUE); // If we made it through the ASSERTs, we're OK.
}
#endif
```

Notice the surrounding #ifdef that removes the function for the production compilation. This prevents clients from verifying the function during production testing, causing potential failures and maintenance problems.

Road Map

Figure 12.9 is the road map for the message polling test script class.

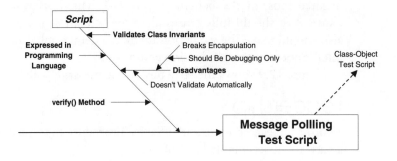

Figure 12.9 Road map for the message polling test script class.

INTEGRATION TEST SUITE

Integration Test Suite

An *integration test suite* represents a series of tests run against an integrated foundation component or cluster of software components. Thus, another name for the integration test suite is *cluster test suite*. A *cluster* is a collection of two or more software components that relate to each other through messaging relationships. The tests in the test suite usually each test a specific component and its integration with other components comprising the cluster. Usually a specific integration test suite relates to a specific software component, even though it may need to execute or use components from other systems to test the primary components fully. Much of this structure depends on how you integrate your components.

When you add a component to a system, and more particularly when you put the component under version control, you are *integrating* the component. Integration can happen as often as once a day (recommended for most systems) or as infrequently as once per implementation iteration. (you're risk prone, so don't go to Vegas anytime soon.) Nightly integration and testing provides a good level of productivity for both testers and coders. The automated integration environment (see Chapter 21) owns the components and builds them automatically, running the integration test suites as required. A foundation component is comprised of a cluster of one or more classes providing a cohesive set of services. Ideally these services are capable of being reused in different systems. Frameworks, libraries, and functional subsystems are examples of foundation components. They are quite literally the foundation components for many different potential systems.

Ch. 21

Automated
Integration
Environment

The ultimate cluster is the system, all the technical components working together. The difference between an integration test suite that tests the whole system and a system test is that the latter tests the system as a whole, not as the sum of various parts. Doing so entails some specific kinds of tests outside the scope of the integration test suite; it also entails testing in an external environment that mirrors the environment in which you actually will use the system. The integration test suite does not require testing in a complete environment in this way. See Chapter 14 for more information on testing the system as a whole.

Ch. 14

System
Component
Test Suite

The integration test suite is a concrete class. There are two specialized kinds of integration test suites, both of which derive from specializations of the partitioning scheme of the cluster.

- **Functional Test Suite:** Tests the vertical integration of a cluster of software components; that is, the way the cluster implements specific functions from the requirements.
- **Abstraction Test Suite:** Tests the horizontal integration of a cluster of software components; that is, the way the cluster abstracts a service contract into an application programming interface (API).

Many less common partitioning schemes exist for specifying the set of components in your cluster.

For example, perhaps some portion of the system has a special set of relationships between the classes (company people versus outside people in the DTS, for example). This may correspond to a separate UI or some kind of subject-related, conceptual relationship that you want to test separately. This is a *technical* partition.

Another possibility is that you will deliver part of the system ahead of other parts as a consequence of resource loading and scheduling in the project plan. This is a *project* schedule partition.

Yet another possibility is that you have several teams working on different aspects of the very large system, and you want to break up the testing to follow the team-based integration efforts. This is *organizational* partitioning.

A related kind of partitioning is when you actually subcontract out part of a system to a contractor and require him or her to test the partition: This is *contractual* partitioning. Generally, contractual partitioning is done as a component, but it may be possible to break very large components into pieces. This kind of clustering is probably fairly risky, however, and restructuring into separate clusters reduces the risk substantially.

Finally, it may make sense to test a cluster of classes that spans two or more systems, essentially creating an orthogonal system across the physical system organization. For example, in the DTS, the Problem and Product systems interrelate quite strongly, and you'd find it hard to construct a test suite that tests a cluster of classes from one of these two systems without testing the other.

Deciding on the partitioning leads into deciding on the nature of the tests. Integration testing could easily duplicate a lot of work done before integration. You should test only integrated components that have gone through requirements and design reviews to ensure that you have the right set of requirements and components as a benchmark. You also should ensure that you have put the component(s) through full suites of hierarchical-incremental and conditional tests. If you don't have a firm foundation, you're going to spend a lot more time in integration testing than you need to finding and fixing all the problems with requirements, design, and coding of the individual classes. This stuff is basic, so let's emphasize the point: **TEST OBJECTS BEFORE TESTING CLUSTERS OF OBJECTS!** Make sure your classes are safe by themselves before throwing them to the wolves. Having made the individual class safe, you then can focus on the risks associated with integration rather than combining local and foreign risks.

Two abstract categories of tests test more than one class at a time, and these test script classes focus your attention on integration risks as opposed to requirements, design, and coding risks:

- **Class-to-Class Test Script:** A test script that tests the interactions between two classes based on a message relationship; includes protocol-interface tests, synchronization tests, and exception handling tests.

- **UI Test Script:** A test script that tests the UI components of the cluster and the software components on which they depend; includes true-time tests, character-recognition tests, and widget-playback tests.

Sections on these classes and subclasses of the test script follow.

The other aspect of integration that affects testing directly is the way in which you go about integrating. Because of the interdependencies, there is a "natural order" to the way the parts fit together. If you're building a house, it's not a good idea to ignore the natural order of things. But with software, you can fool mother nature, at least for a while. You can stub out methods or entire classes with minimal implementations that just return fake data, or you can just not make the calls until you're ready to supply the called parts. You do less overall work building in the natural order, but scheduling and resources often make that inefficient from the perspective of the larger project.

Integration approaches can proceed in order from the bottom up (called classes and methods integrated first, then the ones that call them, then the ones that call them, and so on until you have a complete system). Or they can proceed from the top down, building and discarding stubs as you go. Many object-oriented systems do pieces here and there, driven more by available resources and scheduling issues rather than architectural issues. Reusable classes, when you integrate them into the system as opposed to just calling them from the system, may fill in holes in the natural hierarchy in random ways as well.

All of these approaches have direct implications for developing the integration tests. Some integration test approaches make sense only when you have the entire group of classes in place. Others can start when you integrate just two or more classes. Your test planning needs to track the integration planning in engineering, and you will need the flexibility to respond to schedule changes and architectural changes that affect integration order. This is a key point for project communication, because if the integration tests aren't ready, you can do a lot of spinning on the code integrated before you get to testing. Integration testing, and integration in general, is a *team* effort and a *team* responsibility.

You should design your test suites carefully around your project management requirements, among other things. If the test suite (a collection of test scripts) can't run against the current integration because all the classes in the cluster aren't there, you've wasted a build.

For integration testing purposes, your test model should reflect all the equivalent relationships between classes, including those between classes in different systems. This may mean repeating tests in several clusters if the relationships involve two-way roles with mutual visibility (that is, where each class "knows" about the other class, instead of one knowing about the other but not vice versa—got that?). This repetition lets you integrate systems separately without worrying about the completeness of your test plan. You should note, however, that if you integrate a system that other systems depend on, you need to perform integration testing on all the systems involved, not just the single one you are integrating.

Integration testing also brings under test the passive components of the system, such as data files, resource files, and databases. Since these are passive, you really can't test them until you integrate them with the active objects that use them. The specific test scripts that make up your integration test suite should contain tests of the use of these objects through the test model. You also can use the various kinds of reviews to test the structure and contents of these objects—always a good idea.

Dynamic relationships exist as well, because objects relate to each other through possibly concurrent messaging protocols operating in multiple, coexisting scenarios. Although each object in itself may be relatively simple in its internal dynamic behavior, from the perspective of state-transition models for the classes in the system the possible combinations of objects linked through messages is staggering. You can use such models effectively to test individual classes in isolation, but using them to test integrated components or systems quickly becomes impossible. In addition, dynamic binding and concurrency imply the impracticality of fully specifying the full set of relationships between objects, so integration testing must of necessity use scenarios, or *use cases*, to test components.

Integration testing finds these kinds of *messaging* errors:

- Failure to meet requirements, such as an interface not containing a method required to send or receive a message
- Message sent to the wrong receiver
- Wrong type of message sent (sequential, synchronous, asynchronous)
- Incorrect message priority
- Incompatible message and method in sender and receiver
- Incorrect event timing between object actions
- Incorrect initialization of objects with respect to other objects
- Incorrect destruction of objects with respect to other objects

Integration testing finds these kinds of *user interface* errors:

- A given sequence of user actions (a use case) does not have the desired effect on the component
- The timing of events received from the user results in the incorrect functioning of the component
- Failure to meet functional requirements, such as an external interface not containing a command needed to access part of the component
- Failure to meet performance requirements of the component

As with any test suite and test model, you need to base your testing on your acceptable level of risk rather than comprehensively testing every aspect of the system. In the case of integration testing, identifying and covering high-risk test objects is particularly important doing so requires reference to a technical risk analysis and risk management plan.

Some integration testing is conceptual in nature and thus requires inspection rather than automated testing. For example, comparing the source code with the design to verify that the code reflects the design decisions is usually a matter of inspection rather than automated comparison, as most designs are paper-based, not automated.

Figure 13.1 shows the class design for the integration test suite.

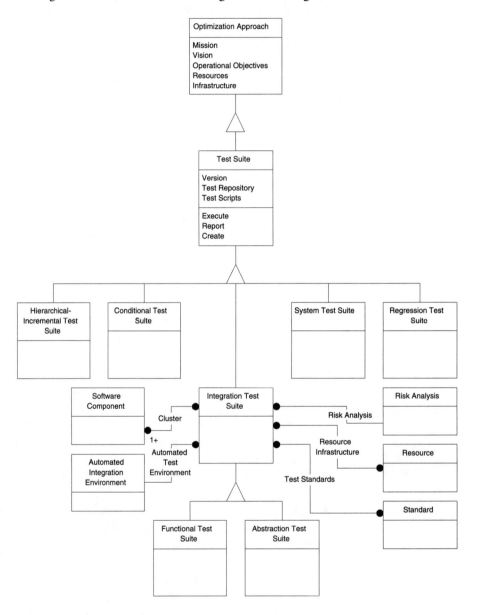

Figure 13.1 Structure of the integration test suite class.

Leadership

Vision: A reusable, robust software cluster of components that meets its requirements.

Mission: To validate and verify to an acceptable level of risk the internal and external interfaces in a cluster of software components.

Objective 13.1: To test the cluster to make sure it's doing the right thing; to validate the cluster against its requirements.

Approach 13.1: Build a test model based on requirements use cases for the cluster of components and test each test object in that model with a test script, recording both failures to meet requirements and the inability to match a component feature against requirements.

Measurement 13.1: Ratio of failed requirements to total requirements, where a failed requirement is either a requirement associated with one or more test script failures or a test object that does not correspond to any known requirement.

Objective 13.2: To test the cluster to make sure it's doing the thing right; to verify the cluster to an acceptable level of risk.

Approach 13.2: Extend the test model with test objects that make the clustered components fail to your acceptable level of risk, then create test scripts that cover the test model.

Measurement 13.2: Test model coverage, the ratio of test objects tested to total test objects.

Objective 13.3: To improve productivity and quality of integration testing through automation.

Approach 13.3: Build the test scripts and data into an automated testing environment and document the objects, data, and procedures to encourage reuse of the tests in other test suites and systems.

Measurement 13.3: Effort per execution of the integration test suite, including that of executing the manual test scripts.

Automating your testing has all kinds of benefits. See Chapter 21 for more details.

Structure

CLUSTER

The integration test suite tests classes and other software components in a particular *cluster* and, through it, the relationships of the objects in that cluster to each other. This can involve several components.

AUTOMATED TEST ENVIRONMENT

Ch. 21

Automated
Test
Environment

Because the integration process benefits in many ways from complete automation, the integration test suites that execute as part of the integration process require an *automated test environment*. See the "Automated Integration Environment" section in Chapter 21 for more detail. Not every script takes advantage of automation; some are manual inspection scripts. However, because it fulfills a specific objective for the class, this relationship is important enough to be an attribute of the class.

RISK ANALYSIS

It is usually impossible to test all the possible relationships between objects in the component, and it is certainly unlikely that you will have the time or resources to do so with a component of any size. The *risk analysis* identifies the parts of the component most likely to fail, then provides a cost-benefit analysis of the tests involved in reducing that risk. Risks not suitable for risk reduction through review or other nonautomatic techniques are then candidates for automated integration testing. You need to identify the acceptable level of risk you are willing to tolerate; this in turn lets you simplify the test model to set the risk of failure to that level. Setting this level is usually a subjective judgment on your part. No one has devised a system of risk metrics capable of quantifying this sort of analysis for software. See the section on risk analysis for details on what you can do here.

INFRASTRUCTURE

To create integration test suites, testers need tools that identify the objects to test and their relationships to one another. Such tools include class browsers, interactive debuggers, and other software inspection tools that are part of the software development environment. You can make use of automated test script generators to build test scripts, though there are few of interest at the integration level.

At that level, you need test standards that specify how robust the cluster must be to call integration successful. Generally this means setting the acceptable level of risk with reference to a specific threshold of failure for the cluster.

Example

The Person system of the DTS is a base system in that it refers only to the database access libraries and system libraries, not to other application systems. There are no relationships from the Person system to other application systems such as Product and Problem. Those systems do have links to Person, but Person does not have links to them. Person gets data from and puts data into the database.

After each day of implementing the Person system, the programming and test development teams turned the system over to the integration team by checking in all the system files and test scripts to the version control system before leaving for the day. The automated testing environment automatically built the system, recompiling all changed components, then executed the integration test suites. The automated suite generated a report on failures and sent the report to the integration test team, the integration autarch, and the project manager.

The ODBC component of the DTS, which is part of the Port library, was beyond the expertise of the DTS system team. They contracted out this part of the library to a small company that specialized in ODBC interfaces. The contract listed a set of requirements for integration testing that treated the work as a system within the DTS, even though it is part of a larger system, the Port library. The contract would perform the tests on this system, and the DTS would perform tests on the rest of the Port library. The ODBC tests were a contract deliverable, and the team integrated the test scripts into the regression test suite for the Port library after accepting the system from the contractor.

Road Map

Figure 13.2 shows the road map for the integration test suite.

FUNCTIONAL TEST SUITE

One way to partition a system for testing purposes is to focus on a specific function of the system. You define functions by use cases or scenarios from the requirements for the system. Various classes in the system support parts of the function, and the *functional test suite* is a kind of integration test suite that focuses on how well the system implements the requirement realized in the use case or cases that the script tests. The test scripts must construct the

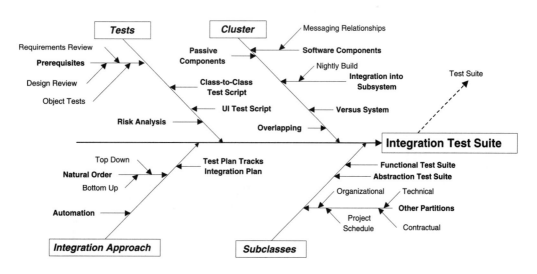

Figure 13.2 Road map for the integration test suite.

appropriate objects, call the indicated methods, and compare the results to expected results, all as the use cases or requirements require.

Another term for this kind of test is *vertical integration test.* The term "vertical" refers to a vertical path through the containment hierarchy of the system representing the objects involved in the use case.

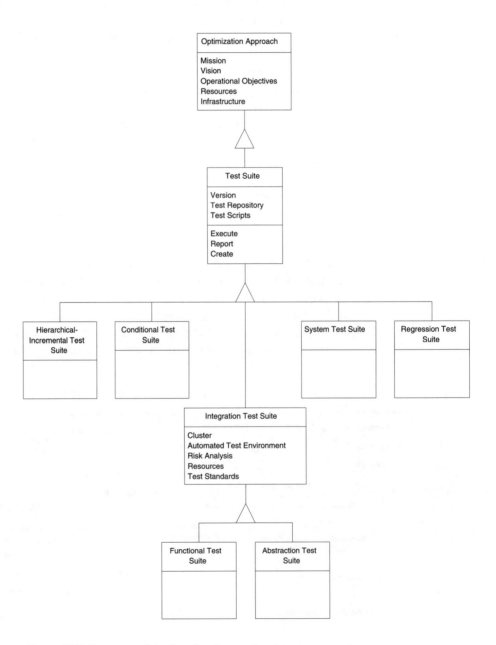

Figure 13.3 Structure of the functional test suite class.

You will find it difficult to perform this kind of partition if the system designers did not keep the functional requirement in mind. Object-oriented design techniques often ignore functional requirements, reconstituting them as part of the overall working of the system. You should focus on other ways to cluster your tests if this is the case with your system. System testing will then test the use case requirements—with any luck.

Figure 13.3 shows the structure of the functional test suite class.

LEADERSHIP

Vision: A reusable, robust software system that meets requirements.

Mission: To validate and verify to an acceptable level of risk the functional interfaces in a cluster of software classes.

Objective 13.4: To test the cluster to make sure it's doing the right thing; to validate the cluster against its functional requirements.

Approach 13.4: Build a test model based on requirements use cases for the cluster of classes and test each test object in that model with a test script, recording both failures to meet requirements and the inability to match a component feature against requirements.

Measurement 13.4: Ratio of failed functional requirements to total functional requirements.

Objective 13.5: To test the cluster to make sure it's doing the thing right; to verify the cluster to an acceptable level of risk.

Approach 13.5: Extend the test model with functional test objects that make the clustered classes fail to your acceptable level of risk, then create test scripts that cover the test model.

Measurement 13.5: Test model coverage, the ratio of functional test objects tested to total functional test objects.

STRUCTURE

There are no new attributes for this class, though there are restrictions on the system and the use cases. You must define the system functionally, and there must be only a single use case associated with the test. The test objects are generally functional protocols that correspond to class-to-class test scripts or possibly, though rarely, UI test scripts.

EXAMPLE

The DTS partitioned into library systems using a connection heuristic that used database relationships between tables to decide where the class belonged, resulting in several systems that coalesced around certain basic classes of object: Person, Product, Problem, Port, and Tools. The Port system contained the framework portability layer, an abstract layer encapsulating the Microsoft Foundation Library classes and the ODBC connectivity classes.

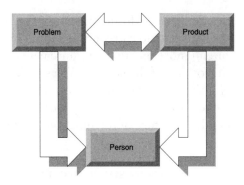

Figure 13.4 DTS system visibility relationships.

Figure 13.4 shows the relationships between the systems. The Product and Problem systems used elements of the Person system, which knew nothing of the other systems. The Product and Problem systems used each other's objects but were loosely coupled through just a few direct relationships between objects.

To test the functional system integration, the DTS testers needed to develop scenarios of use through the requirements. The requirements document that addressed the requirements of technical support for the DTS provided some use cases for the Problem system:

Technical Support is a part of the software producer that handles the interface between the customer and the software producer. Technical Support shall be able to enter failure reports (Reporter responsibility role) containing the following information:

- A unique identifier for the failure
- The software product that failed, including the name of the product and the specific version of the product that failed
- Customer reporting the failure, with information sufficient for Technical Support to contact the individual who reported the failure with updated information
- Date of report
- Person reporting the failure
- Description of the failure
- Description of the hardware and software configuration under which the software failed
- Any supporting materials (test cases) required to reproduce the failure

The use case for entering a failure report looked like this:

```
1. Create a Failure object.
2. Assign a unique identifier to the failure.
3. Assign a Product object to the failure.
4. Assign a Customer object to the failure.
```

5. Assign today's date to the failure.
6. Assign a Technical Support Engineer object to the failure.
7. Create a String object containing text that describes the failure and assign it to the failure.
8. Create a String object containing text that describes the hardware and software configuration under which the software failed and assign it to the failure.
9. Create OLE objects for any supporting materials required to reproduce the failure and assign links to those objects to the failure.
10. Insert the failure in the database.
11. Repeatedly handle events from the UI that affect the object (see additional use cases).
12. Update the database as required and repeat handling events.
13. When the document closes, or on deletion of the failure in the database, or on closing the application, destroy the failure object.

There was one functional test script for each of the use cases based on these requirements (and on other requirements that affected the system). For the failure entry use case, a test script created a Failure, assigned the various data items, inserted the object into the database, and destroyed the object. This script functionally exercised all the parts of the system required by the use case (and the requirements).

ROAD MAP
Figure 13.5 shows the road map for the functional test suite.

ABSTRACTION TEST SUITE
The *abstraction test suite* is a kind of integration test suite that verifies the services of an abstract layer of the system. Abstraction, in this case, is horizontal: It refers to the abstraction of a service layer or application programming interface from an underlying set of objects, or even functions. This could be called a *horizontal integration test*, as it deals with a horizontal line through the containment hierarchy of the system, representing the API. The test tests the integration of the API layer with the underlying classes and functions that it abstracts. The test scripts

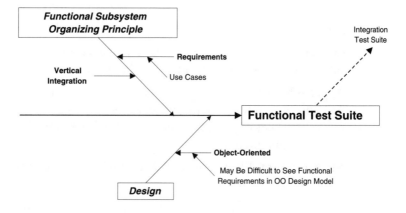

Figure 13.5 Road map for the functional test script.

must construct the required objects, call the methods indicated by the use cases in the requirements, and then destroy the objects.

An example of this kind of partitioning of the system is an API that encapsulates the necessary programming to access a DBMS product. Most such products have no C++ API and rely on a functional programming interface. Many object-oriented systems build a system devoted to encapsulating the necessary features in a set of classes such as Table, SQLStatement, and so on. Another way to encapsulate this is to create a *model layer* that represents the basic objects in the system and encapsulates the database calls within standard methods on the objects. See the "Example" section below.

Again, you will find it difficult to perform this kind of test if the architect did not keep the API in mind during design. An encapsulating API could span systems for any given use case. Generally you can regard this as a design flaw, but if justified by other requirements, you should focus on other aspects of architectural testing and ignore this one. That is, pay attention to project politics here.

The test scripts in the abstraction test suite tend to overlap conceptually with some class-object test scripts from the hierarchical-incremental test suite. If, for example, a use case involves only messages to a single object, then hierarchical-incremental testing should have already exercised those methods. But the purpose of abstraction testing is to verify the abstraction, not to test the methods; the hierarchical-incremental test could well have stubbed out the underlying code, testing only the code the developer actually put into the object. The abstraction test actually exercises the underlying code to make sure its operation satisfies the requirements for the API. Also, the abstraction test can add intermediate objects of other classes and calls to those objects to provide a more realistic test of the abstraction. See the example that follows.

Figure 13.6 shows the structure of the abstraction test suite class.

LEADERSHIP

Vision: A reusable, robust software API layer that meets abstraction requirements.

Mission: To validate and verify to an acceptable level of risk the API.

Objective 13.6: To test the API to make sure it's doing the right thing; to validate the API against its functional requirements.

Approach 13.6: Build a test model based on requirements use cases for the API and test each test object in that model with a test script, recording both failures to meet requirements and the inability to match a component feature against requirements.

Measurement 13.6: Ratio of failed functional requirements to total functional requirements.

Objective 13.7: To test the API to make sure it's doing the thing right; to verify the API to an acceptable level of risk.

Figure 13.6 Structure of the abstraction test suite class.

Approach 13.7: Extend the test model with API-related test objects that make the API fail to your acceptable level of risk, then create test scripts that cover the test model.

Measurement 13.7: Test model coverage, the ratio of API-related test objects tested to total API-related test objects.

EXAMPLE

The DTS used an ODBC layer as part of the Port library to provide a horizontal layer of database access services. Because this layer underpinned the object layer of Faults, Failures, and Persons, the DTS testing team tested it separately as a layer and also tested the integration of the object layer with the ODBC layer as a cluster/abstraction test. The ODBC classes did not connect to the other classes in the Port library. For example, all ODBC connections went through a single class, the Connection class, which encapsulated the MFC library interface to ODBC as the Connection API:

```
// Class:                        Connection
// Description:                  Encapsulates a framework ODBC connection
// For MFC, encapsulates a "CDatabase" object. Opening the connection
// prompts for the ODBC data source and connects to it.
#include <afxext.h>             // CFormView class
#include <afxdb.h>              // include MFC ODBC classes
#include "port.h"               // portability library header
class Connection
{
public:
    Connection(void);
    ~Connection();
    HDBC        handle(void) const;      // return the MFC connection handle
    BOOL        begin(void);             // start a transaction
    BOOL        commit(void);            // end a transaction with COMMIT WORK
    BOOL        rollback(void);          // end a transaction with ROLLBACK WORK
    BOOL        isValid(void);           // is the connection valid?
    void        handleError(HSTMT handle, RETCODE returnCode);
protected:
CDatabase * pDatabaseObject;
};
```

While testing the Port system, the DTS testing team needed to develop an abstraction test suite to test the ODBC layer. This particular class abstracted three basic features of ODBC: connecting to a database server, handling transaction management commands, and handling server errors. The abstraction test suite tested these three abstracted functions with class-object test scripts that exercised the required features. For example, one script connected and disconnected to a specific server, ORACLE7. Another script connected, performed a basic transaction, and committed. Another rolled back. Another created an error situation and handled the error through the **handleError** method. Most of these scripts happened to overlap with hierarchical-incremental test suite scripts, since the single class contained all the features. Some of them involved things outside the class, such as the work done in the transaction, which required a SQL statement and the features involved in executing it on the server. Technically, then, this was an integration test, not a hierarchical-incremental test, though it could happen during a hierarchical-incremental test suite if you wanted it to. Ordinarily, though, the programmer would provide a test stub for the lower-level calls to ODBC during hierarchical-incremental testing of the Connection class.

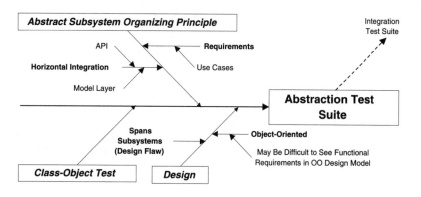

Figure 13.7 Road map for the abstraction test suite.

ROAD MAP

Figure 13.7 shows the road map for the abstraction test suite class.

Class-to-Class Test Script

Class-to-class testing tests the compatibility of classes by focusing on the messages between objects. The *class-to-class test script* is an abstract class that tests the *internal interfaces* between any two classes, including the primary interfaces that other systems call (often termed the *system Application Programming Interfaces* or system APIs). The term "class-to-class" comes from the fact that message-related integration tests are essentially two-class tests: A message has a sender and a receiver. These can be objects of the same class. The actual test refers to objects, but you are testing the classes.

You can see each class as an API, or you can see clusters of classes as APIs if doing so makes conceptual sense. The functional test suite, a kind of architectural test suite, tests such APIs conceptually, while the *interface test suite* tests the class-based parts of the APIs. You can organize class-to-class *interface and protocol test scripts* within a framework of architectural testing to ensure systematic testing of the API.

Timing is an important part of messaging, especially in systems that support concurrent or parallel behavior (*multitasking, multithreading,* or *concurrency*). A *synchronization test script* tests the timing requirements and behavior of objects. These tests also verify the behavior of objects that "receive events," really messages from external objects.

Finally, objects in many object-oriented systems can raise or throw *exceptions,* program anomalies handled by exception handlers in the object or in objects that have sent messages to the object. An exception is a reverse message that sends information from a receiver back to a sender. The *exception test script* should test possible exception conditions and handlers. It's also the place to test the whirlwind you reap when you sow your concurrent program with exceptions in parallel classes. Dynamic binding has nothing on this situation. Figure 13.8 shows the class design for the class-to-class test script.

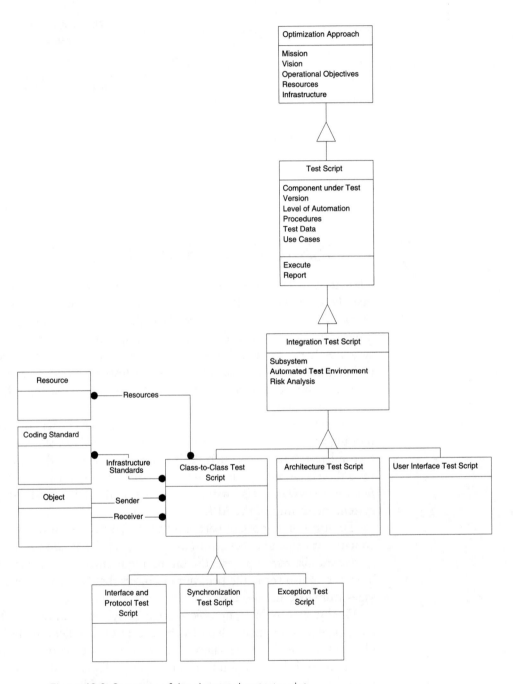

Figure 13.8 Structure of the class-to-class test script.

Leadership

Vision: A system of compatible classes that work together cooperatively and correctly to satisfy requirements.

Mission: To verify the internal interfaces between classes in the system.

The subclasses define the operational objectives relevant to the particular sort of class-to-class test.

Structure

SENDER

The class-to-class *sender* is an object of the class that sends a message from one of its methods to the receiver.

RECEIVER

The class-to-class *receiver* is an object of the class that receives a message from the sender. The receiver object can be an object of the class or of any subclass of the class. If the subclass overloads the method the message refers to, you have a dynamically bound message. That means you can't determine the exact class (and hence the exact method that executes) until you get there.

RESOURCES

Class-to-class testing requires a knowledge of the programming language in which you construct the classes. It also requires training in the kinds of testing involved in testing object methods.

INFRASTRUCTURE

Standards for protocol definition, documentation, and calling may exist that you will need to apply in checking the protocol and interface.

Road Map

Figure 13.9 is the road map for the class-to-class test script.

Interface and Protocol Test Script

The *interface and protocol test script* tests the messages sent from objects of one class to objects of another class (technically, the objects can be of the same class) for compatibility and validity.

One class can interact with other classes in the system through messages in an infinite number of ways. *Interface* testing tests the ways they actually *do* interact; its purpose is not to create jobs for interface testers. To develop these test scripts, you need to know how one class calls other classes, and you need to build test scripts based on that knowledge to test the compatibility of the actual message with the method of the receiver. The techniques you use are similar to those you use in testing object methods: equivalence classes of arguments, testing boundary conditions, and so on. The tests and results must take into account the sending class context,

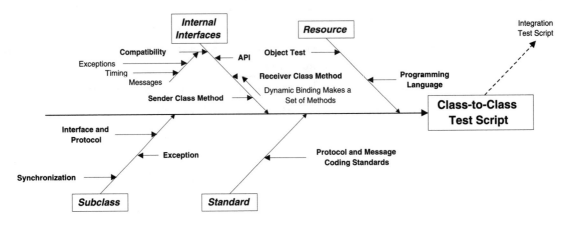

Figure 13.9 Road map for the class-to-class test script class.

however, and must provide an appropriate set of equivalence classes for the message parameters that almost certainly differs from the single-object tests. You can get a lot more accurate if you know how the sending class constrains the message. But you are at least one step removed, as you are calling the methods that call the methods you are testing; that means that you must necessarily be vaguer about the exact call itself.

Put another way, the interface test is similar to the abstraction test script in that you are testing the underlying integration, not just the class under test. Your focus is on the request for service that the sender class provides to the receiver class in terms of compatibility, consistency, and correctness.

Dynamic binding creates the possibility of a set of messages (sender and receiver combinations), which means you need several tests instead of one to test a specific message.

The flip side of testing this class-to-class relationship is the *protocol test*, the testing of the contract between the classes. The focus here is on the service that the receiving class provides to the specific sender and whether that service fulfills the contract. This requires an understanding of the contract that design and requirements use cases define. The contract consists both of the relationship between the classes (such as supporting one-to-many or many-to-many relationships) and the requirements for the service that the receiver performs.

You also should make sure that the objects create and destroy the appropriate nested objects by sending the appropriate constructor and destructor messages. A common flaw in object-oriented programming is failure to *initialize* an object properly by constructing the objects it contains at the appropriate time. Another, very common flaw is to fail to destroy these objects at the appropriate time, which leads to *memory leaks*. Some construction and destruction gets done "on the fly" through compiler initialization (such as through static initializers in C++) or on the stack when you send a message, passing parameters by value instead of by reference. Your test script should verify the appropriate construction and destruction under all these circumstances.

Again, you actually are using objects with the test scripts, but you are testing the classes and the class relationships.

Figure 13.10 shows the structure of the interface and protocol test script.

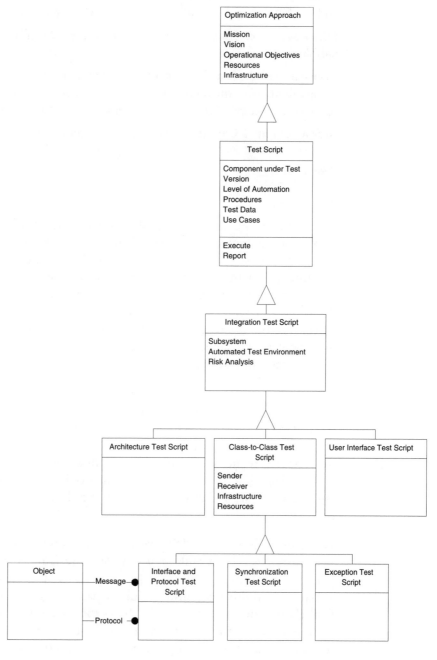

Figure 13.10 Structure of interface and protocol test script class.

Vision: A pair of compatible classes in a contract-fulfilling client/server relationship.

Mission: To test the interfaces and protocols between the classes to validate and verify the contract and its implementation as a method.

Objective 13.8: To discover the maximum number of failures due to incompatibility of classes.

Approach 13.8: Test the messages sent from an object to another object for compatibility with the methods of the receiver, and test the performance of the receiver on receipt of the message to ensure it performs the required services.

Measurement 13.8: Number of interface compatibility or service failures.

Structure

PROTOCOL

The *protocol* is the definition of the message structure (the *method protocol*) as it exists in the receiver; this is an element of the class. It provides whatever details are necessary about the protocol to decide whether a specific message is compatible with the receiver. This information includes the name of the method, the list of arguments, and the return object. The argument specifies the name and type of the data passed from sender to receiver; the return object specifies the type of the data passed from receiver to sender on return of control to the sender. Different programming languages may add additional specifications to the protocol.

MESSAGE

The *message* is the combination of data elements that the sender sends to the receiver as a test case. This message may test whether specific combinations of parameters are compatible with the receiver, or that the receiver performs the service as requested, or that the appropriate action occurs somewhere else (such as handling an exception or a synchronized event set off by the message). The message is also an element of the class.

EXAMPLE

Faults and failures in the DTS related to one another with a many-to-many relationship, causes. A fault *causes* one or more failures in a product, while a failure *is caused by* one or more faults in a product. The *Fault* and *Failure* classes represented this relationship with a separate object that maintained a unified relationship set. Figure 13.11 shows the contract between the classes.

In this kind of two-way relationship, the DTS testing team needed to test the class-to-class relationships from the perspective of each class, and they

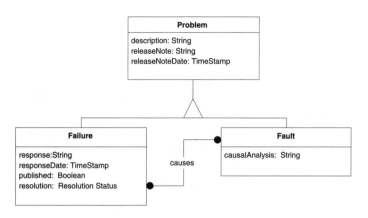

Figure 13.11 Contract between DTS Fault and Failure classes.

needed to test the two objects working together. Was it possible, for example, to relate a fault to a failure without the reverse relationship also being true?

- Add a fault to the failure it causes and check that both know about the relationship.
- Add a failure to the fault causing it and check that both know about the relationship.
- Remove a fault from the failure and check that both remove the relationship.
- Remove a failure from the fault and check that both remove the relationship.
- Set up several relationships, then verify that you can access them from both sides of the relationship.

The Fault class had the responsibility for maintaining the relationship between faults and failures (a contract assumption). The team needed to test the implementation of the Fault class wherever it used the interface of the Failure class. The compiler validated the correctness of the data types, but testing had to go further to verify that the arguments came from valid domains. For example, when you tried to associate a fault with a NULL failure, or if the failure did not yet exist in the database, the testing had to ensure that the Fault class raised an error, or at least hit an assertion, rather than just going down in flames when you access the null pointer.

```
RETCODE Fault::addFailure(Failure & failure)
{
  RETCODE returnCode = SQL_SUCCESS;
  ASSERT(!failure.isNull());
  // Add the failure to the list of failures caused by the fault
  causedBy.add(failure);
  // Tell the failure to add self to the list of faults that cause it
  returnCode = failure.addFault(*this);

  // Since adding the fault verifies both the Fault and the Failure
  // in the database, this is sufficient to validate the Failure,
```

```
                    // and it also has updated the relationship in the database, so
                    // there is nothing left to do. Just return the return code.
                    return (returnCode);
            }
```

The test script then checked the results in the data structures and in the database to verify that the method actually performed the indicated service.

A more extensive example shows the extent of interface and protocol testing based on the entire Failure class:

```
// Class:              Failure
// Description:        A Failure is a failure of this company, as opposed to a customer.

#include "problem.h"  // Problem base class
#include "emp.h"      // Employee     class
#include "faultlst.h" // FaultList and FaultItr classes

class Fault;

// static constants for lengths

static const size_t   cResolutionLength      = 26+1; // Type of failure length + NULL
class Failure : public Problem
{
public:
                        Failure(Connection &            connection,
                                SDWORD                  id,
                                const String &          description,
                                const Person &          reporter,
                                const TimeStamp &       reportDate,
                                SWORD                   published,
                                const Employee &        monitor);
                        Failure(Connection & connection, // query constructor
                                SDWORD id);
                        Failure(const Failure & Failure); // copy constructor

                        ~Failure() {}   // destructor

Failure &               operator =(const Failure &);    // assignment operator
Failure &               operator =(SDWORD id);          // query assignment operator

// Access Methods

const String &          getResponse(TimeStamp &responseDate)    const;
const String &          getResolution(void) const {return resolution;}
const Employee &        getMonitor(void) const {return monitor;}
FaultItr &              getFaults(void) {return causedBy.getIterator();}

// Insert and Delete Methods

RETCODE insertObject(void); // insert the Failure into the database
RETCODE deleteObject(void); // delete the Failure from the database
// Update Methods
RETCODE                 updateResponse(const String & response,
                                       const TimeStamp & responseDate);
RETCODE                 updateResolution(const String &resolution);
RETCODE                 updateMonitor(const Employee & monitor);
RETCODE                 addFault(const Fault & fault);
RETCODE                 removeFault(const Fault & fault);
};
```

To test the various protocols of this class, the testers examined the original contract for the class to determine whether the protocol conformed to the contract requirements. For example, a contract for this class might contain the following requirements:

- Construction
- Destruction
- Assignment by value and by database identifier
- Access to response and response date
- Access to resolution text
- Access to the monitor person
- Access to the list of faults that cause the failure
- Ability to insert and delete failures from the database
- Ability to update the response in the database and timestamp it
- Ability to update the resolution text in the database
- Ability to update the monitor associated with the failure in the database
- Ability to add a fault to the list of faults causing the failure in the database
- Ability to remove a fault from the list of faults causing the failure in the database

For each element of the contract, the tests found some part of the protocol that satisfied the requirement. The testers built a test script for each requirement that validated the class by finding and verifying the appropriate method protocol in the class. The test suite then ran several such interface tests to verify that the implemented methods fulfilled the class contract.

ROAD MAP

Figure 13.12 is the road map for the interface and protocol test script.

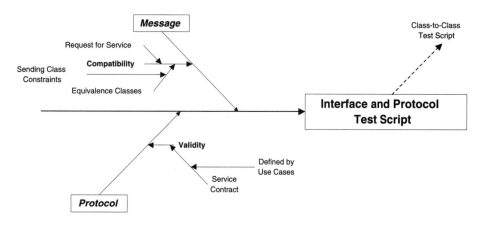

Figure 13.12 Road map for the interface and protocol test script class.

Synchronization Test Script

Several kinds of synchronization are possible in a software system using current programming technology. Synchronization testing could consume an entire volume this size if dealt with in detail. This section summarizes some of the issues, but if you confront a system rife with synchronization requirements, you will need to investigate specific texts on the subject, preferably in parallel. The *synchronization test script* is a kind of class-to-class test script that tests concurrent behavior.

Concurrency in a system permits interacting objects to proceed with their behavior simultaneously. Many different technologies implement this behavior, and there are many different ways of modeling the interactions between concurrent objects. The objects may not actually act simultaneously; for example, in a multitasking or multithreading environment on a machine with a single processor, only one instruction (more or less) executes at a time. In this case, the operating system manages the instructions to simulate the appearance of concurrent behavior. On the other hand, the behavior could be simultaneous: a database server operating asynchronously with many clients, for example.

A common form of synchronized behavior is the interaction of several clients accessing a database at the same time. *Transaction processing* provides a logic for the timing of write and read access to the data. If a class implements some kind of transaction processing or depends on the existence of such processing, you need to test that this works in interaction with another object. Doing so can involve multiple processes on different machines, which might be more appropriate as a system test. You can a lot of these transaction issues by testing only the implementation of the transaction design in a given pair of classes, usually a data object and a database server interface object.

A specialized kind of asynchronous behavior is the event or interrupt. This can be a hardware event, such as a hardware interrupt to the central processing unit (CPU), or it can be a software event, such as the program interpreting user-interface behavior in an event loop as part of the software system. In any case, the raising of the event effects a transfer of control that often depends on timing and synchronization. If there are multiple devices capable of interrupting, for example, timing conflicts between them can disrupt the operation of the program. Or if a particular sequence of things happens as a result of the software event, and some other incompatible event queues first, you can generate a system error by interpreting the wrong event. You need to test the timing of events and interrupts by carefully analyzing the requirements use cases for timing requirements, then testing these requirements as implemented in your system through a synchronization test script. This sort of thing is very common in communication systems software.

Figure 13.13 shows the structure of the synchronization test script class.

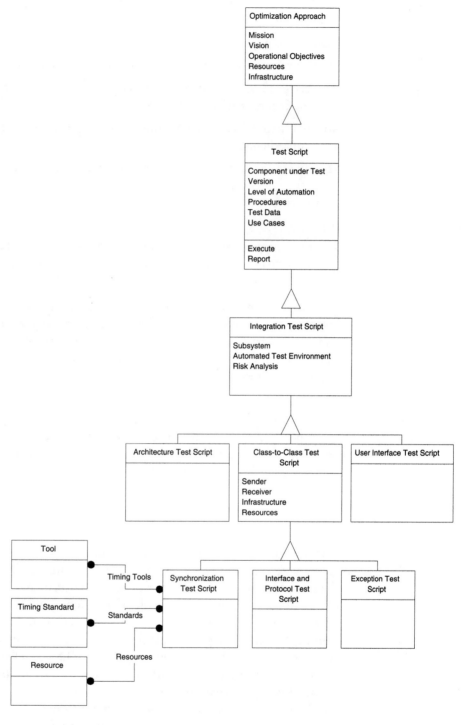

Figure 13.13 Structure of the synchronization test script class.

Vision: A compatible pair of classes operating in a synchronized fashion.

Mission: To test the synchronized behavior of two classes.

Objective 13.9: To discover the maximum number of failures due to the dynamic incompatibility of classes.

Approach 13.9: Test the synchronization of messages and events against timing requirements.

Measurement 13.9: Number of synchronization-related failures.

STRUCTURE

USE CASES

The *timing requirements* are the specific use cases that the test script tests. You need to have these use cases well understood before you can write a test for it.

RESOURCES

Synchronization testing is relatively specialized and requires specialized knowledge about concurrency, transaction processing, events and event handling, and interrupt processing. It may even require some knowledge of hardware. Skimping on skill training in this area will result in poorly understood and specified test scripts.

INFRASTRUCTURE

A system that depends on synchronized operation usually has standards for such operation that you must check against the implementation. You also may need specialized tools to inspect the parallel behavior of the system, such as database transaction monitors, event monitors, or even hardware monitors.

EXAMPLE

There were no specific timing or sequencing issues in the DTS due to the single-task nature of the system. However, the DTS was a fully functional client/server application, and as such it had to use transaction management to manage multiple clients accessing and changing the database at once. Synchronization testing therefore had to ensure that all the equivalence classes of transactions were capable of interacting in the correct way; another way to say this is that the DTS testers had to test all combinations of transactions in the system that exercised significantly different paths to transaction completion. For example, the DTSSQLObject class that centralized the transaction commit or rollback in a single place in the system needed five test objects and scripts:

1. Two transactions overlapping and committing
2. Two transactions overlapping and rolling back
3. Two transactions simultaneously committing

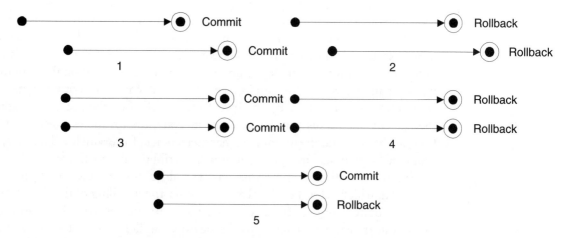

Figure 13.14 Testing transactions synchronicity

4. Two transactions simultaneously rolling back

5. Two transactions, one committing and one rolling back simultaneously

Figure 13.14 shows the timing diagram that describes the use cases for these tests.

ROAD MAP
Figure 13.15 is the road map for the synchronization test script.

Exception Test Script

An *exception test script* tests the raising and handling of an exception between two classes. An *exception* is an explicit or implicit (anomalous) instruction to

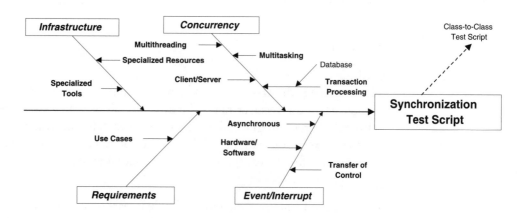

Figure 13.15 Road map for the synchronization test script.

transfer control during the execution of a method. The method raises the exception, then control transfers to an *exception handler* defined for the exception. Just as with transaction and concurrency, there are different models of exception handling. The most common one handles the exception through the nearest handler, where "nearest" means the handler most recently registered by a calling object (that is, by an object in the stack of method calls leading to the current one). This handler executes its code, then resumes execution (in C++, at the next statement after the handler's block, for example). The exception may be an object in its own right with attributes and methods.

Exception testing as a class-to-class test does not test the *raising* of the exception, which is local to the class, but rather the handling of the exception. The component under test is a message sent to the receiver that raises an exception, transferring control to the nearest handler. The test ensures that the right handler executes when the receiver throws the exception and that the right behavior happens in the handler. Part of this testing is to make sure that the exception object contains the right attributes given the combination of sender and receiver.

Figure 13.16 shows the structure of the exception test script class.

LEADERSHIP

Vision: A compatible pair of classes cooperating in handling exceptions.

Mission: To test the exception-handling behavior of two classes.

Objective 13.10: To discover the maximum number of failures due to the incompatibility of classes with respect to dynamic exceptions.

Approach 13.10: Test the exception handling between classes to ensure that a method raises exceptions as required and that the system handles the exception appropriately.

Measurement 13.10: Number of exception-handling failures.

STRUCTURE

USE CASES

The *exception* is the class of object returned from the receiver to the exception handler when the receiver raises the exception. The actual structure may vary between different programming languages, as each has its own model of exceptions and exception handling. The test script refers use cases that state the requirements for the exception, not to the actual exception class or structure.

HANDLER

The exception *handler* is the block of code (a part of an object) that handles the exception raised in the receiver. The sender class may own this code, or it may be code in a caller of the sender class. In any case, the test must clearly identify

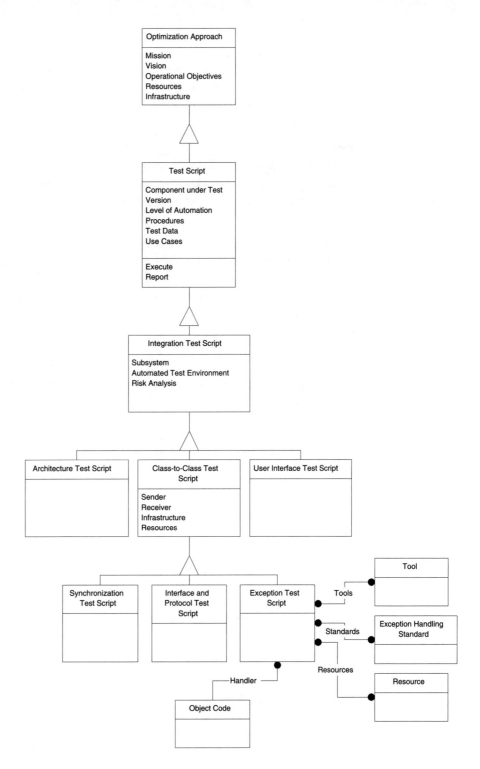

Figure 13.16 Structure of exception test script class.

the handler, or at least the group of possible handlers, that might handle the exception. When the receiver raises the exception as a consequence of a message from the sender, the handler handles it. If there is more than one possibility, the test script should test all possible paths. It is usually better to structure the test script to preclude all but one possible handler. This means you must have a series of test scripts for the equivalence classes of exception handler.

RESOURCES

Building exception test scripts requires, in addition to the standard programming language and design knowledge, a grasp of the model of exception handling in the programming language or library.

INFRASTRUCTURE

There may be standards for exception structure and handling (such as a limit on the number of stack levels before handling or a requirement to handle all exceptions in the sender). For manual testing, you will need a debugger that understands exception handling and shows you the appropriate transfers of control and data.

EXAMPLE

The following code implemented the constructor for the Connection class of the DTS, which encapsulated the MFC CDatabase object. The call to the Open member of the CDatabase class could have raised two possible exceptions. The CDatabaseException told the caller of a server error preventing connection, while the CMemoryException told the caller that there was not enough memory to open a connection.

```
#include "connect.h"
Connection::Connection(void)
{
    pDatabaseObject = new CDatabase();
    if (pDatabaseObject)
    {
        TRY
        {
            pDatabaseObject->Open(NULL);
        }
        CATCH(CDBException, pDBException)
        {
            TRACE("Database exception %s on opening connection \n",
                pDBException->m_strError);
        }
        AND_CATCH(CMemoryException, pMemException)
        {
            TRACE("Memory exception on opening connection\n");
        }
        END_CATCH
    }
    else
    {
        AfxThrowMemoryException();
    }
}
```

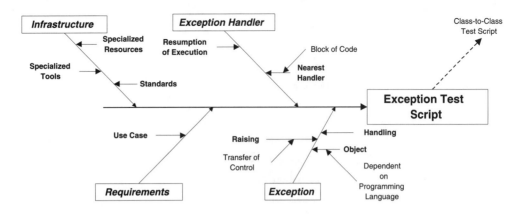

Figure 13.17 Road map for the exception test script class.

The exception test script for testing the class-to-class connection between the Connection class (the sender) and the CDatabase class (the receiver) set up one exceptional situation, then tested it to make sure the sender handled the exception when the script raised it. For this method, there were two exceptions and hence two test scripts.

ROAD MAP
Figure 13.17 is the road map to the exception test script class.

UI Test Script

UI testing tests the way the user interacts with the system. The UI *test script* applies only to systems that allow direct user interaction; UI testing tests the *external interfaces* of the system. Not all systems have external interfaces; some serve as internal APIs, while others are utility systems that serve other systems.

The UI script is both a kind of integration test script and a kind of system test script. In its integration form, the test script tests a specific UI component and the components of the underlying system with which it interacts. The automated integration environment runs the test script to verify the integrated behavior of the system and to validate the implementation against the requirements use cases. For system testing, the UI test script becomes part of the larger set of test scripts that tests the overall UI against requirements such as the UI specification and system use cases. Figure 13.18 shows the class design for the UI test script.

The UI test script class is an abstract class with three subclasses (Kepple, 1994; Symons, 1994):

- True-time UI Test Script: A test script that verifies exact behavior in the UI.
- Character Recognition UI Test Script: A test script that verifies behavior allowing for specific differences such as fonts or relative pixel location.

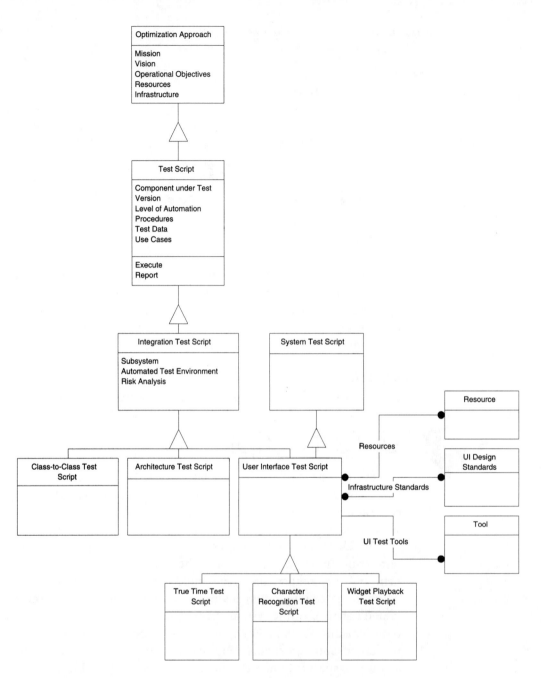

Figure 13.18 Structure of the user-interface test script class.

- Widget-Playback UI Test Script: A test script that verifies behavior of objects rather than collections of pixels.

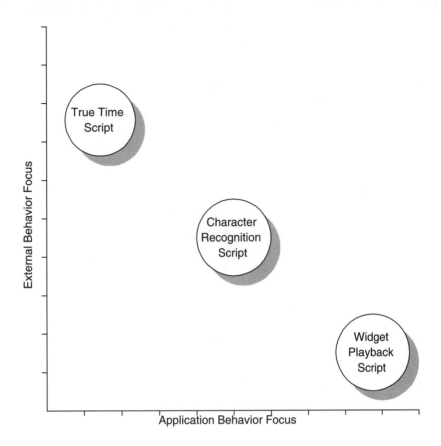

Figure 13.19 Focus of user-interface test script subclasses.

The difference among these three types is largely in the focus. True-time scripts focus on the external behavior; character recognition scripts focus on application behavior within strong external constraints on external behavior; and widget playback scripts focus entirely on application behavior. Figure 13.19 shows the two dimensions of focus for UI testing, focus on external versus application behavior, and the positions of the three kinds of UI test script along those dimensions.

Figure 13.20 shows the class designs for the three subclasses of UI test script, which themselves have no additional attributes or methods. Often you can switch between these kinds of tests by changing an option in your testing tool.

UI testers usually can generate UI scripts in two ways, depending on the particular tool or scripting language you choose to use. First, you can record a series of manual actions into a script, which then faithfully reproduces the actions. Second, you can program the series of actions directly into the script. Often you can start with a recorded script and change it manually by adding or changing actions in the script.

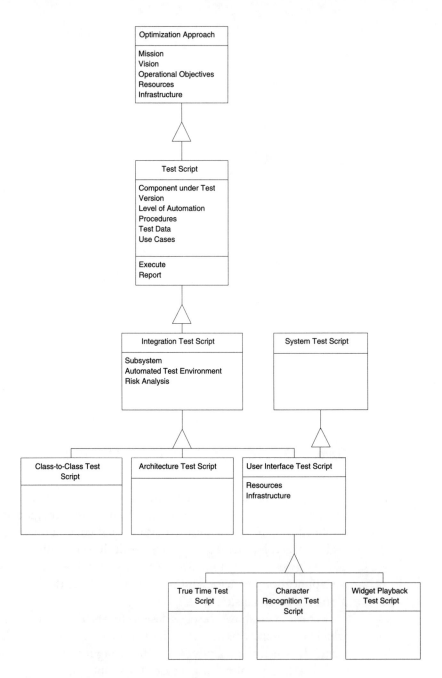

Figure 13.20 Structure of the user-interface test script subclasses.

Leadership

Vision: A robust user-interface system that satisfies external interface requirements.

Mission: To verify the operation of a UI component of the system and to validate the UI design against the requirements; to test external interfaces.

The subclasses define individual operational objectives.

Structure

RESOURCES

User-interface test tools usually are separate from other testing tools and hence require special training for building the test scripts. Resources who build user-interface test scripts should have both training in the UI testing tools and a general familiarity with UI programming and standards.

INFRASTRUCTURE

Automated UI testing requires special tools that interpret user events and take an appropriate test action. It also requires reference to user-interface design standards and guidelines.

Road Map

Figure 13.21 is the road map for the UI test script class.

True-Time Test Script

The *true-time test script* tests keyboard and mouse events exactly as you recorded them. The script assumes a fixed set of pixel images on the screen, and if anything at all changes from the recording (such as the position of a dialog box or button or the a menu font), the test script regards it as an error. Usually the test script executes with the exact timing of events during recording on the assumption that you want to perform the test as a simulation of a real user.

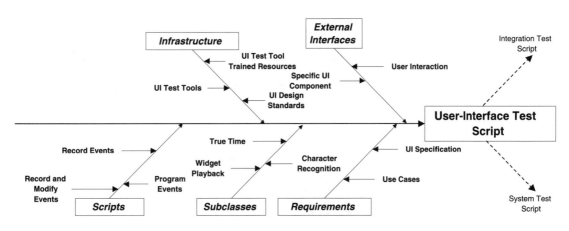

Figure 13.21 Road map for the user-interface test script class.

The timing test and the focus on external events are the strengths of this type of test. You use this kind of test script to test very specific timing requirements. You also can use this test to test very specific drawing requirements: that is, whether the same sequence of actions results in exactly the same output on the screen, pixel for pixel.

The weakness of this type of test is related to its strength: If you are primarily interested in the application behavior rather than the external events, timing, or external output, you will find that the test script becomes unusable very quickly as the application changes. If a dialog moves by one pixel, if you change a font, if you change the underlying timing, if even if you use a monitor with a different resolution, you have to record the script all over again.

LEADERSHIP

Vision: A robust user-interface system that satisfies exact external interface requirements for event timing and graphical output.

Mission: To verify that a UI component and its underlying objects exactly match behavior requirements.

Objective 13.11: To discover a maximum number of behavioral incompatibilities.

Approach 13.11: Record a test script, then play it back automatically and match the resulting behavior with the recorded behavior exactly.

Measurement 13.11: Number of mismatches between expected results and actual results on a pixel-by-pixel basis.

EXAMPLE

The DTS had the ability to store and display objects required to reproduce failures. One option was to make these objects display exactly where the tech-

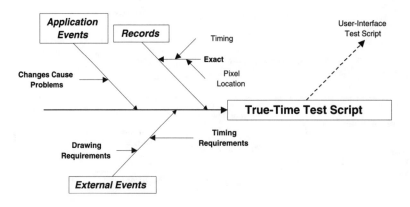

Figure 13.22 Road map for the true-time test script class.

nical support engineer or customer positioned them on a screen. This let the system transmit the object in its context to the developer for debugging.

A true-time UI test script tested this feature to ensure that the object displayed in exactly the same place each time.

ROAD MAP
Figure 13.22 is the road map for the true-time test script.

Character-Recognition Test Script

The character-recognition test script has a focus intermediate between the external events and the application behavior of the system. This kind of UI test script manipulates areas of the screen without requiring an exact match between the recorded sequence of events and outputs and the actual test results. It recognizes characters rather than clumps of pixels and doesn't require that the characters look exactly the same from test to test. You can change fonts or locations of objects without creating a failure.

The advantage of this approach comes when you are interested in basic application testing rather than exact pixel testing. It is particularly advantageous if the screen objects appear in different locations or with different fonts (according to requirements). Since these changes are normal, you can ignore the changes and still run your test script.

But the character-recognition approach is still quite limited in terms of application testing. Change the interface too much, and the test script stops working. You can't change a text line's wording, for example, without rerecording the script. If that's what you're testing, then it's fine.

LEADERSHIP

Vision: A robust user-interface system that satisfies external interface requirements and internal application behavior requirements.

Mission: To verify that a UI component and its underlying objects satisfy behavior requirements.

Objective 13.12: To discover a maximum number of behavioral incompatibilities with maximum productivity.

Approach 13.12: Record a test script of object interactions, then play it back automatically and match the resulting behavior with the recorded behavior of the objects.

Measurement 13.12: Number of mismatches between expected results and actual results.

EXAMPLE

Many of the user-interface elements of the DTS were straightforward dialogs and windows that changed very little from release to release. Their structure, however, depended on certain option settings. For example, the user could change the display font for words in lists. The user could move the objects around the screen, resize them, and so on. A character recognition test tested these objects without needing changes under slightly differing conditions.

ROAD MAP

Figure 13.23 is the road map for the character-recognition test script.

Widget-Playback Test Script

The *widget-playback test script* focuses entirely on the application behavior of the system, referring to external events only as abstract instructions that drive the application behavior. It ignores the display images as such and tests only the application behavior through the UI objects, though that may involve specific display events. Usually the scripting language lets you name the various UI objects and thus puts a level of indirection between the object and the screen.

You use widget-playback testing when you want to test the UI solely as a driver for the underlying application behavior. This procedure is most appropriate when the behavior does not involve further display on the UI, but you also can test a sequence of object changes that the UI displays without worrying about the display format, just the content.

This test script lets you build scripts that are portable across GUI platforms, for example. Even though the UI looks different, the underlying objects are the same and the behavior is the same. The widget-playback script works correctly no matter what platform you're testing. This makes the script more reusable and enhances your productivity.

LEADERSHIP

Vision: A robust user-interface system that satisfies external interface requirements and internal application behavior requirements.

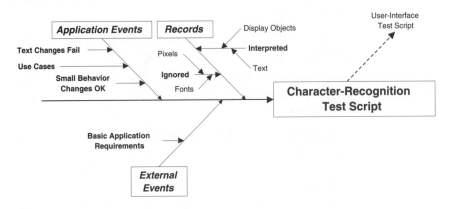

Figure 13.23 Road map for the chaacter recognition test script class.

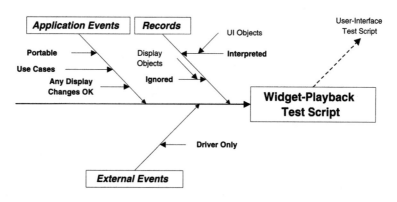

Figure 13.24 Road map for the widget-playback test script class.

Mission: To verify that a UI component and its underlying objects satisfy behavior requirements.

Objective 13.13: To discover a maximum number of behavioral incompatibilities.

Approach 13.13: Record a test script, then play it back automatically and match the resulting behavior with the required behavior.

Measurement 13.13: Number of mismatches between expected results and actual results.

EXAMPLE

Many of the entry screens in the DTS through which the user entered the basic data of the system resulted in specific entries into the DTS database. When testing these entry screens, the tester didn't really care about the external behavior of the screen, just that the entered data got into the right tables in the database. The widget-playback UI test scripts to enter the data logically ran on all the platforms that the testing tool supported. For example, to test data entry of a failure through the Enter Failure dialog, the tester created a test object from that dialog called **Enter_Failure** and built the test script around testing the values entered and the values that changed in the database.

ROAD MAP

Figure 13.24 is the road map for the widget-playback test script.

CHAPTER 14

SYSTEM COMPONENT TEST SUITE

System Component Test Suite

The *System Component Test Suite* may reuse any of the test suites, use cases, and scripts previously developed and executed for safe foundation components and classes. It also will include test suites specific for this SUT (System Under Test). The two major subclasses of system test suites are the System Acceptance Test Suite and the User Options Test Suite (see Figure 14.1). You begin to develop the System Acceptance Test Suite early in the project, during requirements analysis.

In a very real sense system testing begins and progresses in parallel to the requirements analysis activity. High-level use cases are developed to model the system requirements during requirements analysis. Detail is added to the use cases to reflect the feedback from future users of the system about their requirements. The review and refinement of these use cases parallels and enhances the development of the final set of requirements. Theoretically, a complete set of use cases will represent a set of test scenarios that defines and covers the entire set of system requirements. When you have produced this complete set, you also will have produced a set of acceptance criteria with which to system-test your final application. As the developers design, code, and test their components, the system testers design, code and document the system test suite. This involves the design of executable test scenarios (test procedures), the coding of input data (test messages), and the documentation regarding how to execute the test scripts and evaluate the output.

There are several major differences between the integration testing of the system and/or foundation components and the system test proper. First and foremost is that the entire system will be tested as a whole, in an environment which duplicates as much as possible the real world end-user environment. This involves hardware and software configurations that simulate the end-user environments with loads and stresses on the system likely to be encountered in the real world. This sounds straightforward enough, but in practice it is very difficult (and expensive) to actually simulate all of the end users' environments.

The complexity and flexibility of modern software systems makes it cost prohibitive to actually simulate the hardware and software environments of the entire end-user community. For much of the shrinkwrap software industry, it is simply impossible to account for all the variations of system configurations the application is likely to encounter. As a practical matter, we create equivalence classes of configurations and live with some risk. The more we deviate from the end-user environments in our system test environment, the greater the risks we take.

To help manage the risks, we divide out system testing into two broad test suites:

- **System Acceptance Test Suite:** A test suite derived from the set of use cases covering the system requirements.

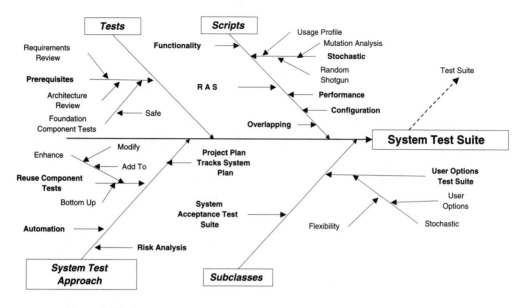

Figure 14.1 System test suite.

- **User Options Test Suite:** A test suite based on the probable usage patterns of the features and functions delivered with the system. This suite is designed to simulate ways in which the end users will combine the discrete features and functions of the system to synthesize new and different (unknown, unforeseen and unexpected) usage patterns.

Our basic system test approach assumes that your project has implemented much of the hierarchical approach. If your project has not deployed some form of hierarchical testing approach, you now have the opportunity to do all the integration and function testing during the system test phase. This is the expensive and risky way to test; precisely what this book is designed to help you avoid in the future! It is assumed that you have test suites and scripts that you can reuse, override, and overload. You may enhance, modify, or add to these existing suites and scripts. You should have some degree of test automation in place, but if you don't, you still have an opportunity to automate your system test scripts. If your system application is likely to go through at least several major revision cycles while in production, then it is both cost effective and wise to design some system test automation procedures. Experience shows that the time and effort you invest in designing and implementing automation will start to pay dividends by the third or fourth reuse of a test suite.

Some specific test scripts need to be included for the system test. These include (but are not limited to) the following test scripts.

Functionality - The basic features and functions of the requirements. The tests for this script should be inherited from the class and integration test cases as well as the requirements' use cases. Do not neglect error testing. At least one test should be executed for each system error message with an acceptable termination or exit action.

Reliability - The reliability requirements should have been stated and verified with system test scenarios. These test scripts often require the most imagination and greatest system resources. Review the risks and plan carefully.

Availability - If there are specific requirements in this area, this is your first and best opportunity to test them. A common strategy is to install a "beta" version of the system for a subset of the user community and to measure down time (system availability). Recovery testing, of particular importance to safety-critical types of systems, is a special kind of availability system test. Simulate or cause system failures and implement the recovery procedures. Compare the results to the system requirements or specification.

Another form of availability testing concerns maintainability. What are the maintenance procedures? How long do they take? What is the impact on the availability of the system? These are questions that can only be answered in system test or in the field.

Security - Design and execute test scripts that attempt to compromise the security of the system.

Performance - You must have specific measurable system requirements in this area to execute performance test scripts. If you do not, and you are measuring the performance of the system, then you are bench marking but not testing. There is nothing wrong with bench marking, we think it is a good thing to do, but without previously specified performance criteria you have no objective way to determine if the performance is acceptable. Invariably you will resort to subjective criteria. Usually, the customers and the developers have different ideas about what is acceptable. Hint: the customers are always right! Specify measurable performance criteria and system test to those requirements.

Stress testing involves placing significant and realistic loads on the system. Volume testing involves specified volumes of data under specific conditions. There should be threshold values specified in the requirements and/or specifications. Performance test to establish acceptable performance in the eyes of the end users.

Configuration - There are three major areas of configuration testing: hardware and software variations, compatibility requirements, and installation tests. Scripts for every hardware and software combination are impractical, so design with equivalence class coverage in mind. Creating a matrix (use a spreadsheet) of required hardware and software requirements and designing configuration test scripts to cover all the required components first is recommended. Then evaluate the probability of specific hardware and software combinations and evaluate the risk of not testing those combinations. Usually you can combine the compatibility requirements with the hardware and software configurations to get more testing productivity. Installation test scripts must be developed for a percentage of the possible configurations. It is best to categorize potential installation configurations as high, medium, and low probability of occurrence. Use risk analysis to guide your design of these test scripts.

Usability - There are at least four distinct areas of usability testing: the user interface, help information, user documents, and flexibility. The user interface can and should be tested as an integration component. The test script should already exist. Consider it as a regression test script within system test. Specific use cases for using help information should have been developed during requirements analysis. These become part of the system test. Scripts to test the user documents whether online, or hard copy, or both, should be executed and evaluated in light of the usability requirements. Pay particular attention to examples used in the documentation. Every example must be verified during the system test. The flexibility requirements are a new and specific type of requirement that object or component-based systems enable. The stochastic test script is used to test these requirements. The stochastic test script *object* is discussed later in this section.

Leadership

Vision: Serious system failures at the customer sites will be virtually eliminated.

Mission: Verify and validate the SUT (system under test) against explicit requirements and specifications. Discover faults that are likely to cause failures and fix them before delivering the SUT to your customers.

Objective 14.1: Verify and validate that the system requirements have been met.

Approach 14.1: Execute the System Acceptance Test Suite.

Measurement 14.1: Failures per unit of execution.

Objective 14.2: Discover faults that are likely to cause failures.

Approach 14.2: Execute the User Options Test Suite.

Measurement 14.2: Potential failures per unit of execution.

Structure

System Under Test (SUT)

The SUT is either the final application system or a stand-alone system component. There is no reason why we should not apply everything said about the system test suite to one or more system components. Remember, everything is a system. Your test focus, the SUT, is a matter of how you choose to focus and define "system."

System Acceptance Criteria

The ideal situation is to use or transform your use cases, test scripts, and test suites as the system acceptance criteria. Developing these criteria along with the system requirements and using them as a form of final system acceptance criteria is advo-

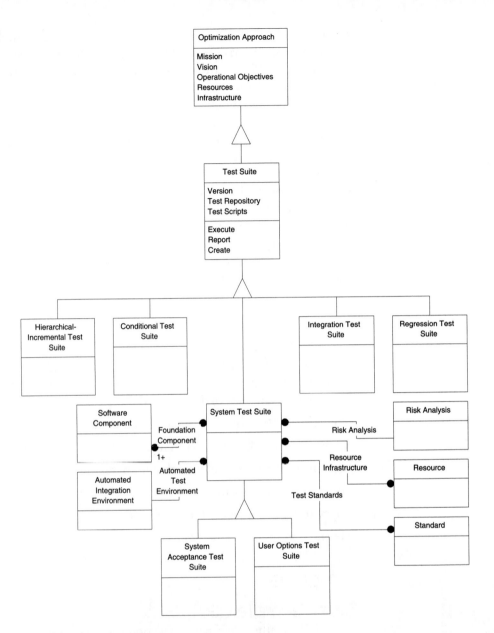

Figure 14.2 System test suite road map.

cated. Regard the tests as a contract between the end users and the developers of the system. If you do a good enough job of modelling the requirements in your use cases and test scripts, then transforming them into executable suites and actually running them as the objective system acceptance criteria makes perfect sense.

SYSTEM TEST ENVIRONMENT

The actual hardware, and software installed and running. The environment also includes time and access to the system test environment. We have encountered more than a few situations where the developers and testers shared the system test environment and the activities of each impacted the other. The system test environment takes real resources in real time. Plan on it, implement it and have it debugged and ready in so far as that is possible.

Road Map

Figure 14.2 is the road map for the system test suite.

Stochastic Test Script

A key aspect of this type of test is illustrated by the general purpose Process Planning application. A major system testing concern was "how to predict in what wonderful and ingenious ways the flexibility of this system will be applied by a user/customer base when it (the user) discovers the power and flexibility of the system." In other words, for any general purpose flexible system that enables the user community to invent applications for their specific needs, how can the development community know what combinations of functionality will be meaningful? How can one test flexibility in areas in which the users have no current domain specific knowledge? Stochastic Test Script can be seen in Figure 14.3.

LEADERSHIP

Vision: The development team will solve user problems before they become serious problems for the users.

Mission: Anticipate how the flexibility in the system will be used by the end users.

Objectives: Fix potential faults before they manifest as failures for the users.

Approach: Establish a usage profile, execute random stochastic tests, analyze the results, mutate the original test parameters, and run more stochastic tests.

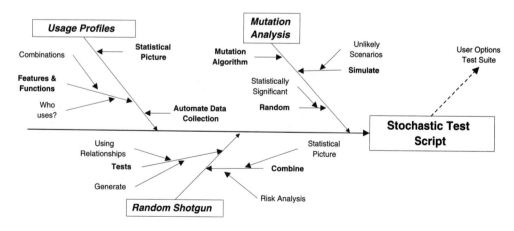

Figure 14.3 Stochastic test script.

Measurement: Number of potential faults and or failures per unit of effort.

STRUCTURE

USAGE PROFILE

A Usage Profile tests the functionality actually used by the user community expressed in relative percentage terms. It involves creating a set of usage profiles and using the results to make decisions about how to allocate testing and development resources.

This is not a new technique, (and is central to reliability modeling). It is also an essential technique to apply to complex and flexible OO systems. The profiling is performed by polling, survey, questionnaire, interviewing, or other means. The best way to get this information is to put counters in your product and to have an agreement with the users to monitor the usage. The end result is a profile of the relative use of the functionality in your system. This profile takes the form of a set of matrices that illustrates the many different segments of the user population using different aspects (features, functions, etc.) of the system in different proportions. Use the information to prioritize your testing and drive the choices of what combinations of classes and methods to test and how thoroughly to test them.

MUTATION ANALYSIS

Directed Mutation Analysis tests combinations of functionality that result from the flexibility designed into the system. This is useful for shaking out bugs that you just could never imagine. Testing involves random but significant (based upon usage profile and risk assessment) combinations of use relationships between classes and then applying a mutation factor based upon application domain specific knowledge. It is especially useful where flexibility and freedom are designed into the system, and for computing legal combinations between classes based upon use relationships . Set up your test bed so that it reflects the statistical usage of the system and then weigh it based on the risk factors you can identify. You will need to hand check the results of each run.

If you don't find bugs, then randomly mutate system parameters (combinations of values used by the methods) and rerun the same using relationships. If after significant mutation runs there are no bugs in the random combinations, save the results file and use it as a meaningful regression test set. After applying a mutation factor always re-set the results file to enable future automated results checking.

For example, if methods A,B,C,D,E...Z are visible to methods a,b,c,d,e,...z, then you can determine which methods are most likely to use what others from the usage profile. You would run random combinations of these high usage relationships varying (mutating) the values for specific methods. The mutation values will follow a pattern based on the type of application it is. So an air traffic control system might vary the number of planes on the runway, and the amount of noise in the communication system, and the air temperature, moisture content, etc. The amount that a value is mutated should be randomly chosen from the domain of acceptable values for the parameter. All of the methods' values are simultaneously being mutated so that you are simulating different and strange scenarios.

DYNAMICS

CREATE USAGE PROFILE

EXECUTE RANDOM SHOTGUN

Random Statistical Shotgun is described as follows.

- **Tests:** Reliability of combinations of using relationships.
- **Involves:** Risk analysis and combination of random statistical testing.
- **Description:** Perform Risk analysis and then generate statistically significant but random combinations of using relationships between classes. For buggy relationships or where errors are found, use a shotgun approach and develop more cases for those situations. The additional cases should be developed based upon an analysis of what methods failed and why.

CHAPTER 15

REGRESSION TEST SUITE

A *regression test suite* is a series of tests run against a previous version of the component under test (foundation component, system, or whatever). The current version exists either because of maintenance (fixing faults in the component) or enhancement (adding features to the component). The suite is a regression suite because you are applying the tests to a software revision. This is not an innate quality of the suite itself, which is the same as when you ran it against the original version of the component.

The regression test suite contains test scripts of any type.

During integration, you can run regression test suites independently of the new tests, or you can add the new tests into the regression test suite. Integrating old and new tests permits you to optimize resources by integrating the work involved, but the productivity improvement is probably not significant. Also, regression tests are almost always automated tests; usually it is not cost effective to perform manual tests over and over again unless they are particularly effective at discovering failures or are the only way to test some part of the system. The former case is a good candidate for optimization, and the latter is probably a warning flag to look more closely at the design.

Figure 15.1 shows the class structure for the regression test script.

Leadership

Vision: A software component free of faults introduced by maintenance and enhancement and a validated set of failures resolved by maintenance.

Mission: To perform previously executed tests against revised code.

Objective 15.1: To find failures introduced by changes to a tested software component.

Approach 15.1: Sediment test scripts into an automated regression test suite, where possible, or a manual one, where not, and run the test suite against every revised version of the software component.

Note: There are other approaches to these objectives. The leading one is review, walkthrough, or inspection of the component. Reviews let you think about how a change may affect other elements. Other possibilities include deferring tests of individual components such as classes to the system test (or even user test), but this, as with all test deferrals, will raise the cost of fixing the problem.

Measurement 15.1: Number of new failures per execution of the test suite.

Objective 15.2: To fail to reproduce old failures claimed to be fixed by maintenance.

Note: It is not a goal of regression testing to *verify* that the software component is correct. You cannot do that by testing, regressive or otherwise.

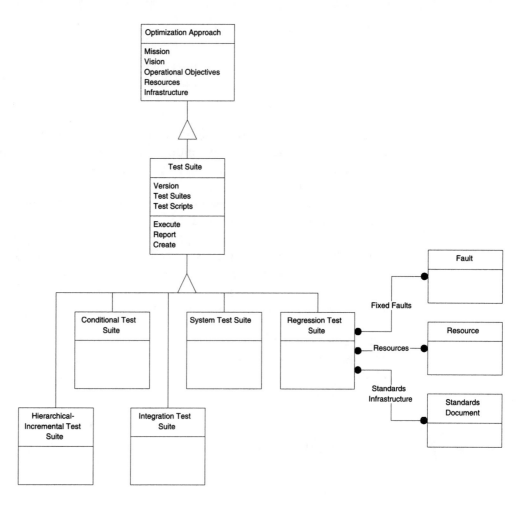

Figure 15.1 Structure of the regression test suite class.

Approach 15.2: Check the set of known fixed faults against the test results of the regression test and report any failures that correspond to faults supposedly fixed.

Measurement 15.2: Number of fixes validated by an execution of the test script.

Structure

Fixed Faults

One objective of the regression test suite is to validate fixes to faults that resulted in failures in previous versions of the component (and therefore in previous executions of the test scripts in the suite). The regression test script suite contains a list of fixed faults and the corresponding failures that they fix. You can use this list in more sophisticated automation systems to tell developers what fixes didn't pass the regression test.

Resources

Unlike most test suites, regression test suites require no deep knowledge of either the test or the code. By definition, the work of creating the suite in relationship to the component is complete; only the execution and evaluation of the suite remains.

For an object-related regression test, the logical resource is the maintenance engineer or developer who coded the changes to the class, who can use the regression test as a debugging component of the maintenance or enhancement effort. All you really need here is somebody capable of executing the test script.

For an integration- or system-related test, the logical resource is usually a QA engineer or release engineer. The release engineer is usually the person responsible for building the system and running the basic regression tests.

Infrastructure

Usually standards or processes in the life cycle mandate various aspects of executing appropriate regression tests after certain events (recompiles, rebuilds, alpha release, and so on).

Dynamics

Execute

You can execute either the entire collection of scripts in the suite or an equivalence class of those tests. You can base the decision on an equivalence-class analysis showing that the tests are equivalent under the change or on your estimate of the probability of encountering a difference in failure frequency. That is, if you know that the change has almost no chance of affecting some part of the component (99.999 percent), then you don't need to run tests of that part of the component. The regression test execute method thus looks at the risk management plan to determine whether the test is necessary.

One battle-scarred veteran of system software engineering in the old days (that is, the 1960s and 1970s) described one database system he worked on as a table full of marbles. When you added a new marble, one fell off; you just didn't know where. This kind of system needs lots of regression testing. Another classic example of this kind of decision was the choice not to test a small change to some telecommunications code that brought down most of a major telecommunications network for hours.

This decision is a risk analysis based on the risk of failure versus the consequences of failure and on the cost of performing the additional tests. If the costs of performing the tests are minimal, run them even if you don't think you'll find anything. If the costs are substantial, and the consequence of not detecting a failure is acceptable, ignore the tests. Automation helps a great deal here, since it dramatically reduces the costs of additional testing. With extensive manual testing, however, you may have to choose where to spend your time with regression testing. Focus on the objectives: to find failures caused by changes or to validate the fixes to the component.

Report

The report for a regression test suite should contain a note of the successful completion of the specific tests for faults fixed in this version of the component. (See the earlier "Fixed Faults" section for details.)

Randomize

Systems get tuned to regression test suites rather rapidly. If you use regression test suites from one version to another or run the same suite over and over withour finding many errors, try mixing it up. You should regularly replace up to 25 percent of the tests in a regression test suite with tests that cover the same things but with different data values and in a different order or execution. Just randomizing the order of execution often can help shake out problems. How often and how much you randomize is up to you; it is a good and cost-effective practice.

Example

For version 1.1 of the DTS, the corporation enhanced the class Failure with a new attribute, marketingSeverity, that described the severity of the failure with respect to the marketing programs of the corporation. The developer knew that just adding the attribute and the corresponding access method **getMarketingSeverity()** would have no regressive consequences. The method **updateSeverity**, however, got a new, optional parameter to add this new severity to the other ones in a single update. The developer decided to run a regression test to make sure the test scripts involving update of severity had no new failures.

The testing approach in this case separated new tests from regression tests, and because this was an enhancement with no consequences outside the class (as a domain analysis shows), there was no need for specific integration or system regression tests. The general QA automated system regression test did run some test scripts that touch on the Failure class, and QA decided to run them anyway as they took only five minutes.

At another point in the project, the DTS integration team had completed the Problem system beta baseline after fixing many problems that the alpha

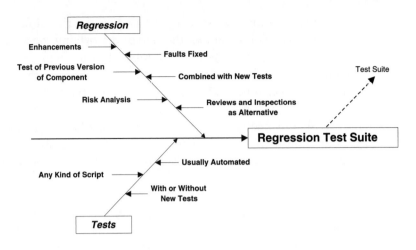

Figure 15.2 Road map for the regression test suite class.

baseline test suite had uncovered. The team randomized the test scripts in the alpha regression test suite and ran it, uncovering three new problems; according to the criteria for the beta baseline, the test failed and the system went back into development. After another week, the developers again checked in the system, randomized the test suite again, and this time successfully met the test exit criteria for the beta baseline for the system.

Road Map

Figure 15.2 shows the road map for the regression test suite.

CHAPTER 16

TEST

EVALUATION

W. Edward Deming's Third Point sums up the purpose of the quality system: Cease dependence on inspection to achieve quality. Eliminate the need for inspection on a mass basis by building quality into the product in the first place. Having spent most of the book to this point discussing how to inspect and test, this chapter is all about the test evaluation: how to improve the test process to build quality into the product in the first place.

Lowell Jay Arthur makes the point well in *Improving Software Quality* (1992): Inspect code to find defects in the *software process*, not to find defects in the *code* (p. 141). If you limit yourself to finding faults (inspection and testing), you get a high-quality product; if you eliminate the root causes of the faults in the process, you get many such products with much less effort. That's what the test evaluation object is all about and, in fact, what the quality system as a whole is all about.

The *test evaluation* is the development document that the testers and developers produce after the execution of a test suite. The document summarizes the test results output into the test repository and the metrics for the test scripts and suites. It provides lists of the failed tests and the faults that caused the failures (if you know them).

The analysis section of the document evaluates the test completion criteria for the test suite and judges whether the testing of the components under test is complete. It provides an analysis of the root causes of the failures detected, identifying any specific faults for fixing. Based on this causal analysis, the authors propose changes to the test approach, test content, and/or the test optimization. The report finally identifies the test scripts that become part of the regression test suite.

To produce the document, you step through several distinct tasks in order. (See the "Dynamics" section below for details.)

- **Fault analysis:** Determine the faults from the failures.
- **Test completion status:** Is this test suite done?
- **Root causal analysis:** What are the underlying reasons for the failures and faults?
- **Test approach optimization:** How can you improve the approach to testing?
- **Test content optimization:** Given the new approach, what needs to change in the test models and objects?
- **Optimization approach optimization:** Step back and look at the whole test system to see if you can improve it.

Figure 16.1 shows the class structure of the test evaluation class.

Leadership

Vision: An optimizing test system that contributes its share to the quality system.

Mission: To optimize the test system to achieve better alignment with the overall quality system and its objectives.

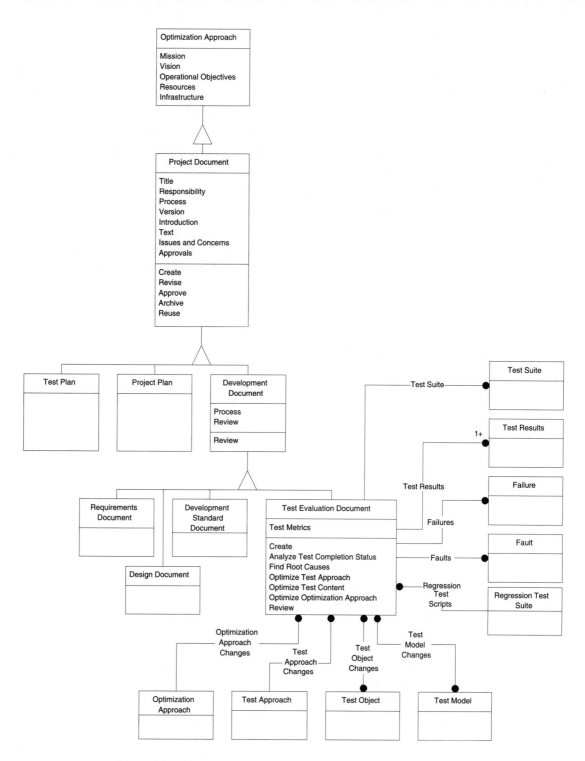

Figure 16.1 Structure of the test evaluation document class.

Objective 16.1: To optimize value contributed by the test system during an accounting period with respect to the business objectives of the quality system during that period.

Approach 16.1: Analyze the results of execution of the test suite and use that analysis to optimize the contribution of the test system to total system quality by improving the test approach, test content, and optimization approach.

Measurement 16.1: Return on investment in test evaluations during the accounting period.

Objective 16.2: To optimize productivity in the test system with respect to value during an accounting period.

Approach 16.2: Analyze the results of execution of the test suite and use that analysis to optimize the contribution of the test system to total system productivity by improving the test approach, test content, and optimization approach.

Measurement 16.2: Testing effort-hours per function point during the accounting period.

Structure

Test Suite

The *test suite* is the set of test scripts you executed to get the test results.

Test Results

The *test results* are the outputs of the test scripts in the test repository.

Test Metrics

The *test metrics* are the statistics you gather from the measures for the different test scripts and the test suite, including things such as number of failures, expected failure rate, and model coverage. You use these metrics to judge the quality of the test suite and its scripts and to determine whether the test suite meets its testing completion criteria.

Failures

The *failures* list is a list of the test scripts that failed to execute according to expectations. The test results provide the raw data for this list. First, testers must compare the actual test results to the expected test results. Often the test script or suite makes this comparison automatically through the testing tool and provides the comparison results. The testers should then probe a bit into each failure to gather any additional data that might help them or the developers to identify the faults that caused the failure. Any conclusions or hints belong in this section of the report.

Faults

The *faults* list is a list of the actual code, design, or requirements faults that the testers discover as a consequence of analyzing the failures from the test results. Not all failures become faults, either because of revisions to expectations or because the preliminary analysis can't identify what caused the failure. There has to be something left for the debugging gurus, after all.

You may want to use code inspection techniques to discover the faults behind the failures.

Regression Test Scripts

The list of *regression test scripts* is the set of scripts from the test suite that succeeded and that should execute against future versions of the components under test as part of a regression test suite.

Test Object Changes

The *test object changes* are your recommended changes in the individual test objects (additional test objects, fewer test objects, or changes to a test object).

Test Model Changes

The *test model changes* are your recommended changes in the test models for the test suite, such as modifications of the model to correct flaws, adding more models to the suite, or removing models from the suite.

Test Approach Changes

The test approach changes are your recommended changes in test approach for the suite, such as using a different kind of test model or changing the completion criteria for the suite.

Optimization Approach Changes

The optimization approach changes are your recommended changes in optimization approach for the suite, such as changes or additions to measurements or objectives, or even major changes in vision and mission for the test suite.

Dynamics

Create

Starting with the test results, construct the basic report with the metrics and the lists of failures and faults. This task includes the analysis of the failures to get the list of faults. You then execute the following subtasks in order: test completion status, root cause analysis, test approach optimization, test content optimization, and optimization approach optimization.

Analyze Test Completion Status

The first step in analyzing completion status is to look at the test metrics. Each test suite has one or more specific metrics that measure how well it achieves its objectives. Similarly, each test script has metrics for objectives. You should look at the results of the test to judge the quality of the test suite and its scripts. To do this, usually you need benchmarks of test suite and test script quality and test standards. If the suite as a whole fails to meet its objectives, go directly to jail without passing go—you should have caught this in a test review. Don't bother to continue analyzing the test, but go directly to optimizing the test approach and test content. Try, try again. If an individual script looks too good or too horrendous (that is, there are too few or too many failures or whatever other measure you have established), analyze it for script quality before assuming the code to be terrific or terrible in the next step.

If the metrics are what you expected and hoped for, it's time to figure out whether you need to expand the testing further. Dig out your test plan and look at the test standard for this kind of test suite (or this test suite specifically, if planning went that far).

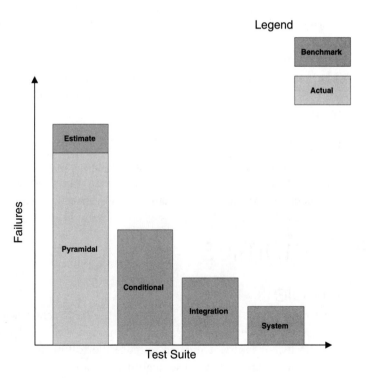

Figure 16.2 Example of number-of-failures completion criteria.

Testing standards can include several different specific ways of measuring the progress of testing:

- Whether you've spent enough time testing according to your manager or your manager's manager (not the best criterion, at least from the quality perspective if perhaps not from the job-retention perspective).
- Whether you've run all your test scripts at least once (a weak criterion, especially if there is no accompanying metric of model coverage and suite quality; remember, you are not testing anything completely, but rather indirectly through models of models).
- Whether you've achieved an acceptable level of risk, demonstrated by having found a number of failures comparable to reasonable benchmarks of failure discovery. (Figure 16.2 shows a typical graph of failure discovery versus a benchmark.)
- Whether you've achieved an acceptable level of risk, demonstrated by having begun to find fewer failures per effort-hour of testing. (Figure 16.3 shows a typical graph of failure discovery per effort-hour with the inflection point and the stopping point labeled.)

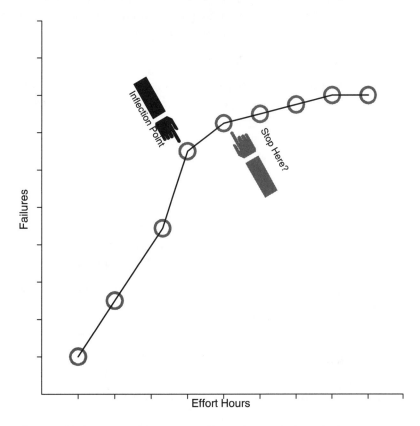

Figure 16.3 Example of failures-per-effort-unit completion criterion.

Which criteria you apply to this test suite depends on the nature of the test suite. For a hierarchical-incremental or conditional test suite, you can use expected failure rates to benchmark your level of risk, as the suite has measures of test coverage based on the appropriate test models you've selected. For integration or system or regression test suites, you should use some combination of expected failure rates and the rate of change of failure discovery with respect to testing effort, since the test models are more diffuse.

Ch. 17

Test
Standards

See the section on test standards in Chapter 17. This is the point at which you start the Implement method of the test standard for each test object you are evaluating. The resource responsible for the evaluation is also responsible for following the standards.

In any case, the data you collect from the test suite and its execution give you the information you need to evaluate whether you've caused enough pain to the developers, or whether to continue the torture. As a consequence of this decision, you decide whether to optimize the test suite or to let it go because you've reached an acceptable level of risk—at least, for this test suite. Often this decision is a key one that permits the life cycle to move to a new phase. For example, if you decide that the hierarchical-incremental test suite has reduced the number of failures in individual classes to a reasonable level, the developers and testers can begin integrating the classes and running the integration test suite.

Find Root Causes

Identifying root causes for failures and faults requires both persistence and an intuitive ability to recognize the obvious. The primary tool for causal analy-

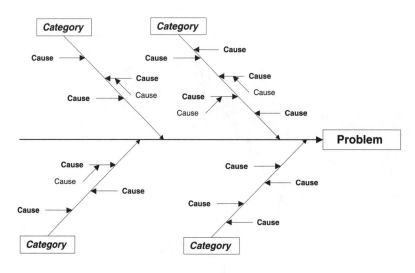

Figure 16.4 Example of causal analysis fishbone diagram.

sis is the fishbone diagram, with which you should be reasonably familiar by this time. Figure 16.4 shows a prototype of a causal fishbone diagram (an Ishikawa diagram, to the cognoscenti). The main bone is the problem statement, the major side bones are the categories you want to investigate, and the rest of the bones are the causes of the problem in a particular category. Don't let the hierarchical format keep you from overlapping categories—there are no rules here. Also, as with most brainstorming activities, root cause analysis usually benefits from having more than one person involved in an interactive, group session.

The main way you figure out the root cause is to ask "why" until nobody can answer the question or until the answer begins to smack of metaphysics. Probing into the decisions made and the "way it works" invariably yields significant insights into special and common causes of problems. Be careful to avoid circularity, though; as with any procedure, an infinite loop is not useful. If you find yourself explaining something in terms of something else in the diagram, make sure you aren't going to explain the something else in terms of the first something. The snake eating its own tail is a stock metaphysical concept. Stick to facts.

It's also useful to keep track of the ancillary issues that come up in the analysis, even if they turn out not to apply to this test suite. Feed such issues back into the quality system on a formal or informal basis.

Optimize Test Approach

Having identified root causes of the problems, think about the way you approached the testing in the test suite. See the individual sections on test suites for discussions of the various modeling decisions you can make. Your approach depends on what kinds of risk are important or likely. Go back and examine your assumptions in the light of what you've learned from the test. Also, think about the mission and objectives of the different parts of the quality system that you affect through the test model and make sure you are closely aligned with those objectives. Come up with a list of changes and append them to the test evaluation report.

Optimize Test Content

Once you've settled in the approach, apply it to the models to determine what the changes mean in specific terms. First, decide what should happen to the test models. Do you need a new model for any technical component? Was there something missing that seems to have contributed a good many failures? Is a particular model deficient in content? Did your state-transition model fail to take certain states into account? Did your transaction-flow model miss some basic tasks in a transaction?

After listing the model changes, list any changes to test objects. Derive new test objects from the new or changed test models. Correct any faults in the test objects that already exist. Take a second look at your equivalence classes and decide whether some additional test objects would be useful. Often you will find a gaggle of failures comes from a misunderstanding or perhaps a misstating of the equivalence relation over some domain.

Optimize the Optimization Approach

Finally, think back over everything you've seen and done and decide whether the optimization approach itself needs adjustment.

Operational objectives (objective-approach-measurement triples) tell you about the specifics of what you want to achieve. Do you still want to achieve exactly that? Will changing the objective or the measure help you get to a higher return on investment (ROI) or productivity rate? Can you think of a better way to achieve the objective than the current approach?

You even can change your vision and mission for the test suite if you figure something out that revolutionizes the way you think about your testing system. Take care, though, not to be too influenced by temporary fads. Vision and mission statements should be reasonably stable, because they should represent some values basic to your quality system. If they don't, think about why they don't. (Hint: Root causes *can* be metaphysical on occasion, or perhaps ethical or value-based are better terms.)

Review

After completing the test evaluation document, you need to review it as you would any development document. You should conduct the review just as you would a test review, but you should carefully put the review in the context of the quality system optimization effort stemming from your analysis and proposals for optimizing the optimization approach, if any.

Example

The thirty-third run of the DTS Problem system integration test suite ran overnight, and the autarch and project manager came in the next morning to find the test results in their email. Running the test evaluation report, the autarch generated a first draft of the report with the current failures and metrics.

The test results reported 15 failures. Looking at the failures, the autarch identified six faults, two of which were responsible for six failures. The autarch entered the faults into the database and left the five other failures to the test review for resolution into faults by the project manager.

Looking at the current test suite and script metrics, the autarch and project manager were satisfied that the suite was on track. The ratio of failed requirements to total requirements had gone to zero after the twenty-fifth test run (a debacle, that one—78 requirements still not satisfied). The ratio of test objects tested to total test objects had increased to 0.97 from 0.85 at the last test run; it looked as if the test team was finally catching up with test development. The effort per execution of the test suite was down to six hours from its initial 60 hours, which meant that the test team had managed to automate the remaining manual tests; that new C++ test framework was finally paying off.

The test suite contained a series of functional, interface, synchronization, exception, and widget-playback test scripts. Each contributed several failures to the total number of failures. The project manager looked at the failure discovery rate graph in the draft report. The test run took a total of 50 hours of effort, including test development and the six hours required to run the test, including manual test scripts. The rate of discovery, 0.3 faults per effort-hour, was definitely declining, confirming that the inflection point from the previous test was in fact a decline in the rate. It looked as if the system was stabilizing. The project manager reflected on the test completion criteria: 100 percent model coverage and an estimated fault discovery rate of 0.04 faults per effort-hour. Not there yet; at least one more run, possibly two, would probably do it. By the next run, the test team should have better than 100 percent coverage; they also should have found most of the remaining faults, especially now that the requirements had stabilized. The project manager adjusted the project schedule to reflect two more test runs, down from the five she had previously estimated.

Turning to optimization, the autarch now looked at the integration test approach. The decision made after the last review to add the synchronization tests by improving the concurrency design model and adding concurrent test operations to the classes had proved itself, finding five failures in the last test run. The objectives and metrics for the approach still looked good compared to the overall system testing objectives: lowering the overall risk of failure to an acceptable level.

The test models seemed to be adequate, covering the requirements use cases and providing a good, measurable set of test objects. The test objects still seemed a bit weak; perhaps a bit more work with equivalence classes in the functional and interface test models would help. The autarch scheduled a meeting with the project manager and the testing team to discuss further optimization.

The autarch and project manager then discussed the overall approach and agreed that the mission and vision were still in line with the goals of the project and the company and that there was no need to change at this point. The project manager noted in the report that the proposed change in product focus being considered by the chief executive probably would have an effect on the optimization approach for the DTS product, as the numerical targets for ROI would change. But since nothing had happened there, it was premature to change the objectives of the project.

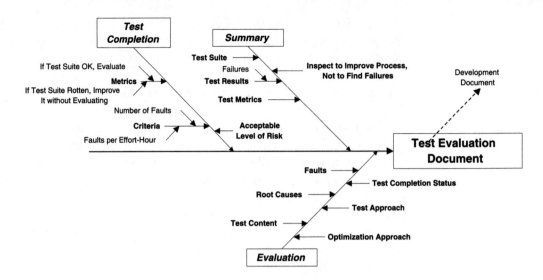

Figure 16.5 Road map for the test evaluation document class.

Road Map

Figure 16.5 is the road map for the test evaluation document class.

CHAPTER 17

TEST STANDARDS

Test Standards

Standards enable reuse. Standards inhibit creativity. Sounds like "tastes great, less filling." Throughout history, standardization has carried technology to greater levels of implementation and availability. Numerous examples exist: Telephones, automobiles, computer keyboards, operating systems, graphical user interfaces: all have benefited from the adoption of some level of standardization. Why not testing practices, and for that matter software development at large?

Giant bureaucratic institutions have developed around standards. Political systems (communism comes to mind), religious systems (we leave the identification of specific religions to the reader), social systems (the welfare system in the US as of 1995) and corporations (IBM of the 1980s) have stagnated as a result of too much standardization and the ensuing lack of freedom and creativity. The problem is not one of standards; rather, it is having the right standards for the right objectives with the right implementation approach.

Standards come in different flavors. Certain standards are or amount to *law*. Deviation from them is regarded as unacceptable behavior. Other standards represent excellence or describe a *desirable behavior*. This is the spirit behind the standards we are proposing in the hierarchical method. Still other standards are recommended practices; desirable but not required practices, these usually are referred to as *guidelines*. *Conventions* are de facto standards. There is general agreement about how to do something and mostly everyone does it that way. Your current development culture is based on convention. In order to implement the hierarchical method, you will have to replace many of your current conventions with new standards. You will need a plan to succeed! Plan on a one-to-seven-year transition period.

This book contains a series of classes, all of which derive from a single class, the optimization approach. Each class contains a vision, mission, and set of operational objectives that reflects the contribution that the class makes to the quality system. Your modifications of these objectives to suit your own optimization cycles and needs provides you with a comprehensive set of objectives and measures for evaluating how well you are doing. Standards provide a quantifiable way of setting the success threshold for your optimization objectives. The measurement in each objective, by itself, does not report success or failure; only when you compare it to a criterion for success do you know whether you have achieved your objective. That's the role standards play: They are the criteria by which you judge success. Your optimization approach for each kind of object is viable only to the extent you can establish a good set of objectives and a standard for evaluating them. Testing standards thus consist of the standards for each test object's operational objectives plus any additional criteria that can play a role in optimizing the quality system.

Also, note that this book defines test standards as optimization objects in their own right with their own mission, vision, and operational objectives. That means that you optimize standards as you would any other object in the quality system. Now, at some point quality begins to eat its own tail: That's where common sense comes in. When you start seeing the need for standards that standardize standards for standards, step back, take a deep breath, have a cup of coffee, and throw everything away to start from scratch: You've gone overboard, and nobody's going to pay attention. Focus on value and productivity, not standards; optimization, not criteria; success, not numbers.

How your organization chooses to present a testing standard depends on its corporate culture. Medical applications subject to FDA regulations or financial applications subject to government laws will have a strict attitude to certain standards. Government contractors and military applications find it easier to introduce and follow standards than developers of shrink-wrap software. If your corporate culture centers on group consensus, you should introduce standards as guidelines, then try to evolve them into enforced standards by reaching a consensus on their value and applicability. Use good sense and be sensitive when suggesting the standards.

Following is a list of guidelines for bottom-up implementation of testing standards.

- Choose a project that is likely to succeed anyway.
- Never, never, NEVER make anyone go back and change already completed work to conform to your standards. (If they do it on their own it is a sure sign that they value and have bought into the standard.)
- Choose a rollover date: one that all work from this date forward will come under the new standard.
- Inspect to standards.
- Delay deployment of any standards that slow down progress enough to put the project schedule in jeopardy.
- New standards are best introduced on new projects, before the project starts to be late.
- It is better to have half a testing standard than none at all.
- Tools that automate documentation are well worth the money.
- If the word "standard" is too strong in your development culture, change it to "guideline."
- Always measure the productivity gains and or increased product value associated with standards.
- Conduct postproject reviews and evaluate standard practices.
- When the project fails and the project team did not follow the standards, point out how a standard could have helped.
- Evolve your standards: Adjust and improve them as part of the optimization cycle of the object to which they belong.

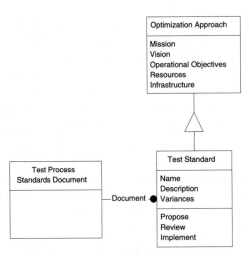

Figure 17.1 Structure of the test standard class.

Figure 17.1 shows the structure of the test standard class.

Leadership

Vision: A standard, reusable criterion for test success that improves productivity and system value.

Mission: To define the reusable criterion for success of a test objective.

Objective 17.1: To set or reuse a standard criterion for test success for a test object that optimizes productivity and system value.

Approach 17.1: For a specific test object, identify and deploy the appropriate test standards that you believe will achieve optimal levels of value and productivity when you implement the test object. Measure the results and verify that the standards do have their desired effect.

Measurement 17.1: Compare productivity and quality metrics from a system that uses the standard to benchmarks that use other standards or none at all.

Structure

DOCUMENT
The *document* is the test standards document that contains the standard.

NAME
The *name* is a unique, meaningful identifier, just like coded objects.

DESCRIPTION
The *description* defines the standard, referring to the object to which it applies and to any specific operational objectives for which it is the success criterion.

Variances

The *variances* list defines the conditions under which you may waive, bypass, or amend the standard.

Dynamics

Propose

Propose a standard that clearly defines the criterion for success of a test object objective. Get consensus on the standard, both about acceptance of the underlying philosophy of value and about any competing standards. When you have such a consensus, review the standard.

Review

It is important to give the users of a standard a say. This may be a long and painful process, or it may be relatively easy. It depends on your corporate history and culture. Listen carefully to what the reviewers are saying about the proposed test standards; often it is not the standard they object to, but the lack of resource to implement the standard. Solve the resource problem and you have a much better chance of the standard taking root.

Implement

Implementing a standard requires an ongoing process that kicks in whenever you are evaluating the results of using some test object. You must be sure to refer to this implementation process from the evaluation object, thus ensuring that you are following the standard. The resource with the responsibility for the test evaluation also must be responsible for following the standard.

Example

The DTS project manager, having made the decision to add the hierarchical-incremental test suite to the test model possibilities for the DTS project, assigned the quality assurance team the responsibility of setting a standard for these tests. After training in the test technique, the test team decided that the key to achieving the objectives for the test suite was the standard for model coverage. The general criterion for all test models in the hierarchical-incremental test suite became 100 percent: Tests would have to cover all test objects in the test model at least once.

This general standard then translated into specific standards for each of the test models: state-transition, transaction-flow, exception, control-flow, and data-flow.

The team proposed the standard and compared it to the prior standard of covering all the statements in the code at least once (statement coverage), showing the rest of the team how that level of coverage was simply insufficient to reduce the risk of failure to the required level. Several communication

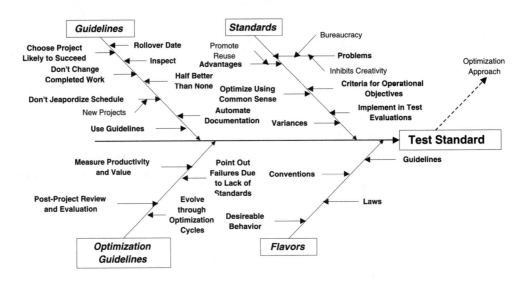

Figure 17.2 Road map for test standard.

meetings were required to convince all the developers that their coverage analyzers were inadequate, but eventually everyone came around and the project manager held a review. The project team accepted the proposal, and the test team wrote the new standards into a new section of the test standards document. The team built the appropriate checks into the test evaluations so that the evaluation would always apply the correct standard.

Road Map

Figure 17.2 is the road map for the test framework class.

Test Standards Document

The *test standards document* is a kind of standards document. It contains the standards for test models, objects, scripts, and suites, including the testing objectives and criteria and any standards for test object documentation and reports. As with any object in the quality system, if you can reuse a document from another project, your productivity and value go up. It pays to stabilize your standards and reuse them from project to project, as you don't have to redevelop them for every project.

Figure 17.3 shows the structure of the test standard document class.

Leadership

Vision: Minimal effort required to communicate test results and evaluations to those concerned.

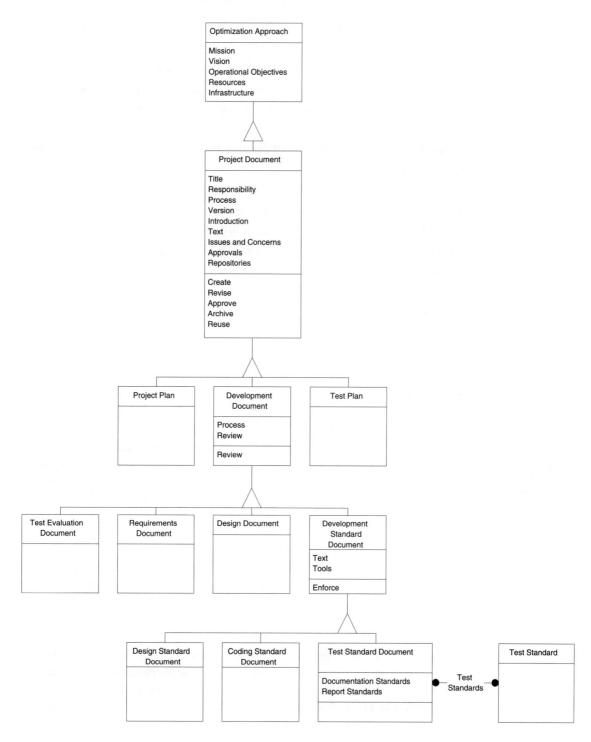

Figure 17.3 Structure of the test standard document class.

Mission: To reduce the chance for error and to improve communication of testing results.

Objective 17.2: To reduce the risk of error in testing.

Approach 17.2: Standardize test criteria, documentation requirements, and report formats to reduce the risk of failing to achieve the intended results of testing.

Measurement 17.2: Number of failures resulting from lack of compliance with testing standards.

Objective 17.3: Improve communication of test results.

Approach 17.3: Standardize documentation requirements and report formats that communicate test intentions, contents, and results effectively.

Measurement 17.3: Number of communication failures due to lack of test standard compliance.

Structure

TEST CRITERIA

The test criteria are the test standards that apply to specific test models, test objects, test scripts, and/or test suites. See the preceding test standard class for more details.

DOCUMENTATION STANDARDS

The documentation standards are the standards for commenting on or describing test scripts, test objects, and test models in the test repository. These standards may also apply to ad hoc comments you enter for a particular test run through the test framework interface. (See Chapter 17.)

REPORT STANDARDS

The report standards are any content and format standards that apply to test reports that report the results of a test run. You need to make sure all the relevant information to evaluate the tests is present in the test reports, and the test report standards give you a place to do that.

Example

Since the DTS is not the first project to use most of the test environment, it reused much of the test standards document from previous projects. The project team modified the initial test standards document to include some additional test standards (See the "Example" section above.) The team reused in their entirety the sections on documentation and report standards.

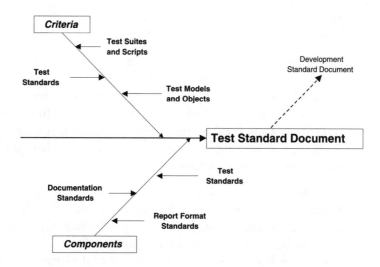

Figure 17.4 Road map for the test standard document class..

Road Map

Figure 17.4 is the road map for the test standard document class.

Part 3 References

1. Lowell Jay Arthur. *Improving Software Quality: An Insider's Guide to TQM.* John Wiley & Sons, New York: 1992.

This book introduces you to Total Quality Management (TQM) and its tools. If you don't have a background in TQM, Arthur's book serves as a good preparation for this one. The approach in this book doesn't take the overall system into account, however, so be aware that optimization requires something more than it recommends.

2. Boris Beizer. *Black Box Testing: Techniques for Functional Testing of Software and Systems.* John Wiley and Sons, New York: 1995.

This is an introductory textbook on the techniques and theory of functional or black-box testing, which includes many of the test models and test objects this book uses to test object-oriented systems. This book is a useful reference to have on hand while building test scripts for your object-oriented system.

3. Boris Beizer. *Software System Testing and Quality Assurance.* Van Nostrand Reinhold, New York: 1984.

This book is a thorough reference to the process of software quality assurance (SQA). It goes into detail on all aspects of SQA and overviews the test techniques for each kind of testing. The reviews of the objectives and strategies in the different modes of testing is very worthwhile.

4. Boris Beizer. *Software Testing Techniques*, 2nd ed. Van Nostrand Reinhold, New York: 1990.

The reference on testing techniques, this book is essential to have close at hand when you are developing tests. Although it does not distinguish object-oriented technology, you can apply the techniques Beizer presents to most testing in this book. In any case, familiarity with Beizer is an essential part of a tester's education.

5. Robert V. Binder. "Design for Testability in Object-Oriented Systems," *Communications of the ACM* 37:9 (September 1994): 87–101.

This article is an excellent survey of the work being done on class testing and class design for testability. It is particularly good on the way to build testing into the class; it suggested the conditional test model to us.

6. Donald G. Firesmith. "Testing Object-Oriented Software," available from Advanced Software Technology Specialists, 17124 Lutz Road, Ossian, IN 46777.

This article introduces a different view of object-oriented testing. We use some of its concepts in Chapter 16.

7. Donald C. Gause and Gerald M. Weinberg. *Exploring Requirements: Quality before Design* Dorset House Publishing, New York: 1989.

This book gives you the tools to understand the why of building software: requirements. It focuses on removing ambiguity and adding missing requirements, giving you many specific techniques. If you ever have to do a requirements document, read this book first. Read it anyway, even if you don't have to do a requirements document; you'll benefit.

8. David Harel. "Statecharts: A Visual Formalism for Complex Systems, *Science of Computer Progamming 8* (1987): 231–274.
David Harel. "On Visual Formalisms," *Communications of the ACM* 31:5 (May 1988): 514–530.

These two articles introduce a notation for state-transition diagramming that has revolutionized the art, literally: Pictures now become capable of representing extremely complex models that you could previously represent only through tables. The secret is to use an inheritance-like scheme for nesting states, thus allowing a more complete logical language for showing multiple transitions and either/or situations. Anyone seriously considering state-transition diagramming should read these articles. Also see the OMT dynamic modeling adaptation of the techniques in Rumbaugh et al., *Object-Oriented Modeling and Design*.

9. Mary J. Harrold and John D. McGregor. "Incremental Testing of Object-Oriented Class Structures." In *Proceedings of the 14th International Conference on Software Engineering*, 1992.

This article defines some useful ways of looking at testing in the context of an inheritance hierarchy.

10. Richard Helm, Ian M. Holland, and Dipayan Gangopadhyay. "Contracts: Specifying Behavioral Compositions in Object-Oriented Systems," *ECOOP/OOPSLA '90 Proceedings* (October 21–25, 1990): 169–180.

This article lays out the formal concept of the contract: "a set of communicating *participants* and their *contractual obligations*. Contractual obligations extend the usual type signatures to include constraints on behavior which capture the behavioral dependencies between objects." We extend this to include class invariant constraints.

11. Ivar Jacobson, Magnus Christerson, Patrik Jonsson, and Gunnar Overgaard. *Object-Oriented Software Engineering: A Use Case Driven Approach*. Addison-Wesley, New York: 1992.

A pragmatic and comprehensive method for object-oriented software engineering in all its aspects, this book is a must for anyone seriously considering an object-oriented development project. The section on use cases is useful in showing you how to go about requirements analysis, though it doesn't go very deep. (See Gause and Weinberg above.) The section on testing is also of interest.

12. Laurence R. Kepple. "The Black Art of GUI Testing," Dr. Dobb's Journal (February 1994): 40–46.

A good introduction to GUI testing techniques.

13. Virginia Klenk. *Understanding Symbolic Logic*, 2nd ed. Prentice-Hall, Englewood Cliffs, NJ: 1989.

An introductory textbook on symbolic logic that is extremely well written and useful for both teaching and self-study. The first part of the book deals with sentential logic of the sort we use for conditional modeling; the rest of the book deals with proofs and predicate logic (logic involving quantifiers such as "for each" and "for all"). A strong logic background is very useful to testers; conversely, being weak in understanding symbolic logic is likely to lead you to take more risk than necessary.

14. John D. McGregor and Douglas M. Dyer. *Selecting Functional Test Cases for a Class*. Clemson University, Clemson, SC: 1994.

Seminar class notes. This course goes into a lot of detail on state-transition testing and ways to make it more useful in the context of testing classes.

15. Kurt Mendelssohn. *The Riddle of the Pyramids*. Praeger Publishers, New York: 1974.

The first book on pyramid testing, though the pyramids in question are real, not abstract ones. Mendelssohn takes an architectural archaeological approach to understanding the pyramids and their construction, especially the rhomboidal "bent" pyramid at Dashur. This understanding is the inspiration for the pyramidal testing method in the current book. The rhomboid produced a "SAFE" pyramid, according to Mendelssohn. The techniques learned in building this pyramid influenced the successful, larger pyramids at Giza.

16. Bertrand Meyer. "Applying "Design by Contract," *Computer* (October 1992): 40–51.

This article contains a full analysis of the place of conditional "contracts" in object-oriented programming, including a discussion of assertions and exceptions. The Eiffel programming language includes these as part of the language, not just as part of the debugging environment.

17. Glenford J. Myers. *The Art of Software Testing*. John Wiley and Sons, New York: 1979.

This book is one of those small, succinct, extraordinary books that get published from time to time in spite of the best efforts of publishers and academics. Although now years out of date and in many ways "quaint," it still has more of interest cover-to-cover than most testing books twice or thrice the size and is a good, practical accompaniement to Beizer's more thorough and theoretical books. The serious tester would do well acquiring this book.

18. James Rumbaugh, Michael Blaha, William Premerlani, Frederick Eddy, and William Lorensen. *Object-Oriented Modeling and Design* Prentice-Hall, Englewood Cliffs, NJ: 1991.

We have chosen to adopt the object-oriented modeling notation of this book largely because of its popularity in the object-oriented community. While the modeling techniques have some flaws, such as the lack of a notation for generic templates, tasks, and exception handling, and some flaws in the methods for object-oriented design, overall this is a good, well-written book that gives you serious tools for modeling and design. In any case, you must become familiar with the notation as one of the major communication mechanisms in the literature.

19. George J. Symons. "Capture/Playback Techniques," *Dr. Dobb's Journal* (February 1994): 42.

A short article describing the terms "true-time," "character-recognition," and "widget-playback tests."

PART 4

THE SOFTWARE DEVELOPMENT SYSTEM

The *software development system* is the part of the quality system that relates to *software development*: the specification, design, and building of the software system. This system contains the software itself and the things you use to build it.

Figure P4.1 shows the inheritance hierarchy of the software development system. As with all the different parts of the quality system, all the classes have the *optimization approach* as the root; see Part 2, "The Process System," for details on that class. Each class can and should go through optimization cycles to optimize value and productivity.

The *project document* hierarchy is partially in this system (*development document* and its subclasses) and partially in the project management system (project document and project plan and its subclasses). See Part 5 for details on the different parts of the project document. There are

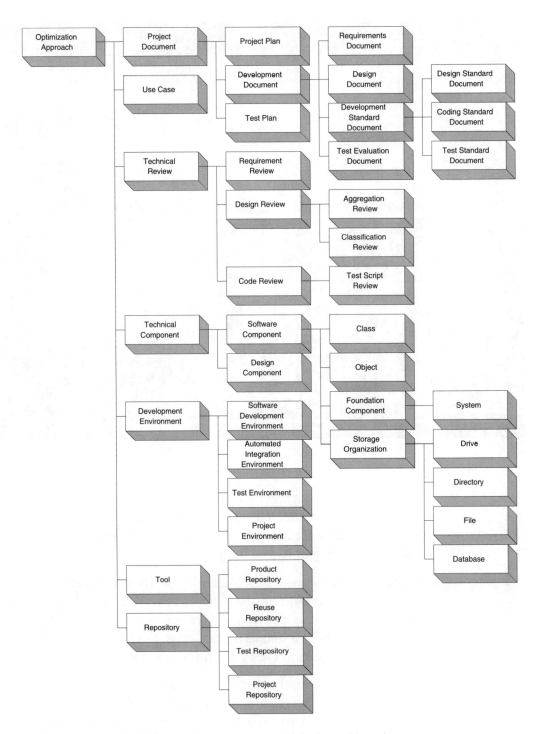

Figure P4.1 Software development system inheritance hierarchy.

four kinds of development document: *requirements*, *design*, *standards*, and *test evaluation*. Two kinds of standards document are of interest to software development: the design standard and the coding standard. See Part 3 for details on test evaluation and test standard documents.

The *use case* is the primary element of requirements documents; it is a sequence of transactions from the point of view of system users playing different roles in using the system.

Technical reviews include reviews of *requirements*, *designs* (including both composition and inheritance hierarchies, the *aggregation* and *classification* reviews, respectively), and *code*. Test script reviews are a kind of code review; see Part 3.

Technical components include both *software* and *design components*. The technical component is an abstraction that represents a technical "thing" to which various parts of the system refer. In other cases, parts of the system refer directly to software or design components. Software components include *classes* and *objects*, unsurprisingly; most object-oriented programming systems have these components. A great deal of software development concerns collections of classes and objects as well; the *foundation component* (a meaningful collection of classes) and its subclass *system* (a meaningful collection of foundation components) represent such collections. Finally, the *storage organization* (*drives*, *directories*, *files*, and *databases*) represent the static data component of software.

Software development happens in the context of a *development environment*. There are four types of environment: the *software development* and *automated integration environments*, of interest to developers; the *test environment*, of interest to testers; and the *project environment*, of interest to project managers. See Parts 3 and 5 for details on the latter two environments. The tool and repository are both components of the development environment and thus part of the infrastructure of software development (as well as of testing and project management). There are four kinds of repository:

- **Product Repository:** Contains the software and data for the product itself.
- **Reuse Repository:** Contains reusable software and data.
- **Test Repository:** Contains test scripts, plans, data, and results.

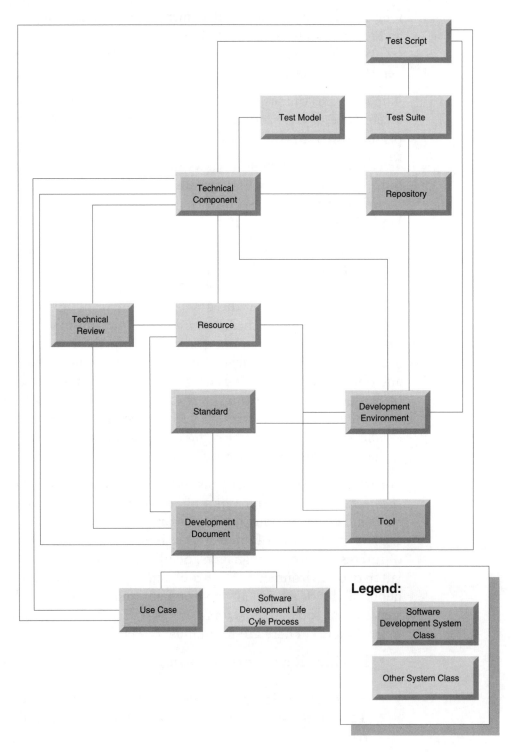

Figure P4.2 Software development system containment hierarchy.

- **Project Repository:** Contains project documents and data.

Figure P4.2 shows the containment relationships between the classes at a high level.

The central objects in the containment hierarchy are the technical component and the development document, which relate to most of the other classes in the system. Components and documents drive the software development system. The technical aspects of the system (components, reviews, and documents) all sit on top of the system infrastructure, the standards, resources, and tools that are part of the development environment.

Technical reviews relate development documents to technical components. The technical component connects to the test system directly through links to test models, test suites, and test scripts, and both technical components and test suites are part of a repository of stored objects.

Development documents relate to use cases and to the software development life cycle process in the process system.

CHAPTER 18

DEVELOPMENT DOCUMENT

Development Document

A development document is a project document that the development team creates and uses during the software development life cycle. The abstract class development document sets the structure and generic content of all the different kinds of development documents, adding to the project document structure. See Chapter 22 for details.

Ch. 22

Project Document

This chapter, an overview, presents the different kinds of development documents that you use to optimize the quality system. There are doubtless many other kinds of development document, but they are less relevant to productivity and value. See the military software development standard DOD-STD-2167A for a careful and complete, detailed, and very bureaucratic vision of development documentation.

The two main process documents of interest to the quality system are the requirements document and the design document. The *requirements document* is an explanation of what you want the software product to do. The *design document* is an explanation of how you intend to build the software to do what you want it to do.

The *development standards document* details, for some domain, the rules and suggestions and criteria for success that you intend to use in building the software product.

Ch. 16

Test Evaluation

The *test evaluation document* contains the analysis and details of the results of running a test suite. This evaluation, the subject of Chapter 16, contains the feedback that optimizes the test and quality systems.

The rest of this chapter contains one section on each of the first three subclasses of development document: the requirements, design, and development standards documents.

Development documents are a part of the product repository, and you can consider them part of the project repository as well.

Figure 18.1 shows the structure of the development document class.

Leadership

Vision: A written document that improves the quality and productivity of software development.

Mission: To improve quality and productivity of software development by means of written words and illustrations.

Objective 18.1: To improve the quality of the development process.

Approach 18.1: Create, review, revise, and approve a development document for a software development life cycle process. The review process involves several team members in addition to the document author, which improves quality through team critiques and brainstorming.

Measurement 18.1: Number of failures associated with the development process object.

Each subclass of the development document operationalizes the vision and mission with specific productivity objectives for the particular area of the system the document improves.

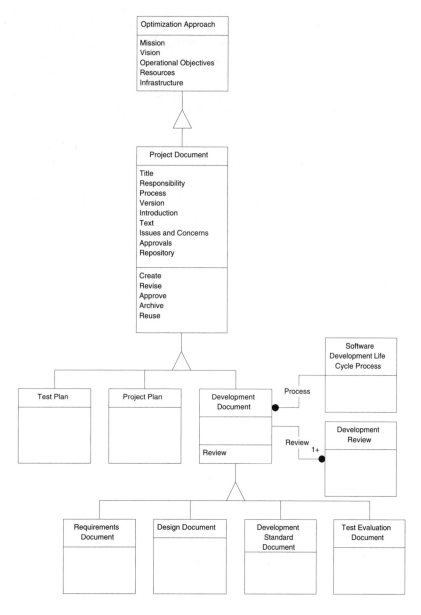

Figure 18.1 Structure of the development document class.

Structure

PROCESS

The process overloads the project document process to limit the process object to be a software development life cycle object.

Each document applies to a single process object in the software development life cycle or to the life cycle as a whole. If you find yourself creating a document that spans two or three process objects, you're probably not organizing your work and thinking. You're probably not focusing on the process model that you're using, which is generally a bad idea, or at least suboptimal. Think of development documents as process documents and align them with your model of how you organize development work. This process is part of the overall system with which you must align your work to optimize productivity and value.

In particular, as the primary objective of a development document is to improve the quality of the process, you should focus on a single process to measure the results and optimize the process in an optimization cycle. It is never a good idea to optimize more than one process in an optimization cycle, as the increased variance creates too much noise in the optimization data.

Ch. 19

Technical
Review

REVIEW

The development document review is the review object you create when you review the document. This object contains the reviewers, minutes, action item list, and other review elements; see Chapter 19.

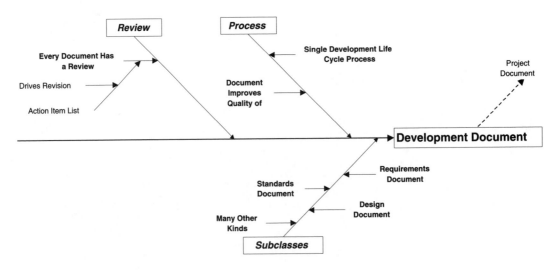

Figure 18.2 Road map for the development document class.

Dynamics

REVIEW

The review task is a development review of the document. All completed development documents go through a development review. As the document is reviewed, the review object is created, which is part of the development document object. See Chapter 19 for details on the structure of reviews. The action items of the review drive the revision task. As with any review, the consensus of the reviewers can be to have another review after revisions.

Road Map

Figure 18.2 is the road map for the development document class.

Requirements Document

Donald C. Gause and Gerald M. Weinberg (1989) put it very succinctly in their book, *Exploring Requirements*: "If you tell what you want, you're quite likely to get it. If you don't tell what you want, you're quite unlikely to get it."

As Don Gause is fond of saying, the ability to "disambiguate" is the essential dynamic underlying all requirements work. Don explains "disambiguate" as the process of removing ambiguities from the requirements. (Gause and Weinberg 1989) How to do it takes them another 300 pages to explain in detail, and there is probably a lot more to be said. For example, their concept of requirements analysis does not include the use case that Ivar Jacobson (1992) developed to structure the connection between requirements and the rest of the development process less ambiguously. The use case is such an important part of the requirements document that later we break it out as a separate object. This book is not, however, about requirements analysis, it's about testing.

Testing focuses on discovering the myriad ways that software can fail. Many failures derive fundamentally from requirements in that they are failures precisely because the software doesn't do what you wanted. On the other hand, if you don't do requirements analysis very well, many failures derive from contradictions introduced by developers not knowing what you wanted. To paraphrase Gause and Weinberg, you have to explain what you want clearly before you can hope to get it.

Validation is the process of determining whether a software object conceptually meets the set of requirements to which it owes its life. It addresses the issue of whether you are developing the right objects. Every kind of test script involves some kind of validation, usually through a relationship to one or more use cases. Validation may be accomplished statistically as in an inspection or review.

If the software object doesn't do what the use case needs done, a *validation failure* arises. Compare the validation process to the *verification* process, which determines whether the software object implements the required functionality correctly. This is usually accomplished by the dynamic execution of tests against software.

A *requirements failure* arises from not knowing the correct requirements. It represents the later discovery of a requirement problem when the design or implementation fails. This kind of problem can be a missing or an ambiguous requirement (one that does not adequately specify what you want to the developer, which leads to failure).

Why is a requirements failure especially problematic? Why should we put so much effort into a requirements document? There are two answers to this question.

First, it is much less costly to fix a requirements error in the requirements process than in later processes. Barry Boehm, in *Software Engineering Economics* (1981), studied the relative cost of fixing a requirements failure in different phases of his waterfall development process. Fixing it at the design stage is about five times more costly; fixing it at the coding stage is about ten times more costly. Fixing it during maintenance is anywhere from 40 to 1,000 times more costly, depending mostly on the size of the product. Gause and Weinberg (1989, pp. 17–18) point out that this probably underestimates the problem because it takes into account only *successful* projects! Thus the impact of requirements failures on the project cost can be dramatic later in the development life cycle.

But, second, requirements failures prove in practice to be a sizable portion of the variability of development process quality. Boehm (1981) estimated requirements failures to be 8 to 10 percent of the total number of failures — again, for *successful* projects. Our experience has been 10 percent to 30 percent. A related problem, creeping requirements, affects over 70 percent of medium-to-large applications, according to Capers Jones (1994). *Computerworld* (1995) recently reported the results of a survey showing that incomplete requirements was the number-one reason for software project failure. (Lack of user involvement and unrealistic expectations were in the top five.) Optimizing the requirements process thus has a lot of potential for improving overall system quality.

One way to improve requirements quality is to reuse requirements. Tested, reviewed, unambiguous requirements for a feature of the product could eliminate virtually all requirements failures. Without some form of a requirements document, it is unlikely that you will ever be able to reuse requirements in this way. Also, if the project represents an enhancement of an existing system, you should reuse the original requirements, adding the new ones. The requirements for a system feature must exist as long as the feature does.

Figure 18.3 shows the structure of the requirements document class.

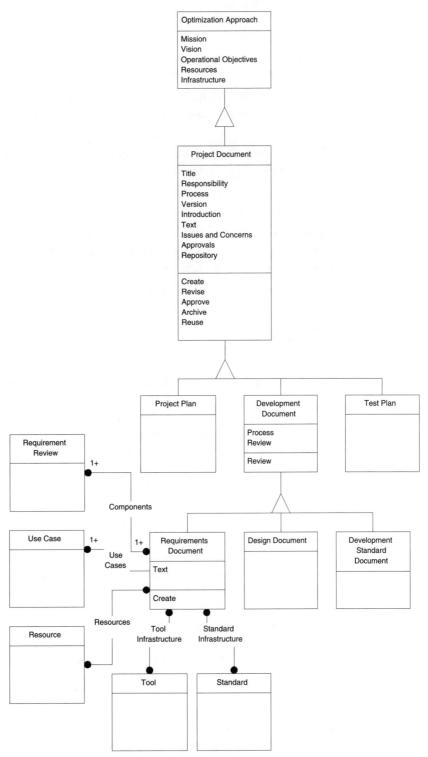

Figure 18.3 Structure of the requirements documents class.

Leadership

Vision: A written requirements document that improves the quality and productivity of software development.

Mission: To improve quality of the software product and the productivity of the development process by fully documenting what you want the product to do.

Objective 18.1: To handle the quality component of this mission, with the accompanying approach and measurement items.

Objective 18.2: To improve productivity of the development process by reducing the number of requirements failures.

Approach 18.2: Explore requirements thoroughly, document them in a requirements document, and review that document with the users of the software; or reuse such a document.

Measurement 18.2: Number of requirements failures per life cycle process.

Structure

TEXT

The text of the requirement document describes or summarizes requirements beyond what the use cases detail. This text is often useful for gaining a complete understanding of what users want, as often use cases are difficult to absorb into a big picture. It also may include illustrations, such as network designs, maps, or other details, that will help the developer understand what the user wants. It also may contain text examples of situations the software must handle. Finally, it may contain the visual and textual specification of the user interface (menus, dialogs, scripting languages, and so on) to whatever extent that's appropriate for the stage in the development life cycle. This part of the requirements document is usually called the functional specification, though in the case of an object-oriented system that's something of a misnomer. We prefer the term "external specification."

USE CASES

The use case is a systematic textual analysis of a requirement for the product. The following section entitled "Use Case" provides details. Each requirement document has (or should have) a set of use cases that link to any number of tests throughout the development life cycle.

RESOURCES

Creating a requirements document requires special training both in understanding what users want and in expressing those needs in clear, unambiguous language or use cases. The system analyst is one person who performs this sort of work. The analyst also may need specific domain knowledge to enable him or her to understand the nature of the users' needs.

INFRASTRUCTURE

Special tools may aid in creating requirements. For instance, graphical requirements methods, such as data-flow diagramming and Specialized System Design tools, are supported by Computer Aided System Engineering (CASE) tools. These tools can integrate with your word processing or document preparation systems to produce requirement documents by integrating the text and graphics automatically.

Your organization may have standards for requirements specifications, especially if you are using some kind of graphical method.

Dynamics

CREATE

The **Create** method overloads the standard document method to create the use cases and other components of the requirements document. The heuristic for creating a full set of use cases follows these steps:

1. Produce a list of initial user requirements in text form.

2. Determine the set of users and customers of the system.

3. For each user, identify the roles he or she may play in interacting with the system; this is the set of actors for the system. (See the following "Use Case" section.)

4. For each actor, develop a single base-flow use case with a state-transition graph and a textual description of the sequence of transactions.

5. Iterate over each base flow to identify variants or possibly separate use cases.

6. For each use case, develop *extends, abstract use cases*, and *uses relations* to structure the set of use cases as the requirements become more complete. (Again, see the "Use Case" section.)

Example

The DTS team used a combination Object Modeling Technique (Rumbaugh 1991) and data-flow diagramming approach to specifying requirements, along with a comprehensive set of use cases. (An example follows.) The OMT Object Model and Dynamic Model specified the high-level interface objects and the data model objects (people, faults, and so on). The OMT Functional Model specified the use cases using data-flow diagrams.

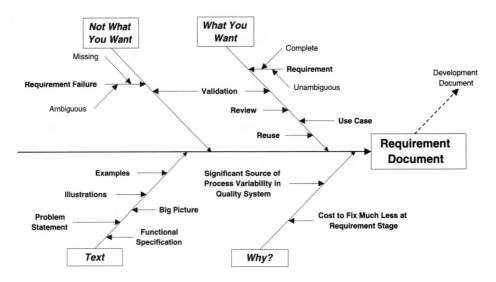

Figure 18.4 Road map for the requirements document class.

Road Map

Figure 18.4 is the road map for the requirements document class.

Use Case

The *use case* is an unambiguous description of a requirement as a sequence of transactions between an actor and the system. Jacobson (1992) invented the use case as part of his **Objectory** method for object-oriented analysis and design. Its aim is to be more systematic about usage profiles than a simple, textual, problem statement. By breaking down a requirement into a scenario of actor and system actions, the use case states completely and unambiguously what the system must do to be successful.

An *actor* is a role that the user plays in the system. (Not the user him- or herself, just one or more roles that a real user may play.) The actor is thus an external agent who stimulates the system by creating a dialog. A *transaction* is a series of actions that an actor initiates through a stimulus of some kind. The transaction ends when the system awaits another stimulus. The sequence of such transactions for an actor is a *use case*. An actor may own many use cases, or ways of using the system. The set of all actors and their use cases is the set of use requirements for the system. You can describe a use case with a state-transition diagram: the stimulus from the actor is a state change.

Jacobson (1992) has developed a sophisticated structure for use cases that makes the use case a kind of class, with operations, a variation on inheritance, and instances. A use case can have internal variants, and you can structure it by including extensions or "extends" or by a uses-relation between an abstract use case and a concrete one. The details of these relationships are beyond the scope of this book; see Jacobson's *Object Oriented Software Engineering* (1992), pp. 152–169.

You identify use cases through actors. The requirements document dynamics include a process for constructing the proper set of use cases; see the discussion earlier in this section for more details.

Figure 18.5 shows the structure of the use case class.

LEADERSHIP

Vision: A series of scenarios that comprehensively show what the system must do to be successful as a product.

Mission: To represent a scenario requirement completely and unambiguously.

Objective 18.3: To prevent requirements failures.

Approach 18.3: For each requirement, build a use case out of the sequence of user and system actions that make up the scenario for the requirement.

Measurement 18.3: Number of requirements failures

Objective 18.4: To allow design and code validation

Approach 18.4: Link the use case to the appropriate design and code components to allow validation of the design and implementation.

Measurement 18.4: Number of validation failures due to missing use cases.

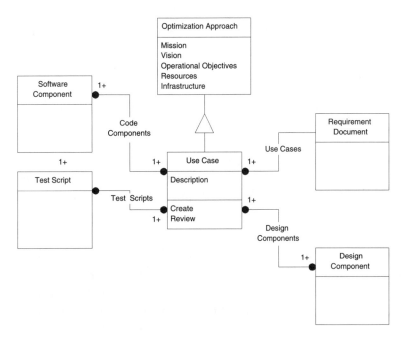

Figure 18.5 Structure of the use case class.

STRUCTURE

DESCRIPTION

The use case is a description of an ordered sequence of transactions, with each transaction consisting of a set of actions that do not request input from the actor. The transaction ends with such an input request. You can represent transactions and actions as descriptive text, as a state-transition model, or as any other kind of model capable of representing this structure.

DESIGN COMPONENTS

The use case relates to one or more *design components* (sections in a design document) that represent the architecture for implementing the usage scenario represented by the use case. All design objects should relate to at least one use case. The use case justifies the existence of the design object.

CODE COMPONENTS

The use case relates to one or more software *code components* that represent the implementation of the usage scenario that the use case represents. All software components should relate to at least one use case. The use case justifies the existence of the component.

TEST SCRIPTS

The use case also relates to one or more *test scripts* that validate a software component against the use case. Not all test scripts relate to use cases, but a substantial number of integration and system test scripts do.

DYNAMICS

CREATE

Creating the use case transforms a part of a problem statement into a complete, unambiguous series of actions. The format of the use case depends on the requirements standards you've set. It can be a simple, textual description of the scenario, or it can be a functional model or data-flow diagram or any other appropriate notation for representing a process. The **Create** method of the requirements document starts this method for each use case it creates.

REVIEW

The use case review is part of the larger requirements review. The reviewers walk through the use case step by step to make sure it is complete and unambiguous. This procedure is essential for validating the use case, as which then becomes the foundation for the validation of the rest of the system. After review, the use case gets revised and archived with the rest of the requirements document.

EXAMPLE

The requirements document that addresses the requirements of Technical Support for the DTS provides a simple problem statement for the Problem system:

Technical Support is a part of the software producer that handles the interface between the customer and the software producer. Technical Support shall be able to enter failure reports (Acting in the reporter responsibility role) containing the following information:

- A unique identifier for the failure
- The software product that failed, including the name of the product and the specific version of the product that failed
- Customer reporting the failure, with information sufficient for Technical Support to contact the individual who reported the failure with updated information
- Date of report
- Person reporting the failure
- Description of the failure
- Description of the hardware and software configuration under which the software failed
- Any supporting materials (test cases) required to reproduce the failure

The requirements use case for entering a failure report might look like this:

1. Create a Failure object.

2. Assign a unique identifier to the failure.

3. Assign a Product object to the failure.

4. Assign a Customer object to the failure.

5. Assign today's date to the failure.

6. Assign a Technical Support Engineer object to the failure.

7. Create a String object containing text that describes the failure and assign it to the failure.

8. Create a String object containing text that describes the hardware and software configuration under which the software failed and assign it to the failure.

9. Create OLE objects for any supporting materials required to reproduce the failure and assign links to those objects to the failure.

10. Insert the failure in the database.

11. Repeatedly handle events from the user interface that affect the object (see additional use cases).

12. Update the database as required and repeat handling events.

13. When the document closes, or on deletion of the failure in the database, or on closing the application, destroy the failure object.

Each step is a transaction that ends with a request for input from the actor. Figure 18.6 shows the data-flow diagram representation for this use case; each process bubble is a transaction, and the data flows represent transitions from transaction to transaction. The individual steps correspond to the data-flow process circles, and the process description language elaborates the individual steps in detail. Notice that steps 3-6 and 7-8 combine into single process steps; the asterisk indicates that these processes decompose into a series of smaller processes in another diagram, which is standard data-flow diagram technique.

You also could represent this use case as a state-transition diagram, with the states of the class being the states and the transactions being the transition/action pairs.

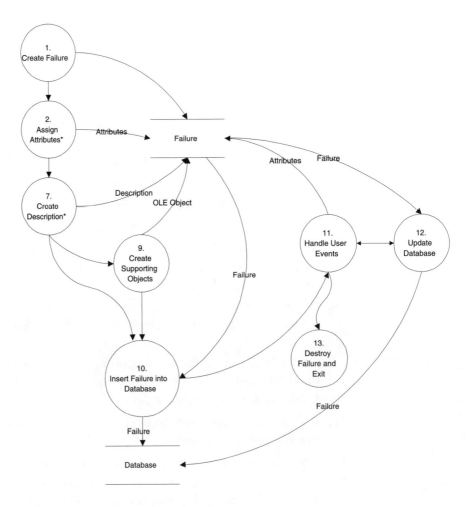

Figure 18.6 DTS use case data-flow diagram.

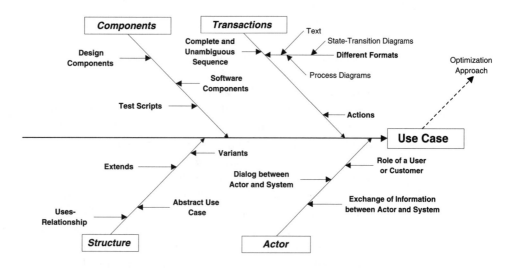

Figure 18.7 Road map for the use case class.

Road Map

Figure 18.7 is the road map for the use case class.

Design Document

A *design document* is a project document that specifies how to implement a set of requirements. An object-oriented design document usually consists of several kinds of information:

- A class model that shows the inheritance and containment structure of the classes in the system
- A behavioral model for each class that shows how objects of the class respond to messages and events
- A process model for the system that shows how the objects interact to satisfy requirements (use cases)

Different design methods have different ways of structuring these elements. You can organize the elements in whatever way makes the most sense: into systems, alphabetically, by the inheritance or containment hierarchies, by the work being done or by the resources assigned to the work, or by whatever method most software architects around you use to structure design documents.

Usually there is more than one design document in a product repository, as they tend to get quite involved as you get into more detailed system architecture.

Most architects distinguish three subclasses of design document:

- The *system architecture* or *high-level design document*
- The *detailed* or *low-level design document*
- The *data architecture document*

The *system architecture document* shows the major classes and their relationships, both inheritance and containment, without going into detail about attributes and methods or detailed system behavior. It specifies whether classes are abstract or concrete. The document shows the different systems and how they interrelate and the major classes belonging to each system. The objective of this document is to show how the pieces interrelate and to break the system up into major parts. Collaboration scenarios may describe how the major parts of the system work together as a process.

The *detailed design document* shows all the classes in detail, with attributes and methods and pseudocode describing the behavior of each method. It specifies the protocol for each method and the parameters for templates. It usually has state-transition diagrams showing the life cycle of each object, which the state-transition test scripts use. It may have process diagrams showing how the design relates to the use cases in the requirements document. It also specifies the test framework you use to run the test scripts for the class, including the appropriate drivers and stubs.

The *data architecture document* shows the major data structures and any relational or object-oriented database designs (tables and columns, data types, and so on). This document usually contains entity-relationship diagrams or object model diagrams of some kind.

A design failure occurs when you find a problem in the software that is a result of either a missing or a badly specified design component. If a component is missing usually the design must be reworked to add the missing parts; if the design is badly specified, the bad design and any consequences resulting from it must be reworked. Some examples of bad design:

- Failing to make necessary data visible to an object
- Making too much data visible to an object, enabling it to access parts of the system when it should not
- Organizing the objects in ways that impact productivity, performance, or reuse
- Introducing unnecessary complexity and thus decreasing maintenance productivity and increasing the risk of implementation faults

Figure 18.8 shows the structure of the design document.

Leadership

Vision: A systematic exposition of system and detailed object architecture that satisfies the requirements for the system and provides unambiguous plans for implementation and testing of the software components.

Mission: To document the complete and unambiguous architecture of the system to improve system value.

Objective 18.5: To eliminate failures in constructing classes.

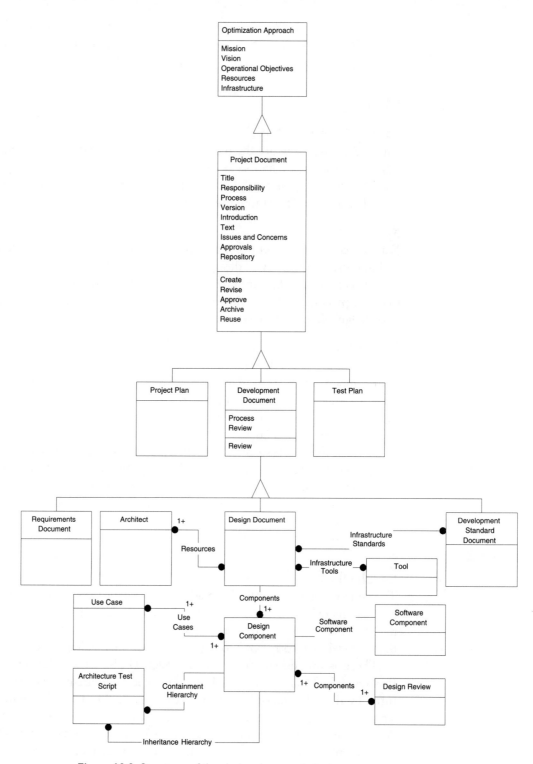

Figure 18.8 Structure of the design document class.

Approach 18.5: Design classes and systems using standard design techniques and tools, documenting the results for later use in constructing the classes.

Measurement: Number of design failures.

Structure

DESIGN COMPONENTS

The *design components* are the individual sections of the design document that describe the classes, database tables, systems, and other software components. Each design component should relate to a software component, and each should relate to one or more use cases.

RESOURCES

Experienced system architects are usually required to develop system-level architecture. Lower-level design requires knowledge of object-oriented design techniques. Data architecture is the realm of database design experts. Overall, producing design documents requires a high degree of specialized knowledge and experience.

INFRASTRUCTURE

Many tools are available for creating design documents; this is the focus of the entire upper-CASE software industry. Most major CASE vendors offer the standard object-oriented design methods, and most integrate with word processors and document production systems to let you automate the process of building the design document.

Because there are so many alternatives in the world of object-oriented design, most organizations need standards for the design method and structure. Some organizations take this further and specify the exact detail items each section in the document needs. In any case, you should be thoroughly familiar with your organization's set of design standards before proceeding with your design document.

Example

The design documents for the DTS adhere to the basic OMT design method with its object model, dynamic model, and functional model components. Each class in the DTS has an object and dynamic model, and each system has a series of functional models that correspond to requirements in the requirements document.

There is one design document for each DTS system (Person, Product, Problem, Tools, and Port). Each document is a hierarchy of sections structured by the inheritance hierarchy of the system. Most DTS systems have a single root class, so the document organization begins with the next level down as main section headings, with the root class serving as the introduction. For example, this is the structure of the Person System design document. (See Figure 2.3 for the class hierarchy.):

Title
Responsibility
Version
1. Introduction
1.1 Executive Overview
1.2 Scope
1.3 Assumptions
1.4 Person Class
1.4.1 Object Model
1.4.2 Dynamic Model
2. Customer Class
2.1 Object Model
2.2 Dynamic Model
3. Employee Class
3.1 Object Model
3.2 Dynamic Model
3.3 Manager Class
3.3.1 Object Model
3.3.2 Dynamic Model
(and so on through the subclasses)
4. Functional Model

The database design document for the DTS uses the OMT object model to model the database objects, then translates them into relational tables specified with ANSI standard SQL **CREATE TABLE** statements.

Road Map

Figure 18.9 is the road map for the design document class.

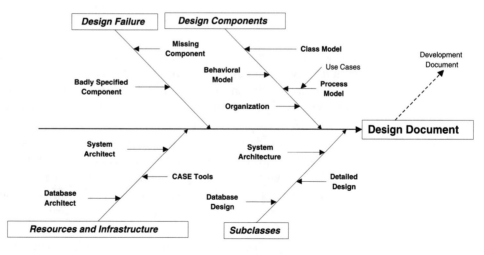

Figure 18.9 Road map for the design document class.

Development Standards Document

Development standards documents are a kind of development document used by developers to standardize certain methods for doing their jobs (or more prosaically, imposed by the organization on developers as a part of the corporate bureaucracy).

Anything that exhibits the human characteristic of choice is a potential target for standardization. The line between effective standards and bureaucracy is a fine one; like most fine lines, you may not be able to explain it, but you always know which side you're on. Standards make the trade-off between encouraging individual creativity on the one hand while limiting the risk of technical failure and enhancing team communication on the other. We make development standards, as are all other aspects of the quality system, a kind of optimization approach. You need to specify your vision, mission, and goals for each standard and measure their effectiveness.

Standardization may be a solution to an optimization problem, but it can be an optimization problem itself: What to standardize, and to what extent? For example, some methods may require enforced standards, while others just require guidelines that developers can follow as they wish.

The three main kinds of standards of concern to software developers are design, coding, and test standards. There also may be development and project document guidelines. There are thus three subclasses of standards document:

- **Design Standards Document**
- **Code Standards Document**
- **Test Standards Document**

Design standards specify a design method and any specific design issues that the architect should resolve in a certain way. For example, some software shops outlaw multiple inheritance on the theory that it leads to unworkable complexity. Others require that all methods spell out parameters in detail, with data types and an input/output specification.

Code standards specify a standard programming language or languages (C++ and SQL, for example, with some modules in C) and rules for using them. Some examples include:

- Use static data members to store data shared between all objects of a class, not global data or static data scoped to the file.
- Use only constant string literals that cannot change at runtime.
- Use default arguments where possible to simplify messages (a guideline).
- All programs should use a standard set of primitive data-type names from **dts.h**.
- All SQL table names should use the singular noun form, not the plural (Person, not People, for example).

See *C++ Programming Guidelines* by Thomas Plum and Dan Saks (1991) for a sample C++ code standard.

Ch. 17

Test
Standards

Test standards specify the test object test standards and the test documentation and report standards. See Chapter 17 for more detail on test standards, which are part of the test system.

It's usually a good idea to put the code standards, and perhaps the design standards, in an online document or help file to allow architects and developers easy access as they work. The more accessible a standard, the more the team follows it.

Figure 18.10 shows the structure of the development standards class.

Leadership

Vision: Minimal effort required to communicate correct decisions and information throughout the organization.

Mission: To reduce the chance for error and to improve communication through design and code.

Objective 18.6: To reduce the risk of error in design and coding.

Approach 18.6: Standardize design and code techniques that reduce the risk of design or code failure.

Measurement 18.6: Number of failures due to standard compliance errors.

Objective 18.7: Improve communication through design and coding.

Approach 18.7: Standardize design and code techniques that communicate most effectively (or eliminate techniques that obscure communication).

Measurement 18.7: Number of communication failures due to standard compliance errors.

Structure

TEXT
The text of the standard contains the various standard items, usually organized by subject area.

INFRASTRUCTURE
CASE tools often are capable of enforcing many standard design and code rules.

Dynamics

ENFORCE
If you don't enforce your standards, they aren't standards. Generally it is a good idea to automate standards checking. Having a set of rules built into your CASE design tool, or having a code-checking program scan all code on

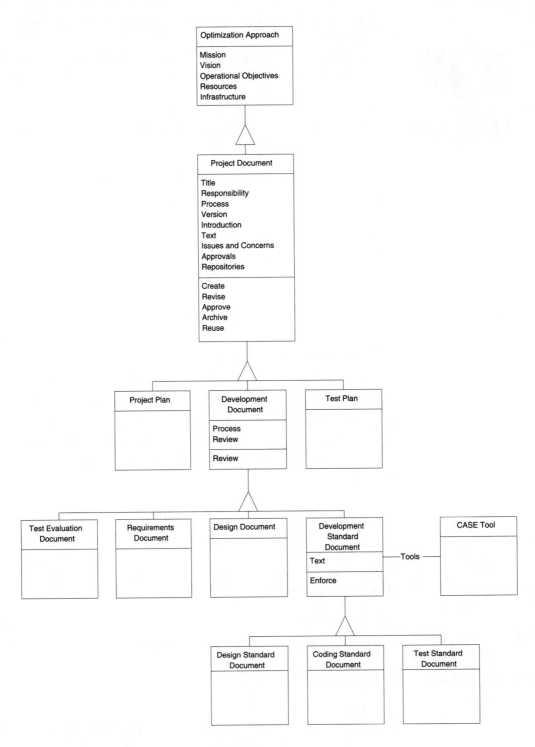

Figure 18.10 Structure of the development standards document class.

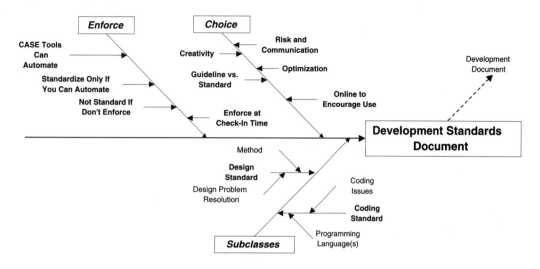

Figure 8.11 Road map for the development standards document class.

check-in to the version control system, will greatly reduce the chance of standards compliance failures. Note that you should standardize only those things you can automate, because other standards will be much harder to enforce. Your only recourse is reviews.

Unenforceable rules are an optimization cycle opportunity. Again, if you don't (or can't) enforce standards, they aren't standards.

Example

The DTS design standard is to use the OMT method and its notation as implemented in a particular CASE tool. The tool enforces scripted rules on the design when you check the design into the configuration management system; each rule applies to a clearly identified risk of technical failure in the DTS risk assessment.

The DTS coding standard follows the Plum and Saks (1991) standard with some additional features that apply to the DTS style of coding, again based on risk assessment. When you check in the code, the configuration management system calls a command-line program that checks the coding standards.

Road Map

Figure 18.11 is the road map for the development standards class.

CHAPTER 19

TECHNICAL REVIEW

Technical Review

A *review* is an inspection of an object in order to evaluate it. The key terms in this generic definition are "inspection" and "evaluation."

There are two meanings for "inspection." An *inspection* can be an official examination, with "official" connoting the heavy stamp of authority and legitimacy in the context of the political system. But an *inspection* also can be a simple, careful, and critical examination, with no political connotation. The latter meaning is the one that applies in the case of the technical review; the former is the one that applies in the case of the project review, such as the schedule or milestone approval review.

Evaluation is, by definition, always in the context of some kind of value or quality. When you critically inspect something, you are evaluating its quality according to whatever system of values applies in the context. In the quality system, you evaluate objects based on the vision, mission, and objectives of the object.

Putting all this together, a *technical review* is a careful and critical examination of a technical object with respect to its objectives. If you think about it, a critical evaluation of work, particularly by other people, is always an excellent way to ensure that the work is of high quality. Formalizing this evaluation and aligning it with the objectives of the object (and hence with the quality system objectives) is a key part of the quality system.

A technical review can be formal or informal. *Formal reviews* have written evaluations of the object and formal responsibility for the quality of the evaluation. It can involve one person or a team of reviewers. Generally, technical reviews in the context of an object-oriented software project are formal, team reviews of technical components, with written minutes and an action item list. Each reviewer is responsible for full, open participation in the review and for the completeness and correctness of the minutes and action items.

This chapter provides an overview of the technical review. See any book on software engineering management for more information, but in particular you can benefit from the third edition of the *Handbook of Walkthroughs, Inspections, and Technical Reviews* (by Daniel P. Freedman and Gerald M. Weinberg (1990). This book is a highly readable and very detailed account of the different kinds of technical reviews.

The difference between walkthroughs, inspections, and reviews is largely pragmatic. *Walkthroughs* generally step through a series of objects, while *inspections* focus on single objects. The term "review" is more generic. The exact format of a review is clearly a matter for an optimization cycle and depends on the objectives for the specific review. The technical review class is thus an abstract class with concrete subclasses for the different types of review:

- **Requirements Review:** Review of the requirements specification and use cases

- **Design Review:** Review of design components
- **Code Review:** Review of code components
- **Test Script review:** Review of test code components (test scripts)

A few general guidelines derive from formal meetings in general:
- Keep the meetings to two hours or less with at least one break. Count the meeting and preparation time against standard project accounts; this is real work, not overtime catch-up work.
- Keep participation to a minimum; the more people you have, the harder it is to reach a conclusion or consensus. In particular, try to eliminate managers from reviews, as they tend to transform an evaluative review into an authoritative one. Managers should participate only in a technical capacity, if at all.
- Distribute the review materials in advance with sufficient time for all participants to prepare themselves, and hold the participants responsible for two to four hours of preparation.
- Review objects at a stage where they can accommodate changes; otherwise, you're wasting your time critically examining them.
- If there are automated ways to inspect an object, do that before the review; there is no point in substituting the valuable time of a real person for the cheap time of a computer. Note that people can and should validate the automatic checking; software checking may be cheap but it's seldom perfect. But what is?

At the end of the review, the review leader should get consensus from the participants about whether the reviewed object needs further review. If there is no consensus, or if everyone agrees that the object needs further review, a further review of the object should be scheduled, after whatever revisions the action item list indicates.

Figure 19.1 shows the structure of the technical review class.

Leadership

Vision: A critically evaluated technical object of high quality.

Mission: To critically evaluate technical objects with respect to their vision, mission, and objectives.

Objective 19.1: To evaluate a technical object to find technical failures relative to its objectives.

Approach 19.1: Determine the vision, mission, and objectives of the object you are going to review, then review it in a series of two-hour meetings with minutes and action items lists.

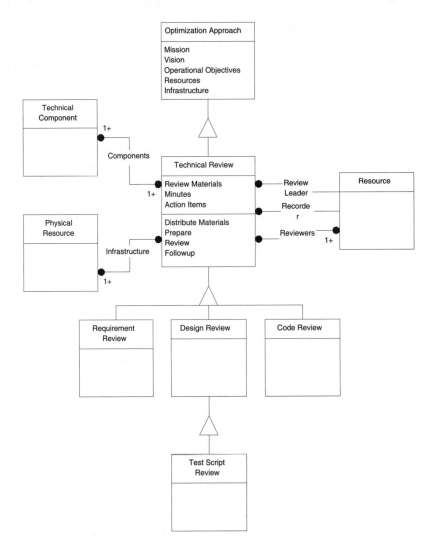

Figure 19.1 Structure of the technical review class.

Measurement 19.1: Ratio of the number of action items per hour of review to the expected rate of failures per hour based on the size of the technical object in function points.

This measurement requires some benchmarking to figure out how many failures to expect from your technical objects per hour of effective review time. Also, it's important to note that you should not collect the number of failures in the technical object as a measure of its quality. As Freedman and Weinberg (1990) suggest, *it's not a failure if it doesn't make it out of the review*. Here you are measuring the success of the review, not of the object you're reviewing. That will come later when you use and test the object.

Structure

COMPONENTS

The *components* of the review are the set of technical components (requirements use cases, design components, code components, test scripts) to review.

REVIEW MATERIALS

The set of *review materials* communicates the technical object or objects that are the subject of the review. The nature of this set of materials depends on the nature of the object; therefore, this is therefore a pure method that each subclass needs to overload.

REVIEW LEADER

The *review leader* is the person with ultimate responsibility for the minutes and action items as well as for the quality of the review itself. The skills this person needs include the ability to understand the technical object and to keep the quality of the review high. In particular, the leader needs to keep the meeting focused and productive given its objectives. He or she needs to report in the minutes the reasons for poor-quality results of the review.

RECORDER

The review *recorder* is the person with responsibility for generating the minutes and action item list. This person needs to be able to listen and summarize points and action items, preferably in a way that is public and immediately available to the participants of the review, such as flip charts or online conferencing. In particular, he or she needs to be able to make decipherable notes, not always an easy-to-find skill among those of us who are graphically challenged.

REVIEWERS

The rest of the *reviewers*, generally no more than six or seven people at most, should be technically capable of evaluating the object. They should have some training in the rules and customs of conducting reviews in your organization.

MINUTES

The *minutes* describe in text format the significant events of the review, including all points of criticism raised and the response, if any. The minutes also should include the subject, date, and names of the reviewers.

ACTION ITEMS

Specific items on which the author of the object (or anyone else) needs to act are *action items*. This textual list contains the set of failures that the reviewers discover during the review. These items serve as the basis for measuring the effectiveness of the review.

RESOURCES

Each technical review has some specific resources associated with it in the list of reviewers above.

INFRASTRUCTURE

The review generally needs some kind of meeting room and the appropriate set of facilities such as a flip chart or other meeting tools.

Dynamics

DISTRIBUTE MATERIALS

The review leader should distribute the review materials with enough lead time for the reviewers to prepare themselves.

PREPARE

The review leader prepares the review infrastructure while the reviewers prepare themselves for the review.

REVIEW

The review method is the actual review meeting or meetings. Such meetings should last no more than two hours at a stretch with breaks as often as needed.

FOLLOW-UP

The recorder publishes the minutes and the action item list so that all the reviewers have a record of what happened and what they need to do. The

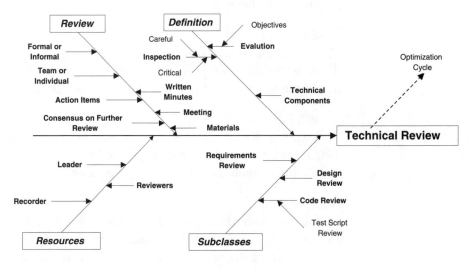

Figure 19.2 Road map for the technical review class.

review leader follows up on the action items or transfers responsibility for them to the appropriate manager to ensure they get done.

Road Map

Figure 19.2 is the road map for the technical review class.

Requirements Review

The *requirements review* is a technical review of one or more requirements components: the requirements document or documents and/or the individual use cases that are part of the requirements document. You should review requirements after you create them and after you make major changes to them following the creation review.

This review identifies requirements failures, missing or ambiguous requirements. See the "Requirements Document" section in Chapter 18 for details on these kinds of failures. Be sure you understand the real objectives of each requirement component; the requirement must satisfy these objectives, not just be internally consistent and correct.

Figure 19.3 shows the structure of the requirements review class.

LEADERSHIP

Vision: A critically evaluated requirement component of high quality.

Mission: To critically evaluate requirements with respect to their vision, mission, and objectives.

Objective 19.2: To evaluate a requirement to find requirement failures.

Approach 19.2: Determine the vision, mission, and objectives of the requirement or requirements you are going to review, then review the requirements in a series of two-hour meetings with minutes and action items lists.

Measurement 19.2: Ratio of the number of action items per hour of review to the expected rate of requirement failures per hour based on the size of the technical object in function points.

Structure

COMPONENTS

The requirements document, or the part of it that you are going to review, is the *component*. You can review more than one requirements document if doing do is appropriate.

REVIEW MATERIALS

The requirements document, or the relevant portion of it is the main *review material* to distribute to the reviewers. You also should distribute any sup-

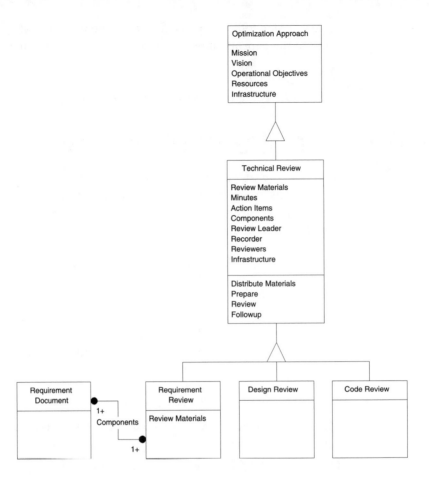

Figure 19.3 Structure of the requirements review class.

porting material, such as problem statements, prototypes, previous versions of the product, and so on.

Example

The DTS project manager completed the requirements document for the part of the DTS that serves Technical Support users, including a set of use cases, and scheduled a requirements review. (See the "Requirements Document" section in Chapter 18 for a sample of the requirements document and use cases.) The project manager assigned a lead programmer to be review leader and the project librarian to be recorder. The review leader chose an additional developer from the DTS team to participate, then arranged for a product marketing participant and a technical support engineer participant as well. The review leader then distributed the requirements document to this group of five people and scheduled a two-hour review meeting for the following week.

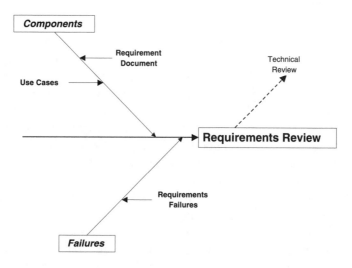

Figure 19.4 Road map for the requirements review class.

All the participants read the requirements document except the marketing reviewer, who was shanghaied into doing a trade show and had no time. After the usual moaning during the initial review meeting, the reviewers rescheduled the meeting for the next day so that the marketing reviewer could catch up.

The review went well, with all participants contributing suggestions and corrections, all of which were relatively minor. The recorder wrote down the points on a flip chart, asking after each person whether it was right, and wrote the action items on a separate flip chart as the group agreed to them. At the end of the review, all participants agreed that no further review was needed.

After the review, the recorder wrote up the minutes and the action item list from the flip charts and sent them to the review leader by email. The review leader distributed the approved minutes and action items to the participants for review, and everyone agreed that they were accurate and complete. The review leader then sent the final minutes and action item list to the project manager for revision of the document.

Road Map

Figure 19.4 is the road map for the requirements review class.

Design Review

The *design review* is a technical review of one or more design components: the design document or documents and/or the individual classes or database tables that are part of them. You should review a design component when you create it and when you make major changes to it after the initial review. Design reviews apply to all kinds of design components, including system architecture documents, low-level design documents, and database design documents.

This review identifies both requirements failures and design failures.

Each design component should relate to at least one use case in the requirements. There is no point in designing components that aren't required. A simple traceability matrix showing the list of use cases that the design addresses is a good addition to the design document. If you think you have discovered a missing requirement, state the requirement and decide whether the design component is superfluous or not based on the review team's reaction to the requirement. If you decide the component is necessary, flag the problem as a requirements failure.

A design failure occurs when a design component fails to achieve its objective or when the design fails to meet the general design objectives your design method and standards impose on the design process. For example, a general rule in design is to avoid alternative designs that achieve the same objective. That is, keep the design simple so that developers can be more productive. Another example is the "abilities": the various qualities that make a good design. Here is a list of the more common qualities:

- **Usability:** The design component should be easy to use.
- **Portability:** The design component should be easy to move to a different operating system or interface framework.
- **Maintainability:** Identifying problems in and making changes to the component should be easy.
- **Reusability:** The design should allow you to easily reuse the component in other applications, where that is useful.
- **Performance:** The design should perform according to requirements.

Your standards documents should have a check list of these kinds of design issues.

Ultimately, the design review should answer these questions: Is there enough information in this design component for a developer to implement the component? Is the component correct, complete, and consistent?

Two specialized types of design review review architecture:

- Aggregation Review: Reviews the composition hierarchy.
- Classification Review: Reviews the inheritance hierarchy.

These specialized reviews find the following kinds of architectural errors:

- Are any classes missing or incoherently structured with respect to requirements?
- Are the included classes at the right level?
- Are any classes abstract that should be able to instantiate objects?
- Have you included the latest versions of the correct classes?

- Are the parameters to generic classes correct?
- Does the set of inherited attributes make sense given the requirements?
- Do subclasses contain appropriate implementations of overloaded methods? Overridden methods?
- Do the included classes work together without critical failures?
- Are the interfaces and relationships between objects consistent?
- Are the components that use one another compatible?
- Are components of an object correctly created according to the class design?
- Are the owned components of the object correctly destroyed when the object is destroyed?
- Does the object contain all the required components to satisfy its requirements?

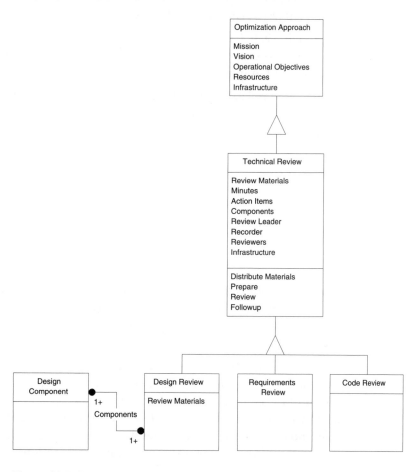

Figure 19.5 Structure of the design review class.

Design reviews also have interesting side effects in the quality system: training and communication. If junior team members participate in design reviews with more senior members, they will learn the ropes and rules quickly and will be exposed to the different techniques your organization uses in design. In addition, the design review exposes the design and its rationales to other members of the team, increasing the team's level of general knowledge about the design.

Figure 19.5 shows the structure of the design review class.

Leadership

Vision: A critically evaluated design component of high quality.

Mission: To critically evaluate design components with respect to their vision, mission, and objectives.

Objective 19.3: To evaluate a design component to find requirements or design failures relative to its objectives.

Approach 19.3: Determine the vision, mission, and objectives of the design component you are going to review, then review it in a series of two-hour meetings with minutes and action items lists.

Measurement 19.3: Ratio of the number of action items per hour of review to the expected rate of requirements or design failures per hour based on the size of the technical object in function points.

Structure

COMPONENTS

The design review reviews design *components*, which are individual sections of a design document.

REVIEW MATERIALS

The *review materials* should include the design document or documents and any prototypes that show how the design component works in practice.

Example

After completing the design of the system for relating faults and failures, the chief architect of the DTS team assigned a developer to head up a design review of the components involved. The review leader chose several developers to participate in the review along with the chief architect in his technical role, and designated one of the developers as recorder. The chief architect, at the request of the review leader, distributed her design document to the rest of the review team a couple of days before the meeting.

The team met and carefully reviewed the class designs using the design document and a simple prototype the architect had put together to show how the list processing features work. The team found one major problem (the one-way linked list needed to be two-way, since the iterators needed to move back and forth through the sets of faults and failures) and several maintainability issues (too many pointers in the method arguments and obscure member names). The team also found in passing that a missing requirement (two-way processing) had resulted in a missing design element. The recorder wrote down the list of design failures on a whiteboard. At the end of the review, the team agreed to review the design again after the architect had revised the requirements and made the changes to the design.

After the review, the recorder wrote up the minutes and the action item list from the whiteboard and gave them to the review leader. The review leader distributed the approved minutes and action items to the participants for review, and everyone agreed that they were accurate and complete. The review leader then sent the final minutes and action item list to the architect for revision of the document. The review leader also notified the project manager that there was to be another review of the fault-failure design component.

Road Map

Figure 19.6 is the road map for the design review class.

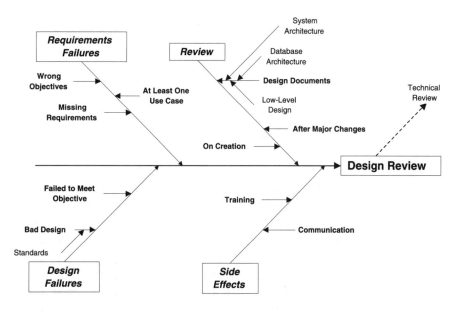

Figure 19.6 Road map for the design review class.

Aggregation Review

The *aggregation review* reviews containment: the "has-a" relationships in the object-oriented design. Each object is a collection of attributes and methods, and some if not all the attributes represent objects elsewhere in the system. The containment, or *aggregation*, hierarchy is the network of such relationships. Reviewing this hierarchy in a system tests the relationships that make the sum of the whole greater than the parts.

The overall containment hierarchy for a system usually breaks into decomposable pieces that loosely connect through messaging. This decomposability can lead to a way of partitioning the system into smaller systems. Each aggregation review should review one such containment hierarchy rather than attempting the whole thing. To review your containment hierarchies effectively, you may have to break even these pieces into smaller pieces. If you experience much of this nested complexity it is probably prima facie a reason to raise an issue in the review. That is, if you can't break your system into reasonably small parts that you can understand in a couple of hours of review, your system is probably too complex, and you should look at ways to reduce this complexity. Reducing complexity is one of the main issues in software architecture.

In the review, you first need to inspect the hierarchy to make sure that it corresponds to the requirements. Doing so may require decisions as to which requirements should apply to this hierarchy and some detours to make sure that you review requirements that don't make the cut in another review and another system.

No visibility of objects outside the system that are not explicit in the design shuld be required in the hierarchy. Also no internal visibility of objects beyond what the design calls for should be necessary. Finally, you should make sure that visibility is consistent and that objects that need to know about other objects always do. In other words, you should inspect the hierarchy to make sure the encapsulation and abstraction of the implemented system are appropriate.

This inspection can be technically quite complex. For example, in C++, you make objects visible by including their definitions in header files—or at least that's the preferred way to do it. If your header files include several class definitions as well as a multitude of constants and other low-level design constructs, often you will find that you have many symbols or names to which you will never refer in the containing object. Given this situation, you need to decide whether to improve encapsulation and cohesion by breaking up the header files into smaller parts or whether the design is cohesive enough to overcome the fact that certain classes don't use all the features of their contained objects. *Do not worry about things like compiler limitations at this stage.* For example, many C++ compilers limit the number of include files that you can nest within each other. Letting these constraints leak into the design is a primary reason for getting stuck with a bad architecture. While you may have to make some compromises during coding if your tools have limits, these limits definitely are not a reason to compromise your design.

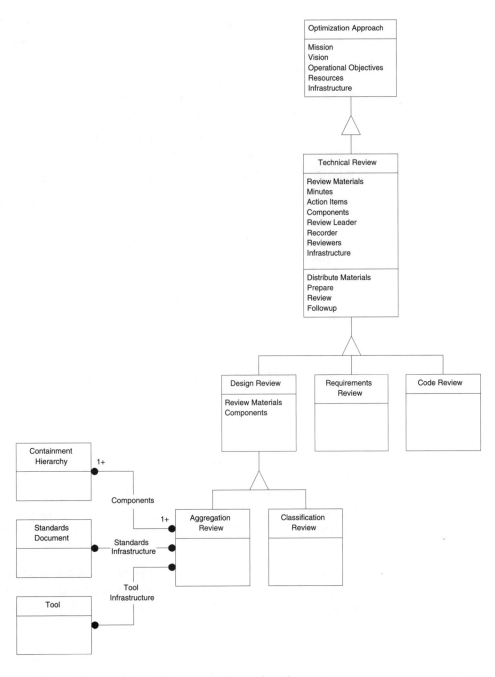

Figure 19.7 Structure of the aggregation review class.

Minimizing visibility is a risk-reduction approach that limits the possibilities for affecting parts of the system or greater system unnecessarily. On the other hand, optimizing visibility encourages reuse by ensuring that an object has the appropriate level of access to information it needs to do its job. That job might even be something that current requirements do not envision.

Figure 19.7 shows the structure of the aggregation review class.

LEADERSHIP

Vision: A class hierarchy design that meets requirements and optimizes visibility, encapsulation, and reuse.

Mission: To validate the system against requirements involving containment relationships between objects and to verify the containment hierarchy's design.

Objective 19.4: To validate the class hierarchy design against its requirements.

Approach 19.4: Trace each property and class back to its requirements use cases.

Measurement 19.4: Number of failures to meet requirements plus number of requirements failures (failures of the requirements to reflect the system needs correctly).

Objective 19.5: To test the hierarchy for appropriate visibility of objects.

Approach 19.5: Inspect the hierarchy design to ensure that all objects are visible to their containers in well-understood ways and that no object is visible that is not required to be visible.

Measurement 19.5: Number of design failures due to inappropriate visibility.

STRUCTURE

COMPONENTS

The *components* relationship in this case is the set of has-a, or containment, relationships between classes. The containment hierarchy as a design component is usually an element or elements of a design document or a diagram or diagrams in the product repository. The optimal representation for review is a single, integrated diagram with associated design explanation and detail.

INFRASTRUCTURE

A standard for the design and documentation of the containment hierarchy may provide criteria for review. The validation aspects of the review task may require special tools for looking at the use cases and/or the design components.

EXAMPLE

As an example of aggregation, part of the DTS Problem system tracks the history of the status of the problem. A problem has a *problem status history*, a time-ordered list of statuses through which the problem has passed. The current

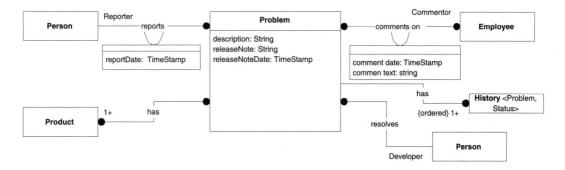

Figure 19.8 DTS Person class design.

status is the most recent, and the initial status is the oldest item in the list. Figure 19.8 shows the class design.

Here's the portion of the Problem class design in C++ pseudocode that relates to the ProblemStatusHistory. The italicized lines are the ones relevant to this review:

```
// Class: Problem
// Description: A problem is a fault or failure that creates a need for service
//              or product development.
#include "sqlobj.h"   // DTSSQLObject base class
#include "dtsstr.h"   // String class
#include "timestmp.h" // TimeStamp class
#include "person.h"   // Person class
#include "pstathst.h" // ProblemStatusHistory class and friends

class Problem : public DTSSQLObject
{
public:
    Problem(Connection & connection, SDWORD id, const String &description,
                  const Person & reporter, const TimeStamp & reportDate);
    Problem(Connection & connection, SDWORD id); // query constructor
    Problem(Connection & connection) : DTSSQLObject(connection), reporter(connection),
                  developer(connection) {nullify();}
    // Return iterator over status history of problem
    ProblemStatusItr & getStatusItr(void) const;
    // Insert and Delete Methods
    RETCODE         insertObject(void); // insert the problem into the database
    RETCODE         deleteObject(void); // delete the problem from the database
    // Update Methods
    RETCODE updateStatusHistory(const ProblemStatus & status);
protected:
    // Primary data members
    SDWORD        id;                   // unique identifier
    String        description;          // description of problem
    Person        reporter;             // person who reported the problem
    TimeStamp     reportDate;           // date on which reporter reported problem
    String        releaseNote;          // text describing problem for publication
    TimeStamp     releaseNoteDate;      // date of release note completion
    Person        developer;            // person assigned to fix the problem
    ProblemStatus HistorystatusHistory; // history of statuses for problem

};
```

Here is the Problem Status History class itself, including the iterator class:

```
// Class:              ProblemStatusHistory, ProblemStatusItr
// Description:        A double-linked list of Problem Status History nodes
//                     and an iterator class for the list class
#include <connect.h>    // Connection class and ODBC defines
#include "prstnode.h"   // ProblemStatusNode class
class ProblemStatusItr;    // forward declarations

class ProblemStatusHistory
{
    friend class ProblemStatusItr;        // access to all elements of ProblemStatusHistory
public:
    ProblemStatusHistory();
    ProblemStatusItr &    getIterator(void);
    void                  addNode(ProblemStatusNode & node);
    void                  removeNode(ProblemStatusNode & node);
    RETCODE               query(Connection & connection, SDWORD id);
};

class ProblemStatusItr
{
public:
 ProblemStatusItr(const ProblemStatusHistory & history) : history(history) {}
    BOOL                          hasNodes(void);
    const ProblemStatusNode &     getOldest(void) const;
    const ProblemStatusNode &     getYoungest(void) const;
    const ProblemStatusNode &     getNext(void) const;
    const ProblemStatusNode &     getPrevious(void) const;
};
```

Here are some issues that might arise during the review:
- Does the concept of problem status history correspond to a requirements use case, and if so, do the methods in that class correspond to well-defined parts of that use case? For example, is there a reason to be able to remove a node from this list? Is there a need for a separate iterator class, or could you move the methods into the problem status history class for simplicity? You could justify both these elements based on reusability and good design standards.
- Can a class outside the Problem class access and change the problem status history (in memory)? This should not be possible, since Problem owns the history.
- Are there any elements in the problem status history structures that the containing class does not use? In this case, apparently not.
- Are there any issues with visibility versus reusability? In this case, encapsulation seems tight enough to guarantee that you could reuse this class, while the semantic content of the class makes it somewhat unlikely. You might consider looking at a further abstraction of the list processing elements and iterator into a more generic form that you could reuse in other list classes.

ROAD MAP
Figure 19.9 is the road map for the aggregation test script class.

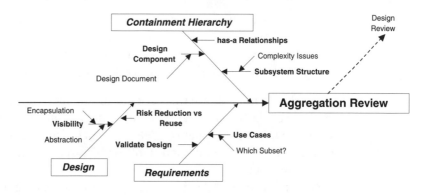

Figure 19.9 Road map for the aggregation review class.

Classification Review

The *classification review* inspects the inheritance relationships between classes. As with the aggregation review and containment hierarchy, the inheritance hierarchy of a system usually decomposes into systems or other clusters more suitable for review than the hierarchy as a whole. The inheritance hierarchy provides a useful way to decompose the system into smaller systems, as long as you take containment into account and place tightly coupled classes together. For example, the DTS problem status history and its accompanying iterator just discussed have no common parent in the inheritance hierarchy. Separating them into separate systems would be folly, since you always use them together.

First, you must ensure that relationships specified by the requirements exist. Next, you should examine these specific relationships between the superclasses and subclasses of the system:

- Cohesion of the classes with respect to superclasses and with respect to other classes in the system (or even outside the system if you can find substantial functional duplication).
- Appropriate breakdown of classes into subclasses; sometimes classes try to combine things that should be separate or vice versa; in particular, look carefully at multiple inheritance, which almost always leads to problems with reuse later, and look at how the inheritance coupling will affect changes to the classes in the future.
- Abstract versus concrete classes as appropriate; make sure that objects in the system are not objects of an abstract class, and/or that concrete classes are in fact concrete in nature rather than an abstract intermediate type.
- Cohesion of the parameters to generic classes or templates, ensuring better reusability. (Sometimes you lose the generic nature of a template or other generic structure because the parameters are incoherent or otherwise unable to handle different possibilities because they are too specific.)

- The overloading and overriding of methods is appropriate; sometimes there is code that does the same thing in subclasses, and sometimes truly different behavioral requirements are overlooked and the class does not provide the overloaded or overridden method that should be there.

You should not confuse this review with the hierarchical-incremental testing of a class. Both classification reviews and hierarchical-incremental testing look at the relationships between elements of a class hierarchy, but the review really concerns the overall picture of the hierarchy rather than the operation of individual objects.

Ramakrishnan (1993) has developed an interesting litany of problem classes:

- **Schizophrenic:** A class that tries to be two or more things at once.
- **Big Brother:** Handles everything for you, regardless of function.
- **Open Heart:** Opens its kimono, giving you access to all its attributes (this is really an aggregation/visibility issue).
- **Single Object:** Only one object in the application or system of this class.
- **Single Function:** Does only one thing and that minimally.
- **Wide Protocol:** Too many functions in a single class.
- **Unfinished:** Missing key elements to make it reusable.

You probably can find many more syndromes.

Figure 19.10 shows the structure of the classification review class.

LEADERSHIP

Vision: A hierarchy of related classes optimized for reuse through optimized cohesion and coupling between superclasses and subclasses.

Mission: To validate the inheritance hierarchy against requirements and to verify the design of the hierarchy.

Objective 19.6: To validate the class hierarchy design against its requirements.

Approach 19.6: Trace each property and class back to its requirements use cases, ensuring that all aspects of the inheritance hierarchy reflect the requirements use cases.

Measurement 19.6: Number of failures to meet requirements plus number of requirements failures (failures of the requirements to reflect the system needs correctly).

Objective 19.7: To test the hierarchy for appropriate cohesion and abstraction of classes.

Approach 19.7: Inspect the inheritance hierarchy design to ensure that all objects are semantically cohesive and abstracted to the right level according to your design guidelines and standards.

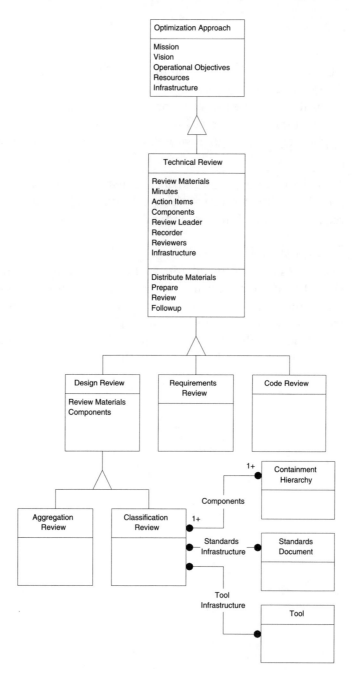

Figure 19.10 Structure of the classification review class.

Measurement 19.7: Number of design failures due to inappropriate inheritance structure.

STRUCTURE

COMPONENTS

The *components* relationship in this case is the set of is-a, or inheritance, relationships between classes. The inheritance hierarchy as a design component is usually an element or elements of a design document or a diagram or diagrams in the product repository. The optimal representation for review is a single, integrated diagram with associated design explanation and detail.

INFRASTRUCTURE

A standard for the design and documentation of the inheritance hierarchy may provide criteria for review. The validation aspects of the review task may require special tools for looking at the use cases and/or the design components.

EXAMPLE

Figure 19.11 shows the inheritance hierarchy of the Person system. The root class DTSSQLObject is in the Utilities system, as other systems also contain classes that inherit from this parent. The classification test suite for this system might have the following test scripts:

- Compare the class to the requirements use cases and make sure there is a class for each kind of person the requirements mention.

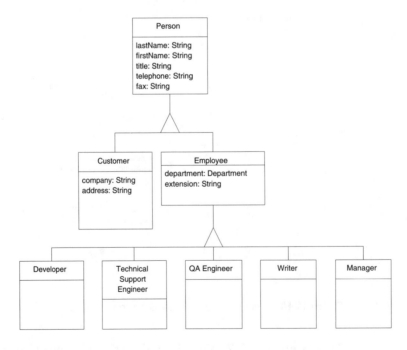

Figure 19.11 DTS Person inheritance hierarchy.

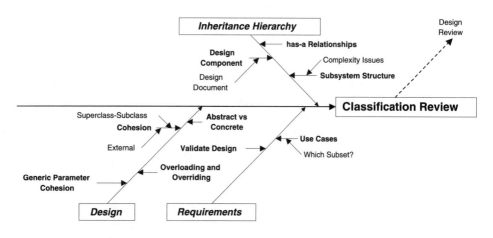

Figure 19.12 Road map for the classification review class.

- Test the cohesion of the classes by examining the different classes for overlaps: Can a single real person be of more than one class at any given horizontal level of the hierarchy? For example, can a customer also be an employee? Can a technical support engineer also be a writer? If so, perhaps you should restructure the hierarchy as a hierarchy of "roles" rather than a hierarchy of "people."
- Test the breakdown of the classes from level to level. Are the levels right for the attributes and methods involved? Are customers and employees, for example, the right breakdown from Person, or would some other division be more appropriate given the requirements?
- Evaluate the abstract versus concrete classes. Person is abstract, so no data attribute in the system should be of that type. (Method parameters can be.) Employee is abstract, since the employee has to be one of the concrete subclasses of employee. Ideally, you should be able to find data attributes that use the concrete subclass definitions, such as Technical Support Engineer or Developer, or perhaps those should be abstract as well.
- Check the series of overridden methods to make sure they are appropriate. In this case, for example, the concrete classes such as **insertObject()**, **deleteObject()**, and **isNull()** should override the virtual methods on the root class, **DTSSQLObject**. Check that the constructors, destructors, conversion operators, and assignment operators all conform to standards at the different levels of the class.

Road Map

Figure 19.12 is the road map for the classification test script.

Code Review

The *code review* is a technical review of one or more software components. You should review a software component when you create it and when you make major changes to it after the initial review. You must register (check) the software component with (into) the configuration management system before distributing it for review. This ensures that you review the correct code and that you can restore your code to the state it was in before the review, if necessary.

This review identifies requirements failures, design failures, and coding failures.

Each software component should relate to at least one use case in the requirements, and each component should relate to a design component as well. As with the design, keep it simple. A traceability matrix that shows the list of use cases applying to the design is a good addition to the review materials. As with design reviews, you can discover missing requirements and design components.

A software failure occurs when a design component fails to achieve its objective by failing to behave as you expect. It also occurs when the code fails to meet the general coding objectives your method and standards impose on the development process.

Your coding standard documents should have a check list of these kinds of coding issues.

One kind of code failure bears some emphasis here: failure to include code that works correctly but does more than the requirements or the design require. Very often reviewers find it difficult to stick to their guns in the face of clever design improvements, such as performance improvements. After all, faster is better, right? Wrong. Faster is usually more complicated and hence more likely to be wrong or to become wrong in the future. Design changes introduced sub rosa during coding without considering the big picture often weaken the overall design. Have you ever found a module in your code that cleverly managed to make it impossible to enhance the system the way you intended? And did requirements drive that code? Variability works as long as you're not interested in optimization; but in an optimizing system, rewarding variability is not a good idea.

Ultimately, the code review should answer two questions: Will the software component do what it should do, and only that? Does the code in the component adhere to all the prescribed standards?

Figure 19.13 shows the structure of the code review class.

Leadership

Vision: A critically evaluated software component of high quality.

Mission: To critically evaluate software components with respect to their vision, mission, and objectives.

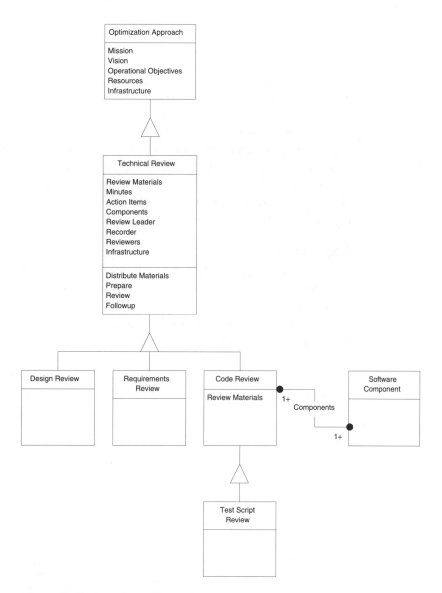

Figure 19.13 Structure of the code review class.

Objective 19.8: To evaluate a software component to find requirements, design, or coding failures relative to its objectives.

Approach 19.8: Determine the vision, mission, and objectives of the software component you are going to review, then review it in a series of two-hour meetings with minutes and action items lists.

Measurement 19.8: Ratio of the number of action items per hour of review to the expected rate of failures per hour based on the size of the software component in function points.

Structure

COMPONENTS
The code review *components* attribute contains the checked-in software components you are going to review.

REVIEW MATERIALS
The *review materials* are the source code in printed or online form, a traceability matrix showing how the component relates to design and requirement components, a standards compliance report from the checking tool, and a compiled version of the component. The latter both offers an opportunity for preliminary experimentation if necessary and demonstrates that the code compiles.

Example
A developer, having finished the coding of the Fault class, checked the code into the version control system and notified the project manager that it was ready for review.

The project manager appointed another developer to be review leader, and the leader set up the review by tapping two other developers and a quality assurance engineer. The author of the class did not participate in the review.

The leader told the reviewers where the code was, and they looked at the source code online for errors. They also inspected the nightly build report for standards violations and integration test errors. The next day, the reviewers met and went over printed copies of the code in a one-hour meeting. They

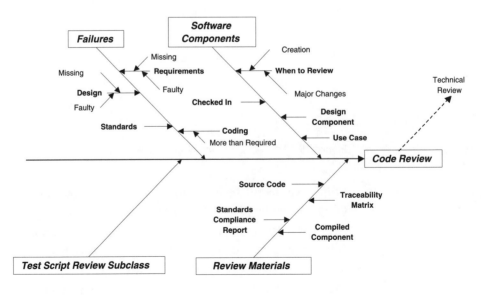

Figure 19.14 Road map for the code review class.

found several minor code errors (missing comments and poor variables names). They also flagged the fact that the author had not included a traceability matrix showing the use cases and design components to which the code related. This stopped the review and sent the code back to the developer. After he worked up the traceability matrix, the reviewers again met and agreed that the code passed muster and needed no further review.

The recorder for the session had written all the points on a flip chart. He turned the chart over to the review leader, who approved it and took it around to the rest of the reviewers, who also approved it. He then gave it to the developer as the action item list.

Road Map

Figure 19.14 is the road map for the code review class.

Test Script Review

The test script review is a kind of code review that applies to the test script, which is not really a software component, as such. Some test scripts can be manual procedures, while others may be testing tool scripts or built-in code in the classes. The test script applies to a software component of some kind, and the review touches on that component as well.

Test script reviews are a bit different from other code reviews. While you're concerned about the correctness of the code and the adherence to standards, just as in a software component review, you also want to know what's missing. A good test script is one that completely tests the thing it tests relative to the test objectives. In a test script review, you're looking for missing test steps and missing test scripts. That means understanding the component under test with enough depth to judge whether the test script really exercises the component. See the section on the test script class for details about the test script.

There may also be test standards against which you must check the script, and you should evaluate the script against its objectives beyond just validating and verifying it. Does the script do what it should do?

As with the code review, you must check the test script into the configuration management system before reviewing it.

Figure 19.15 shows the structure of the test script review class.

Leadership

Vision: A critically evaluated test script of high quality.

Mission: To critically evaluate test scripts with respect to their vision, mission, and objectives.

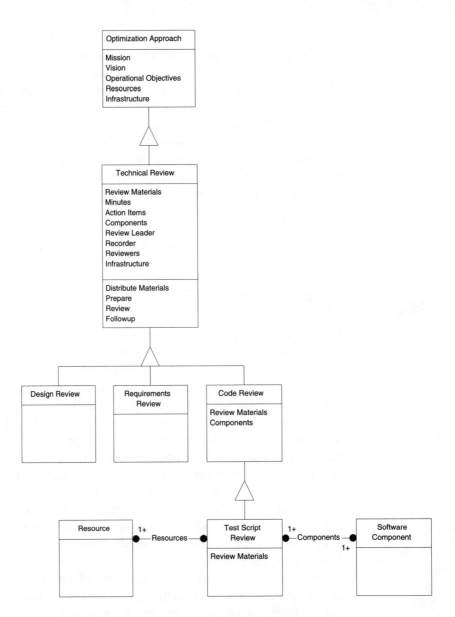

Figure 19.15 Structure of the test script review class.

Objective 19.9: To evaluate a test script to find requirements, design, or coding failures relative to its objectives.

Approach 19.9: Determine the vision, mission, and objectives of the test script you are going to review, then review it in a series of two-hour meetings with minutes and action items lists.

Measurement 19.9: Ratio of the number of action items per hour of review to the expected rate of failures per hour based on the size of the test script in function points.

Structure

COMPONENTS

The component of the review is the test script you are reviewing.

REVIEW MATERIALS

The review materials include the test script in printed or online form and the software component it tests in printed or online form. If you can compile the test script, you also should have access to the compiled test script. For example, in the case of built-in test scripts in the software component, you would need to have the compiled software component.

RESOURCES

Not all developers may be familiar with the test script language. All reviewers should be familiar with both the test script language and the language of the software component.

Example

After working with the programmer to develop a set of built-in tests for the Employee class, the test script developer checked the class into the configuration management system.

She then notified the project manager that the code was ready for review.

The project manager appointed a quality assurance engineer to be review leader, and the leader set up the review by tapping two other QA engineers and a developer. The author of the test script did not participate in the review.

The leader told the reviewers where the code was, and they looked at the source code online for errors. They also inspected the nightly build report for standards violations and integration test errors. (The test script found some code errors, but there were no errors in the test scripts themselves.) The next day, the reviewers met and went over printed copies of the code in a one-hour meeting. They found two assertions to add and one method that had no built-in tests at all. The reviewers agreed that the latter problem required an additional review after the author corrected the class.

The recorder for the session had written all the points on a flip chart. He turned the chart over to the review leader, who approved it and took it around to the rest of the reviewers, who also approved it. He then gave it to the developer as the action item list and notified the project manager of an additional review step for the test script.

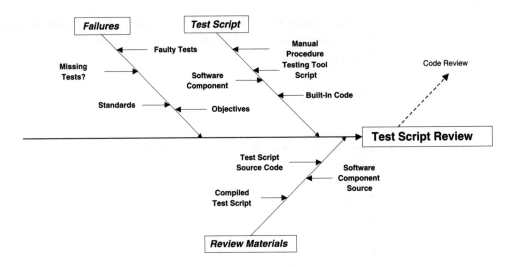

Figure 19.16 Road map for the test script review class.

Road Map

Figure 19.16 is the road map for the test script review class.

CHAPTER 20

SOFTWARE COMPONENT

Software Component

The *software component* is the root class of a hierarchy of software-object classes. This class serves as an abstract placeholder for any software object in the rest of the quality system. The software component is a kind of technical component, an abstract class that includes design components and other technical things that aren't software. Many parts of the software component apply to any kind of software object; that's the role of the software component. Some parts apply to any technical component. This chapter is an overview of the software system, not a complete discussion of all aspects of it; it outlines the things you need to know for the quality system.

The term "software" is a relatively recent word that has little meaning outside the system of computer technology. Software is the complement to hardware: the data that make the machines run.

Qualifying "software" with "component" implies a vision of software as a system. The systems doctrine of the whole being greater than the sum of its parts applies clearly to the software system. The individual class or object, the individual function or method or procedure, the individual module: All of these are parts, or *components*, of the software system.

The object-oriented approach to software aligns the conceptual software system with the concrete software system. Software components in the object-oriented world usually correspond directly to the concrete components of the software system: Objects are objects, classes of objects are classes, and so on. This makes the structure of the system clearer and easier to reuse, but only if you take advantage of the natural organization inherent in object-oriented design. Part of the process of quality optimization, in this case, is aligning yourself with the software system.

Software components relate to several other parts of the quality system, such as use cases, design components, and test scripts. It's important to note, however, that software components do not exist in the software development life cycle prior to a design step. That is, requirements do not correspond directly to software components until you can trace components back to requirements through design components, though the model here expresses the connection directly. Conceptually, you must state requirements without reference to software components (other than the system as a whole or other components with an external interface of some kind, such as initialization files).

The remainder of this chapter lays out four subclasses of software component:

- **Class:** The class of objects is an abstraction of the properties that the objects of the class share; classes can be abstract or concrete, and they participate in an inheritance hierarchy.
- **Object:** An instance of a concrete class that exhibits all the properties of the class and its superclasses, overriding and/or overloading some or all of those properties.

- **Foundation Component:** A collection of classes (one or more) that provides a cohesive set of services and that is the basic unit for hierarchical-incremental and integration testing; a subclass of this is the System, a foundation component that can stand on its own in some sense.
- **Storage Organization:** A conceptual means of organizing data storage, including things such as drives, directories, files, and databases.

Figure 20.1 shows the structure of the software component class.

Leadership

Vision: A system of interacting software components

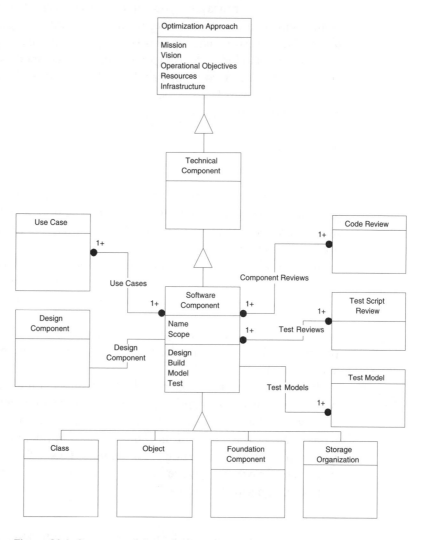

Figure 20.1 Structure of the software component class.

Mission: To provide a cohesive, valuable set of objects to the software system, enabling it to perform its mission.

Objective 20.1: To provide a cohesive, valuable set of objects that satisfy a set of requirements.

Approach 20.1: Implement a quality system of object-oriented software development that ties together requirements, design, coding, and testing into an integrated, productive whole, out of which you can produce individual software components of high quality.

Measurement 20.1: Number of failures associated with the software component.

There are other measures you could use to measure the overall value of the component to the software system, but the number of failures is the most direct. This measurement represents the quality of the component relative to what you expected it to do as expressed in your test models. All of the different kinds of software component inherit this operational objective and hence the measurement of failure based on the specific sorts of test models for the specific type of component.

Structure

NAME

For many different reasons, all software components have *names*. Most names are natural language names (Person, Problem, and so on) or variations on natural languages (CPerson, ProblemClass, or whatever other convention you apply to naming components).

It is a good idea to make component names unique. As with any object, you must be able to refer to the object with a reasonable assurance of getting the right thing. In the software world, this means using unique names. This may or may not be a technological issue: The world of compilers, linkers, and other tools gives you a world of choice in naming and referencing. But on the principle of keeping it simple, you should strive for unique names in your software system.

Reusability also affects naming by providing a context for identifying the object, making names relative to the reusable component (library, class, or whatever). This all works because of encapsulation: The main component name encloses the names of its components, and references use both (or all) names to identify the individual component. This is the concept of scope, to be discussed next. Names are generally unique within a scope, and a system consists of a network of scopes.

SCOPE

The *scope* of the component is the name space in which its name is unique and

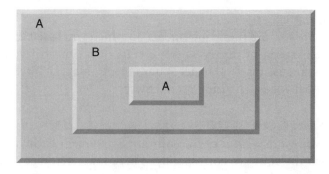

Figure 20.2 Nested naming scopes.

identifying. Figure 20.2 illustrates some of the concepts of scope. Component A (the inner one) nests within the scope that Component B provides, but Component A (the outer one) provides the scope for Component B. Components can have overlapping scopes.

In C++, scope is of three types: file, class, and member/function. The file component contains the classes, variables, and other C++ elements, all of which require unique names within the file. The class component is always within a file, and the file scope always covers the class. For example, when you want to use a class in another class, you include the header file with the class definition, thus making the class definition part of the current file scope. The class conceptually has the scope of every file that includes the file that defines it, thus creating overlapping scopes; practically, though, you are simply duplicating the class in the different files. Some languages such as Ada permit actual reuse of the source without duplication.

Member or function scope makes the names local to a function, the name of which is the scope of the names of the encapsulated components.

Another example of scope is database scope. A SQL column name is unique within its table, and the table name is unique within its schema or module (at least, in the ANSI standard for SQL). You use a special identifier for the scope (the "authorization identifier"). Various SQL implementations add different kinds of scopes ("databases," "users," and so on). For example, the table Person may be in an ORACLE database belonging to the DTS user; the name Person is thus unique within the DTS scope. The column Name is unique within the table scope. You could thus refer to the Name column as **DTS.Person.Name**, uniquely identifying the column in the database context.

A good rule is to make use of scope to avoid cluttering names with prefixes and suffixes that make them universally unique. For example, naming the Name column DTSPersonName makes the name unique but makes programmers crazy every time they have to type it in. It also makes it difficult to reuse the code with other "Name" columns.

USE CASES

The *use cases* are the requirements on which you based the design of the software component. Every software component must have at least one corresponding use case and hence requirement; this guarantees that you develop a minimal system, assuring productivity.

DESIGN COMPONENT

The *design component* of the software component is the part of the design to which the software corresponds. There must be exactly one design component for each software component.

COMPONENT REVIEWS

The *component review* is the code review that reviews the software. See the section on code reviews for full details of this review. Each software component must have at least one code review.

TEST REVIEWS

The *test review* is the test script review that reviews the test script or scripts that test the software component. The software component is part of the review because you need to refer to it to figure out whether the test script is accurate and complete. There must be at least one test review for the component. See the section on test reviews for full details of this review.

TEST MODELS

Ch. 10

Test Models

The *test models* are the abstract models of the software component that help to structure the tests for the component. There must be at least one test model for the component. See the "Test Models" section in Chapter 10 for details on this abstraction. The test models provide the best representation of what you expect the component to do; hence, the tests discover failures that you use to measure the quality of the component.

Dynamics

DESIGN

The abstract Design task creates the structure of the component by building the set of design components.

BUILD

The abstract Build task constructs the component by building the content of the component. Each type of component has its own kind of content: source code, library definition files, physical database definition, or whatever.

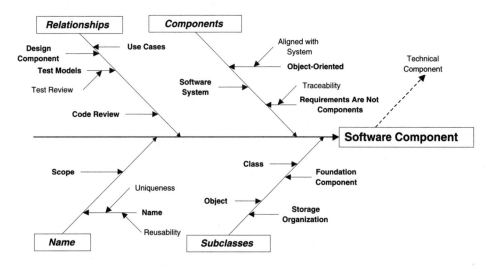

Figure 20.3 Road map for the software component class.

MODEL

The abstract Model task constructs the set of test models for the component. The particular models depend on the particular type of component. The task then builds the set of test objects, test scripts, and test suites as appropriate for the type of component.

TEST

The Test task runs the test scripts you have built from the test models.

Road Map

Figure 20.3 is the road map for the software component class.

Class

The *class* is an abstract software component that represents the properties shared between a set of objects. Properties consist of attributes (data) and operations (behavior). Classes relate to one another through an inheritance hierarchy of superclasses and subclasses. See Chapter 2 for details.

In the testing system, the class enters into the system wherever you you refer to source code, such as in code reviews. It also is the subject of several architecture test script subclasses through their testing of the class design. These relationships reflect the various relationships inherited from the software component.

Ch. 2

Systems of Objects

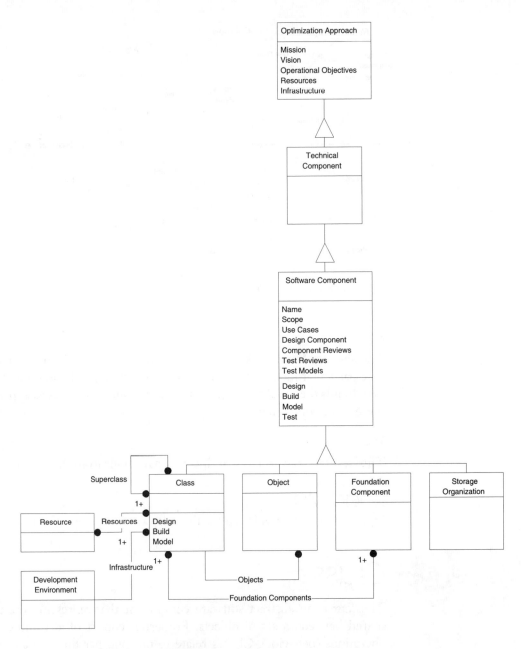

Figure 20.4 Structure of the class class.

Figure 20.4 shows the structure of the class class.

Leadership

Vision: A system of cohesive, interacting objects classified into sets.

Mission: To provide a cohesive set of objects to the software system, enabling the software system to perform its mission.

Objective 20.2: To provide a cohesive set of objects that satisfy a set of abstract requirements.

Approach 20.2: Abstract the requirements use cases into collections of data attributes and methods: classes.

Measurement 20.2: Cohesion index (rate the structural components of the class for cohesiveness on an ordinal scale from 1 to 4: Uncohesive, Inconsistent, Orderly, Cohesive), representing ordinal degrees of cohesion

Structure

The actual *structure* of the class class is very complex. As this book does not focus on building a comprehensive model of the object-oriented software system, the following structure reflects just those parts of the system related to the quality system. We have not tried to represent the containment hierarchy here, for example, as it quickly leads into complex relationships and structures based on programming languages. This is clearly beyond the scope of the book.

OBJECTS

The *objects* are the set of objects with the properties of the class, including objects of subclasses of the class: Each such object includes at least one instance of its parent classes.

SUPERCLASSES

Ch. 2

Systems
of Objects

Each class may have zero or more *superclasses* (parent classes) that provide part of its definition. See Chapter 2 for a discussion of class inheritance.

FOUNDATION COMPONENTS

The class belongs to at least one *foundation component* and possibly to several, since foundation components may contain other foundation components. Foundation components can also overlap, if doing so makes sense. See the following "Foundation Component" section for details.

RESOURCES

Designing a class requires training in the appropriate level of object-oriented design and in the design tools. Building a class requires training in the programming language in which you build the class, and specifically in the compilation and system building tools in the software development environment.

INFRASTRUCTURE

Designing and building a class requires a comprehensive software development environment with design and class construction tools.

Dynamics

DESIGN

The Design task creates the structure of the class by building the object model.

BUILD

The Build task constructs the class by building the structure of the class. This task involves writing source code in any of a number of different construction tools, or even generating the code through precompilers or CASE tools.

MODEL

The Model task constructs the test models for the class. Class test models include any of the hierarchical-incremental and conditional test models: state-transition, transaction flow, exception, control flow, data flow, and conditional. (See Chapter 11 and Chapter 12.) Note that the class itself contains only the model components for that class, not the foundation component of which the class is a part. That means that the full hierarchical-incremental test suite belongs to the foundation component, not to the individual class. See the "Foundation Component" section that follows.

Example

The DTS Failure class is a software component of the Problem system with an accompanying design component (the class design in the DTS Problem System design document), set of use cases, and test models. Both the component and its test models and scripts have gone through reviews.

Overall, the failure class has gone through about ten test reviews. Some

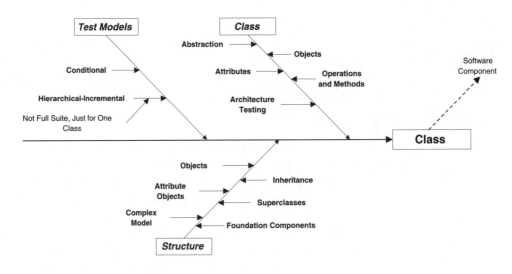

Figure 20.5 Road map for the class class.

reviewed several test scripts; others repeated earlier, failed reviews. (One test script failed to adequately exercise the method called due to a misunderstanding of the requirements.)

Road Map

Figure 20.5 is the road map for the class class.

Object

The *object* is the basic unit in the object-oriented system, not surprisingly. For a system that's oriented toward objects, we spend an amazingly small amount of time dealing with them, but they are an essential part of the system nevertheless. Why do we fail to acknowledge this importance? Because, quite simply, we don't optimize value and productivity through objects. Objects are the outer evidence of the inner workings of the quality system: classes, systems, storage organizations, and all the tests, reviews, and other subjects of this book. Those are the things we look at, think about, and change to achieve productivity and value.

The working software system consists mainly of compiled objects interacting through messages. Class/object testing and class-to-class integration testing use these instances of classes to test how the class of objects performs against requirements and standards. You also can use objects to evaluate classes in reviews.

Figure 20.6 shows the structure of the object class.

Leadership

Vision: A system of interacting objects.

Mission: To provide a software object with the properties of a class to enable the software system to function.

Objective 20.3: To enable the working of the system by making the abstract class concrete.

Approach 20.3: Use software technology to translate the class into a working object.

Measurement 20.3: Number of translation errors from the class source code to the object code (target 0, although sometimes objects can function even with minor translation errors or warnings).

Structure

CLASS

The *class* of an object is the class that represents the properties of the object. The class may have superclass parents from which it inherits some or all of the properties of the object.

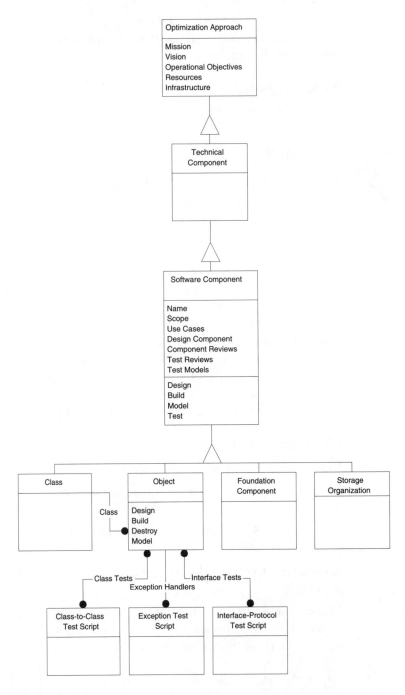

Figure 20.6 Structure of the object class.

CLASS TESTS

The *class tests* are the test scripts that test this object's class as the sender or

Ch. 13

Class-to-Class
Test Script

receiver of a message. See the class-to-class test script section in Chapter 13 for more information.

INTERFACE TESTS

The *interface tests* are the test scripts that test the interfaces and protocols of this object's class. See the interface-and-protocol test script section in Chapter 17 for more information.

EXCEPTION HANDLERS

Ch. 12

Exception

The *exception handlers* are a part of the object that handle exceptions raised during an exception test script. See the exception class-to-class test script section in Chapter 12 for more information.

Dynamics

DESIGN

The Design task refers to the object model you create for the class of which the object is a member.

BUILD

The Build task constructs the object as an instance of its class. The task calls the appropriate constructor method on the class to build the object.

DESTROY

The Destroy task destroys the object by calling the destructor for the class.

MODEL

The Model task does nothing for the object; the class and its test scripts have already done all the work of creating the various tests when you test the object.

Example

The DTS Failure class is a software component with an accompanying design component (the class design in the DTS Problem System design document), set of use cases, and test script. Both the component and its test script have gone through reviews.

The Failure class has 20 or so class-to-class test scripts that test the different messages that objects of the class send and receive. These scripts test the integration of the different classes, such as the ODBC classes, on which the Failure class depends. Each test script corresponds to exactly one object, which the test script creates, though this is not necessarily going to be true of all such scripts.

The class also has about 30 test scripts that test the interfaces and protocols and exception handlers of the class. Again, the DTS testing team created an object in each test script, so each test script corresponds to exactly one object.

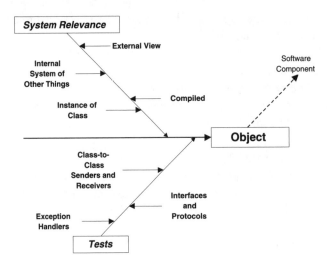

Figure 20.7 Road map for the object class.

Road Map

Figure 20.7 is the road map for the object class.

Foundation Component

If you take the structure of object-oriented programming languages as a guide, you might decide that the fundamental unit of testing was the class. Not so. Although a single class encapsulates its data and operations, it also inherits data and operations and often interacts closely with other classes through messaging. Thus even basic testing of an object often must take into account more than one class. So we need a software component somewhere between the class and the system.

A *foundation component* is a cluster of classes that serves as the basic unit for testing. A foundation component is a system. A foundation component can be one complete class hierarchy, with the classes relating to each other through inheritance. It can perform a core function or represent a logical or physical architectural component, with the classes interrelating through messaging relationships. Most foundation components will consist of classes relating to each other with a combination of inheritance and messaging relationships.

Some *cohesion* always makes the collection of classes a cluster: In a component, no class should be unrelated to the others. You can (indeed, *must*) have relationships between components, but these relationships must be less cohesive than the stronger bonds within the component. This is not cut-and-dried; it's a matter of judgment and good architecture. Good cohesion in software components is one of the basic objectives of good design.

The fundamental testing approach this book advocates, the hierarchical approach, tests foundation components to achieve an acceptable level of risk: A successful test designates the component SAFE. The SAFE collection then becomes the basis—the *foundation*—for additional components. By building your system from safe foundation components built on SAFE foundation components, you carefully construct a system that is safe.

Integration testing of safe foundation components must address only the interconnections between the foundation components and any new composite functionality. You do not need to test all possible combinations of states, flows, and so on, only the connections.

Building the series of foundation components may happen bottom up, top down, or inside out. There is no implied order to the building process. If you want to build top down or inside out, you can stub the components on which the component you're building relies. However, if you take this approach, you can't finish the integration test for the component and recognize its full earned value until you replace the stubs with the real foundation components on which the component depends.

The foundation component also serves as a unit for project management. It becomes a deliverable object in the project plan, and the completed baseline of the component translates to a milestone in the project schedule. See Chapter 23 for details of the project plan.

Figure 20.8 shows the structure of the foundation component class.

Leadership

Vision: A system of interacting classes that serves as a foundation to other components.

Mission: To provide a grouped set of classes to the software system, enabling it to perform its mission.

Objective 20.4: To provide a cohesive collection of classes.

Approach 20.4: Combine the classes, and hence objects, of the system into clusters of classes related by inheritance or messaging.

Measurement 20.4: Number of classes in a cluster unrelated to other classes in the cluster through inheritance or messaging (standard: zero).

Objective 20.5: To provide a reusable subset of objects and classes.

Approach 20.5: Combine the classes of the system into clusters of classes that provide a distinct service or set of services.

Measurement 20.5: Cumulative number of uses of the component from other components in this and other projects.

Note that objectives 20.4 and 20.5 trade off against one another. You can maximize 20.5 by reducing the size of the clusters and 20.4 by increasing the size of clusters. You need to optimize this trade-off. To help, use objective

20.6, which relates to the complexity of the system and relates the system to its requirements.

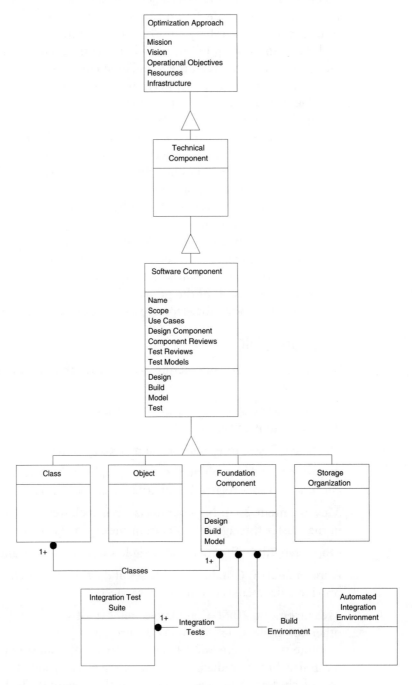

Figure 20.8 Structure of the foundation component class.

Objective 20.6: To simplify the system of objects by partitioning it into loosely connected systems that you can deal with separately

Approach 20.6: Divide the classes of the system into loosely coupled components that you can deal with as a whole even while they are part of a larger component.

Measurement 20.6: Cumulative cyclomatic complexity of the foundation component (sum of the cyclomatic complexity of the methods in the classes that belong to the component).

The objectives of the foundation component provide the key benefits for the hierarchical approach. Objective 20.4 provides value: a cohesive set of services. Objective 20.4 provides productivity: the ability to reuse the services. Objective 20.6 provides both value and productivity: lower complexity, resulting in increased quality (value) and increased maintenance productivity.

Structure

CLASSES

The *classes* are the software components that make up the foundation component. All the classes in a foundation component should relate to one another through inheritance or messaging relationships. Other relationships specific to a programming language are also possible, such as the friend relationship in C++.

INTEGRATION TESTS

Ch. 13

Integration
Test Suite

The set of *integration tests* are the test scripts that apply to the foundation component. They are executed as part of the integration testing process in order to test the component as it integrates into a larger system component. These tests can be automatic or manual. See Chapter 13 for details.

BUILD ENVIRONMENT

The *build environment* is the automated integration environment that builds the component. See the "automated integration environment" section in Chapter 21 for details.

Dynamics

DESIGN

The Design task creates the structure for (architects) the foundation component by analyzing the relationships between the classes of the system and finding the best way to cluster the classes into the component.

BUILD

The Build task constructs the component by identifying the cluster of classes to the product repository and naming the component.

MODEL

The Model task constructs the test models for the foundation component. Component test models include any of the integration test models: object models (interfaces and protocols, synchronization, and exception handling) and user interface models. The classes that make up the foundation component have their own class tests; the Model task adds the relationships between these tests in the full hierarchical-incremental test suite.

Example

The DTS was a small system that had relatively small and self-contained class hierarchies. The main systems consisted of a single class hierarchy with some supporting classes, such as lists and nodes. Thus these systems had only a single foundation component, the system itself.

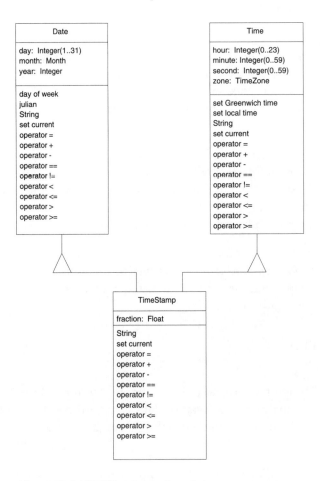

Figure 20.9 DTS TimeStamp foundation component.

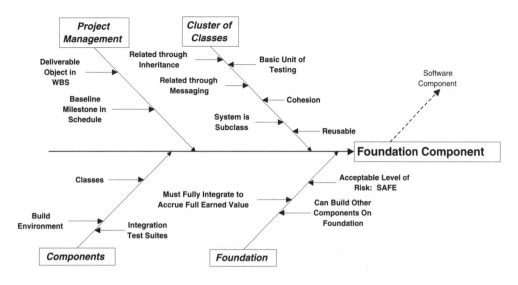

Figure 20.10 Road map for the foundation component class.

The Tools system contained several unrelated classes, each of which became a separate foundation component. The most complex of these was the TimeStamp foundation component, which consisted of the Time class, the Date class, and the TimeStamp class (Figure 20.9). The TimeStamp class inherits from both Time and Date. The test team decided to model this component with a data-flow test model for the hierarchical-incremental test suite and to focus on conditional modeling as the primary test model. These classes have many internal constraints relating to the nature of dates and times, making conditional models an obvious choice. Less obviously, the data and time algorithms are moderately complex and involve many data decisions, so the test team decided to focus on the data-flow model as the best structural model of the class.

Finally, because the foundation component provided a clearly distinguishable set of services, and because the component relied on operating system components, the test team decided to build an integration test suite for the component that fully tested the date-time abstraction in an abstraction test suite against the DTS requirements.

Road Map

Figure 20.10 is the road map for the foundation component class.

System Component

It is becoming more and more difficult to conceive of a software system as a single software entity. The open systems movement in software has enabled software to become less monolithic. The advent of *component technology* such as tool integration backplanes, OLE, and CORBA has made the concept of system much broader than it used to be. For testing purposes, you should think of a software system as an open system of interacting systems. The *system* is a kind of foundation component (perhaps a larger, more complex instance), and all the tests that apply to foundation components apply to systems.

Foundation components are of course systems in the strict sense, but we choose to make a qualitative distinction between foundation components and systems. While a foundation component serves as a test unit for class/object and integration testing, the system serves as the unit for system testing. Certain things happen, qualitatively, when your components get to a certain size or capability: They become working systems rather than components. Perhaps the best way to distinguish such a working system is to ask: Can you use this component independently of other components at the same level in the system? Could you sell this component separately, or does it need other components to deliver its value?

To determine if a set of components is a system component, answer the following questions:

- Does it provide a cohesive stand-alone (complete) set of services?
- Is it a functional subsystem?
- Is it an architectural layer (GUI, database access, etc.)?
- Is it a framework?
- Is it a library or utility system?
- Can the entire component be "plugged in to" another system and provide meaningful services in the context of the new system?

If the answer is yes to one or more of these questions, then the foundation component probably qualifies as a system component. It can be treated as an independent stand-alone system and deserves its own system testing. The system consists not just of a set of classes; it consists of complete, integrated foundation components. Put another way, no foundation component can span more than one system. The foundation component classes that make up a system all share a high level of cohesion compared to components in other systems.

Partitioned systems are an often-overlooked component of a software system, which is too bad: System partitioning can provide more value and productivity than any other decision you might make. In addition to the objectives for a foundation component, the system has the additional objective of providing a minimal set of classes that function as a cohesive whole. By providing the minimal set, the system gives you the biggest bang for your buck: the least complexity that provides the most value.

There is one physical partitioning of the system into physical systems, usually some kind of library such as a DLL that exports a set of symbols (an API or a set of APIs). You also can partition the system into multiple, overlapping partitions for various purposes.

You can use any number of logical principles to partition the system; your choice depends on your objectives. The DTS library partitioning, for example (whose example follows), identifies the systems by looking at the database design and determining what tables have references to what other tables. By moving the classes around to minimize the number of cross-system table references, the DTS system design optimizes the groupings for simplicity and reuse.

Some systems may share certain classes, or foundation components, through inheritance. For example, in the DTS system, the DTSSQLObject class serves as the parent class to all the data model systems (Person, Problem, and Product) because it contains the basic structure for all classes of objects that the system stores in the database. Another example is the standard design approach of all classes in a system inheriting from a single root class, such as CObject in the Microsoft Foundation Classes. Forcing all subclasses of these classes to belong to a single system destroys the usefulness of the concept. You should consider these shared classes as a layer of abstraction that belongs in a separate system (in the case of the DTS, the Tools system; in the case of MFC, in the MFC library DLL).

There are many different ways to divide a system into systems. Some relationships (inheritance or messaging) span systems, no matter how you divide them. In defining systems, you should minimize these spanning connections. If you don't, your integration testing will get very complicated very quickly.

System testing consists of functionality and flexibility testing that relates the system to its requirements. System testing tests the set of qualities that a system as a whole must satisfy, such as usability, reliability, flexibility, performance, security, and so on. The applicability of these qualities marks the qualitative distinction between a system and a foundation component that is not a system.

Figure 20.11 shows the structure of the system component class.

Leadership

Vision: A system of interacting objects that are a decomposable part of the whole.

Mission: To provide a grouped set of objects to the software system, enabling it to perform its mission.

Objective 20.7: To provide a minimal set of classes that function as a cohesive whole.

Approach 20.7: Compose foundation components into a collection that operates as a cohesive whole to provide a complete set of services or to provide an abstraction for such a set of services.

Measurement 20.7: Binary ability to function as a complete system (yes or no).

Structure

SYSTEM TESTS
The set of system tests are the test scripts that apply to this system as part of the

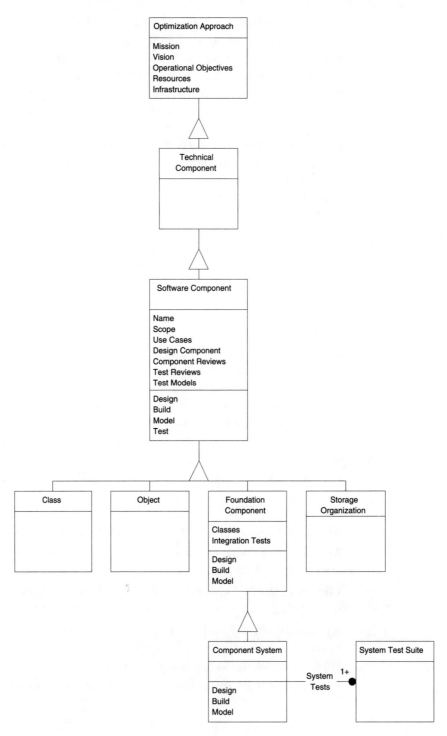

Figure 20.11 Structure of the system component class.

system testing process. These tests can be automatic or manual. See Chapter 14 for details.

Dynamics

DESIGN
The Design task creates the structure of the system by building the architectural model showing the services that the system offers.

BUILD
The Build task constructs the system by specifying the list of classes to the product repository and by building any supporting files, such as the link editor DEF files for a DLL.

MODEL
The Model task constructs the test models for the system. System test models include any of the requirements use cases, the flexibility model, and the capabilities models (performance, security, usability, and so on). The foundation components that make up the system carry along their test models packaged into a system regression test suite.

Example
The main systems of the DTS are the data model systems, including Person, Problem, and Product. Figure 20.12 shows the relationships between these systems. Person is reusable because it does not refer to the other systems internally; Problem and Product are not separately reusable, but you could use the combination of systems elsewhere quite easily. The larger system, composed of three systems, is a logical system, while each of the three systems is a physical Dynamic Link Library.

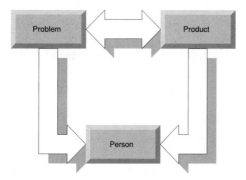

Figure 20.12 DTS system relationships.

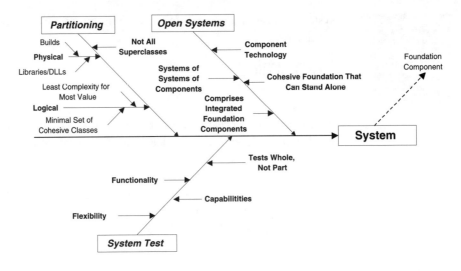

Figure 20.13 Road map for the system component class.

The Tools and Porting Framework systems provide a set of utilities to support the other libraries. Tools provides a string class, the SQL object class, and other such base classes that many other systems use. The Porting Framework contains abstractions that package user interface, operating system, and client/server access facilities for the data model classes.

Road Map

Figure 20.13 is the road map for the system component class.

Storage-Organization

The storage organization is an abstract class that represents the myriad ways that software systems organize and store data:

- **Drive:** A physical or logical volume identifier for a root file hierarchy you access through the operating system.
- **Directory:** A group of files and additional directories you access through the operating system.
- **File:** A sequence of stored data elements you access through the operating system.

Files can have different versions. Usually a version control system stores the initial version of the file and a series of version files, storing the difference between the initial version and the current version (or the last version). The many variations on this scheme have associated advantages and disadvantages. The basic idea is to be able to restore a particular version of a file from the set of versions under control of the configuration management system. The versions also can be part of a database.

- **Database:** A conceptual storage format accessed through a database access language of some kind, either through an API or a higher-level programming interface.

Ch. 10

Test Repository

Ch. 21

Repository

Databases in turn have many types, the most prevalent of which are relational, hierarchical, network, and object-oriented databases. There are also "flat-file" databases that are really just files with additional access mechanisms available.

All the objects in the quality system reside in one kind of storage organization or another, mostly files and relational databases. The system organizes the storage into repositories; see the repositories section in Chapter 10, and also Chapter 21.

Figure 20.14 shows the structure of the storage organization class.

Leadership

Vision: A system of software storage that enables the persistent management of the quality system.

Mission: To provide a means of storing quality system objects, enabling that system to perform its mission.

Objective 20.8: To provide a storage system that enables the quality system to manage its persistent objects.

Approach 20.8: Use the appropriate operating system storage and selected database systems to store the quality system objects.

Measurement 20.8: Number of system failures deriving from storage technology.

In this case, the *system failure* is a failure of the quality system technology rather than the technology it manages. The failure must derive from some disabling of the system due to a fault in the storage technology (or to missing storage technology).

Objective 20.9: To provide a storage system that enables the software system to manage its persistent objects.

Approach 20.9: Use the appropriate operating system storage and selected database systems to store the software system objects.

Measurement 20.9: Number of failures deriving from storage technology.

Structure

DATA MODEL

The data model is the appropriate set of data structures representing the logical structure of the storage organization.

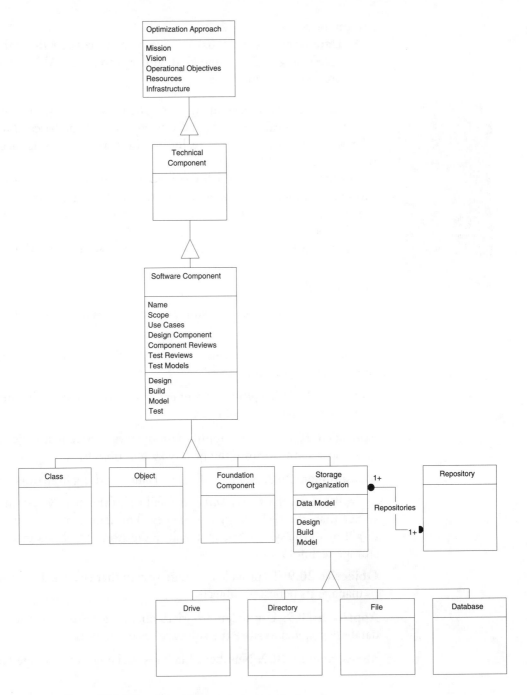

Figure 20.14 Structure of the storage organization class.

Repositories

The repositories are the project, test, and product repositories, all of which require a storage organization.

Dynamics

DESIGN
The Design task creates the structure for the database by building the data model.

BUILD
The Build task constructs the storage organization by running SQL scripts, creating files, or whatever else you might need to do.

MODEL
The Model task does nothing for storage organizations; the data model serves as a test model if you need one.

Example
The DTS automated integration environment uses a combination of file-based technology and relational database technology to store its objects. Test scripts for user-interface testing, for example, are files in the testing tool format, while test data and test results appear in the relational test repository for each system.

The DTS itself is a client/server application that uses ODBC relational database technology as its storage mechanism. It also uses certain files, such as initialization files, on those systems that have standard file elements.

Road Map
Figure 20.15 is the road map for the storage organization class.

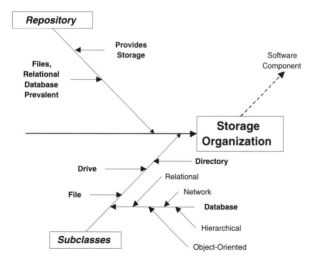

Figure 20.15 Road map for the storage organization class.

CHAPTER 21

THE DEVELOPMENT ENVIRONMENT

The Development Environment

The *development environment* is an abstract class that represents the bulk of the infrastructure of a software development project. A development environment consists of a set of software tools and a series of repositories (databases of information about objects).

There are several kinds of development environment:

- **Software Development Environment:** A development environment that uses tools to design and build software components; we don't discuss this environment any further in this book.
- **Automated Integration Environment:** A development environment that uses tools to integrate software components and test them; see the "Tool" section that follows.
- **Test Environment:** A development environment that uses tools to build, run, and evaluate tests of software components.
- **Project Environment:** A development environment that uses tools to build and execute projects; also includes the external environment and the facilities and communications infrastructure you need to run the project.

These are logical, not physical, distinctions. The storage organization for the test repository in the test environment can exist side by side in the same database or file system with the project repository storage organization in the project environment. Also, some information can be shared between repositories, as it may be of use for different purposes. For example, test evaluations may be of interest to project managers for evaluating project status, and fault reports may be of interest to developers and designers.

A development environment focuses on the integration of the work effort. You could develop software, tests, or project plans with random tools. This book's thesis is that by integrating these tools into a comprehensive environment, you gain the synergy of a carefully optimized process for development in which tools contribute to the objectives of the environment in a measured and optimal way.

One tool that is of vital interest to any development environment is the configuration management system, also known as change management system, source control system, version control system, or document management system, depending on the application. Every development environment requires a configuration management system, so we discuss it separately.

We could devote an entire book to development environments. Perhaps another time. Here we give you a basic approach and describe the various objects without going into much detail. The references at the end of this part provide more information about development environments.

Figure 21.1 shows the class structure for the development environment.

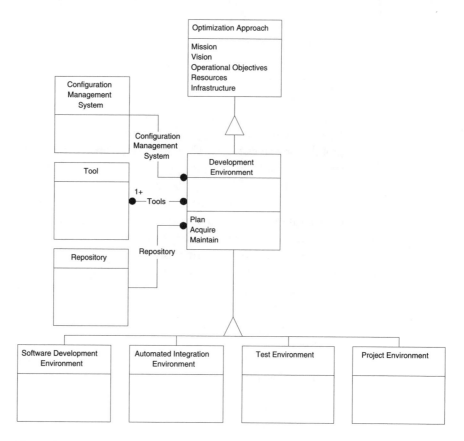

Figure 21.1 Structure of the development environment class.

Leadership

Vision: A comprehensive set of tools and objects for developing software with high quality and productivity.

Mission: To build an integrated system of tools and object repositories.

Objective 21.1: To improve productivity through integrating tools and objects.

Approach 21.1: Combine built or bought technologies with built or bought object repositories to emphasize reuse and ease of use in developing software.

Measurement 21.1: Developer productivity in effort hours per unit of earned value while using the development environment.

Objective 21.2: To improve quality through integrating tools, objects, and tests.

Approach 21.2: Combine tools and repositories with test objects in an automated environment to move failure discovery to as early in the development process as practicable.

Measurement 21.2: Number of faults discovered per hour of testing per development process object.

Structure

CONFIGURATION MANAGEMENT SYSTEM

The configuration management system of the development environment is the tool that manages the configuration of environment product components: software, test scripts, test results, project documents and charts, development documents, and so on. The tool usually has a repository, which you can integrate with one or another of the environment repositories as technology permits. Some tools require separate repositories purely as a technological design decision.

Certain tools are more appropriate for certain purposes than others; few configuration management tools are appropriate for managing all the components you will find in a software development project. Systems that can cope easily with multiple-branching software versioning may not be able to handle large documents with embedded OLE graphics and so on.

TOOLS

The environment tools are the software and hardware tools you use as part of the tasks that the development environment supports. See the tools "class" section (this is the structure section of the configuration management class).

REPOSITORY

The environment repository is the logical storage organization that stores the objects in the environment. It includes the products the environment supports and the by-products of the tools in the environment, including configuration management objects as appropriate. See the following Repository class section for details.

Dynamics

PLAN

As with any optimization process, you need to plan out the scope and contents of your development environment. This method enhances the standard planning that is part of the optimization cycle to include specific planning relating to software tool acquisition and integration, which is somewhat specialized. In particular, you need to evaluate and compare tools carefully to make sure you are getting the best value for your needs. You should work out the tools you need carefully, then plan their acquisition based on the timing required by your project schedule(s) as well as your functional requirements. You may need to put some tools in place earlier than others. You also need to plan for disk space and network availability.

ACQUIRE

This method is the process of acquiring the tools, installing and initializing the tools and repositories, and integrating the tools into a working development environment.

MAINTAIN

After you install the environment, you will need to maintain it over time. This includes network maintenance, system backups and restores, tool and system upgrades, and dealing with the quality problems of software companies. (Not everyone has read and applied the quality approach from this book.) This process consumes a substantial amount of time, so plan for it.

Maintenance benefits greatly from continuous optimization. Use Pareto diagrams to identify particularly troublesome areas, and optimize those areas to reduce maintenance time. The less time you spend maintaining your environment, the more it is fully available for development activities and the more productive is your organization.

Tool

A tool is software or hardware that you use in the tasks your environment supports. It is a kind of optimization approach, and most if not all tools belong to a development environment. This section provides an overview of the various tools that contribute to the development environment. See the "Structure" section for the kinds of tools you might find in such an environment.

To automate your processes fully, all of these tools need to work together. You can buy them, build them, or any combination of the two. You will need toolsmiths to build and integrate tools (see p. 414), and building tools should follow the same processes as building any software product, including the testing approaches discussed in this book. A vital part of the development process is your analysis of the requirements specific to your projects and processes. By providing the criteria by which you can judge or construct the capabilities of the tools the objectives you develop will help you to determine which ones are most appropriate.

You should consider the scalability of the tool relative to the scale of the project. If your project involves a dozen different operating system ports and systems with hundreds of classes, you will need tools that can handle large systems. Limitations in many tools may render them ineffective when confronted with unusual situations—situations that are perfectly usual to your environment. Understanding the scope and size of your project is thus a key element in judging automation tools, so make sure you have your project Statement of Work in place before beginning your automation project.

Figure 21.2 shows the structure of the tool class.

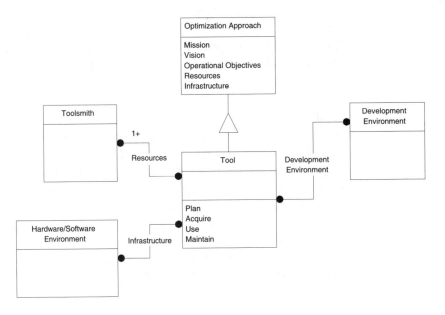

Figure 21.2 Structure of the tool class.

Leadership

Vision: A toolset that enables you to use the right tool for the job.

Mission: To facilitate the performance of a particular task.

Objective 21.3: To increase productivity through automating some aspect of the work process.

Approach 21.3.1: Buy or build software tools that enable work.

Measurement 21.3.1: Earned value of tasks using the tool substantively.

Approach 21.3.2: Buy or build software tools that substantially improve resource productivity.

Measurement 21.3.2: Effort-hours per unit of earned value from tasks that substantively use the tool compared to benchmark productivity.

Approach 21.3.3: Buy or build software tools that substantially improve the ability of developers to deal with technical risk.

Measurement 21.3.3: Risk reduction associated with task when tool becomes available.

Structure

This section briefly describes various kinds of tools you will find in development environments.

Editors provide an environment for creating and modifying any of various kinds of objects, including project documents, development documents, source code, test scripts, graphics, resources (dialogs, icons, and so on), spreadsheets, schedules, and what have you. Computer-Aided Software Engineering (CASE) tools are an extended set of editors, often combined with repositories and engineering tools, that produce development documents and even software objects.

Browsers provide a way to access software objects, tests, or other objects in repositories through some kind of navigational interface that helps you to find what you're looking for.

Build scripts ("makefiles," project databases, or other automated systems for building systems) give you a way to automate local and integration builds of the software. Most let you program commands in one way or another to create incredibly complex systems. This may or may not be a good thing. As with repositories, too much complexity may inhibit the productivity-improving aspects of the tool. Keep your objectives in mind.

Software configuration management systems (aliases: source control systems, version control systems) perform several rather difficult-to-describe functions in managing the progression of changes to source code, documents, or other modifiable objects. These systems also usually provide a way to get information about the sequence of events or status of the system.

Database software and *database access* software lets you build, maintain, and use stored data with much finer-grained structure than a file. This category includes the database server software as well as the application generation, report writing, and database administration tools that work with the server software.

A *report generator* (preferably SQL-based) may come with the database or may be an independent tool that works with various kinds of data formats, including file formats associated with project management systems and spreadsheets. SQL gives you a declarative access language that makes finding and structuring the data you want to report much easier. The report generator combines SQL with report structuring tools (through an editor) that let you format the report just the way you want it.

An *object reuse library* (software and catalog), or reuse repository, can be a special tool that lets you quickly find and reuse software, test, and document components developed by others. This library can involve technology from browsers to fancy text retrieval database systems.

Your basic *file system* provides the simplest storage structure available. Most have hierarchical directory structures. Networked file systems with optional name services (a means of distributing objects across physical storage while still being able to refer to them by simple names) give you an even more sophisticated repository for your objects.

A *test script executor* runs test scripts. This can be external to the software component under test or internal. (See Part 3: The Test System.)

Documentation tools include help systems, "man page" tools, online publishing systems, and multimedia systems. Some of these are helpful; others are more trouble than they're worth, because they suck up toolsmith time while returning very little productivity for developers. Investigate these carefully before diving in.

Project management tools provide help in constructing, executing, and controlling project plans, usually through sophisticated graphical techniques and report writing. Newer tools are beginning to include workflow and process reengineering tools as well as the basic project management functions.

RESOURCES

A *toolsmith* is a person whose primary role in the project is constructing tools that other engineers will use as well as tools for management, if that's appropriate. Each project can benefit from at least one toolsmith, who generally should be a full-time project member dedicated to producing tools. Toolsmiths must understand the tools they are to build and must like building them, but they also need to have a good understanding of the engineering practices and object-oriented methods the tools support. If they do not, you will get tools that never quite do what you want. It would be like having a plumber building the tools you want to use to build a skyscraper. Some results will be better than others, even with a skilled and competent plumber. Get an object-oriented software engineer into this position, and everyone on the team will be happier with the results.

In some teams, each team member builds his or her own tools. That works for small projects, but it doesn't scale up very well. Everyone has his/her own approach. While it's important for an engineer to be able to understand and build his or her own tools, if that's where all tools come from, you're practicing a craft, not an engineering discipline. You need engineering to build projects of reasonable size.

INFRASTRUCTURE

Tools need hardware and software to run. The key things to look for:
- The operating system the tool requires versus the ones you want to run.
- The amount of memory needed to make the tool run reasonably quickly or well (or at all).
- The amount of disk space the tool requires, to store both the software and the results.
- The additional software the tool requires to run (add-on tools, for example, or tools that depend on having some other code available, such as OLE or third-party solutions to connect the tool to other tools).

Never forget that you will need to train people on how to use the tools, so you'll need to buy or build training facilities.

Dynamics

PLAN

Planning and evaluation of tools is a key behavior in the tool object. This method overrides the standard optimization cycle plan method. Your planning process must include careful evaluation of your objectives and the status of your organization. Your evaluation process should compare a vendor's tool with those of other vendors and with the option of building the tool yourself. You also need to decide the quantity of tools and the tool budget.

ACQUIRE

This method overloads the ones in the superclasses, depending on the nature of the tool: You can buy the tool or build. Buying the tool involves standard business practices in licensing software. Building the tool involves standard project management. You then need to deploy the tool to its customers, the developers.

USE

The nature of use depends on the tool. Each tool has a unique way of interacting with its user. The key thing here, though, is to make sure you call the method. Less metaphorically, you need to be sure that developers are using the tool. *Shelfware* is a common affliction in development shops and can be an enormous drain on a tight budget. If your development environment never calls the Use method on a tool, get rid of it; or better, don't acquire it in the first place.

MAINTAIN

As with any software, you must maintain the tool as required. Doing so usually involves maintaining availability on the network, diagnosing and correcting system errors, and installing upgrades from vendors.

Example

The DTS uses a relatively limited tool set running under Microsoft Windows:

- A project management system
- A word processor
- A drawing package that integrates with the word processor through OLE
- A C++ compiler with an accompanying set of development tools such as text editor, text search, file search, compile and execute, a built-in source debugger, and so on
- A version control system that integrates with the compiler environment through a series of menu items
- A static source code checker that checks for common coding error situations, computes complexity metrics, and flags coding standard violations

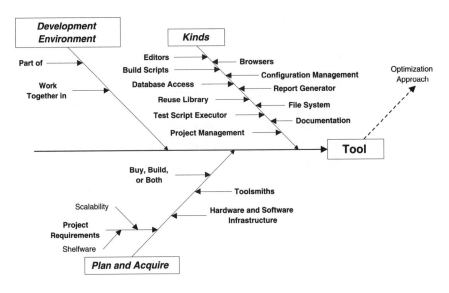

Figure 21.3 Road map for the tool class.

- A database management system (DBMS) that offers both local and server operation
- A graphical user interface (GUI) testing system that lets you write object test scripts
- A DOS file system (and backup facilities) and naming convention for the various systems

All of these tools integrate either through OLE or through various Windows communications mechanisms. The file structure serves as the product, reuse, test, and project repositories. Plans are afoot to move test and project data into the relational database to improve productivity and reporting.

Road Map
Figure 21.3 is the road map to the tool class.

Repository

The word "repository" can indicate a glorious, overarching vision of enterprise data serving the needs of customers; it can indicate a research and development staff itching to move into the bleeding edge of modern, client/server technology; and it probably indicates more than it means.

Here, the term *repository* simply means a database of objects and of information about those objects. This book avoids using the more generic "database" to prevent you from making assumptions about the format of the repository. It can be a structured file system; it can be a relational, object-oriented, or other form of database; or it can be some other kind of organized storage, including pieces of paper in a file drawer.

Where possible, we tend to prefer to use databases because it is easier to get data out of them in a form that's useful. Unfortunately, most tools assume file system storage, using that storage method, it's difficult to get data into the database in any useful form. Thus most repositories will be file structures, with relational or other database systems as the runner-up choice.

At the basic level, you need to set up the database or file system in such a way that an automated (read *dumb*) tool can find what it needs easily. *Consistency* helps here. You also need to set up the system in such a way that a manual (*smart*) tool can find what he or she needs easily. Whether there is a lot of difference between these requirements is not clear.

For example, each system in your overall system should have a clearly demarcated file hierarchy separate from the other systems, plus its own build scripts, test scripts, and other tool files. This permits you to build each system separately without building the entire system. It also clearly identifies where everything is so that someone looking for a file stands a reasonable chance of finding it.

You may find that your tools dictate certain organizing principles. (Be sure to choose tools whose organizing principles are close enough to your organization or project.) Generally it's best to go with the way the tool organizes things by default. This approach minimizes both the customization work for your toolsmith and the risk of running into software failures in the tool. While this may seem constraining, generally this approach will optimize the cost of using the tools you have chosen.

Certain kinds of aggregation can help in organizing your system. For example, many organizations put all the "public" header files (shared constants, class definitions, and so on) in a single directory for the system, then have that single directory in the path for finding header files for the compiler and other tools. This simplification means you don't have to change the include path for different systems. The down side of this approach is you lose the system structure and have more difficulty finding the header file you want among the hundreds in the single directory. It's a trade-off. Another, similar example is putting the system libraries, after they are built, into a single directory for linking with the system as a whole.

We have seen quite complex automation systems sometimes emerge from requirements based on maximum flexibility for the developers. However, this is not necessarily the best way to optimize the automation practices. You may find that limiting flexibility, while it constrains development activities somewhat, has major benefits for the time spent automating the system.

For example, some build systems try to make building on many different operating system platforms totally transparent to the developer. The objective is for the release engineer to give one command that builds the system on all platforms at once. This almost never works in practice without extensive tool-smithing, time that you could better spend on integrating more information into the environment. A simple standard for transferring checked-in objects to different platforms for building there, in a separate system, is sufficient for most cross-platform solutions. Focus on your real objectives to determine whether additional complexity makes sense.

A repository is a kind of tool. There are several subclasses of repository tool:

- **Product:** Contains the product software objects. (This topic is not discussed separately in this book.)

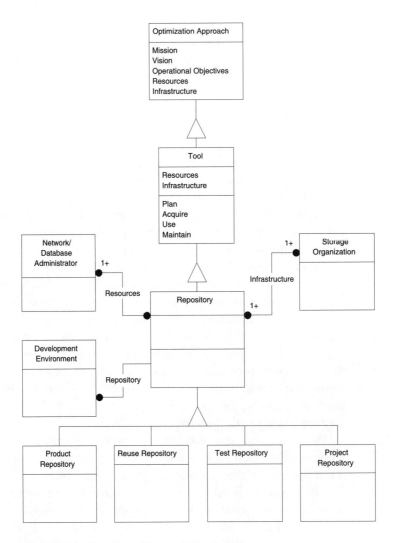

Figure 21.4 Structure of the repository class.

- **Reuse:** Contains the reusable component objects. (Again, this topic is not discussed separately herein.)
- **Test:** Contains the test suites.
- **Project:** Contains project-related data and objects.

Figure 21.4 shows the structure of the repository class.

Leadership

Vision: An effective object storage organization.

Mission: To provide storage services in a manner that promotes productivity.

Objective 21.4: To increase productivity through organizing object storage for easy storage and retrieval.

Approach 21.4: Buy or build a database or file structure that provides storage and retrieval services for product, reuse, test, and project objects.

Measurement 21.4: Developer productivity in effort-hours per function point of product while repository is available.

Structure

STORAGE

Your basic choice in storage technology is between a file system and a relational database. You can easily find proprietary repository technologies, especially for project data, though these can be quite limiting. The file system could be paper-based, of course.

NAMING CONVENTION

In addition to the basic storage options, you need to structure your system using names that help people find what they're looking for. You also need names amenable to automation. (That is, a tool can build the name easily out of component parts or can navigate through a consistently named sequence of hierarchical directories.)

Consistency is the magic word in naming conventions. Whatever you call directories and files, you should use a set of rules, and you should use it consistently. The specific set of rules depends on the tools you use (see the Tool object) and their requirements. You should use an optimization cycle to determine the exact set of rules.

While consistency is essential, you also will find that meaningful names give people using the repository a better clue as to what they're seeing. This situation usually results in higher productivity for those who need to navigate the system. Here are some guidelines for meaningful names:
- Pick a language and use only that language. (This applies to programming concepts too.)

- Align your name choices with the underlying way the system can display names; take advantage of the collating sequences (such as alphabetical order) that the system provides.
- Use only full words or widely accepted abbreviations; use operating systems that let you do this, where possible. Take advantage of commenting facilities to offer an extended explanation of the object.

A small tirade here on operating systems: The eight-character limit that has been imposed on generations of unsuspecting technologists probably has cost the world more lost time because of unreadable abbreviations than any other design flaw in the history of computing. (The one exception may have been the decision to force people to format floppy disks rather than formatting them on the fly through hardware, but that's past history, right?)

- Use upper- and lowercase for readability.
- Make all names unique except for those that represent some kind of consistent concept ("source," "database," and so on). *Do not* consider case in determining uniqueness, even if (*especially* if) your operating system distinguishes between S and s. It may; people don't.
- Use terms that will make sense to the people using the system, not jargon or made-up words.

RESOURCES

If you use a simple file system, you need only be aware of the operating system commands for accessing and manipulating directories and files (or how to use a graphical tool for doing the same things).

If you use a network file system, you may need a *network administrator* familiar with the network software. Network administrators set up file servers and network operating systems on them, then set up the client workstations that use them. Doing so can be similar to setting up shrines to local gods; don't forget to give the appropriate sacrifices to the priest or you may be unlucky. You'll probably be unlucky anyway, but why risk it?

If you use a database, you may need a database administrator who understands how to access and manipulate the database. Usually this will be someone who understands SQL and the particular DBMS you want installed. For sophisticated databases, this person often will also be a network administrator. (This is the *high*-priest level; more sacrifices please.)

INFRASTRUCTURE

You will need the appropriate amounts of memory, disk space, and so on to support your local and server file structures. You also will need file servers and local/wide area network hardware and software to support file or database sharing, possibly even minicomputers or mainframes. This infrastructure can get quite ornate for more sophisticated systems, often exceeding the value of the tools and repositories it enables. Make sure the value you add by using the tools and repositories justifies the cost of the infrastructure needed to support it.

Example

The DTS uses the DOS file system with a simple naming convention (try using a complex naming convention!) to store product components, reuse libraries, and tests. The project management system stores its data in a proprietary file format in that system, but it also lets you export the data into a relational database (plans underway). The data component of the DTS is a local relational database stored in files in the standard file hierarchy. (See the following for discussion on the Automated Integration Environment for a detailed file hierarchy standard.)

Product Repository

The *product repository* contains both the code and the documents that constitute the software product. Code is usually in source, object, and executable form; documents are in source and compiled form (for online documentation, for example).

Often the product repository serves as an ongoing repository associated with more than one project. For example, the first version of the DTS established the DTS product repository as part of the startup DTS project. Maintenance projects followed on to this, building on the product repository, including projects to port the DTS to different operating systems.

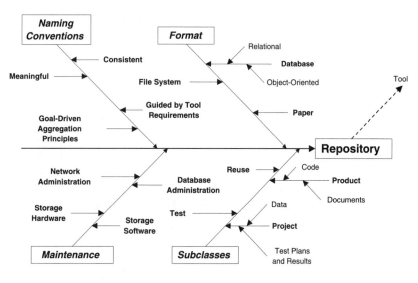

Figure 21.5 Road map for the repository class.

You may want to keep physically separate repositories for product objects and other kinds of objects.

Reuse Repository

The *reuse repository* contains objects such as class implementations, development documents, user documents, and other system components that you can reuse in the process of building new software.

Road Map

Figure 21.5 is the road map of the repository class.

Automated Integration Environment

The automated integration environment is the collection of tools, processes, and standards that you use to build and test an integrated software system. This environment is a kind of development environment, inheriting the tools and repositories.

The integration environment usually consists of a configuration management system, build scripts, a test driver, and a class hierarchy of testing classes that implement your test suites for the system. It also may consist of externally driven test scripts that interact with your system through some kind of programming interface. The environment generates individual, team, and management reports on integration status. It also ties together the tools and repositories you use to integrate your software into the shared development environment. It provides the highway for work to flow from one party to another. Figure 21.6 shows the class structure for the automated integration environment.

The tools you need to build the automated integration environment are by no means standard; in fact, this class is one that will reflect your distinct approach to software development. You should consider the following descriptions preliminary requirements for this software system; as you construct the environment, you will further refine the requirements, adding your own way of doing things. The development process you go through to construct your automation environment will be a nexus for process optimization, standardization, and self-reflection. *You* can choose to integrate the environment fully into the project and process management systems, or use it for simple version control, component integration and basic testing.

The automation effort does require that you have a clear statement of your build process. The first step is to describe your build process; you can then optimize it according to your objectives and automate it.

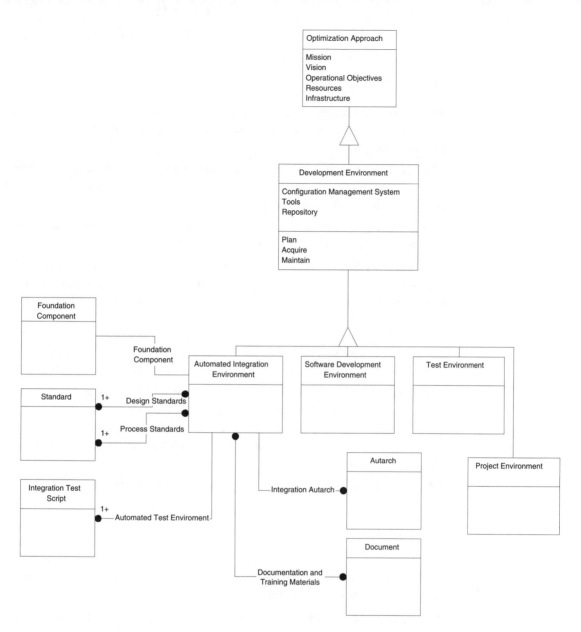

Figure 21.6 Structure of the automated integration environment class.

Minimally, the automated build process compiles and links the integrated (checked-in) components, sets up the system for testing, and executes the test driver, which then takes over. The driver runs the tests and generates a test report. If you are working with a project database, the environment also can generate project status reports based on the tested objects. The automated build process then sends the reports to the appropriate people, either through electronic messaging or by placing the report in a standard location in the file system.

Leadership

Vision: Increased productivity and quality as a result of nightly builds, with automatic reports available every morning to update the team on project progress and problems.

Mission: To automate configuration management, builds, and integration testing to enable, on a daily basis, testing of a system and reports on project and test status to those responsible.

Objective 21.5: To fully automate the configuration management, build, and integration test processes for a software system.

Approach 21.5: Buy or build a software environment that, together with component structure and naming standards, test methods, and project baseline standards, can automatically perform those processes required to integrate a system and test it.

Note that you usually can't automate everything in the integration process. Therefore, you must spell out in detail in the automation environment requirements the manual processes that are still a part of the integration system.

Measurement 21.5: The effort-hours spent in building and testing a system other than that spent checking in finished components.

This measure tells you how much effort you are spending at work that you want to automate; you want to automate all work other than that involved in checking in your work.

Objective 21.6: Optimize the cost of automating integration.

Approach 21.6: Put in place naming, design, and process standards that facilitate automation rather than trying to adapt automation to current practice. Develop the automation environment as if it were a software product using the same project life cycle standards you would for any software project. Use quality optimization techniques to make decisions based on your project objectives rather than on extraneous influences.

Measure 21.6: Marginal cost of automating integration for a new system after the first one.

Objective 21.7: Maximize the adoption of the automation environment across your projects.

Approach 21.7: Document the system as you would any software project. Develop training materials and courses and train all engineers to use the environment. Demonstrate how the environment improves productivity and quality, especially to opinion leaders; and phase in the environment rather than adopting it all at once.

Measure 21.7: Percentage of software system builds automated during a reference time period such as a quarter.

The key to the technical diffusion of the automation environment is to sell it to those who will use it. To do that, you have to have sales materials, and you have to convince the people who will persuade everyone else to use it. Phasing in the system ensures rapid success because it lets you demonstrate the success while giving you a chance to resolve any problems. Phase 1 should focus on a small, successful project; then scale up to ever-larger projects to convince the opinion leaders that the system works.

Objective 21.8: Your specific objectives, approaches, and measures here—this system should address *your* primary objectives. You should state them up front before thinking about the specific tools you want to make a part of the system.

Structure

SYSTEM

The basic input to the automation environment is the *system* to build and test, including the execution of the integration test suite. Note that the ultimate system is the main program that integrates all the other systems. Building the main system is just another integration, but the output software system becomes the main component of the system test suite, the next logical level of testing.

REPOSITORY

The integration environment inherits the repository from the development environment. In the subclass, the repository relates to the individual system rather than to the project system as a whole.

The cost of automating your integration and testing relates directly to the care you take in standardizing your repository. If your repository is a mess, the requirements for automating integration also will be a mess. Try to keep the environment well organized and simple.

The storage objects of the product and test repositories are part of the integration test, as there is some overlap between the contents of the product, test, and automated integration environments. For example, if a configuration management system stores all your software components in a database and provides tools to build the system from that database, your objects are the objects in the database and the database itself.

DESIGN STANDARDS

Certain *design standards* greatly simplify your life when automating. When thinking about system architecture and design standards, think about how your automation environment will handle system building. Again, focus on your objectives to decide when to simplify or complicate your architecture.

For example, most cross-platform development efforts try to keep the code base in a single configuration management system. This is possible because most porting code is limited in scope to a small portion of the system (the "porting layer," for example). Most design standards recommend ways of separating the code into different, encapsulated modules or subclasses so that the port-specific code is completely separate from the generic code. You also can use precompiler directives (**#define**, **#ifdef**, and so on) to tell the compiler when to look at certain parts of each file. All of this means that, while achieving the objectives relating to good architecture such as keeping related objects and methods together, you also accommodate the automation system's requirements for accessing the files in a standard way.

The single most important standard from the automation (and testing) perspective is the way in which you determine your systems. Designing systems with minimal coupling to other systems means that your automation process can be parallel and incremental in nature, which greatly reduces the complexity of the system.

Just as important is the cohesion of your class design. If you are going to automate the reuse process, you will find that meaningful classes tend to be easier to find in repositories than classes that arbitrarily combine functions. Providing documentation that the automation environment can use for searching is also a big step in the right direction for encouraging reuse. Automating class documentation completely with help files, man pages, or online documents means that you can use software tools to figure out what a class is about or to find related classes through hypertext links. Again, all this encourages reuse.

PROCESS STANDARDS

As with the other standards, your *process standards* have a great impact on your automation complexity:

- **Configuration Management Process:** Directly determines which tools are suitable for your objectives.
- **Testing Process:** The specifics of unit and integration testing methods directly determine how your automation system can contribute to automating testing; you also need to know the criteria for successful integration (that is, when does the integration test succeed?).
- **Reuse Process:** All the processes required to build and distribute reusable code and tests have direct implications for the automation system through which you access the reusable objects.
- **Build Process:** All the processes required to build a specific version of a software system, including processes for checking in components, running the build, completing any manual procedures, and generating and distributing reports to the appropriate people.

See the Process System for more detail on process objects.

DOCUMENTATION AND TRAINING MATERIALS

Any software system, including your build automation environment, is only as good as the supporting materials that let people understand how to use it and customize it. The *documentation and training materials* come in various forms:

- **Vendor Tool Documents:** The vendor-supplied documentation, both paper and online.
- **Custom Tool Documents:** Documents you create for tools you create or modify, both paper and online.
- **Tutorials:** Vendor and custom introductions to using the system, both paper and computer-based.
- **Training Materials:** Full-blown courses on using the system, both paper and computer-based.

You also need to provide internal requirements, design, and implementation documents that you can reuse for new systems and that you can use to maintain the system.

INTEGRATION AUTARCH

The *integration autarch* is the leader responsible for the integration process and hence for the automation environment. The autarch is responsible for enforcing the standards, for organizing the processes and infrastructure requirements, for communication, and for encouraging reuse of previously integrated objects.

The autarch is a cross-project leader with specific responsibilities and authority relating to facilitating communication and enforcing standards. These responsibilities are inherently cross-project, because reusing code and communication do not inherently relate to just a single project. Successful autarchs have the following qualities:

- They are highly technical people who understand and sympathize with software engineering and object-oriented methods.
- They should be opinion leaders who command the respect of their development organization.
- They need to know about, or at least how to find out about, available reuse repositories.
- They need to have excellent communication skills and a modicum of diplomacy.
- They should have no other major responsibilities for the foreseeable future!

In setting up an effective communication and feedback mechanism in the integration system, the autarch should work out the details of the following sorts of things:

- Requirements, design, code, and test reviews, inspections, and walk-throughs

- The set of appropriate process standards to follow
- How to handle changes to requirements, design, testing, and coding to facilitate the communication of change to all concerned
- The content and use of one or more reuse repositories

The autarch should have the last word on anything to do with integration or reuse. Giving the person in this role responsibility without authority is a sure way of making the integration process fail to achieve its objectives.

Dynamics

PLAN

You plan the automation system as for any software project. (See the software project management objects discussed in Part 5.) The result of this behavior is to produce a part of the project plan devoted to building the automation environment. Determining requirements in this case is the key piece of planning, as it will determine almost everything else, including which tools you need to acquire or build. Planning is an iterative behavior that goes on indefinitely as you discover new requirements, tools, and processes.

The autarch generally should take responsibility for the overall automation plan, as he or she will almost certainly spend most of his or her professional life working with the results.

If the complexity of the system results in complex problems, you should consider reengineering the system to make it easier to automate. Such complexity almost always indicates a system that is both prone to failure and impossible to maintain over time. While reengineering may add a large amount of time to your schedule, you will recoup it quickly through easier automation and maintainability down the road.

You should plan the technology diffusion of your system explicitly. The phasing in of the system, training, computer-based demonstrations and training, and selling the system to the opinion leaders all have great potential impact on the success of your automation project. Do not neglect this side of the project in favor of the technological side.

BUILD

The iterative building of the automation system constructs the various pieces of the system and integrates them together as your automation environment.

RUN

On a nightly basis, the release engineer takes responsibility for running the integration for one or more systems. His or her main responsibility is monitoring the results to ensure that the system functioned correctly. The actual initiation of the build can occur automatically through scheduling software, but someone must look at the process to make sure it works as expected.

This "run" is the basis for most measurement in this book. Each run generates a set of failures, and generally the number of failures per run is the key metric you want to see.

Report

When the system completes its run, it transmits its results as a series of reports:

- **Log Reports:** Reports that log the outcome of every step of the automated integration process for the release engineer.
- **Exception Reports:** Reports that describe any failures in the integration test suite.
- **Multiple Team Reports:** Reports to individual development teams of failures and optimization measures relevant to the team's responsibilities.
- **Developer-Specific Reports:** Reports to individual developers on the status of checked-in files, including failures associated with those files.
- **Management Reports:** Integration progress reports to project and functional management relaying the earned value of the build, the status of current tasks, and other process measures.

Example

Figure 21.7 shows part of the DTS file hierarchy, which builds each system as a separate DLL in the Library directory for the system. The C++ source code and Visual C++ project database files are in the Source directory, and the compiler creates the object files in the Object directory.

The version control tool maintains a database of files and versions, with revisions being kept as difference files in the system Version Control directory. This tool integrates with the development environment through OLE in-place activation and automation, allowing developers to check code in and out from their workstations. It also provides a scripting language for builds so that the release engineer can start the nightly build before going home, then check an error log report in the morning.

The release engineer, who also serves as the project toolsmith, built the scripts for the nightly integration build along with one of the development team over a six-month period while the project was starting up. When the integration test team had formed and built their test plan for the project, they began to integrate their built-in testing procedures into the build. These tests uncovered many integration problems that would otherwise have waited to interrupt the system test process. The toolsmith team is searching for a tool that lets them integrate the build scripts with the electronic mail system. As they have not been able to find a tool with the right connections to route the

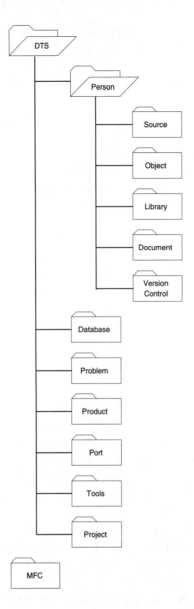

Figure 21.7 DTS file hierarchy.

planned reports, they are drawing up a requirements document as the first stage of a project to build their own.

The team keeps the system-related documents in the Document directory for each system. Other documents are in the DTS Project directory, along with the project management system files and other project repository data.

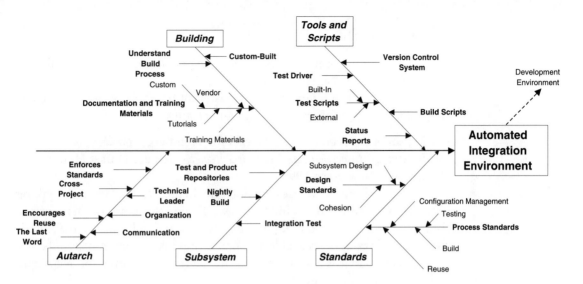

Figure 21.8 Road map for the automated integration environment class.

Road Map

Figure 21.8 is the road map of the automated integration environment.

Part 4 References

1. Barry W. Boehm. *Software Engineering Economics.* Prentice-Hall, Englewood Cliffs, NJ: 1981.

This book is the reference on the waterfall life cycle. It also has a complete analysis of software estimation and costing.

2. Daniel P. Freedman and Gerald M. Weinberg. *Handbook of Walkthroughs, Inspections, and Technical Reviews*, 3rd ed. Dorset House Publishing, New York: 1990.

This wonderful book uses the Socratic method to teach you everything you ever wanted to know about reviews. The question-and-answer format both structures your thinking in the right way and enlivens the presentation to make a thoroughly readable and practical book. There also are lots of real-world standards and suggestions for review procedures and techniques taken from real companies.

3. Donald C. Gause and Gerald M. Weinberg. *Exploring Requirements: Quality before Design.* Dorset House Publishing, New York: 1989.

This book gives you the tools to understand the why of building software: requirements. It focuses on removing ambiguity and adding missing requirements, giving you many specific techniques. If you ever have to do a requirements document, read this book first. Read it anyway, even if you don't have to do a requirements document; you'll benefit.

4. Ivar Jacobson, Magnus Christerson, Patrik Jonsson, and Gunnar Overgaard. *Object-Oriented Software Engineering: A Use Case Driven Approach.* Addison-Wesley, New York: 1992.

A pragmatic and comprehensive method for object-oriented software engineering in all its aspects, this book is a must for anyone seriously considering an object-oriented development project. The section on use cases is useful in showing you how to go about requirements analysis, though it doesn't go very deep. (See Gause and Weinberg above.) The section on testing is also of interest.

5. Capers Jones. *Assessment and Control of Software Risks.* Yourdon Press, Englewood Cliffs, NJ: 1994.

Laid out as a medical compendium, this book is a definitive road map to the world of software risks. The alphabetical presentation and lack of index are somewhat difficult hurdles, but diving into the specific risk topics pays immediate benefits in risk management.

6. Julia King. "Sketchy Plans, Politics Stall Software Development," *Computerworld* (June 19, 1995): 81.

This short article describes the current state of project failure in the software industry, also reporting a survey giving the top ten reasons for failure. Hint: For some reason, not knowing what you are doing and why seems to cause projects to fail; that and not having enough people to do what you don't know you are doing. And there seems to be a lot of ways of not knowing what you're doing.

7. Thomas Plum and Dan Saks. *C++ Programming Guidelines*. Plum Hall [609-927-3770, plum@plumhall.com], 1991.

A coding standard, prepackaged and ready to go. Why work if you can get somebody else to do it for you? Of course, you will always want to add your specific rules and regulations to the generic ones here, and some of these rules may seem too restrictive for your environment.

8. Niranjan Ramakrishnan. *Building Quality Software in C++*. Pacific Northwest Software Quality Conference, Workshop 5. October 18, 1993.

This course is an excellent overview of the issues involved in building quality software, mostly in the areas of requirements and design. Available from Pantheon Systems, Inc., 4800 SW Griffith Drive, Suite 300, Beaverton, OR, 97223.

THE PROJECT SYSTEM

The *project system* is the part of the quality system that relates to the managerial structure of the system: the way the system plans and controls software development. The project system contains the project document, project plan, and project environment classes. This part is an overview of the system, not a complete dissection of all aspects of project management.

Figure P5.1 shows the inheritance hierarchy of the project system. The *project document* is the basic document class in the quality system and is the root class for all the other document classes in this book. The *project plan* is a kind of project document.

The statement of work, schedule, resource plan, risk management plan, and milestone are all parts of the project plan. A *statement of work* lays out the scope, or extent, of the project, including the project requirements, the test plan, the documentation plan, and the work breakdown structure (WBS). The *schedule* takes the work breakdown structure tasks and *milestones*, specifies the dependencies

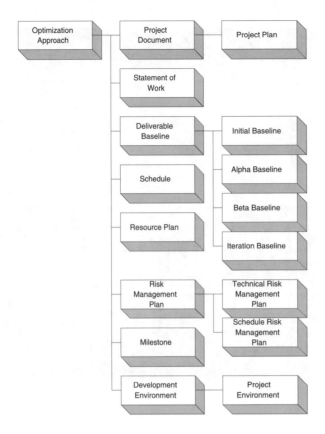

Figure P5.1 Project system inheritance hierarchy.

between tasks and assigns resources to tasks, then specifies the timing of tasks based on estimates of effort, dependency relationships, and resource availability. The *resource plan* lays out the organizational and authority structure of the resource system. The *risk management plan* analyzes risk in the *schedule* or *technical* components and provides a plan for managing that risk.

There are several types of baseline. A *deliverable baseline* is a configuration of technical components, usually under the control of a configuration management system, that gives you a foundation on which to build additional baselines. The ultimate baseline is the system baseline when you finish coding and testing your system. The *initial baseline* is your "first draft" of a component. The *alpha baseline* is your "final draft." The *beta baseline* is the production release to external users. The *iteration baselines* are the iterations on this final release to fix problems or add features as your life cycle continues.

It is vital to understand that these baselines include not only the standard waterfall phase deliverables but also delivery of the smallest foundation component. *Every* component of the system goes through baselining in the hierarchical approach to guarantee that it can serve as a reusable foundation for further work.

The *project environment* provides the infrastructure for project planning and control.

Figure P5.2 shows the containment relationships between the classes at a high level. This is only an overview of the project system, not a detailed model. The containment hierarchy shows only

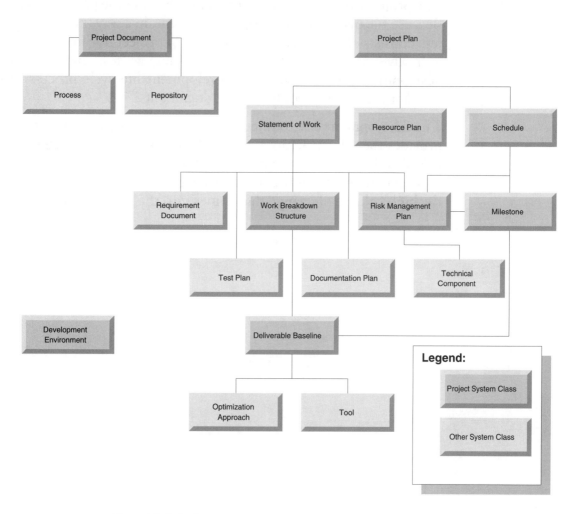

Figure P5.2 Project system containment hierarchy.

the relationships to other parts of the quality system, not the extensive internal relationships between different kinds of things in the project system.

The project plan is the main object in the project system, as it contains most of the other components of the system.

The work breakdown structure, a major part of the statement of work, itself comprises a list of the deliverable baselines. As Chapter 23 notes, there are many ways to build a work breakdown structure; we recommend building it from deliverable baselines, but that is not the only way.

The project document is another major object in the project system. Because the plan is itself a project document, in a way the whole system consists of documents. Other kinds of project documents, however, live mainly in other systems, such as test and software development, and the software development life cycle process and relevant repositories contain those documents.

The development environment, the final component of the system, provides the infrastructure for the project and project management. It is also the source of the unique dynamism (a polite way of saying "extreme insanity") of the software development project because of the high volume of change that comes into the system from outside.

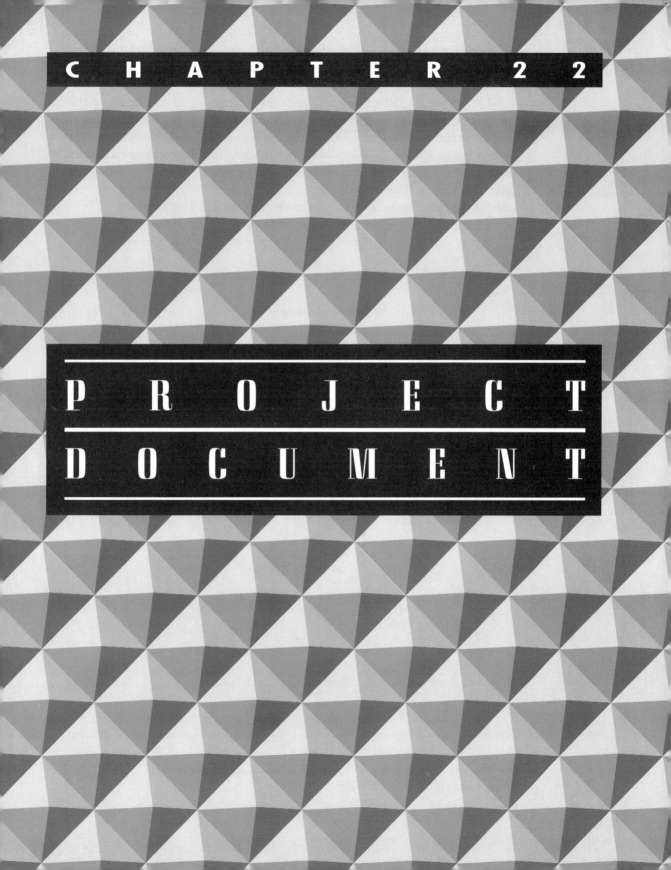

CHAPTER 22

PROJECT DOCUMENT

The project document is an abstract kind of optimization approach that standardizes the structure of all documents relating to a project, including the project plan and the set of development documents.

The project document serves to unify the structure of all documents on the project. A unified structure assists project team members both by standardizing the useful components of documents (such as a version number) that might otherwise be left out or overlooked and by enabling the creation of project document templates that reduce the amount of effort you need to produce a given document. The class also serves as the abstract parent of the more specific document classes; it is the general document class for the system.

The project repository should contain all project documents.

Figure 22.1 shows the structure of the project document class.

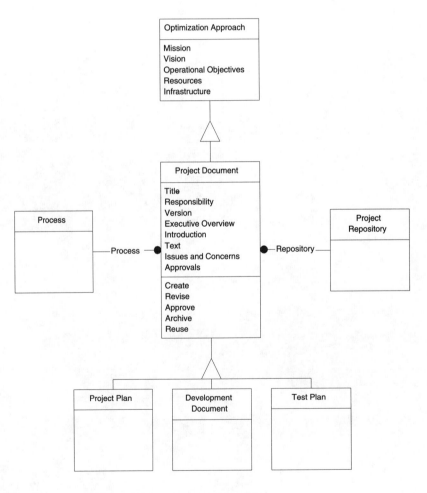

Figure 22.1 Structure of the project document class.

Leadership

Vision: A set of well-structured and communicative project documents.

Mission: To create a standard format for project documents of any kind that enhances the consistency, communicative value, and productivity of project documentation.

Objective 22.1: To have a high level of communicative value in project documents.

Approach 22.1: Standardize the basic format and layout of all project documents so that all contain the basic elements that the project team needs to communicate.

Measurement 22.1: Survey the project team during each accounting period, asking the question "Does the current standard for project documents help you to produce clear, consistent documents?

Objective 22.2: To increase productivity in producing project documents.

Approach 22.2: Standardize the basic format and layout of all project documents to facilitate document creation and to minimize rework due to missing elements.

Measurement 22.2: Ratio of effort spent creating project documents to a benchmark of such effort without the common standard.

Structure

Title

The *title* of the document is the name by which you refer to it. It should be unique among all your project documents (ignoring the version number, to be discussed). You can have a title with multiple parts, including the project name, the document name, a subtitle, and even a document number for the numerically inclined. The point of the title is to identify the document without ambiguity.

Cautions

If your document requires cautions warning readers of confidentiality, copyright, trademarks, and other legal restrictions on it, you usually put them on the page following the title or at the bottom of the title page. You can put confidentiality warnings on each page in the header or footer or printed in gray-scale across the page.

Responsibility

The *responsibility* of the document is the person or persons responsible for its contents, getting approvals, and so on. Ordinarily this will be a single person, but occasionally it may make sense to allow more than one person to take responsibility for a document. If you have a responsibility matrix for the project, the responsibility for a given project document should appear there.

Process

The *process* that creates the document may be any kind of project or development process. Documents that are not the result of a process are generally subjects for optimization; you probably just haven't made the process explicit. Doing so is a good idea.

Any given document belongs to a single process, but a process may produce more than one document. For example, the architectural design process may produce an architectural design document, a database design document, and an external interface design document. The exact structure depends on the process you put in place.

Version

Every document should have a *version* number. This number lets you indicate the specific revision of a document, if that is important in a given context. Version numbers usually have two parts, a major revision number and a minor revision number. Major revisions occur when you make a lot of changes; minor revisions are for corrections and minor expansions of material.

Test Plan Introduction

The *introduction* provides the context for the document, communicating the who, what, why, when, and where of the document to its readers. It provides the context within which the plan details make sense. The introduction gives you a clear and shared understanding of the broad overview of the document scope. It includes the following subsections:

- Overview of the subject
- Scope of the work to perform
- Summary of assumptions made by the test planners
- Approval rights over the information in the plan

You can hand a good introductory section to someone who knows nothing about the project and provide them with enough information to be able to read the rest of the plan and not need to ask too many questions about the details.

To test your introduction, find three people who are not very familiar with your project, and ask them to read it. Note the questions they ask; there should be few about why the project is in fact a project. If they have many high-level questions, the introductory section has failed. Try this out on an executive type. If he or she can read the section in a couple of minutes and expresses satisfaction with the information, the introduction works. If not, ask what questions or concerns are and seriously consider rewriting the section.

The introduction should state what the document covers and what it does not cover. You should summarize any assumptions you make and refer to the detail in the assumptions section.

Refer to existing standards or guidelines acceptable to your organization for the type of work the document proposes. If no standards or guidelines exist, then state how you will measure the successful application of the work. This is usually tied to the milestones.

The introduction should finally set out (again, based on any standards or guidelines) the approval process for the document; see the following "Approvals" section.

Executive Overview

The *executive overview* section is usually one or more paragraphs, as many as are necessary, that describe the background of the project. These paragraphs should provide just enough information so that someone not familiar with the project can review the remainder of the document and understand directly its content in context of the project. Often there is a short description of the project with its major deliverables and customers. A terse statement of what the document does and does not cover is desirable. If other major sources of information provide more detail, you should refer to them in this section.

Assumptions

This section enumerates every conscious assumption that the test planners can identify. Whenever and wherever possible name names, be specific. For example: "We assume that every developer will test his or her code to Safe Class status." State the impact to the testing effort if the assumption is not true.

Approvals

List the organizational units and the names of the persons in charge who have approval rights over this plan. The approval sections requires some careful thought. You can grant approval rights over the entire plan to each of the listed approvers. If you do this, then your plan may wind up in limbo for a long time if one or more of the approvers is out of town, too busy to review the plan, or a political enemy. A second approach is to ask for approvals over the sections that affect a specific functional area or individual. Overall plan approval resides with the project manager and test plan owner. This approach enables individuals to focus on their specific responsibilities and to raise issues in that regard, without holding up the overall test plan.

Text

The abstract attribute *text* represents the actual contents of the document; it may have an arbitrary internal structure for each specific kind of document.

Issues and Concerns

Every document should list any *issues and concerns* with the content. An issue is a point of discussion or dispute, something you think other people should talk about to resolve. A concern is something you worry about but do not necessarily need to resolve.

The issues and concerns are usually the most interesting parts of a document that everyone reads, either for their humorous content or to find out what's really happening, kind of like a talk show. It is hoped you can raise the level a bit beyond that.

Unfortunately, issues always will arise. Most can be resolved. If something changes that affects your test plan and the requisite parties refuse to commit to delivering something you need, *escalate*. Doing so usually means going to the first-level customer, which is almost always development management. The politics can get tricky, but if you have an accepted vision, mission, and objectives, resolution is usually possible. Remember, project documents are living documents. They are used day to day and week to week to guide decisions and prioritization of activities so that the project quality goals can be met. When you use project documents in this way, productivity may increase dramatically across the project because you can allocate resources more directly to tasks that relate to the project objectives.

Approvals

The *approvals* for the project document are the signatures that project or company policy requires to authorize commitment of resources to the actions recommended in the document.

The policy situation varies from company to company and from project to project, depending on the perceived need for executive control over the project resources. One project may require signatures and countersignatures, while another may require no signatures at all. The key point to understand about approvals is that they represent authority, and you always should have clear lines of authority in your project organization.

One variation on approval policy requires the signatures of all the participants in the project, signifying a commitment to execute the project to the best of their ability. If you take this approach, you should make clear that you are basing such approval not on authority but on *consensus*: the ability to *live with* the document even though you may disagree with parts of it. You should not use such approvals as go/no-go (authorization) barriers to doing what the document recommends, or you will wind up with a situation similar to the UN Security Council and a very politicized project process.

If a project document has no impact on resources, there should be no need for approvals. On the other hand, if there is no impact on resources, the document is probably a good candidate for an optimization review. There is little point to producing documents that sit on a shelf or on a disk unused.

If you are producing documents for external approval, you also have to take into account the approval process of your client.

Dynamics

Create

Creating the document usually means taking a template for the specific kind of document, filling in the parts that your project's policy requires, and then doing the actual work involved in the process. The result is a first draft document.

Revise

After some event such as a review or a change request or a period of time for letting the content settle in your mind, you come back and revise the document. You invoke the revision process iteratively until the document fully meets your needs or until you run out of time. Every time you issue a revised document, increment the version number.

Approve

Approval of the document implies a commitment to carry out the proposed actions in the document, implicit or explicit. See the approvals discussion in the "Structure" section above. This method does whatever is necessary to approve the document: collect signatures, collect verbal approvals, or nothing at all.

Archive

At some point, you need to put a copy of the document into an archive for later reference, either for historical purposes such as determining what actually happened during your project for legal reasons or for later reuse. If you have the document under version control, you may want to put the entire revision history in the archive.

Reuse

With the document in a repository of some kind, others can copy the document and reuse it in their project if the content applies; but only if it is available in a repository. This repository is best online, so that you can revise and adapt the document easily. (See the "Revise" method above.)

Example

The DTS project document standards called for the following structure:

- A title consisting of the project name (Defect Tracking System) and logo (a particularly funny "bug" that the project manager drew) and the specific document title
- A confidentiality warning to the effect that project documents were not to circulate beyond the company's employees
- A list of the people responsible for the document, including the author and any team members that actively participated in the document

- A two-part version number
- An introduction
- The text
- A section for issues and concerns
- Approvals by the project manager and by any functional managers with affected resources

All documents in the DTS project were online documents. The company had invested in a document tracking system with version control, and the DTS project kept all versions of all documents in that system. When anyone needed a specific document, he or she went through the network to the repository and checked it out. Also, the project manager reused templates created on another project, altering them to fit the above constraints.

The DTS project did manage to reuse several development documents, including a couple of API architecture documents and some test approaches for the test plan. Overall, there wasn't that much reuse, since the process of accumulating documents was less than six months old.

Road Map
Figure 22.2 is the road map for the project document class.

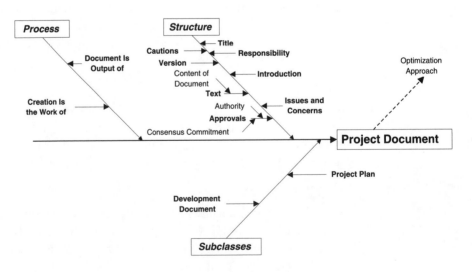

Figure 22.2 Road map for the project document class.

CHAPTER 23

PROJECT PLAN

Project Plan

Ready, fire, aim!

What's wrong with this picture?

The major thing wrong with it as a quality optimization approach is that it is unlikely to succeed in its mission. No matter how much experience the people firing have, they are unlikely to hit much of anything without aiming first.

In a less harrowing setting, the same approach is less obviously wrong, but it always has the same effect: project failure. If there is no planning, or you plan haphazardly and with little attention to detail, the result is that the project resources don't know what they're doing. They can't use their effort to best effect, and they are less productive as a result.

A *project plan* is a kind of project document that lays out and schedules the work and resources of a project. The project plan also includes risk management plans for the technical and schedule aspects of the project. The project plan document should be part of the project repository, as should all its component objects (and all project documents).

The key to planning is to realize that it is the art of *figuring out* what you need to do to succeed, not *doing* it. It's a strategic, analytical process, not a tactical, results-oriented process. Planning is basic to the optimization cycle and so applies to every object in this book. Project planning is quality optimization applied at the highest level to improve the chances of your project achieving its mission.

In every project, there are, three basic things you need to get right. First, you must understand what it is you are trying to do. You must understand the customers and their requirements, what fulfilling those requirements entails in terms of deliverables and tasks, and what technical risks you take in fulfilling them. Second, you have to understand the timing of what the project will do: the dependencies between tasks and resources, how you will assign resources to tasks and what resources you need, how to get feedback on how the project progresses, and what sort of schedule risks there are. Third, you have to understand the organization you will work with during the project, which almost certainly isn't going to achieve its vision without help from people and physical resources. You need to understand how your organization works, who has what authority, who will perform as integration autarch, what capabilities the organization has, and how the culture of the organization works.

A lot of this planning seems obvious to experienced project managers. Nothing says you can't reuse prior planning; quite the contrary. But if you don't have a written plan with this material, your planning is not formal and not likely to be effectively reusable. If you do have a written plan and can't reuse it because it no longer applies to your organization, you really do need to go back and write down the new approaches you will take.

We must stress the importance of the project plan and its components. If the project plan is not comprehensive (whether you reuse parts of other plans or not), it is project management malpractice to approve of and to proceed with the project.

As Chapter 24 discusses in detail, things change or fall apart as part of the natural project environment. That doesn't make it useless to plan, it makes it essential. You also need to plan for change and how to react creatively to it. That's what the risk management plans are for. You also need to keep your current plan up to date in order to communicate effectively with those working on the project.

Project plans are not static, dead documents that sit on a shelf and collect dust. They are dynamic documents that reflect the best and most current thinking about where the project is going. A plan that does not represent the current state of the project is out of date and needs updating. It is also important to understand that a plan is not tablets from the mount, it is simply the current understanding you have of what's going on. It changes with your understanding, which, we hope, does not stand still during the progress of the project.

The plan reflects the fact that, as you look further into the future, your vision dims. You may understand only partially what will happen in six months when it comes time to develop the sixth major system of the project. Events from the project environment may intervene; you and your technical teams' understanding of the technical issues may improve, sometimes radically; you may hire (or lose) the best technical brain on the planet. That's why this book prefers an iterative, incremental approach to project management that benefits from incessant feedback to guide the project toward its objectives.

Figure 23.1 shows the structure of the project plan class. This section and the following ones are not comprehensive, but they do give you a taste of the overall structure of project planning and project management in overview.

Leadership

Vision: A comprehensive but dynamic plan for the project that ensures quality and productivity.

Mission: To progressively analyze the work, schedule, and resources needed to make the project successful in terms of quality and productivity.

Objective 23.1: To understand and communicate what the project needs to accomplish to achieve high quality.

Approach 23.1: Construct and maintain a project plan consisting of a statement of work, a schedule, and a resource plan that comprehensively lay out all of the deliverables, tasks, dependencies, milestones, organizational structures, and physical resources for the project to ensure that the project will accomplish everything necessary for project quality.

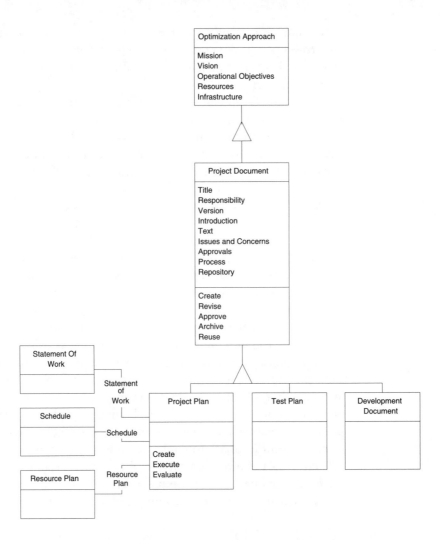

Figure 23.1 Structure of the project plan class.

Measurement 23.1: Schedule performance index (earned value at completion divided by the median plan baseline cost of work scheduled; see the following "Earned Value" section for details).

Objective 23.2: To increase productivity through understanding and communicating how to achieve the project goals.

Approach 23.2: Construct a project plan as in 23.1 that optimizes the effort of project resources through appropriate assignments, understanding of dependencies, and a thorough understanding of the capabilities and culture of the project organization.

Measurement 23.2: Ratio of median project productivity (effort per function point) to benchmark productivity.

Structure

STATEMENT OF WORK

The *statement of work* for the project includes the requirements document, test plans, documentation plan, work breakdown structure, and technical risk management plan. See the following section on the statement of work for details.

SCHEDULE

The *schedule* for the project includes the resource assignments, dependencies, time line, milestones, plan baseline date and effort estimates, and the schedule risk management plan.

See the following section on the schedule for details.

RESOURCE PLAN

The *resource plan* for the project includes the organization chart and its resources and authority structure. It should identify the integration autarch (see the Development Environment Chapter 21). Statements of team and resource capabilities should accompany the chart, as well as a brief analysis of the relevant elements of organizational culture.

The resource plan also includes a list of physical resources associated with the project and its environment. This includes both the machines and software tools as well as facilities for the resources and tasks.

RESOURCES

Planning requires extensive training in several different aspects of project management and software development management. The individual parts of the project plan each require specific skills; see the following sections. The plan as a whole requires training in the quality optimization approach and its techniques and at least an intermediate level of training in general project management.

Dynamics

CREATE

The Create task is the activity that starts the whole optimization approach for the project in motion. Creating the project plan requires creating its components, which in turn create their components, and so on until you have a complete plan for doing the project. This task also creates the standard project document elements (title, introduction, version number, and so on).

EXECUTE

The Execute task is the activity that drives the software development life cycle from start to finish. Executing the project plan requires the project manager and the functional managers to direct and control resources to deliver their assigned deliverable objects in the work breakdown structure (WBS) on the time line from the project schedule. It also drives the revision process for the plan by incorporating feedback on progress and success of tasks.

EVALUATE

The Evaluate task comes at the end of the project and is its last task. It closes the optimization cycle for the project by reviewing the entire project and feeding back the results of this review into the project and functional organizations. This task is also sometimes called a project post mortem, though the implications of this term are too static for the truly alive, dynamic quality of the review.

Example

The DTS project plan was a comprehensive document that included the project document details (title, responsibility, version, introduction, and so on). The project manager reused a resource plan from a prior project, just updating the resources and their capabilities to reflect some training and hiring that the organization had done since the previous project. The project manager spent the most time on the statement of work, as the schedule was not of the essence in the project, but the quality of the software deliverables was paramount. The project manager built the schedule in the corporate project management software using templates for the life cycle processes.

The initial project plan took three months to build, as the requirements process and test planning took a good deal of interaction with the very busy customers for the system. The project manager presented the plan to the senior executives, who approved it with some suggestions for changes in the organization authority structure designed to improve the responsibility/authority mixture for part of the project.

After approval, the project manager maintained the various parts of the project plan as online documents in the project repository, updating the plan once a week and validating it at every major deliverable baseline milestone. The changes were mostly due to requirements changes from customers as they saw the intermediate prototypes and went through usability sessions. A couple of major changes were required organizationally because of capability problems. It turned out the project manager had not asked the right people about the resource capabilities. The project manager's assumptions about schedule risk also assumed too much authority on the part of the project manager, at least according to the vice president involved in the emergency meeting that resulted. Once resolved, the plan baselines reflected the dropping of one major customer requirement by mutual agreement, which all the participants in the project felt would be impossible to achieve with the current resources. This led to a diminished earned value ratio for the project but preserved the productivity ratio at its intended level.

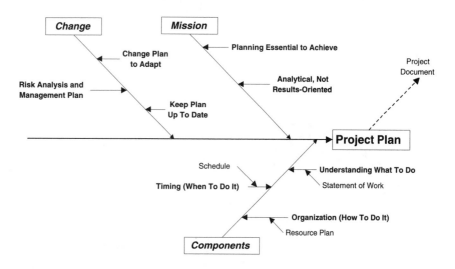

Figure 23.2 Road map for the project plan class.

Road Map

Figure 23.2 is the road map for the project plan class.

Statement of Work

The *statement of work* for the project is a collection of project documents that together define the *scope* of the project as a project document. The statement of work includes these components:

- The requirements document
- The test plans
- The documentation plan
- The work breakdown structure
- The technical risk management plan

These can be individual project documents collected together as a project plan, or they can be sections of the larger project plan. The latter strategy provides a thoroughly integrated approach and assumes that approvals apply to the whole plan, not just to individual parts. If you want a unified approval, make the statement of work a subclass of project document. Because the requirements document and test plan components are discussed individually herein, they are treated as separate documents with individual approvals and structures.

Note that the test and documentation plans do not themselves have any scheduling and resource information (other than requirements). Schedules,

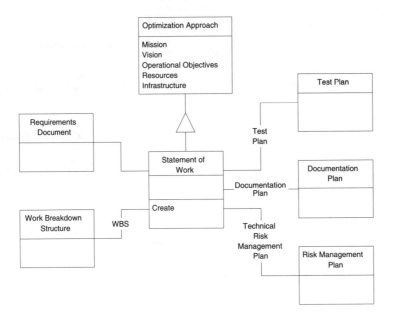

Figure 23.3 Structure of the statement-of-work class.

organizational structure, and resource assignments are part of the schedule and resource plan components of the project plan.

Figure 23.3 shows the structure of the statement-of-work class.

Leadership

Vision: A comprehensive statement of the deliverables and work for the project that ensures the quality of the deliverables and the productivity of the work.

Mission: To analyze and accomplish the scope of the project to ensure quality and productivity.

Objective 23.3: To understand what specific things the project needs to deliver to achieve high quality.

Approach 23.3: Construct a statement of work consisting of a requirements document, work breakdown structure, test plans, documentation plan, and technical risk management plan to ensure that the project will accomplish everything necessary for project quality.

Measurement 23.3: Cost variance at completion (estimated at completion minus budgeted at completion); see the "Earned Value" section on page 472 for details.

Objective 23.4: To increase productivity through understanding what tasks the project must accomplish to meet its goals.

Approach 23.4: Construct a statement of work as in 23.3 that states clearly what work to do and how to go about doing it (approach, standards, methods, and so on).

Measurement 23.4: Cost performance index (earned value divided by actual cost of work performed); see the "Earned Value" section on page 472 for details.

Objective 23.5: To accomplish the planned product deliverables of the project.

Approach 23.5: Construct a statement of work as in 23.3 that states clearly what work to deliver, and use that statement to track delivery according to the plan using earned value for each task.

Measurement 23.5: Schedule performance index (earned value divided by plan baseline cost of work scheduled); see the "Earned Value" section on page 472 for details.

Measurements 23.3 to 23.5 are continuously available throughout the project so that, as project manager, you always can tell how you are doing with respect to the work you planned to achieve.

Structure

REQUIREMENTS DOCUMENT
The *requirements document* is a development document that states what the deliverables of the project need to do. It includes the requirements use cases for the software system. See the requirements document class section for details.

WORK BREAKDOWN STRUCTURE
The *WBS* has many different forms, but its essence is a hierarchy of categories and tasks, with the tasks being the leaves of the tree. There are many ways to structure the WBS:

- Break down the structure starting with functional organizations (usually called an organizational breakdown structure).
- Break down the structure starting with the life cycle processes.
- Break down the structure starting with subprojects for producing different components of the product, such as contracted systems.
- Break down the structure by deliverables.

All of these have more or less validity depending on what you are trying to optimize. For object-oriented software products, we feel that breaking down the structure by deliverables has much more impact on quality and productivity than any other approach. For example, tasks relating to risk management appear together with the tasks that produce the deliverable that is at risk. See the example in this section for a part of such a WBS.

A *task*, or *work package*, is the smallest unit of work that is manageable or on which other tasks depend. That is, you want to break down the deliverables into packages of work that are both manageable and that reflect the actual structure of the process you need to manage.

In this way of creating a WBS, the deliverables are categories, while the tasks required to produce the deliverables are the leaves of the structure. The life cycle process thus becomes a path through the leaves of the WBS. Note that you should not assume that each task occurs only once in the schedule. For example, using a spiral life cycle, you could iterate through several repetitions of a prototype/risk-analysis task set, though they might be just two tasks on the particular class you are developing. The WBS does not map directly into the schedule with a one-to-one mapping from WBS task to schedule task. It represents the logical set of tasks associated with a deliverable, not the actual set of tasks to accomplish.

The WBS is a dynamic document that reflects your current understanding of the structure of the project deliverables. You can foresee only so much in advance. As you progress through the project, you should revise the WBS to include more details or to reflect new ideas about how to structure the system.

Usually a software development task should take no more than two weeks and no less than a day, although some tasks, such as meetings, may take less than a day. You should cluster tasks into *deliverable baselines*, groups of deliverable objects that provide a basis for further development. These baselines become objects in the WBS as a separate category of baseline objects. See the following "Deliverable Baseline" section for details.

You need to use your judgment and your objectives for the WBS and its tasks: value and productivity, both for the deliverables and for management resources. If a manager is spending all his or her time updating time to compete tasks in a database, he or she is not going to be very productive in managing the people doing the work. Conversely, if the tasks go on so long that you risk technical or schedule failure because you have no time left to recover, management of the project becomes impossible.

TEST PLANS

The *test plan* is a project document that lays out the approach, resources, methods, and tools that the project will use to ensure that some software component meets its objectives. See the test plan class section for details.

DOCUMENTATION PLAN

The *documentation plan* is a project document that lays out the approach, resources, methods, and tools that the project will use to create the system components that help the users to use the system. This plan might include manuals, online help, tutorials, examples, and other products that contribute to understanding the system rather than to achieving the requirements of the system directly. The documentation approach should include the structure of the document set (what books, what help files, what examples, and so on) as a statement of the work to accomplish.

The further development of this class is beyond the scope of the book.

TECHNICAL RISK MANAGEMENT PLAN

The *technical risk management plan* details the risks associated with the failure to meet requirements. In other words, it assesses the risk that the deliverable software won't work right.

For each task related to a software deliverable, the risk management plan assesses different technical risks. If any risk exceeds the project risk avoidance criterion (usually a combined probability of failure and consequence of failure of over 50 percent), then the risk management plan contains an approach to avoiding the risk. This approach specifies the actions or tasks that help the project to avoid the risk, which should become part of the WBS. The standards and methods we associate with almost every object in this book build in many risk management procedures. The technical risk management plan gives an overview of specific risk and risk management by object.

A good deal of the test plans deal with the management of technical risk. After all, testing is one clear way to manage the risk of failure. In fact, testing is the process of making the system fail to find and fix faults that contribute to the risk of failure. Similarly, reviews are a way to limit technical risk by applying the synergy of multiple viewpoints to risky single-viewpoint tasks.

This book assumes that while you manage technical risk, you don't *eliminate* such risk. Despite whatever you do, there is always a statistical chance of technical failure. If the impact of failure is very great, such as multiple human deaths, irreparable environmental damage, or immediate loss of your job or reputation, you may want to manage to this impact by being a lot more careful, testing more, sending out résumés, and so on. People who think that by doing this they are eliminating risk completely are fooling themselves.

Dynamics

CREATE

The Create task is a simple process of gathering the individual components together into a unified document of some kind, whether a paper one or an online one of some kind. To create the statement of work, you can create the documents that are a part of it; this drives the process of project planning and requirements analysis.

Example

Upon getting approval for the project, the DTS project manager began the various processes associated with developing the requirements document, test plans, and documentation plan by requesting the documents from the development, QA, and documentation team managers. After reviewing and revising those documents, the project manager created the WBS by specifying the systems (including the documents) that would comprise the overall DTS system. Working with the system architect, the project manager broke the requirements down into an initial class hierarchy and partitioned it into systems. Because there were some special work requirements, including a contracted ODBC system and an abstraction partition related to ODBC, there were some overlaps in the resulting WBS structure. There were also some partitions that related to project requirements rather than user requirements.

Working with the different functional managers, the project manager broke the work categories down into fundamental objects that represented four to six weeks of work. The project manager added deliverable baseline components to these fundamental objects.

Having completed the first pass on the WBS, the project manager created the technical risk management plan. For each task in the WBS, he performed a technical risk analysis, looking at the various elements that might have contributed to the failure of the task to achieve its technical objectives. Most risks for the DTS tasks involved a lack of relevant technical experience and training, creeping user requirements, low quality, or inadequate configuration control (some of the typical risks for MIS projects). The project manager added tasks to compensate for these risks, including many reviews, technical training, testing, and a full-scale subproject to develop an automated integration environment with configuration management tools.

Figure 23.4 shows a piece of the WBS as a graphical tree display. This particular chunk of the WBS shows three system components of the Person system: the Person class, the Person class-to-class test suite, and the Person integration test suite. The diagram starts with the system, breaks down into the different components, then the subcomponents, then the tasks associated with the components and subcomponents.

The Person class is a software component of the system that satisfies user requirements for dealing with people in the system. It has the tasks Code, Test, Integrate, and Review. The design document for the system goes through the standard process of creation, review, revision, approval, and archiving. The WBS fragment shows one component of the design document, the Person class design component, which you create.

The Person hierarchical-incremental test suite contains two test models, a dynamic (state-transition) model and a transaction-flow model. Each has a Create and a Review task. Each model contains one or more test objects (state-transition life cycles or transaction flows, respectively), which has a Create task. Each object corresponds to a test script, which you create, execute, and report on. As an optimization, the project and QA manager decided to forgo code reviews of the test scripts in this case. Instead, they relied on

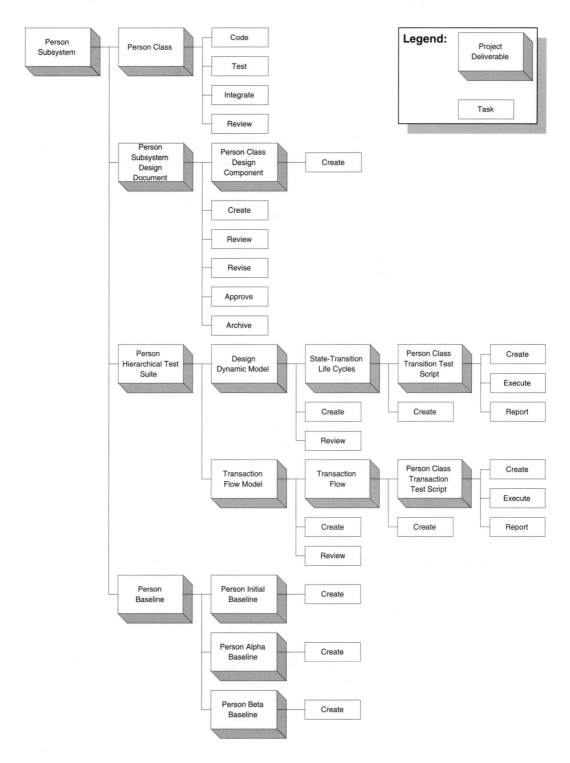

Figure 23.4 Portion of DTS WBS for Person class.

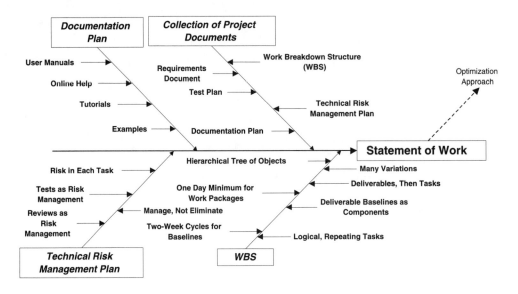

Figure 23.5 Road map for the statement-of-work class.

the model reviews, based on statistical error rates in test scripts being minimal or zero in past projects using the same people.

Finally, the Person baseline object consists of three baselines of the Person class hierarchy, the initial baseline, the alpha baseline, and the beta baseline. Additional, iteration baselines could be added to this component if needed. Each baseline has a Create task.

Road Map

Figure 23.5 is the road map for the statement-of-work class.

Deliverable Baseline

Deliverable objects include everything from the project plan itself, to requirements documents, to design components to classes to architectural test suites to system test evaluations. All have *deliverable baseline* configurations: the project plan baseline, the requirements baseline, the Person class hierarchy baseline, the Problem architectural test suite baseline, and the system test baseline, respectively. The deliverable baseline is a configuration of deliverable objects that meets some set of exit criteria. *Exit criteria* are standards in a standards document that define the acceptable level of risk through operational measures such as test model coverage or failure rates. Typically you place the baseline version of the objects under configuration management control. Also typically, further development tasks can use the resulting object, so it must be in some sense complete and tested, depending on what kind of object it is. Since, by definition, a baseline represents something you build on, you want that something to be stable and safe. In the case of classes, that means at the minimum achieving full coverage of the class-related test models and preferably some level of successful integration testing.

You can build a foundation object such as a class hierarchy and its associated test objects or a development document, typically, in about four to six weeks. This grouping level provides a clear sequence of deliverable baselines for your WBS. If you structure your WBS in these clusters, you can develop a baseline sequence that represents the progress of the baseline over the development period. There are four kinds of deliverable baseline: initial, alpha, beta, and iteration. These are subclasses of the main abstract baseline class that have special exit criteria. (see the "Exit Criteria" section that follows).

The *initial deliverable baseline* contains a complete description of the components of the baseline. It may have stubbed methods and no functionality, outlined headings without accompanying text, and so on: a high level of detail only. It will contain the first pass at the content and the accompanying risk management objects, such as class test scripts or use cases.

The *alpha deliverable baseline* contains the first draft of the core functionality or content but not a lot of detail items such as cross-references, error handling, or other i-dotting elements. You should have the first revision of things like test scripts.

The *beta deliverable baseline* contains the full functionality or content of the baseline objects, including full test model coverage or quality assurance techniques such as proofreading or spell-checking. The baseline should represent a usable component at this point.

The *iteration deliverable baseline* revises a previous baseline of the objects to evaluate the reusability of the objects, to rework or reschedule any missing or incomplete content, to complete tests or quality assurance, and so on. You should plan for at least one and possibly more iteration baselines to adapt the objects in the baseline to changes that occur as the project progresses.

It shouldn't take more than two weeks of work at any given time to get to one of these baselines, and you should choose your level of work breakdown to reflect this timing requirement. You may have to rework parts of the WBS to reflect better effort estimates after you build the project statement of work. See the section on the WBS in this section.

Figure 23.6 shows the structure of the deliverable baseline class.

Leadership

Vision: A collection of deliverable objects that provides a safe foundation for further work.

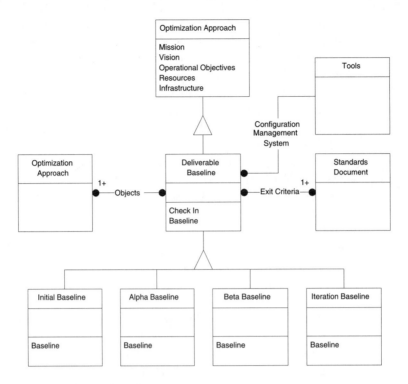

Figure 23.6 Structure of the deliverable baseline class.

Mission: To combine deliverable objects in a collection that meets standard criteria for achieving an acceptable level of risk.

Objective 23.6: To provide a collection of deliverable objects that has an acceptable level of risk.

Approach 23.6: Place the deliverable objects under configuration management control and test them against standard exit criteria in a standards document to determine whether the collection has an acceptable level of risk. Declare the baseline when the collective risk falls below the threshold risk that the exit criteria express.

Measurement 23.6: Ratio of risk to the risk threshold defined in the exit criteria; this may be a simple ratio of values or a complex heuristic that combines multiple criteria such as test model coverage and failure rates.

Structure

OBJECTS

The deliverable objects are the actual objects that you are putting under configuration management control. These may be technical components, project documents, or any other object that is part of the software development project: any optimization approach.

EXIT CRITERIA

Although the exit criteria more properly belong in the infrastructure section, as they are part of a standards document so fundamental to the baseline that we define them as a component of the structure. The exit criteria for a baseline are the specific meters against which you measure the level of acceptable risk for the package of objects. Since there are several kinds of baseline, you must supply exit criteria for each kind: what constitutes a valid initial baseline, what constitutes a beta baseline, and so on. The Baseline method that follows applies the appropriate level of exit criteria to the collection of objects for the specific baseline you are declaring.

INFRASTRUCTURE

Putting the objects under configuration management control requires a configuration management system, which may be part of the larger automated integration environment. However, some deliverables, such as user documents, requirements documents, or other "paperware," as opposed to software, may require additional configuration management tools appropriate to the format.

Dynamics

CHECK IN

The Check In task puts the baseline objects under configuration management control by checking the objects into the configuration management system. This task makes no assumptions about the quality of the deliverables; it just puts the objects under change control. For auditing reasons, once you check in an object, that version of that object always remains in the configuration management system.

BASELINE

The Baseline task, for a specific type of baseline, verifies that the collection of objects satisfies the threshold of acceptable risk implied by the exit criteria applying to that type of baseline. Having baselined the objects, the collection now provides the indicated type of foundation for further work. You can baseline the collection using the appropriate level of baseline as often as you change it for the change.

Example

When the project architect finished the architectural design document for the DTS system, she put it under configuration management control in the document management system. The project manager scheduled a design review and held it to verify that the design (1) covered all the requirements, (2) reused all possible components from the reuse library, and (3) was internally consistent and complete. These three exit criteria from the design standards document provided the review team with specific metrics for these risk factors in the design.

The reviewers found five unsatisfied requirements, a couple of possible reusable items from the reuse library, and six internal inconsistencies. All of these were under the threshold for the initial baseline for the architectural design document (ten requirements, ten reusable components, and ten internal inconsistencies, respectively). To achieve the alpha baseline, the architect had to get the faults down to two or fewer, and so the revision process began. Two weeks and two reviews later, the architectural design document became a beta baseline for the project. Later in the project, the architect revised the document twice to accommodate new requirements added during the later design stages, reviewing the changes and creating iteration baselines for the document.

Road Map

Figure 23.7 is the road map for the deliverable baseline class.

Schedule

The project *schedule* is the part of the project plan that lays out the timing of the project. It shows how resource assignments and logical dependencies

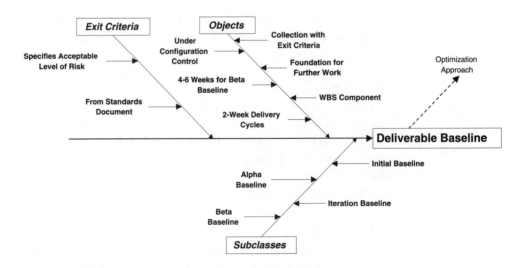

Figure 23.7 Road map for the deliverable baseline class.

between tasks affect the sequencing of tasks. It also contains the time line for tasks and milestones, the plan baselines for effort and time and the earned value metrics that come from them, and the schedule risk management plan.

The statement of work provides a clear statement of the work to do in the project. The project schedule provides a clear statement of *when* to do the work. The WBS tasks are the inputs into the scheduling process. To these you add *milestones*, points in time that represent key events, such as the accomplished delivery of a major deliverable in the project. Milestones let you distinguish clearly the important events that you need to manage as project manager. They are not tasks, nor does anyone have responsibility for them. If you follow the iterative, incremental style of project management we propose in this book, the deliverable baselines in your WBS become the milestones in your schedule. Alternatives include making the completion of phase steps milestones, or creating milestones from externally derived events. We do *not* recommend this latter course, except perhaps for payment or penalty events or other events that might affect the success of the project, and specifically ones on which project tasks depend.

There are several different ways to show a project schedule, depending on your purpose. The schedule itself consists of a series of tasks from the WBS with associated start and end dates and dependencies between the tasks. How you represent this structure depends on what you're trying to accomplish.

A simple spreadsheet representation, a table of tasks with their start and end dates, lets you present and track the project as a straightforward check list of items to do. Usually you present the schedule in this fashion in combination with the WBS structure, showing how the project will accomplish the deliverables and their tasks.

If your interest lies in the time aspects of the schedule, you need to present the tasks in a calendar of some kind. There are two representations for this: the Gantt chart and the calendar chart. See the following attribute section on the schedule time line for details.

If the logical relationships of the tasks (how one task depends on another) concerns you, you can use a critical path chart or PERT chart dependency diagram. See the following attribute section on the schedule dependencies for details.

The plan baseline information for the schedule provides a way to estimate your progress toward completing the project through the earned value metric. See the two attributes below for details, and be aware that these elements of the schedule are potentially the most important for project success, as they let you get solid, informative feedback about progress as you work your way through the project. Also, please don't confuse plan baselines with deliverable baselines; the former is a time or cost amount planned, while the latter is a collection of objects under configuration control.

Finally, the risk management plan provides a clear statement of how you intend to manage the risk of failure to meet your scheduled milestones. We

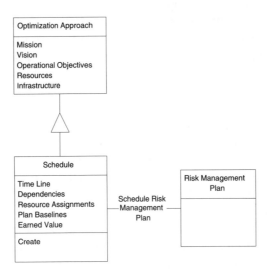

Figure 23.8 Structure of the schedule class.

prefer to focus on milestones rather than on individual tasks to assess schedule risk, as it is difficult to manage both technical and schedule risk at the same level of detail.

As with the entire plan, the schedule is iterative and incremental in nature. Things in the near term are likely to be more accurate than tasks that are months away. As the WBS changes, the schedule changes. Life in an open system is full of surprises; with the schedule in place, you have a good shot at recovery.

Figure 23.8 shows the structure of the schedule class.

Leadership

Vision: A comprehensive, iterative statement of the timing of work for the project that ensures the quality of the deliverables and the productivity of the work.

Mission: To analyze and to accomplish the timing of the project to ensure quality and productivity.

Objective 23.6: To understand how to arrange the timing of tasks to achieve high quality.

Approach 23.6: Construct a schedule of tasks using the appropriate resource assignments and an analysis of the logical dependencies between tasks to ensure that each task has the resources and prior work deliverables it needs to ensure quality.

Measurement 23.6.1: Number of plan baseline changes.

Measurement 23.6.2: Number of changes in dependencies.

Objective 23.7: To increase productivity through understanding when the resources must accomplish the tasks to achieve the project goals.

Approach 23.7: Construct a schedule as in 23.5 to ensure that resources have everything they need to accomplish the task, including an appropriate amount of work time.

Measurement 23.7: Schedule performance index (earned value divided by the plan baseline cost of work scheduled).

For example, if you have an earned value of $600,000, but you intended by this time to have earned $1 million, then you are $400,000 dollars behind (and you can translate that directly into productivity).

Objective 23.8: To accomplish the work of the project according to the schedule.

Approach 23.8: Construct a schedule as in 23.5, baseline it, and use the earned value metric to measure the value each task contributes to the project goals.

Measurement 23.8: Schedule variance percentage (earned value minus plan baseline value divided by plan baseline value) at a point in time.

Structure

TIME LINE

The schedule *time line* shows the tasks with their start and end dates, providing the timing for the tasks, and the milestones that represent deliverable baselines. You can build a simple spreadsheet with this information, or you can graphically represent the time line with a Gantt or calendar chart.

The Gantt chart (see Figure 23.9) presents the tasks as horizontal bars along a time line, with the left edge of the bar representing the start date and the right edge of the bar representing the end date. You can fancy this diagram up with dependency lines, critical path designations, float indicators, and plan baselines. (See your local project management software for examples of these.) The basic idea, however, is to show the timing of the tasks relative to one another along a time line.

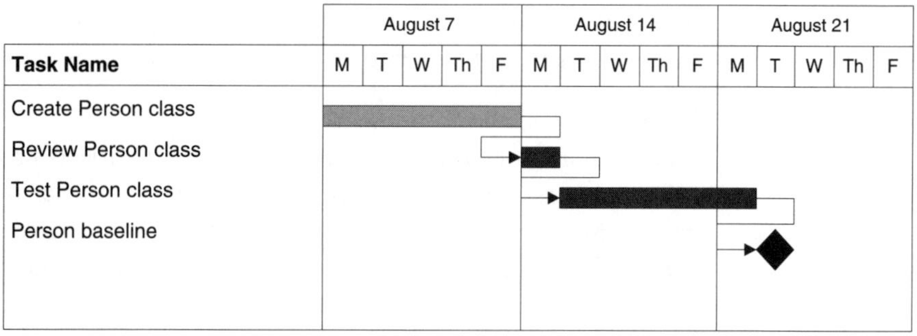

Task Name	August 7					August 14					August 21				
	M	T	W	Th	F	M	T	W	Th	F	M	T	W	Th	F
Create Person class															
Review Person class															
Test Person class															
Person baseline															

Figure 23.9 Sample Gantt chart.

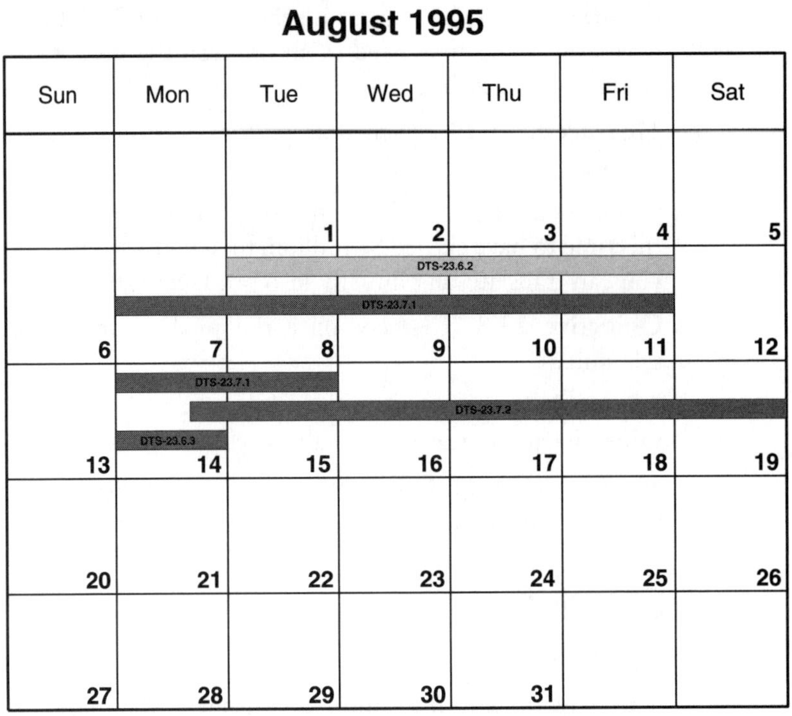

August 1995

Sun	Mon	Tue	Wed	Thu	Fri	Sat
		1	2	3	4	5
6	7	8	9	10	11	12
13	14	15	16	17	18	19
20	21	22	23	24	25	26
27	28	29	30	31		

DTS-23.6.2 Create Person class

DTS-23.6.3 Review Person class

DTS-23.7.1 Create Person integration test suite

DTS-23.7.2 Test Person class

Figure 23.10 Sample of calendar chart.

The calendar chart (see Figure 23.10) provides the same graphics but with the time line as a rectangular calendar rather than as a straight line. The more familiar calendar format can be an aid to understanding how the tasks organize into weekly work. Most project managers use the Gantt chart as it is more compact and easier to read once you understand the conventions.

DEPENDENCIES

The schedule dependencies are the logical relationships between the tasks. Often one task requires as input the output of another task. Less often, tasks can begin or end based on some kind of timing relationship with another task, such as both tasks starting at the same time, or one task starting some fixed amount of time before or after another. The dependency relationships between tasks provide a structural context for determining the timing of tasks

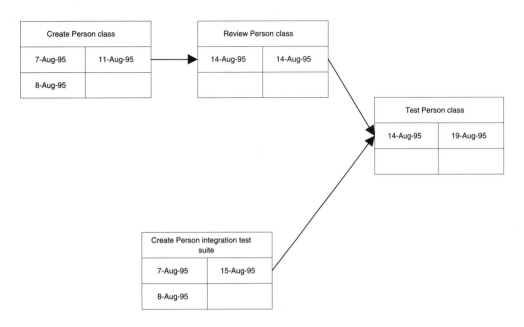

Figure 23.11 Sample PERT chart.

in the schedule. You can't really schedule tasks until you understand the dependencies because they constrain the sequencing of tasks.

As with the time line, you can represent dependencies in a simple spreadsheet format if your interest is in tracking the relationships. Each task can have an associated list of predecessors or successors. You also have the type of dependency (start-start, finish-finish, start-finish, finish-start) and any lead or lag time.

You also can display the dependencies graphically in a network diagram, of which there are two varieties, the task-on-node method and the task-on-arrow method. PERT charts (see Figure 23.11) are an example of the former, and CPM charts (see Figure 23.12) of the latter.

These charts show the tasks as nodes in a connected network of arrows (or, conversely, the tasks as arrows between the nodes that connect them). You usually attach labels to the task nodes or arrows showing the start and finish dates and other information about the task. You can even arrange the chart along a time line to get the best of both worlds, although this makes for a less compact and less readable diagram than a simple Gantt chart with dependency lines between the bars.

An *issue* (part of the issues and concerns section of a project document; see Chapter 22) is when two or more individuals or functional areas cannot agree on some item in the plan. Resolution must come from a third party, preferably someone who has higher responsibility for the tasks or what will result

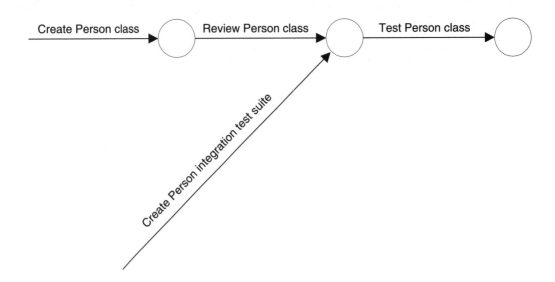

Figure 23.12 Sample CPM chart.

if the task is completed. A *concern* is different from an issue in that it involves speculation. Someone might be concerned that the protocol design document for a library class will be available for the first time next Tuesday and that the designer and responsible party has planned an extensive vacation in Bora Bora beginning on Wednesday. (Here we do mean the very next day.) Any reasonable party would and should be concerned. The concern becomes an issue when the designer states that the protocol design is trivial and any idiot will be able to understand and use it, when in reality he has been working on it for four months and nobody has seen any part of it. We encounter this situation all too often (except it usually isn't Bora Bora). The objective of the issues and concerns sections is to record unresolved items in a place where there is enough visibility for them to be addressed by the appropriate parties in an appropriate time frame. Issues and concerns that reflect relationships that might affect the schedule should become formal dependencies in the project schedule.

RESOURCE ASSIGNMENTS

You can produce a perfectly complete and usable schedule using only the time line and dependency information. In practice, software development projects usually have schedules that depend on three additional factors:

- How the project shares resources with other projects going on at the same time
- How the project uses the time of resources with specific skills or availability

- How the productivity level of individual resources affects the effort for a task

In other words, the resource assignments for a project often determine its schedule.

A *resource assignment* is a relationship between a resource (labor, physical, or whatever) and a task in the WBS. There are many different ways to express this relationship, but common elements include the amount of work effort each resource devotes to the task and the specific timing of that effort (how many hours on which days).

Resource assignments and the attendant technical issues can be incredibly complex. The basic optimization issue is to assign resources (1) not to exceed their *availability*, based on their individual calendars, working shifts, and phases of the moon, and (2) to work to their *capacity*, based on productivity and availability. *Overtime* is the way out of having too few resources or too many tasks. You can summarize all of this in a simple histogram that shows a line representing availability and columns that represent the effort spent or scheduled for a given time period (see Figure 23.13). The process of moving tasks and resources around to optimize this chart is *resource leveling*, the reduction of the chart columns below the availability line.

PLAN BASELINES

A *plan baseline* is a budget for time, effort, or cost. To set a plan baseline, work out a schedule for a set of tasks, then save the estimated start and end dates, effort estimates, and cost estimates for the tasks. As you progress through the tasks, you record the actual start and end dates, effort spent, and cost of each task. You can then compare these values to the plan baseline for the task to judge how well the project has performed.

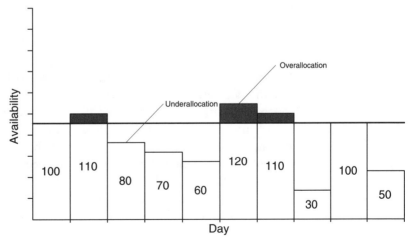

Figure 23.13 Sample resource histogram.

Effort or cost plan baselines are fundamental to the concept of earned value; see the following section, on "Earned Value," for details.

You can have more than one plan baseline for a project, but you need to understand clearly what purpose it serves. If you have too many plan baseline versions, the notion becomes meaningless; too few, and the schedule becomes meaningless. As Chapter 24 illustrates, change is everywhere in a project environment. But a plan baseline assumes a perfectly static environment, providing a clear way to measure your effectiveness. Unfortunately, your employers and customers are likely to judge you ineffective if you don't respond to change well but keep perfectly to your plan baseline.

Here are some hints for changing plan baselines. First, you should try to isolate the effects of environmental change as much as possible, as it disrupts both measurement and motivation. If you change all your plan baselines religiously once a week, your earned value statistics will be meaningless. You should not change a plan baseline for a task unless the schedule change is in direct response to an environmental change or you can gain major benefits from the change, such as shortening the schedule by a significant amount. Second, make changes only for requirements changes, not for cost changes. Don't change an effort or cost plan baseline just because you have to assign a less productive resource or prices go up for physical resources. Third, you should maintain records for all your plan baselines to provide a way to measure the impact of environmental change. Fourth, you should maintain records for each change detailing why you made the change; such information will prove extremely valuable during optimization cycles in understanding what happened in your project.

There are four kinds of plan baseline change (Fleming, 1983, pp. 103–105):

- **Internal replanning:** Changing the plan baseline for specific tasks without affecting the overall budget (time, effort, or cost) for the project; tends to be informal, though you should minimize such changes, as previously noted.
- **Reserve use:** Taking some of the management reserve budget (the "fudge factors") and applying them to the plan baseline, increasing the plan baseline values without increasing the overall budget by decreasing the costs associated with the reserve.
- **Contract changes:** Changing the plan baseline through formal contract changes, usually through a change management system of some kind; usually this affects specific tasks, not the entire project, and is a result of environmental change, such as requirements creep.
- **Formal replanning:** Changing the plan baseline for specific tasks, increasing the overall budget, because the original plan has failed; this is "formal" because it requires customer reapproval of the budget.

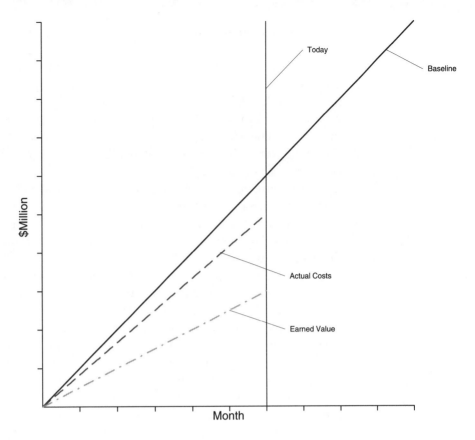

Figure 23.14 Sample earned value graph.

EARNED VALUE

Earned value is the plan baseline value of the tasks you accomplish during some period of time. That is, when you finish a task, the baseline cost or effort for the task becomes the earned value of a task.

Figure 23.14 illustrates the concept of earned value graphically. The chart shows the progress of a project over the course of a year. The current time is at the vertical line. The plan calls for spending $1 million per month, which the top, solid line represents (the plan baseline). The middle, dashed line represents the actual spending to date. The bottom, dashed-dotted line represents the earned value, the planned or baselined cost achieved by finishing tasks. Clearly, even though the project has spent less than planned, it has achieved even less than that, so earned value is much less than planned. So a project can be under budget but still in trouble in terms of the actual value achieved.

You can represent value either in terms of cost (dollars spent) or in terms of effort (person-hours spent). Many software development projects do not have actual cost budgets but rather focus on effort budgets, so the effort earned value is often more useful for software development projects. You also can translate earned value into schedule terms. Schedule variance is the difference between earned value and the plan baseline value at a point in time. You can convert this to a percentage by dividing it by the plan baseline value (that is, EV-BASELINE)/BASELINE, or the schedule variance percentage), by which you can then multiply the time period to get the schedule variance in terms of time. Cost variance is the difference between the earned value and the actual cost at the current date; dividing by the earned value gives you the cost variance percentage.

To optimize your system, you may want to consider a more sophisticated system of valuation based on requirements. This kind of valuation system is more complicated and requires much better record keeping and systematization of your development efforts, but the rewards in terms of value and productivity can be substantial.

Instead of using cost estimates in dollars or effort-hours, you can use a weighted percentage of delivered function points as your earned value metric. A function point is a measure of functionality you deliver to the user in response to a requirement, and you can size the system by developing function point metrics from your requirements use cases. To turn function points into earned value, you must connect your use cases (and therefore the function point valuations attached to them) to your deliverables in the WBS through a traceability matrix. You can then allocate a weighted percentage of the value for each use case to the tasks. You could base the weight on a standard division of effort between the set of tasks on the deliverable (30 percent design, 30 percent coding, 40 percent testing, for example). You could base it on the statistical means or median effort or cost divisions of similar tasks in other projects. You could assign value by risk, giving the more difficult tasks more value. In any case, when you finish, each task should have a baseline value in function points that accrues when you finish the task. You need the connection to the use case to allocate the value to the tasks, and you need to maintain the connections to handle changed allocations as you change the WBS and the requirements.

When you finish the last task associated with the last deliverable that affects a particular requirements use case, your earned value for that use case should equal the value in function points unless you canceled part of the functionality without replanning the baseline or reengineering the use case. When you finish the project, your earned value should be equal to the value in function points of your requirements. You can then compute performance metrics by computing cost per earned function point and effort-hour per earned function point.

Using this scheme has three major optimization benefits.

First, the function-point earned value approximates *true value*, while artificial cost or schedule estimates do not. The only measure that would be better would be the notoriously unreliable and complex numbers associated with market estimates of value (how much customers would pay for the work under what economic conditions). Using this better measure gets you closer to understanding the real productivity and value your efforts contribute.

Second, the function-point earned value fully values *reused* components that satisfy requirements. When you have a requirement that you can satisfy by reusing a technical component, you get the full earned value for the requirement. If you used cost, the cost estimate would be near zero, and you would get little earned value from reuse.

Third, the function-point earned value keeps you focused on *requirements*. If you have tasks or deliverables that don't contribute to satisfying requirements, you get no earned value from completing the tasks. They are true overhead. You can, of course, include such tasks in earned value arbitrarily by allocating some kind of overhead earned value ("level of effort" in project management jargon); we recommend against this. You should optimize your system by either improving requirements to include things such as risk reduction, performance, or quality to a certain level of risk or by eliminating tasks and deliverables that are unnecessary to producing customer value.

You can aggregate earned value up through the WBS structure to the higher-level deliverables to produce a good metric to use for the value of those deliverables. Thus, when you deliver all the components of a WBS deliverable, you get the earned value for that higher-level deliverable. You can thus report aggregated earned value at any level in the WBS, making the technique scaleable to large projects.

Earned value and the accompanying variance metrics let you judge the progress of your project. You can measure it to see how the work you have achieved compares to the work you planned to achieve, both in terms of effort/cost and in terms of schedule.

When do you "earn" the value? There are several ways to handle accrual of earned value. The best and most common way is to earn the value of a task when you complete it and not before. That is, until a task is 100 percent complete, you have zero earned value from that task. Another way is to accrue earned value by a percentage of effort spent, but this leads to discontinuities when you discover you're spending a lot more effort on a task than you budgeted for it. A third way is to accrue 50 percent when you start the task and 50 percent when you finish it. There are many more. (See Kerzner, 1995, pp. 820–821.)

Note that earned value changes as the plan baseline changes. If you increase your plan baseline amount by any of the plan baseline change methods, the value you earn from tasks covered by that plan baseline increases, as does the overall total estimate of earned value (the *estimate at completion*). You can measure changes in estimate at completion to show the level of variance due to environmental change in your project. You also can set thresholds for contract reconsideration, rebudgeting, and so on using this measure. The estimate at completion is the cost of earning the value you have yet to achieve, which you can then compare to the plan baseline cost of completion as a variance measure.

SCHEDULE RISK MANAGEMENT PLAN

The *schedule risk management plan* is a kind of risk management plan that details the risks associated with the failure to meet your schedule. In other words, it assesses the risk that you won't accomplish the task by its plan baseline finish date.

For each task related to a software deliverable, the risk management plan assesses different schedule risks. If any risk exceeds the project risk avoidance criterion (usually a combined probability of failure and consequence of failure of over 50 percent), then the risk management plan contains an approach to avoiding the risk. This approach specifies the actions or tasks that help the project to avoid the risk, which should become part of the WBS.

Managing schedule risk usually comes down to one of three things: managing scope, managing productivity, or budgeting.

If the scope of your project changes, then your plan baseline schedule and costs also need to change. You can do this in an ad hoc manner, or you can plan for and manage the changes through a scope change management plan. Change management is a risk management approach; it limits risk by forcing examination and approval of changes to scope or content. It makes sure that, when you propose a change to the schedule, that change is necessary.

Occasionally you may find that particular resources don't perform as well on a task as you estimated they would, or that a task has more work required than you budgeted for that task. For productivity problems, the best answer is reuse. The more software you can reuse, the less you must worry about how productive your programmers and designers and testers are. As Jones (1994, p. 427) points out, a lot of productivity gets lost because of faults not discovered earlier in the process. A strong quality program thus can dramatically improve productivity by removing this source of problems further down the line. Training, good working environments, good tools, effective development methods (particularly object-oriented ones), and formal reuse programs such as the autarch approach we suggest all control or prevent the risks associated with productivity failure.

Estimation failure is a topic for a book, or several. The combination of training in estimation methods and good tools for estimation is the best way to address the risk of estimation failure. If you have not taken a course or read a book on cost/schedule estimation for software projects and if you are not using a tool for producing such estimates, you are not doing all you can to manage schedule risks by getting the estimates right in the first place. A good place to start learning about this subject is Tom DeMarco's classic *Controlling Software Projects* (1982).

Infrastructure

If you have more than 15 to 20 tasks, using project management software to manage the information in this object is generally a good idea. Most good project management software provides a full range of tools for time lines, dependencies, and resource assignments as well as for the WBS and other components of the project plan. Also, if you are serious about managing schedule risk, you should have one of the many software cost estimating tools on the market.

Dynamics

Create

The Create task builds the project schedule as a document that contains the schedule and resource assignment data and the accompanying time lines and dependency charts, along with the risk management plan.

Baseline

The Baseline task creates a plan baseline value (cost or time or function-point percentage) for one or more of the schedule tasks. This task also should archive the previous plan baselines for the tasks and update any stored values for estimate at completion.

Revise

The Revise task formally revises the schedule, either as a result of change control procedures or as part of a formal replanning process.

Compute Earned Value

The Compute Earned Value task computes the earned value for the schedule at a given point in time based on the completion status of the tasks in the project. We recommend you accrue 100 percent of the earned value when you complete a task and not before.

Example

The DTS project manager, having finalized the WBS, now put the structure into a project management system along with the available resources from the resource plan. The project manager used the software to link dependent tasks to one another and added schedule milestones for the key process events. Using a software cost estimation system with historical data from previous projects, he estimated the effort required for all the tasks in the project. The project manager validated the estimates by having knowledgeable engineers and managers review them.

Working carefully through the milestones, the project manager did a full schedule risk analysis for the cluster of tasks leading to each milestone.

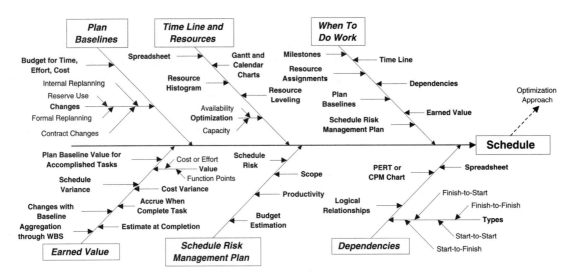

Figure 23.15 Road map for the schedule class.

Working with the project autarch, he identified several tasks that the team could eliminate in favor of reusing software from other projects or off-the-shelf software. The QA department abandoned development of the "nifty little test generator" in favor of buying a package that did the same thing, for example. The project manager emphasized the quality program for requirements and design and identified several team members who could benefit from object-oriented design and programming courses. He also recommended hiring a database administrator with experience in the database approach (ODBC) the DTS software was to use. The connections between all of these approaches to managing schedule risks and the relevant milestones to which they applied became the basis for the schedule risk management plan.

The project manager, working with the functional managers, then assigned resources to the tasks and leveled the resource assignments using the software. After some manual optimization, the managers and the project manager expressed satisfaction with the results during a project review of the Gantt chart.

Road Map

Figure 23.15 is the road map for the schedule class.

Resource Plan

The resource plan consists of the organization chart and the resources, authorities, capabilities, and culture that are a part of it. The plan also lays out the machines, software tools, and other physical resources the project needs to succeed.

Figure 23.16 shows the structure of the resource plan class.

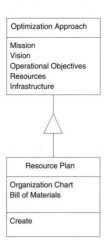

Figure 23.16 Structure of the resource plan class.

Leadership

Vision: A coherent resource organization that provides the labor and material infrastructure you need to achieve your goals.

Mission: To organize labor and materials into a comprehensive system that you can use to produce valuable products in a productive way.

Objective 23.9: To apply resources to the project *congruently*, taking the appropriate actions at the appropriate times with the appropriate skills.

This objective is a bit summary for a complex system of human and material resource management, but a full discussion is beyond the scope of the book. Weinberg's three-volume set *Quality Software Management* (1992, 1993, 1994) provides an excellent introduction to the issues in resource management and congruency.

Approach 23.9: Build a resource plan that clarifies the availability and capability of resources in the context of the organizational structure that assigns authority and in the context of the culture within which the resources operate.

Measurement 23.9.1: Median work-hours per unit of earned value (productivity).

Measurement 23.9.2: Labor turnover rate (number of resources leaving the project in a time period divided by the maximum number of labor resources for the project in that time period).

Measurement 23.9.3: Material delays (number of hours you must delay tasks because of unavailability of material resources).

Structure

ORGANIZATION CHART

The *organization chart* and the accompanying materials provide an overview of the organization of labor resources and how it can address the work needs of the project.

The chart itself shows the authority structure of the organization and is a comprehensive list of the resources available for work during the project. As with all plans, this one changes as you hire and fire resources, rearrange authority, or increase capabilities and responsibilities. Chapters 3 to 5 of Kerzner (1995) contain excellent introduction to the varieties of project organizational and authority structures in his, and the PMBOK from the Project Management Institute (1994) has an excellent two-page summary of the possibilities.

One aspect that should appear on the organizational chart is the breakdown of the resources into development teams. Additional charts showing how resources participate on individual teams and the authority structure of those teams may be required here.

Also, the organization chart must clearly identify the integration autarch, the person with the authority and responsibility to direct the integration and reuse of software components into systems.

To accompany the organization chart, you should have a summary list of the capabilities or skills of the people in the chart, including their skill level. This list will help you in assigning the appropriate individuals to work on specific deliverables. It also will help you to see where the technical and schedule risks lie, as lack of capability through lack of training or knowledge is one of the main contributors to these kinds of risk.

It also would be a good idea to summarize the aspects of the organizational culture that will have an impact on the way the project progresses. Does the culture stress individual initiative over teamwork? How do corporate politics affect quality optimization? Are there adequate informal feedback channels for technical and managerial information?

BILL OF MATERIALS

Projects, even software projects, are not just about people doing work. Programmers need computers and software tools, production needs paper and reprographic facilities and disk copying facilities.

The *bill of materials* for a project specifies the list of particular material resources you will need to accomplish the tasks of the project. You should be very careful to specify the items that create dependencies. For example, if you need to buy a specific testing tool in order to start testing a particular UI component, you must acquire the tool before the tasks for the testing can start. If you don't know you need the tool until the task is ready to start, you'll have to delay the task,

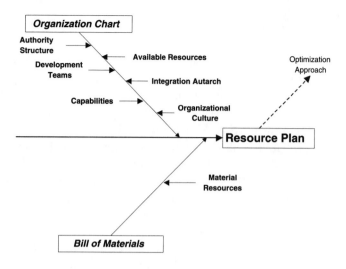

Figure 23.17 Road map for the resource plan class.

possibly delaying the project if the task is critical. Similarly, if your deliverables require a lot of memory and system resources, you will need to make sure you have the requisite machinery and the people to maintain them.

Dynamics

CREATE

The Create task builds the resource plan as a document that contains the organization chart and the bill of materials along with any supporting materials needed to manage the resources during the project.

Example

The resource plan for the DTS project was relatively easy to develop. The various teams involved had all worked together on a previous project, so the project manager reused the resource plan for that project, updating it with the few team resource changes that had taken place. A complete integration automation system was added to the bill of materials; the project manager felt it would effectively manage the schedule risks associated with integration delays that had occurred on other projects. Some additional hardware requirements also were needed for compatibility with the chosen integration system.

Road Map

Figure 23.17 is the road map for the resource plan class.

Risk Management Plan

A *risk management plan* is an assessment of the risks of a set of tasks and a statement of the approach you intend to take to minimize any risks that meet the project risk avoidance criteria.

Two subclasses of risk management plan are of interest to this book:

- **Technical Risk Management Plan:** Those risks associated with the probability of failure to meet the technical objectives (user requirements) for the software system; a component of the statement of work.
- **Schedule Risk Management Plan:** Those risks associated with the probability of failure to meet the milestones in the project schedule; a component of the project schedule.

This section is not a comprehensive discussion of risk analysis and management. If you need more detail, consult Charette (1989), Jones (1994), and Roetzheim (1988).

Jones (1994, p. 604) defines risk as "the probability that a software project will experience undesirable events." Charette (1989, p. 55) notes that risk has an associated loss, uncertainty, and choice. The loss is the impact of a failure; the uncertainty is the chance of the failure occurring; and the choice implies that you can do something about it. (Otherwise, it wouldn't need risk management.)

Risk analysis is the determination of the specific loss and uncertainty in a situation. The object of analysis may be a single task, a set of tasks, or a component. Once you know the loss and uncertainty, you then have to figure out how to manage that risk by making choices. Risk management approaches make up the risk management plan. This plan is a compendium of specific risks and the things you intend to do to reduce the loss or the uncertainty to acceptable levels.

To assess the impact of failure, you need to brainstorm the consequences of failure of the task or object. Are there physical consequences, such as loss of life or property? Legal consequences, such as torts or criminal violations? Market share issues? Public relations issues? Political issues? Governance issues? Will you still be able to conduct business after a failure?

Without delving into the complexities of measuring social harm, you can set up a simple scale from zero to one that measures the consequence of failure. Zero represents no consequence, while one represents devastating consequences. You usually can partition the scale into categories (high/low, critical/severe/moderate/low/none, and so on). Assign the categories values between zero and one (1, .75, .5, .25, 0 for the critical to none scale, for example). Now you can assign the category number to be the impact of failure for the object.

To assess the probability of failure, you need to develop a statistical model of the chances of failing. How often do you use the object? How much do you know about the type of failure? What is the history of failure for similar components? The history of the development team for the object? Any data from the field or other products? How complex is the object?

Again, create a partitioned scale that rates the probability of failure from zero to one; high, medium, and low will do fine (.75, .5, .25 as numbers, for example). If you use statistical techniques, use the probability value you find is most likely. Assign the number to the estimated probability of failure.

If you now multiply the impact by the probability, you get a metric for risk. For example, a low probability of failure and a moderate impact yields a risk of .13 (.25 times .5). A high probability of failure and a severe impact yields .56 (.75 times .75).

As part of your project standards, you must set a risk level that indicates whether to manage the risk. For example, if your threshold is 50 percent, you would manage the high/severe risk (56 percent) but not the low/moderate risk (13 percent). You need to set this threshold to your acceptable level of risk.

You can categorize project deliverable risks in any number of ways. A common one that we use is to divide risks into those relating to technical failure, schedule failure, and cost failure: not delivering the technology or features, not delivering on time, and not delivering the features for the budgeted amount. We don't include costs in this book.

Capers Jones (1994) provides a comprehensive list of the most important software risks. Here are some of the most important:

- Canceled projects
- Cost overruns
- Creeping user requirements
- Error-prone modules
- Excessive paperwork
- Excessive schedule pressure
- Excessive time to market
- Friction between customer and producer
- Harmful competitive actions
- High maintenance costs
- Inadequate configuration control
- Inadequate cost estimating
- Inadequate user documentation
- Litigation expense
- Long schedules
- Low productivity
- Low quality
- Low user satisfaction
- Unused or unusable software

Figure 23.18 shows the structure of the risk management plan class.

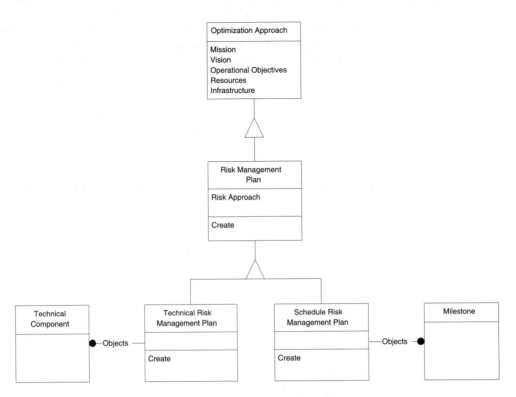

Figure 23.18 Structure of the risk management plan class.

Leadership

Vision: A plan for managing risk to an acceptable level.

Mission: To analyze and plan for risks beyond an acceptable threshold.

Objective 23.10: To create a plan that reduces the unacceptable risks in the project WBS and schedule to an acceptable level.

Approach 23.10: Analyze the probability of occurrence and the impact of failure for each target object in the WBS and schedule, then create a management approach for each risk that exceeds the acceptable threshold of risk for the project.

Measurement 23.10: Number of technical and schedule failures beyond the acceptable risk threshold.

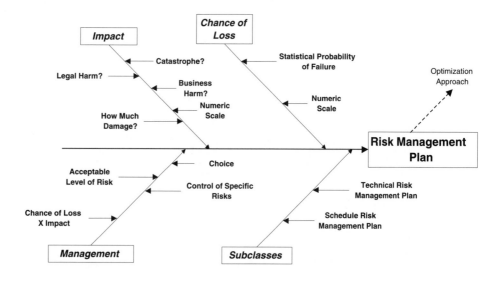

Figure 23.19 Road map for the risk management plan class.

Structure

RISK APPROACH

The risk approach specifies a particular set of actions to take to reduce a particular risk in a particular situation. This connects the approach to a kind of object that depends on the type of risk involved. Technical risks associate with technical components; schedule risks associate with milestones in the project schedule.

Dynamics

CREATE

The Create task builds the risk management plan as a document that contains the risk approaches.

Road Map

Figure 23.19 is the road map for the risk management plan class.

CHAPTER 24

PROJECT ENVIRONMENT

The project environment is the set of external factors that make project life interesting. Every project is an open system that interacts with the external world. In the case of software development, that means interacting with changes, working somewhere, and communicating. This chapter gives a brief overview of this open system environment.

The project environment is a kind of development environment that also includes the project repository.

Figure 24.1 shows the structure of the project environment.

Leadership

Vision: A seething mass of uncertainty and risk channeled to help the quality system survive as a system.

Mission: To encompass external events and things in a system that control uncertainty and risk to an acceptable level.

Objective 24.1: To accommodate change feeding back into the quality system.

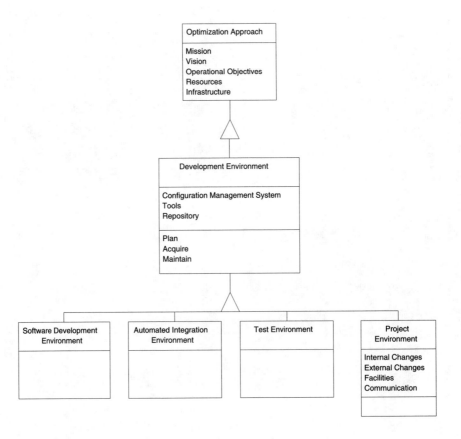

Figure 24.1 Structure of the project environment class.

Approach 24.1: Pay attention to and track changes in a comprehensive way that lets you react to the changes quickly and with assurance.

Measurement 24.1: Earned value from tasks added due to changes in requirements or other external changes.

Objective 24.2: To build an infrastructure capable of supporting the project.

Approach 24.2: Build a collection of facilities and communications channels that provides you with the infrastructural capabilities your project needs to succeed in its objectives.

Measurement 24.3: Survey the project team to determine whether the project infrastructure was sufficient or whether the lack of such infrastructure significantly impeded their productivity or imperiled the quality of the deliverables.

Structure

Internal Changes

One worry of the functional manager is to handle internal changes in teams. People retire, quit, even die; work goes on. Both the functional and project managers must forecast their personnel needs and make sure that they get the resources when they need them.

Internal functional changes often happen because software development is not a cut-and-dried, snap-the-pieces-together process. It's mostly still practiced as an art (most regrettably not an engineering practice), and like most artists, people working on software get creative from time to time. This creative dynamic always creates changes that project managers and functional managers must deal with. Working with object-oriented software seems to encourage such creativity because it makes you think about the real relationships between things and the "one right way" to do things. At least, that's the impression we have after hanging around a lot of object-oriented software conferences and team meetings. Managers have to be able to accept change and work it into their project plan to take full advantage of working in this dynamic environment.

External Changes

If the internal environment for a project is dynamic, the external environment is wild. The technical revolution brought about by computers and the subsidiary revolutions of personal workstations and object-oriented software have created a hurricane of change in the technical world. Every object-oriented software project must take *external changes* into account. An enormous array of such changes feeds back into the open quality system:

- Changing standards of value based on changing technology (you find all of a sudden that you really do need a trash can icon or nobody will take you seriously; or you discover that you're apparently the last one to hear that all your customers have gone to Windows NT instead of UNIX; or a third party comes out with a new application framework that does 80 percent of what you had planned to code in C++).

- Changing requirements from customers who finally understand what you're giving them and want more.
- Changing laws (a lot of that going on these days).
- Changing economics (ditto).
- Changing minds (a new marketing manager comes on board . . .).
- Changing bodies (the customer contact you worked with quit and somebody new replaced him with a completely different idea about the application).

Facilities

It is not yet possible for a project to exist entirely in cyberspace, though it may be getting closer to reality. That's because, as technology transfer speeds up, the world is building a massive infrastructure of computer technology and communications that can replace the infrastructure in many companies. For example, electronic mail through the Internet is now pretty much free for anyone with a personal computer and a modem, and more and more people have that as standard household equipment.

As the technological requirements of doing business in today's world expand, what companies used to take for granted as things they had to pay for are increasingly becoming part of our societal infrastructure. But there are still some basic *facilities* that any project must have to succeed.

At the top of the list is workspace. Workspace is as varied as the companies that provide it. We have worked in cubicles, sitting at tables with other engineers, in private offices, in semiprivate offices, and at home. Some workspaces are more effective in promoting productivity than others. DeMarco and Lister (1987) have a great book that deals well with these environmental issues, such as do-not-disturb buttons on phones and private offices with doors.

Next on the list is meeting space. If you have more than one person working on a project, you have to have someplace to meet. Small projects can meet in large offices (thus keeping the senior management in the loop, since they usually have the large offices). Large projects can share meeting rooms with other projects or even rent space in public places. You also of course have to have access to a softball field . . . or at least to a ping pong table. Foosball? A lot of good project meetings have happened over the foosball table.

After these big ones comes communication facilities, such as networks, phones, video systems, sound systems, and all the other pieces of the communications infrastructure. Face-to-face communications are the best for project success, but in today's world you often have to accept second best. If the infrastructure isn't there to support you, you will find yourself very frustrated and your project unsuccessful. For example, if you have a remote site, possibly on another continent, you will be very frustrated if your electronic mail system can't get the mail back and forth on the same day. This does happen, surprisingly.

COMMUNICATION

Not all *communication* is infrastructure. Two things in particular need to get some attention if your project is to succeed: meeting minutes and the project room.

MEETING MINUTES

Meeting minutes are those things that nobody does in meetings. They should. Minutes can provide both a record of what happened and a means of communicating what happened to people not at the meeting. Minutes consist of a list of the people attending the meeting, the agenda of the meeting (yes, you should have one of those too), the date and time and place of the meeting, a summary of the points made under each agenda item (and any made additional to the agenda), and a list of action items.

You also can use meeting minutes as a source for metrics, if you measure things such as number of agenda items on particular modules or number of action items to fix problems in documents.

Primarily, though, you should use minutes to remind people of what was said or to communicate what happened to people who either were unable to attend the meeting or weren't invited.

THE PROJECT ROOM

The project room is a meeting room, a bulletin board, or even an electronic bulletin board or forum that provides up-to-date information about the project for anyone who wants it. Obviously this room must be at the same level of security as the project itself, since you don't want anyone getting project information who shouldn't see it. Otherwise, this room should tell all: Everyone needs to know how the project is doing in terms of schedule, budget, and technical success. Have a computer in the room that runs the latest build for people to demonstrate and experiment. Have the wonderful charts from your favorite project management system scattered all over the walls, and *keep them up to date*.

There is nothing more demoralizing to a software project than to have a project room with project charts and information six months out of date. This communicates loud and clear to the team that the project as such is unimportant to management. If you can't keep things up to date, don't have a project room. But if you don't have a project room, be ready to explain to everyone who asks why you can't give them any information about the project.

Project Repository

The project repository contains project-related documents and objects:

- Project management documents
- Test plans
- Measures
- Baselines
- Project management data (tasks, resources, dependencies)
- Software change records identified by time and resource stamps
- Automated build and test results identified by time stamp

Resources

To understand and control change, you need to know about it. To know about it, you need to have people looking for it, such as product marketing professionals, technical consultants, and other people whose job it is to look outside the project rather than inside at its technology.

To have a working infrastructure, you need to have resources capable of providing and maintaining it. A facilities manager is essential to any project, whether shared between projects or dedicated to one. Technical employees such as systems managers, network managers and engineers, and help desk support may be essential in keeping the more technical aspects of your infrastructure in operating order. A good purchasing manager can save you thousands of dollars in project expenses for infrastructure, even though you may not like all those plastic chairs he or she bought at a fire sale. And think of all those plane tickets you'll need to visit the teams in Taiwan and Sydney.

Example

The DTS project encountered several technology changes during the course of the project, including the availability of a new ODBC framework that made it unnecessary to contract out the work, the standardization of certain kinds of test data by an international standards body, and the advent of a new version of the chosen database manager that was incompatible with the previous six versions. Some changes in copyright and patent law also motivated the company to apply for a patent on part of the system, which in turn motivated the designers to use different algorithms and architectures to facilitate the patent application process. An architect had published a paper on the main algorithm before the company realized it was patentable.

The DTS work environment was a model facility, especially for the developers, who all got to work at home and come in only for project meetings. Only the testers suffered, working in cubicles. The documentation team had to use old, 286 PCs running Microsoft Word for DOS, but this situation improved when the company got $20 million in venture capital and bought everyone a high-end Macintosh desktop system. The email system was from a vendor that lost mail again and again until the company finally replaced it with direct Internet connections between individuals.

The DTS project room was also the foosball room, thus guaranteeing a constant level of activity, though perhaps not on project work. The project charts festooned the walls, as did pictures of everyone on the development team in various silly positions. There was also an espresso machine for the fanatics and a microwave for the merely hungry. All this worked well to promote communication about both the technical aspects of the system and about the project schedule and work process.

Road Map

Figure 24.2 is the road map for the project environment class.

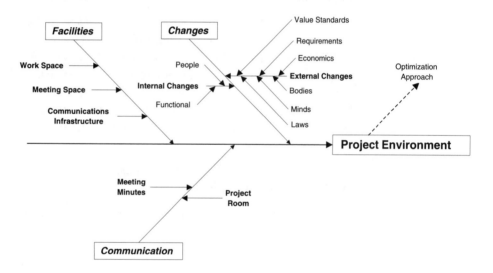

Figure 24.2 Road map for the project enironment class.

Part 5 References

1. Robert N. Charette. *Software Engineering Risk Analysis and Management*, Intertext Publications, New York: 1989.

This book is the major textbook on software risk analysis as a process; use it in conjunction with Capers Jones's book to get the full picture.

2. Tom DeMarco and Timothy Lister. *Peopleware: Productive Projects and Teams*. Dorset House, New York: 1987.

The funniest and best book available on how to really motivate software developers, or anybody else for that matter. Every project manager should first read this book, then do what it says.

3. Tom DeMarco. *Controlling Software Projects: Management Measurement and Estimation*. Yourdon Press, Englewood Cliffs, NJ: 1982.

4. Quentin W. Fleming, *Put Earned Value (C/SCSC) into Your Mangement Control System* (Worthington, OH: Publishing Horizons, Inc., 1983).

This is a thorough exposition of the C/SCSC system by one of its main proponents and gives you a complete and comprehensive picture of how earned value works in the context of controlling costs and schedules. C/SCSC is a cost control method for large projects, and much of the material in this book has to do with such projects, though a lot is of interest to any project.

5. Tom Gib. *Principles of Software Engineering Management*. Addison-Wesley, Wikingham, England: 1988.

6. Capers Jones. *Assessment and Control of Software Risks*. Yourdon Press, Englewood Cliffs, NJ: 1994.

This book is the most complete reference on the risks you incur in developing software. Every practicing software manager should own a copy. Jones, while opinionated, provides the detail you need to make your own decisions about the risks you should take. Along with some introductory material the book provides an alphabetical list of the 59 most important risks in developing software.

7. Harold Kerzner. *Project Management: A Systems Approach to Planning, Scheduling, and Controlling*, 5th ed. Van Nostrand Reinhold, New York: 1995.

This is *the* reference book on modern project management. It has few specifics for software projects and tends to assume you are dealing with large projects, but nevertheless if you are a professional project manager, you should own this book.

8. Project Management Institute. "A Guide to the Project Management Body of Knowledge (PMBOK)." Exposure draft. (Upper Darby, PA: Project Management Institute, August 1994).

This pamphlet is a draft of the new PMBOK, which is a well-structured summary of the range of things a competent project manager must know. The PMI bases its Project Management Professional certification examination on this material. The new draft fits in very nicely with our approach to project management. At publication time, the final version is not yet available from PMI.

9. William H. Roetzheim. *Structured Computer Project Management.* Prentice-Hall, Englewood Cliffs, NJ: 1988.

This short book on project management stands out in the project management literature for its thorough integration of risk analysis and management. Read this book to get a clear understanding of the position of risk analysis and management in the overall project life cycle.

10. Gerald M. Weinberg. *Quality Software Management*, Volume 1: Systems Thinking. Dorset House, New York: 1992.

11. Gerald M. Weinberg. *Quality Software Management*, Volume 2: First-Order Measurement. Dorset House, New York: 1993.

12. Gerald M. Weinberg. *Quality Software Mangement*, Volume 3: Congruent Action. Dorset House, New York: 1994.

This three-volume set is the most readable work on software management that we know. It focuses on organizational and people issues because those are often the most important ways to improve quality. The first volume introduces systems thinking and characterizes software organizations as behavioral patterns or cultures, focusing on quality and steering toward objectives. The second volume focuses on observations and measurement of organizational systems and quality. The third volume focuses on congruent action, using systems thinking to show managers how to act in appropriate ways at appropriate times. If you manage people or work with people who manage people, you should read these books.

INDEX

A

abstract classes, concrete classes versus, 164
abstraction, defined, 18
abstraction test suite, 236, 247–51
abstract methods, 164, 165
ad hoc tests, 127
aggregation reviews, 362–66
Align task, test approach, 99
alpha deliverable baseline, 41, 461
APIs (Application Programming Interfaces), 251
approach to optimization. *See* optimization approach
approvals, project document, 443, 444
Arthur, Lowell Jay, 294
Art of Software Testing, The (Myers), 143
assertions, 227–29
   in class-object tests, 175
   in conditional test suite, 217
attributes, defined, 18–19
autarch, integration, 427–28
automated integration environment, 37, 408, 422–31
   components of, 422
   documentation and training materials, 427
   dynamics, 428–29
   example, 429–30
   integration autarch and, 427
   leadership, 424–25
   road map, 431
   structure, 425
   training materials, 427

automation of test scripts, 159
availability test script, 280

B

balance, optimization and, 62
Baseline task, 463
base models, 136, 137
Beizer, Boris, 141, 143, 155, 183, 191, 195, 216
beta deliverable baseline, 41, 461
bill of materials, 480
Black-Box Testing, 195
Boehm, Barry, 330
branch coverage, 166
browsers, 413
build process, 426
   automated integration environment and, 422–23
build scripts, 413

C

C++, as type-safe language, 26
calendar chart, 465, 467–68
cautions, in project document, 441
change management system. *See* configuration management system
character recognition UI test scripts, 267, 269, 273–74
Charette, Robert N., 482
class bang approach, 95–97
class diagrams, 34
classes, 37, 380, 385–89
   abstract versus concrete, 164

D

Firesmith, Donald, 217
fishbone diagrams, 4–6, 28, 301
fixed faults, regression tests and, 289–90
foundation components, 37, 100, 381, 392–97
    example, 396–97
    leadership, 393–95
    road map, 397
    structure, 395
foundation component test plan, 109
Freedman, Daniel P., 350, 352
functionality test script, 279–80
functional test suite, 236, 243–47, 251

G

Gantt chart, 465, 467, 468
Gause, Donald C., 329
global functions, 19
graphical user interface for test framework, 126

H

Harel, David, 193
Harrold, Mary J., 164
hierarchical approach, 100–106
    example, 106
    leadership, 102–3
    road map, 106
    structure, 104–5
Hierarchical Incremental Test (HIT) Script, 67–68
hierarchical-incremental test

suites, 104, 152, 157, 164–75
    dynamics, 168–71
    example, 171–74
    leadership, 166–68
    road map, 174
    structure, 168
hierarchical method, 31, 38
hyperlink road maps, 5

I

Improving Software Quality (Arthur), 294
INFACT! test framework, 128
infrastructure section specification, 4
Infrastructure subsection, 61
inheritance, 20–21
    multiple, 21, 34
initial deliverable baseline, 41, 461
initialize method, 127
inputs, in processes, 73
inspections, 350
instance, defined, 17
integration autarch, 427–28
integration environment, automated. *See* automated integration environment
integration testing, 158
    interface errors found by, 239
    messaging errors found by, 239
integration test suites, 104, 153, 157, 236–43
    example, 242–43
    leadership, 241

user options test suite, 279

V

validation, 329
value, 17, 28, 58. *See also*
    optimization approach
    earned, 472–75
vendor tool documents,
    automated integration
    environment and, 427
version control system, 402
virtual functions, 23
visibility, 25

vision statement, 59

W

walkthroughs, 350
waterfall model, 76
Weinberg, Gerald M., 329, 350,
    352
widget-playback UI test scripts,
    268, 269, 274
work breakdown structure
    (WBS), 435, 455–58
workspace, 490